A European Central Bank? Perspectives on monetary unification after ten years of the EMS

The Italian Macroeconomic Policy Group

The Italian Macroeconomic Policy Group first met in 1986. It consists of a small group of Italian economists who wished to promote discussion of economic policy issues that are relevant not only to Italy, but also of more general interest. The Group periodically commissions papers from economists based in Italy and elsewhere. Subsequently these papers are discussed by an international panel at meetings convened by the Group.

Current members of the Group are:

Giorgio Basevi
Marcello de Cecco
Mario Draghi
Francesco Giavazzi
Alberto Giovannini
Mario Monti
Paolo Onofri
Antonio Pedone
Luigi Spaventa

Centre for Economic Policy Research

A European Central Bank?

Perspectives on monetary unification after ten years of the EMS

Edited by
MARCELLO DE CECCO
and
ALBERTO GIOVANNINI

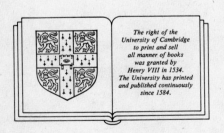

The right of the
University of Cambridge
to print and sell
all manner of books
was granted by
Henry VIII in 1534.
The University has printed
and published continuously
since 1584.

CAMBRIDGE UNIVERSITY PRESS

Cambridge
New York   New Rochelle   Melbourne   Sydney

Published by the Press Syndicate of the University of Cambridge
The Pitt Building, Trumpington Street, Cambridge CB2 1RP
32 East 57th Street, New York, NY 10022, USA
10 Stamford Road, Oakleigh, Melbourne 3166, Australia

First published 1989

Printed in Great Britain by The University Press, Cambridge

British Library cataloguing in publication data

A European Central Bank?: perspectives on
monetary unifcation after ten years of the EMS
1. European Community countries.
Monetary systems Integration
I. De Cecco, Marcello
II. Giovannini, Alberto
332.4'566'094

Library of Congress cataloguing in publication data applied for

ISBN 0 521 37171 6 hard covers
ISBN 0 521 37623 8 paperback

CE

Contents

Figures

Tables

Preface

This volume represents the second in an annual series of collaborations between the Italian Macroeconomic Policy Group and the Centre for Economic Policy Research. It contains the papers and proceedings from a conference on 'Monetary Regimes and Monetary Institutions: Issues and Perspectives in Europe', held at Castelgandolfo on 17/18 June 1988. The first volume of this series, *High Public Debt: The Italian Experience*, edited by Francesco Giavazzi and Luigi Spaventa, was published by Cambridge University Press in June 1988.

The programme committee for the conference were the members of the Italian Macroeconomic Policy Group. The participation of CEPR in this project stems both from the great interest in the topic of the conference outside Italy, and from the involvement of members of IMPG such as Francesco Giavazzi and Alberto Giovannini, who contribute to the activities of CEPR as Research Fellows, and Giorgio Barevi, a Governor of the Centre.

We are grateful to Euromobiliare SpA, Centro Europa Ricerche, and Prometeia, who provided financial support for the conference series, and to the Ente Nazionale Idrocarburi, who hosted the meeting at Villa Montecucco in Castelgandolfo. We are especially grateful to Paul Compton at CEPR, for extremely fast and efficient handling of all the arrangements necessary to publish the volume, and to John Black for his efforts as production editor.

Marcello de Cecco
Alberto Giovannini

Conference participants

Alberto Alesina *Harvard University and CEPR*
Giorgio Basevi *Università di Bologna and CEPR*
Giuseppe Bertola *MIT*
William Branson *Princeton University and CEPR*
Samuel Brittan *The Financial Times*
Franco Bruni *Università Bocconi, Milano*
Michael Bruno *Bank of Israel*
Guillermo Calvo *IMF*
Carlo Carraro *Università di Venezia and CEPR*
Alessandra Casella *University of California, Berkeley*
Daniel Cohen *Centre d'Etudes Prospectives d'Economie Mathématique Appliquées à la Planification, Paris, and CEPR*
Remy Cohen *Euromobiliare SpA*
Franco Cotula *Banca d'Italia*
Clive Crook *The Economist*
Carlo D'Adda *Università di Bologna*
Marcello de Cecco *European University Institute, Firenze*
Rudiger Dornbusch *MIT and CEPR*
Mario Draghi *World Bank*
Allan Drazen *Princeton University*
Barry Eichengreen *University of California, Berkeley, and CEPR*
Jonathan Feinstein *Stanford University*
Renato Filosa *Ente Nazionale Idrocarburi*
John Flemming *Bank of England*
Francesco Giavazzi *Università di Bologna and CEPR*
Alberto Giovannini *Columbia University and CEPR*
Charles Goodhart *LSE*
Vittorio Grilli *Yale University*
Daniel Gros *Centre for European Policy Studies*
Carl-Ludwig Holtfrerich *Freie Universität, Berlin*

xvi

Lucio Izzo *European Investment Bank*
Norbert Kloten *Landeszentralbank im Baden-Württemburg*
Rainer Masera *Banca d'Italia*
Stefano Micossi *Confindustria*
Jeffrey Miron *University of Michigan*
Mario Monti *Università Bocconi, Milano*
Paolo Onofri *Università di Bologna*
Fiorella Padoa Schioppa *Libera Università Internazionale degli Studi Sociale, Roma*
Tommaso Padoa Schioppa *Banca d'Italia*
Marco Pagano *Università di Napoli and CEPR*
Antonio Pedone *Università di Roma*
Torsten Persson *Institute for International Economic Studies, Stockholm*
Edmund Phelps *Columbia University*
Giovanni Pittaluga *Banca d'Italia*
Richard Portes *CEPR and Birkbeck College, London*
Wolfgang Rieke *Deutsche Bundesbank*
Nicola Rossi *Università di Venezia*
Massimo Russo *IMF*
Fabrizio Saccomani *Banca d'Italia*
Maria Teresa Salvemini *Università di Roma*
Valeria Sannucci *Banca d'Italia*
Luigi Spaventa *Università di Roma*
Alan Stockman *University of Rochester*
Guido Tabellini *University of California, Los Angeles, and CEPR*
Niels Thygesen *University of Copenhagen*
Gianni Toniolo *Università di Venezia*
Giacomo Vaciago *Università di Ancona*
José Viñals *Banco de España and CEPR*
Charles Wyplosz *Institut Européen d'Administration des Affaires, Fontainebleau, and CEPR*
Stephen Yeo *CEPR*

1 Does Europe need its own central bank?

MARCELLO DE CECCO and ALBERTO GIOVANNINI

1 Introduction

The initiatives to discuss the establishment of a centralized monetary authority in Europe, coming from government officials, have caught observers by surprise. The European Monetary System (EMS) has proved to the whole world to be a viable arrangement, and has been able to withstand the sizeable international financial shocks of the early 1980s: an immediate threat to the EMS is thus not evident. These initiatives, however, should all the more be applauded, since they signal the concern of governments with the fast evolution of the European economies and capital markets. The renewed debate on a European central bank reopens the questions of whether current monetary institutions will be obsolete and incapable of functioning in the face of the seemingly unstoppable trend towards market integration, and of the viability of new institutional arrangements among central banks.

In the significant body of research on the EMS there is little concern with the issue of a European central bank. Existing work concentrates on interpreting EMS experience, and evaluating the performance of that system. Hence this book represents a first attempt at analysing the various aspects of the problem of a centralized European monetary authority. While by no means exhaustive, this book brings the perspectives of both economic analysis and economic history to bear on this issue. The purpose of this essay is to describe the background to the question of monetary unification, the arguments according to which Europe would need its own central bank, and the problems of designing viable institutional arrangements, in the light of historical experience.

In Section 2 we list the reasons why the institution of a central bank is viewed – at least by some – as a desirable step to take in Europe. These include a desire to further the process of monetary unification that the EMS has not contributed to accelerate, and concern with the potential

1

disruptive effects of the complete liberalization of financial markets planned for 1992. Section 3 surveys the contributions of this volume to the theory of optimum currency areas. Section 4 discusses the historical experience, and Section 5 considers proposals for institutional reform.

2   Background

It is possible to identify two separate arguments for the creation of a European central bank. The first stems from the recognition that the EMS has failed to spontaneously bring about monetary unification. This observation leads to asking the reasons for this failure: was the system ill-designed; did member countries wilfully resist monetary unification; or is the very concept of gradualism unworkable in the case of monetary reforms?

The second argument relates directly to the way monetary policy has operated during the EMS years: countries have not eliminated inflation differentials, and have resorted to periodic exchange-rate realignments to avoid ever-growing divergences in relative prices. The 'weak-currency' countries have preserved stability in their domestic financial markets by systematically resorting to capital controls: these capital controls have been essential for the smooth working of the EMS. The complete liberalization planned for the year 1992 would then seriously destabilize domestic financial markets, unless market participants perceived countries' commitment to a European monetary union as a credible one. According to this argument, the only credible commitment to a monetary union is the monetary union itself.

2.1   The EMS and the commitment to monetary unification

The EMS was viewed by its creators as an intermediate step towards monetary unification. The Conclusion of the Presidency of the European Council of 4 December 1978 stated:

> The purpose of the European Monetary System is to establish a greater measure of monetary stability in the Community. It should be seen as a fundamental component of a more comprehensive strategy aimed at lasting growth with stability, a progressive return to full employment, the harmonization of living standards and the lessening of regional disparities within the Community. The Monetary System will facilitate the convergence of economic development and give fresh impetus to the process of European Union.

The 'transition' role of the EMS is apparent in the features that represented institutional novelties over the experiments that preceded it in the second postwar period: the Bretton Woods System and the Snake.

Unlike its predecessors, the EMS is characterized by a special 'money' – the European Currency Unit (ECU)[1] – and by an institution to control the issuance of this money, the European Monetary Fund (EMF).

The ECU's functions, as laid out by the Resolution of the European Council on the establishment of the EMS (of 5 December 1978), were to serve: as numéraire for the EMS exchange rate mechanism (to establish bilateral central rates); as the basis for the indicator of divergence; as the numéraire for central ba. financial operations; and as a means of settlement between monetary authorities in the European Community. The 1978 Resolution also established a two-year deadline after the start of the EMS for the full utilization of the ECU as a reserve asset and a means of settlement.

The role of the European Monetary Cooperation Fund was also much enhanced by the Resolution establishing the EMS. The Fund was supposed to provide a supply of ECU that served as means of settlement of central bank transactions, against the deposit of 20% of gold and 20% of dollar reserves held by member countries' central banks. Hence the Resolution created an embryo of a European central bank.

Has the EMS actually provided the 'fresh impetus to the process of European Union' hoped for by its creators? The experience of the last ten years suggests a plainly negative answer to that question. The symptom of the inability of the EMS to boost monetary unification is the lack of any substantial role played by the European Fund and the ECU. The former remained just an account at the Bank of International Settlements, used for the clearing of the bilateral credits arranged through the Very Short Term Financing Facility. The latter never rose to perform the functions of a European money, but has been used, in official and private transactions,[2] only as an accounting unit.

Indeed, the functioning of the EMS in its first ten years strikingly resembles the functioning of other fixed exchange rates regimes:[3] the gold standard and the Bretton Woods regime. Like the earlier experiences, the conduct of monetary policy was under the control of a 'centre' country – West Germany. The other countries either largely accommodated Germany's monetary policy, as did Ireland, at an allegedly high price in terms of domestic employment and welfare,[4] or achieved temporary monetary independence with the use of capital controls, as did France and Italy. This pattern also characterizes also earlier experiences: monetary policy was dominated by the United Kingdom during the gold standard and – at least to some extent – by the US during the Bretton Woods years.[5] Capital controls were also used by countries other than Britain during the gold standard,[6] and by the European countries, including West Germany, during the Bretton Woods years.

Was the failed promise of the EMS due to defective design of the institutions? Analysis of the regulations governing the EMS suggest that the institutions were clearly not designed to bypass the sovereignty of individual countries' monetary authorities, as would be needed to achieve monetary unification. The rules governing the use of the ECU and the European central bank, as well as the rules governing intervention and central bank financing, were loose enough to allow independent manoeuvre by individual countries. For example, the compulsory intervention in the foreign exchange market that is required by the EMS when two currencies reach bilateral fluctuation bands, does not impose any constraint on monetary policies, since countries can freely sterilize reserve flows.[7] The ECU has not functioned effectively as a common benchmark for monetary policies, since countries were not compelled to take specified corrective actions when the so-called divergence indicator reached the predetermined thresholds. These corrective actions were just presumed.[8] Similarly the EMS guidelines, while not precluding future enhancements of the role of the European Fund, do not in any way state the ultimate purpose of that institution.

In summary, the implementation of a monetary union is only a 'good intention' in the rules governing the EMS. The careful exclusion from those rules of all the features that could have brought about an infringement of monetary sovereignty have prevented any further autonomous evolution of the EMS.

2.2   Liberalization and the instability of financial markets

The second argument for a European central bank is based on the view that liberalization of international capital flows would make the EMS collapse. This view is re-proposed by the contribution of Rainer Masera in this volume.[9]

The collapse of a system of fixed (but adjustable) rates with perfect capital mobility could be caused by two sets of factors. First, there is the presence of different trends in monetary growth in the member countries. Although since 1979 inflation rates and monetary growth rates have converged significantly in Europe, countries like France and Italy are still viewed as 'weak' members, since their inflation rates are still roughly double those in West Germany. These countries afford higher inflation than West Germany by severing domestic financial markets from the rest of the world, and thereby preventing or minimizing the speculative attacks that take place in anticipation of the inevitable exchange rate depreciations.[10] The second set of factors which could account for the collapse of a system of adjustable parities with perfect international capital mobility is the possibility of *self-fulfilling* speculative attacks, that is runs on central banks that are not justified by divergent trends in monetary policies, relative to money demands. In the presence of self-fulfilling speculation, the very existence of different currencies – which is the implicit recognition that, at least remotely, their relative valuation can be changed – is enough to trigger speculators' activity.

What is the effect of speculation? The analysis of Euro-currency markets at times of turbulence provides a vivid illustration. When realignments of the order of 3–5% are expected to occur, short-term interest rates shoot up to 40–60% in the currencies expected to depreciate. These movements are fully consistent with the expectations about currency realignment: if the devaluation is expected to be 5% within one month, interest rate differentials on one-month deposits should be 60% (5% times 12) on a per-annum basis, to compensate for the expected capital loss. Hence it is safe to assume that, if international capital flows were fully liberalized, such short-term interest rate swings would affect domestic financial markets as well.

Supporters of the trend towards financial liberalization claim that free capital markets will force central banks to converge, without any need to unify the currencies by law. Historical experience, on the other hand, has shown that in times of crisis central banks have most frequently resorted to a temporary abrogation of the 'rules of the game' imposed by international monetary arrangements: this happened during the gold standard when the Bank of England suspended the convertibility of banknotes into gold in 1847, 1857 and 1866 (as Keynes, 1930; de Cecco, 1974a, and Dornbusch and Frenkel, 1984, documented), and has happened during the Bretton Woods years and the EMS years, when countries have resorted to various forms of regulations to stem speculative inflows[11] and outflows.[12] Since liberalization of capital controls cannot strip central banks of the right to make regulations concerning financial intermediaries and the use of currency, in times of crisis central banks would still have the option of temporarily invalidating international arrangements. Thus we are led to conclude that the liberalization of financial markets does indeed present a most serious threat to the stability of the existing monetary institutions in Europe.

3   Costs and benefits of monetary integration

Quite independently of the problems raised by the evolution of the EMS, the European currency question involves also the issues associated with the theory of optimum currency areas. The theory of optimum currency areas, started by Robert Mundell, considers the costs and benefits of common currencies, and by extension the relative desirability of fixed and flexible exchange rates. Assuming indeed that a system of adjustable exchange rates will not survive full liberalization of international capital markets, the theory of optimum currency areas can provide a guide to determine whether monetary unification might – or might not – be superior to a return to flexible exchange rates among European countries.[13]

The benefit of a common currency is that of a common medium of exchange among countries, i.e. a lowering of transactions costs. Casual empiricism suggests that the benefits from using money might be quite large: the opportunity cost of holding cash is large, and yet banknotes are a major means of payments in all industrial countries. Similarly, the benefits of a common currency are perceived to be very high by international traders and producers in different countries. The case of the monetary compensatory amounts in agriculture – a blatant exception to the principle of free trade in Europe – provides a good example of the aversion to exchange-rate changes.[14] Unfortunately, economic models which offer a convincing account of the welfare effects of money in modern economies, and a consistent justification of the costs of different moneys used by trading nations, are still lacking. Similarly, econometric evidence on the effects of exchange rate uncertainty on international trade is scant.

The costs of common currencies were seen by Robert Mundell as those of unemployment and inflation, caused by country-specific shocks that are not offset by movements of factors across the frontiers, nor by exchange rate changes. Mundell's theory relies on the presence of downward wage and price rigidity, which prevents adjustment of demand shocks in the goods and labour markets, and gives exchange rate realignments the power to affect relative prices.

The papers in the first half of this volume provide some interesting new perspectives on the theory of optimum currency areas. They concentrate on three sets of issues: the costs of relinquishing monetary independence, the determinants of factor mobility between countries, and the coordination problems of central banks in a monetary union.

Allan Drazen analyses the interactions of inflation convergence and capital markets liberalization from the perspective of public finance. Free capital markets and inflation convergence will force many European countries to a substantial restructuring of tax revenues, with direct and indirect taxes replacing the inflation tax. Drazen analyses the optimal transition to this steady state. He shows that maintaining inflation tax revenue high through increases of reserve requirements imposed on financial intermediaries might worsen public finances, by discouraging intermediation and the accumulation of productive capital.

The costs of relinquishing monetary independence are also analysed by

Vittorio Grilli, who discusses the empirical evidence on the use of the inflation tax by European countries. He documents the presence of asymmetries in the use of seigniorage, and explores the public-finance motivations to use different inflation rates in Europe. Grilli's results question the long-run sustainability of current budgetary policies in a number of European countries: such potentially disruptive divergences highlight the importance of an integration of public finance aspects into the discussion of the benefits and costs of common currencies.

The paper by Giuseppe Bertola deals with an important building block of the theory of optimum currency areas: the determinants of international factor mobility. Bertola proposes a new and potentially far-reaching theory of factor mobility. Rather than assuming *ad-hoc* adjustment costs, he argues that uncertainty is likely to be a major determinant of the international mobility of factors. By showing that, in general, the reallocation of factors in response to changes in relative prices is larger, the smaller the uncertainty about future changes in relative prices, Bertola indicates that there might exist increasing returns to stabilization activity. This insight suggests important new directions for empirical and theoretical research, aimed at quantifying the extent to which stabilizing nominal exchange rates might improve welfare. As he correctly emphasizes, the analysis is crucially affected – and complicated – by the assumptions about nominal price stickiness.

The problems of coordination of monetary policies are the focus of the papers by Alessandra Casella and Jonathan Feinstein and Carlo Carraro. Casella and Feinstein explicitly model central banks' objectives under alternative international monetary arrangements. They note that in a regime of fixed exchange rates monetary authorities have an incentive to free-ride on the partners' commitment to peg the exchange rate, and conclude that fixed exchange rates can be dominated, in a welfare sense, by flexible rates. Casella and Feinstein also offer a formal model of a common central bank, managed with a system of 'proportional representation.' They find that even in the presence of a central authority, the distortions that characterize a fixed exchange rate system are still present.

Carraro attempts to infer the tastes of European central bankers from time-series data on inflation, output growth, and other relevant macroeconomic variables. Evidence of this type is necessary to determine the scope for international policy coordination, and the sustainability of alternative cooperation schemes. Carraro's main results are that central bankers appear to have very short policy horizons, thus making cooperative outcomes difficult to sustain. He also does not find significant differences in central bankers' policy targets, a factor that facilitates policy coordination.

4   The lessons of history

Having surveyed the theoretical costs and benefits of a European Monetary Union which includes some form of common monetary authority, we should stop to consider the way in which it can actually come about, that is, its institutional feasibility. In this task, it is usually enlightening to bring back into focus some historical facts. The German and Italian experiences in the 19th century – described in the papers by Carl Holtfrerich and Valeria Sannucci, respectively – might be of interest as examples of monetary unifications, while the creation of the Federal Reserve system in the early 20th century – whose process and effects are analysed in Jeffrey Miron's paper – is an example of the creation of a 'federal' central bank.

The German and Italian experiences with monetary unification are deceptively similar at first glance. In both cases one state, Prussia and Piedmont, actively promoted political unity and, having achieved it through military victory, proceeded to establish its monetary system over the whole territory of the unified country.

But the similarity ends there. The Reichsbank and the Banca Nazionale nel Regno d'Italia (BNRI) managed to obtain a dominant position over bank note issue. The Reichsbank was a state institution, whose creation coincided with the proclamation of the German Reich. The BNRI, on the contrary, was a private bank (though its connections with the Government were close) while the banks of issue of the Kingdom of the Two Sicilies were public banks. This difference between the two cases helps to understand why the Italian monetary experience was much more chequered than the German one. The New Reich, moreover, started with hefty gold reparations of 5 billion francs paid by France, while the Kingdom of Italy began its life with a huge pile of public debt and an equally huge fiscal deficit. Even more important, before unification, Germany had become an integrated economic area and a united currency area, which was based on a silver standard. Italy, on the contrary, was a patchwork of economically heterogeneous states which, at the time of political unification, traded much more with foreign countries than with one another. Unlike the German states, they were not united by a network of railways. And the two main components of the new state, Piedmont and the Kingdom of the Two Sicilies, had currencies based on different standards, the former on bimetallism (like the French), the latter on a pure silver standard.

We have thus two cases that are extremely relevant for the present debate on European monetary union. The Italian case shows political and monetary unification preceding economic integration. The German case shows economic and monetary integration leading to political unification.

We are the latest in a very long line of researchers believing that Italian unification was a sudden and largely unexpected event, while German unification was a long and gradual process which occupied the best part of the 19th century. This basic difference can go far toward explaining the great difficulties which the new Italian state experienced in the economic and monetary fields, and in particular the long and difficult process of building a modern banking system around a publicly-controlled central bank. On the other hand, the great success of the German Reich can be attributed to the economic and monetary unification which preceded political unity. The influence of the immediate past over the present and future, both in the case of Germany and Italy, seems to have been overwhelming.[15]

Early attempts at European monetary unification, like that promoted in the Werner Report of 1970, can be likened to Italy in 1860 or even 1870. Economic and financial unity was not advanced enough in either case to justify the great step forward represented by monetary union. The economic integration of Europe in 1988 is arguably much greater than it was at the time of the Werner Report. The motorway network (which has had an impact on integration comparable to that of railways in the 19th century) is now much more complete than it was then, and it allows greater economic and social interchange (witness the much smaller size of firms engaged in intra-European trade). Total intra-European trade has stabilized for many years at a very high level, so that the interpenetration of the economies is much greater (witness the increased trade in intermediate, semiprocessed and component goods among EC countries). This evolution reminds us of Germany's experiences.

All three historical papers very clearly point out that monetary union, in its 19th century incarnation as free circulation of coins among states and in its present reincarnation as joint floating plus liberalization of capital flows, is altogether possible without political unification. A central bank to control monetary policy over the whole area of the Union, however, is the single most important step into uncharted territory, when it is not preceded by political union: Niels Thygesen convincingly raises this point in his remarks.

How were local interests reconciled by central monetary authorities? The Federal Reserve Charter, the Federal Reserve Act of 1913, is the expression of a much more heterogeneous economic reality than the Reichsbank foundation law, the Bank Act of 1871. The plurality of the Federal Reserve Banks witnesses that clearly, as it had been the case with the National Banking Act of 1861. But the problem of discretionary money creation was solved by the US decision to adopt the Gold Standard, just as it was solved by the German States by adopting silver convertibility and by the Reich by switching to the Gold Standard. The inelasticity of a commodity standard was, however, taken into account by the Federal Reserve Act and by the Bank Act, by allowing a possibility of exercising discretionary money creation. It is precisely that possibility that permitted the interest stabilisation which Miron attributes to the Fed and criticises as the Fed's main policy target. Interest stabilisation was one of the main policy targets of the pre-1914 Reichsbank too, widely admired, as the similar policy adopted by the Banque de France, by the members of the National Monetary Commission, and favourably contrasted with the vagaries of US and British interest rates.

Thus both the US and Germany worked on semi-automatic commodity standards, which gave central banks a wider discretionary space than is normally remembered in today's discussions. It might be useful to consider also that the Fed's regional pluralism over the conduct of monetary policy was imitated by the (American) designers of the present-day German central bank. Even this diffusion of power, however, is altogether different from what is at stake with the creation of a European Central Bank. In both the German and the US cases the greater devolution of powers over monetary policy takes place within the context of one Government and one currency. Neither has yet been achieved in Europe.

5   Feasible institutional reforms

What should then be the shape of a European monetary authority? As Rainer Masera suggests in his remarks, it is perhaps more useful to think in terms of a common monetary authority for Europe, rather than of a European Central Bank. This is what the Single European Act does, when it mentions the EC Monetary Committee and the Committee of Governors of the Central Banks as 'bodies to be consulted regarding institutional changes in the monetary area.' The distinction between a European Monetary Board (as Masera calls it) and a European Central Bank is not merely semantic. Without political union we can be quite sure that a European Central Bank, even one shaped like the Federal Reserve System or the Bundesbank, will not be feasible. An institutional step of this size implies a once-and-for-all abdication of monetary sovereignty which it is very unrealistic to expect from the EC countries.

But will such a loose arrangement be able to stand the pressure coming from the effects of intra-EC liberalization of capital movements? If 1992 brings about, as there is every indication that it will, the integration of European banking – freedom of establishment by European banks wherever they want on EC territory – another large chunk of traditional monetary sovereignty will have been eroded. A full application of the right of establishment for banks and other financial institutions brings with it a series of problems of banking supervision and of the management of the lender of last resort function. Also in these cases, agreements can be struck among the central banks which have full legal status and are far enough from the glare of macroeconomic policy, but at the same time profoundly relevant to it. These agreements are essential to help establish a truly European payments network, which will make the re-cycling of balances much easier and much more casual among European regions:[16] as Cohen suggests in his paper, intra-European balances of payments could thus become just a statistical curiosity.

The panel discussions by Masera, Russo, Rieke and Thygesen offer a number of interesting views, and a number of actual proposals, on the practical implementation of a European monetary authority. Rather than summarizing their views here, at the risk of misrepresenting them, we prefer to leave the task of interpretation to the readers. One aspect of the panel discussion that has struck us is the surprising homogeneity of the proposals. This homogeneity could be a good sign that agreement on the institutional reforms to be undertaken in the years to come might – in principle – not be hard to work out.

NOTES

1 The ECU is defined as a basket comprising the currencies of the countries members of the European Economic Community, hence it includes currencies, like the Greek drachma and Pound sterling, which are not part of the EMS.
2 The issuance of bonds dominated in a basket of currencies identical to the ECU has boomed in recent years in the Euromarkets.
3 The fluctuation bands that characterize the EMS have also been a feature of the gold standard and the Bretton Woods regime. For example, under Bretton Woods, the maximum fluctuation of bilateral European rates was 4%, versus 4.5% in the EMS. The lira is of course an exception to the rule.
4 See Moore (1988).
5 See Giovannini (1988) for a formulation of this hypothesis, and empirical evidence supporting it.
6 In the form of manipulation of gold points, and limited convertibility of banknotes into gold for exports.
7 In fact, intervention at the fluctuation margins has been just a small fraction of total intervention.
8 In practice, the divergence indicator has a host of additional problems originating from the asymmetric weights of the different currencies. It has played no significant role in the functioning of the EMS.
9 A formalization of this argument is provided by Obstfeld (1988).
10 Giavazzi and Giovannini (1989) provide a survey of Italian and French controls on international capital flows, and a formal analysis of their effects.
11 As in the case of Germany in 1960.

12 The French and Italian experience in 1968 and 1969, as well as in the more recent years, is relevant.
13 On these questions, see also de Cecco (1974b).
14 As Giavazzi and Giovannini (1989) point out, the system of monetary compensatory amounts in agriculture is explained by the concern of agricultural producers with fluctuations of the price of their output induced by exchange rate movements, which are automatically and equiproportionally reflected in output prices by the Common Agricultural Policy, which fixes Europe-wide prices in a common unit of account.
15 Another important factor was that the BNRI, as the first and especially the Second Bank of the United States, was a commercial bank trying to establish itself, with some backing from the government, as a central bank. The Reichsbank, by contrast, was confined to the public good by its charter. This contrast, while historically pertinent, is not useful for the present-day debate. Central banks are now firmly established as public banks, and no-one can think of giving back to them a commercial banking function.
16 It will also reduce the tasks of national central banks as lenders of last resort in their own domestic markets.

REFERENCES

De Cecco, M. (1974a). *Money and Empire*, Totowa, NJ: Rowman and Littlefield, (1974b), 'Optimum Currency Areas and European Monetary Integration' *Journal of World Trade Law* **8**, pp. 463–74.
Dornbusch, R. and J. Frenkel (1984). 'The Gold Standard Crisis of 1847', *Journal of International Economics* **16**, pp. 1–27.
Giavazzi, F. and A. Giovannini (1989). *Limiting Exchange Rate Flexibility: The European Monetary System*, Cambridge, MA: MIT Press.
Giovannini, A. (1988). 'How do Fixed-Exchange-Rate Regimes Work: The Evidence on the Gold Standard, Bretton Woods, and EMS.' CEPR Discussion Paper No. 282.
Keynes, J.M. (1930). *A Treatise on Money*, London: Macmillan.
Moore, M. (1988). 'Deflationary Consequences of a Hard Currency Peg,' mimeo, Research Department, Central Bank of Ireland.
Obstfeld, M. (1988). 'Competitiveness, Realignment, and Speculation: The Role of Financial Markets,' in F. Giavazzi, S. Micossi and M. Miller (eds.), *The European Monetary System*, Cambridge: Cambridge University Press.

2 Monetary policy, capital controls and seigniorage in an open economy

ALLAN DRAZEN

1   Introduction

Several European countries rely heavily on inflation tax revenues to finance their expenditures. Seigniorage accounted for between 6 and 12% of government revenues in Greece, Italy, Portugal, and Spain in the period 1979–86 (in contrast to generally less than one percent in most of the rest of Western Europe over the same period). These countries argue that reliance on the inflation tax is made necessary by a poorly developed tax base for regular taxes. The potential loss of seigniorage as a revenue source under alternative monetary and capital market arrangements is therefore a prime concern to these countries in analysing such arrangements. For example, the loss of revenues from a decreased inflation rate is crucial in a decision by some of these countries of whether or not to join the EMS.

A look at the data on revenue from money creation reveals that the issue is more complex than simply the revenue loss from reducing the inflation rate. The four high-seigniorage countries not only have higher inflation rates than their Northern neighbours, but have significantly higher monetary bases as well. (See Table 2.1, based on Giavazzi, 1988.) Disaggregating the monetary base, one sees that the significant difference is not in currency to GDP ratios, but in bank reserves (relative to GDP) which are an order of magnitude higher. The last two columns of the table explain why this is so. High bank reserves do not reflect much larger banking sectors, as evidenced by bank deposits as a percentage of GDP not being significantly higher in the 'Southern' countries; instead, the higher monetary base reflects a ratio of bank reserves to deposits several times as high in the 'Southern' relative to the 'Northern' countries. Hence significant revenue from money creation in the Southern countries depends on a high demand for reserves by financial intermediaries.[1]

The high reserve to deposit ratios (that is, high demand for reserves)

13

	Seigniorage (% of tax revenues) 1979–86	Monetary Base (% GDP 1986)			Bank Deposits % GDP 1986	Reserve to Deposit ratio %
		Total	Currency	Bank Reserves		
Greece	9.1	22.6	9.8	12.8	48.6	26.5
Italy	6.2	18.6	6.8	11.8	66.6	17.7
Portugal	11.9	20.5	9.5	11.0	38.6	28.6
Spain	5.9	19.3	7.5	11.8	60.2	19.6
Belgium	0.4	8.2	7.8	0.4	33.4	1.2
France	1.3	5.9	4.5	1.4	38.5	3.8
Germany	0.8	9.9	5.8	4.1	53.2	7.8
UK	0.5	4.6	3.6	1.0	45.7	2.1

Table 2.1 *The importance and sources of seigniorage revenues*

Notes: This table is drawn from several tables in Giavazzi (1988).
Sources: Seigniorage is the change in the monetary base, line 14 from *International Financial Statistics* of the International Monetary Fund. The definition of seigniorage is as in Fischer (1982), not the more general notion of total revenue from money creation suggested in Drazen (1985).

Tax revenues are from *Revenue Statistics of OECD Member Countries*. They include personal and corporate income taxes, employers' and employees' social security contributions, and property, consumption, and excise taxes.

Currency is line 14a from *IFS*.
Bank reserves is line 20 from *IFS*.
Bank Deposits are demand, time and savings, and foreign currency deposits, lines 25 and 26 from *IFS*.

reflect primarily government regulations or portfolio restrictions. (See for example Welch, 1981.) Foremost among these of course are higher reserve requirements, though other portfolio restrictions play a role. Understanding the effect of alternative monetary regimes on seigniorage (broadly defined) therefore means understanding how demand for reserves, especially the ability of countries to impose restrictions generating a demand for reserves, would be affected.[2]

The importance of portfolio restrictions in generating demand for reserves and thus government revenues has two key implications. First, it is opening up capital markets (rather than simply reducing inflation rates *per se*) which would largely remove seigniorage as a revenue source. If capital market liberalization makes it impossible to impose different regulations on financial intermediaries across countries, maintaining the competitiveness of local banks would compel governments to match the least restrictive regulations in force, causing reserve holding and seigniorage to fall sharply. In the absence of open capital markets, on the other hand, inflation tax revenues can be maintained in the face of reductions in the inflation rate by the imposition of capital controls and high reserve requirements. The case of Italy is instructive here. As Giavazzi (1988) points out, simultaneous with the sharp reduction in the inflation rate subsequent to Italy's joining the EMS was an increase in reserve requirements (and thus the monetary base) so that the revenue from money creation fell far less than the inflation rate.

Thus the importance of capital controls in generating seigniorage means that the real threat to this revenue source is the integration of capital markets envisioned in 1992. Expenditures and transfers will have to be financed, at least eventually, by regular taxation in excess of debt service. Countries that have relied on revenue from money creation previously will be able to maintain government expenditures without resorting to bond financing only if debt service is low or the regular tax base is high.

The second implication of the crucial role of reserve requirements in generating government revenues has to do with their long-run effects on revenue. Forcing financial intermediaries to hold a higher fraction of their portfolios as low-yielding reserves reduces the return to saving which will reduce private asset accumulation. Slower accumulation of income-producing (and therefore tax-producing) assets adversely affects the tax base over time. Therefore increasing reserve requirements may increase government revenue today at the expense of reducing government revenue in the future. That is, though using seigniorage heavily is motivated by a low tax base, heavy use in itself may lower the future tax base! *A priori* there is a tradeoff. High reserve requirements can reduce government debt and hence debt service relative to what they otherwise would have been (leading to a better fiscal position), but do so at the possible expense of reducing the base for regular taxation, perhaps so much so to actually worsen the fiscal position. Policymakers must therefore consider the total fiscal effects of policies designed to increase seigniorage revenues.

These two points – the likely loss of seigniorage as a major revenue source after 1992; and the possible detrimental effects of reserve requirements on the future tax base – lead one to ask how monetary policy (specifically required and inflation policy) should be used prior to an anticipated capital market liberalization in order to arrive at the liberalization date in the best possible fiscal position. Looking at the narrow issue of growth in debt and the tax base, should a country 'milk' this revenue source as much as possible while it is still available? Should a country choose a low-inflation path (that is, by joining the EMS) or should it postpone reducing inflation until capital market integration requires a reduction? This paper is a preliminary attempt to address these questions.

Because the model is both simple and specialized, especially in the modelling of the tax base, the analysis should be seen as a number of examples which are meant to be suggestive.

Whether net asset accumulation increases or decreases depends on the whole constellation of monetary policies, specifically how much the contractionary effects of higher reserve requirements are offset by other policy actions. I present two polar cases: one in which other monetary policies are accommodating in that open market operations and central bank lending fully offset the contractionary effects of increased reserve requirements; the second where monetary policy is tight, so that capital formation is 'squeezed'. In the first case, government debt grows less fast and the tax base rises, so that imposing high reserve requirements before a liberalization improves the fiscal position. In the second case, it is shown that under certain conditions the tax base may fall so much that the fiscal position is worsened by use of reserve requirements to generate a high monetary base. On the choice of the inflation rate, a high inflation rate prior to liberalization tends to improve the fiscal position, though for different reasons in the two cases.

As the above discussion indicates, policies will be ranked in terms of their effects on the government's budget position, rather than in the broader sense of their effect on utility. I have chosen this focus because of my interest in the problems policymakers actually perceive themselves as facing. In the case of Italy for example a central policy question is how to restrain the growth of the government debt in the face of limited sources of tax revenue. In many countries with persistent budgetary problems Central Banks view the choice of inflation policy not in terms of broad welfare maximization but in terms of its revenue implications, and very short-term ones at that. The message of the paper is that even if one focusses on the revenue implications of inflation policy, the long-run effects of a policy may be quite different from the short-run effects.

The paper is organized as follows. In the next section the basic model is set out. Section 3 considers the effects on the government's budget position of increasing reserve requirements in anticipation of an expected capital market liberalization at some known future date T, and Section 4 the budgetary effects of alternative inflation policies. Section 5 presents conclusions and an overview.

2   A basic model

The model is built to highlight the preliberalization dynamics in terms of the narrow budget questions outlined above. I will first describe the setup of the economy under capital controls, with special emphasis on how the financial sector is modelled. The workings of the financial sector after capital controls have been removed is then a simple extension. I will then describe government behaviour, both on the monetary and fiscal side. The third subsection describes individual maximization. The modelling of government and individual behavior will yield the differential equations which describe the dynamic behavior of the economy.

2.1 Financial structure of the economy

The economy is initially subject to capital controls which prohibit domestic residents from engaging in capital account transactions with the rest of the world or holding foreign securities. Under a fixed exchange rate regime, the central bank fixes the commercial exchange rate, buying and selling foreign exchange for commercial purposes only. Foreign exchange earnings from current account transactions must be converted into domestic currency at the central bank. With a single consumption good which may be freely imported or exported and with a foreign inflation rate of zero, this fixes the domestic price level as well. Under a flexible rate system, prohibition of capital account transactions implies that the current account must always be in balance. The assumptions on the goods market imply that the commercial exchange rate depreciates at the rate of domestic inflation.

The assets of the central bank are net holdings of foreign securities f and domestic government debt b^{CB}, both in real terms. Central bank lending to financial intermediaries yields offsetting items on both sides of the T-account and is netted out for now. Population growth is set equal to zero, so that variables may be thought of as *per capita*. The central bank values foreign assets at the world price, which remains constant over time and is therefore normalized to one. Liabilities are the monetary base, consisting of currency m and reserve holdings x by financial intermediaries, also measured in real terms. The central bank's T-account thus implies that

$$m + x = f + b^{CB} \tag{1}$$

Monetary policy in an economy with capital controls consists of several aspects. Foremost for our purposes is the required reserve ratio, denoted j, and the rate of change of the money supply. If we denote by μ^F the growth rate of the money supply above that which is necessary to manage the exchange rate, this will also equal the rate of inflation. (The F superscript is used as a reminder that this is not the total rate of monetary growth, but only that part yielding revenue to the fiscal authority.) The central bank may also pay interest on unborrowed reserves, lend reserves to banks, and engage in open market operations. The last two will be relevant here at the time of a change in reserve requirements.

The empirical importance of bank reserves in the monetary base for countries that rely on seigniorage suggests modelling financial intermediaries as having a key role in the saving and investment process. It is therefore assumed that funds to finance investment must be raised through financial intermediaries (rather than assuming that firms can raise capital directly from ultimate asset holders). Placing banks at the centre of the process of financing investment, made here to highlight the effect of reserve requirements on the capital accumulation process, is consistent with a number of the economies discussed above. Intermediaries also hold reserves with the central bank equal to a fixed fraction j of their liabilities s, meaning they hold no excess reserves. Denoting loans to finance capital accumulation by k, we have

$$
\begin{aligned}
s &= k + x \\
  &= k + js
\end{aligned}
\tag{2}
$$

In order to model reductions in the economy's productive assets, it is assumed that these loans are not marketable assets which the financial intermediary can simply sell to another holder. Liquidation of loans in the intermediary's portfolio means that the entrepreneur must reduce his investment, so that a fall in s or an increase in j will lead (other things equal) to a fall in productive assets k rather than simply a transfer in ownership. As in the textbook story, there will be a 'multiple contraction' of deposits. (Technically, k is a control rather than a state variable.)

Under the assumptions of no holding of foreign securities and no direct holding of capital, individuals hold three assets: money; saving deposits (the liability of financial intermediaries); and government bonds, denoted (in real terms) b^P. (I assume that saving deposits are *not* money in order to highlight how a fall in the interest rate to borrowers can constrict investment via a fall in saving done through financial intermediaries.) Total real wealth a is therefore

$$
a = b^P + s + m
\tag{3}
$$

These three equations summarize the T-accounts of government, financial intermediaries, and individuals. It is useful to note that under capital controls the net foreign asset position of the economy can change only via current account surpluses or deficits, with the central bank acting as intermediary for the public.

A further key implication of capital controls is that domestic real interest rates need not equal the world interest rate, r^*. Government bonds and saving deposits must bear the same real rate of interest r. Denoting the return to capital (i.e. investment) by ρ, where ρ is assumed to be constant, competition among financial intermediaries implies that

$$r = (1 - j)\rho + j(i^x - \mu^F) \tag{4}$$

where i^x is the nominal interest rate paid on reserves. Output in the economy is linear in k, namely ρk. The possibility of steady state with no capital controls requires $\rho = \beta \, (= r^*)$.

2.2   Consolidated government behaviour

I first consider the evolution of debt and then discuss modelling of the tax base. The monetary authority is assumed to turn any interest earnings on foreign assets over to the fiscal authority, which in turn is responsible for paying interest on reserves. We then write a single consolidated flow budget constraint for the government as

$$\dot{b}^P = rb^P + g + i^x x - \tau - \mu^F(m + x) - r^*f, \tag{5}$$

where g is government expenditures, τ is taxes minus transfers, and where interest paid on government debt held by the central bank is also returned to the fiscal authority. Using equation (1) this may be written as

$$\dot{b}^P = rb^P + g - \tau - [\mu^F(m + x) + r^*(m + x - b^{CB}) - i^x x] \tag{6}$$

The term in brackets is revenue from money creation. The first two components are those set out in Drazen (1985) for an economy without banks. The first is the real value of newly printed money (above that used to manage the exchange rate) $\mu^F(m + x)$. Seigniorage is often taken to refer to this term alone, as in Table 2.1. The second term is the interest earnings on that part of *previous* issuance which went to purchase interest-bearing assets, $r^*(m + x - b^{CB})$. This term may be easier to understand when one notes that previous money issuance used to finance government consumption was transferred to the fiscal authority in exchange for the sale of government interest-bearing debt to the central bank. As I argue in Drazen (1985) most of the popular measures of seigniorage may be seen as special cases of the sum of these two terms. The last term is an adjustment due to payment of interest on reserves. If, as Pagano argues in his discussion of the Italian case, nominal interest i^x is fixed, positive reserve holding could lead to a *fall* in real revenues when the inflation rate fell. On the other hand, if i^x were adjusted with changes in μ^F to keep the real return constant, growth in the reserve component of the monetary base would yield positive revenue (assuming that i^x were no greater than μ^F).

After some manipulation (and using the fact that $\rho = r^*$), the budget constraint may be written as

$$\dot{b}^P = r^*(b^P + b^{CB}) + g - \tau - (r + \mu^F)m \\ - j(r^* - (i^x - \mu^F))a \tag{7}$$

This equation will summarize the evolution of debt prior to the date of liberalization T, conditional on the evolution of m and a and from the consumer's problem.[3] For future use, I denote total government debt outstanding by $b = b^P + b^{CB}$.

After T, with capital markets fully integrated and controls no longer in force, both reserve requirements and inflation (under fixed exchange rates consistent with EMS membership) are determined by world levels. Assuming for simplicity that these are zero, the budget constraint (5) becomes

$$\dot{b}^P = r^*b^P + g - \tau - r^*f \tag{8}$$

Feasible expenditures after T consistent with no growth in b^P are

$$g = \tau + r^*f - r^*b^P \\ = \tau + r^*m - r^*b \tag{9}$$

Given the discussion in the introduction on the fiscal problem economies perceive they face, I will rank policies in terms of feasible expenditure at T consistent with no growth of government debt.

Since we want to see how the tax base and thus feasible collections change in response to monetary policy, τ must be made endogenous. The modelling of the tax base will be quite primitive. I assume that τ is simply an increasing function of net assets in the economy $a - b$. (Similar results qualitatively would arise if τ were a function of $a - b - m$ which equals k after T). Returning to the stock constraints (1) through (3) one notes that

$$a - b^P = s + m \\ = k + x + m = k + f + b^{CB} \tag{10}$$

so that

$$a - b = k + f \tag{11}$$

It will turn out to be easy to derive dynamics for the quantity $a - b$ and hence for the sum of capital plus foreign securities together, but much more complicated to derive unambiguous dynamics for k and f separately. This is not too surprising as they are the two net income-producing assets in the economy and will yield the same return in steady state under perfect capital mobility. (Consider equation (18) below.)

2.3   *Individual maximization*

The representative consumer's utility is a function of consumption c and money balances m. Given the above assumptions about the financial structure and about output equalling ρk (so that all income can be represented as coming from asset holding), the consumer maximizes

$$\int_0^\infty u(c_t, m_t) e^{-\beta t} dt \tag{12}$$

subject to a budget constraint

$$\int_0^\infty (c_t + i_t m_t) e^{-R(t)} dt \le a_0 - \int_0^\infty \tau_t e^{-R(t)} dt \tag{13}$$

where $R(t)$ is the interest factor, equal to $\int_0^t r(s) ds$, and i_t is the nominal interest rate. The budget is written this way to take account of the change in the interest rate at 0 and at T.

The solution to the consumer's problem is standard except for the jump in the interest rate at 0 and T. The solution may be written

$$u_c(c_t, m_t) = \lambda_t \tag{14}$$

$$u_m(c_t, m_t) = \lambda_t i_t \tag{15}$$

$$\lambda_t e^{-\beta t} = \lambda_s e^{-\beta s} e^{R(s) - R(t)} \tag{16}$$

where λ_t is the marginal utility of wealth and where at points where the real interest rate $r(t)$ jumps (so that $R(t)$ is continuous, but with different right-hand and left-hand derivatives) dR/dt is taken to be the right-hand derivative. Expressing the budget constraint in derivative form we have (for points where a does not jump)

$$\dot{a} = r_t a_t - c_t - i_t m_t - \tau_t \tag{17}$$

where r is defined by (4). Equations (14) through (17) fully summarize individual behaviour for given expectations about the future time path of τ and of course current government policy as summarized by g, τ, j, and μ. Combined with equation (7) giving the evolution of government debt, they determine the movement of the system prior to T. For the policy changes we consider it will often be sufficient to consider only a subset of these equations. It will be especially useful to consider the evolution of $a - b$ between 0 and T, derived by subtracting (7) from (17). Denoting this variable by $\gamma = a - b = a - b^P - b^{CB}$, we have

$$\dot{\gamma} = r^* \gamma - c - g \tag{18}$$

where it is assumed that the government engages in no open market operations after time zero, implying $\dot{b}^{CB} = 0$, so that $\dot{b} = \dot{b}^P$.

One may also note that since (11) implies that $\gamma = k + f$, (18) may be thought of as the equation for the economy's net accumulation of income-producing assets. Under this interpretation (18) can be written as

$$\dot{f} = r^*(k + f) - c - \dot{k} - g \tag{19}$$

so that foreign asset accumulation equals economy-wide income minus absorption.

3   Reserve requirement policy in anticipation of capital market liberalization

We are now ready to consider how government revenue is affected by choice of monetary policy until the date of liberalization T. As the discussion following equation (6) indicated, the two policy variables that affect seigniorage revenues most directly are reserve requirements and the rate of monetary growth. I will concentrate on the first in this section by considering an economy with a fixed exchange rate relative to zero-inflation trading partners, and concentrate on the second in the next section by considering the same economy with flexible exchange rates and a positive rate of inflation.

The main message of this section is that a policy of increasing reserve requirements (raising j) to increase revenue today may do so at the cost of lowering government revenue in the future. Specifically, government debt will accumulate less rapidly, but so will private asset holding, so that on net the tax base may rise or fall. As indicated in the introduction reliance on seigniorage (broadly defined) may exacerbate the problem of raising revenue. I will consider two polar cases to show that depending on the type of monetary policy that accompanies the increase in reserve requirements, the fiscal position at T in terms of increased feasible government spending may either improve or worsen.

Two make things more concrete, let us consider the following scenario. A country which has imposed capital controls knows that its capital market will be integrated at T with countries which have lower reserve requirements (for simplicity taken to be zero). What levels of reserve requirements should it choose prior to T to put the fiscal budget in the 'best possible shape' when capital markets are opened? (The analogous question for inflation will be asked in the next section.) Should it extract large seigniorage revenues by setting high reserve requirements? For expositional simplicity I assume that initially the economy is in a steady state with zero inflation and zero reserve requirements, and consider a choice of a constant j prior to T.

I consider the effects of increasing j until T first for 'loose' and then 'tight' monetary policy, with tax and expenditure policy held fixed. At T free flow of capital is allowed and government spending is chosen to ensure no further growth of debt for the endogenous maximum feasible τ.[4] The elimination of capital market restrictions further implies that reserve requirements must be set at the world level. For simplicity I assume throughout, unless otherwise noted, that the real interest rate paid on unborrowed reserves is zero (that is, $i^x = \mu^F$).

Before considering the precise policy experiments, some characteristics of time paths which are independent of the specific cases may be noted. Before $t = 0$ the economy is in a steady state with $r = \rho = r^*$. Under the assumption of no real interest paid on reserves, the real rate of interest is constant at a level $r = (1 - j)r^*$ until T, at which time it returns to a level $r^* (= \beta)$. The level of k achieved just before T is thus the steady-state level.

Given the assumption about the equality of the discount rate β to the world interest rate r^*, whatever level of domestic wealth a is achieved just prior to T from the consumer's maximization problem is consistent with a steady state. Adjustment of government expenditure g at T implies that the same is true for the level of government debt achieved at T, so that any level of $\gamma = a - b$ is consistent with a steady state. Hence the terminal values of a and b that the economy must hit at T are simply whatever the existing values are. (While γ will not jump at T, its composition between capital and net foreign securities held by the government can change due to capital mobility.)

3.1   *Accommodating monetary policy*

I first consider the case where the central bank fully 'accommodates' any change in the demand for both currency and reserves induced by increased reserve requirements (and hence lower interest rates) at time zero. The discrete increase in the demand for currency is met by an open-market purchase of debt held by the public; the discrete increase in demand for reserves is met by freely lending reserves to financial intermediaries. (After time 0 individuals adjust their money balances via current account surpluses of deficits, as in (19)). Specifically, the central bank lends financial intermediaries whatever reserves they need to meet reserve requirements without their lending to investors being affected. The key implication is that these two accommodative policies imply that capital at the time of the reserve requirement change will therefore be unaffected. With unborrowed reserves remaining unchanged and with b^{CB} rising by the amount of the desired increase in m, net holding of foreign assets f will also remain unchanged, so that γ will also be unchanged at $t = 0$. (One could also derive this from the individual's wealth constraint, by noting that this policy leaves a unchanged and implies that b^P falls by the amount that b^{CB} rises.)

With individual asset holding a unchanged, net after-tax wealth will depend on expectations of future tax policy via its effect on after-tax wealth. Other things equal different expectations of future taxes (more generally different fiscal policies) will clearly have different implications for current consumption and hence future asset accumulation. Since the goal here is to stress the role of monetary policy in determining the time path of consumption and asset accumulation, I will assume that the individual myopically anticipates that with an unchanged tax system (that is, unchanged *function* $\tau(\ )$), the present discounted value of tax payments will remain unchanged. (Strictly speaking, with the tax base being endogenous, an unchanged tax system would imply that present discounted taxes would change as γ changes. Since the evolution of consumption itself affects γ, analysis of this case appears to be quite complicated.

Though it would be preferable to perform the analysis under the assumption of rational expectations about the future path of taxes, as Calvo does for a simplified example in his discussion, the complexity of the analysis with an endogenous tax base dictates the simpler approach and allows me to concentrate on the monetary aspects of the problem.

Even under the assumptions that utility is separable in c and m and that the individual expects the present discounted value of tax payments to remain unchanged, consumption may jump at $t = 0$.[5] Whether

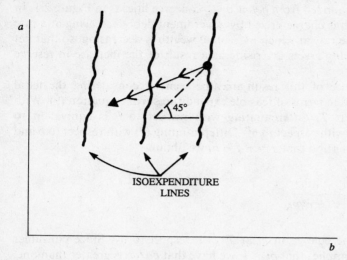

Figure 2.1 Accommodative policy

consumption jumps up or down will depend on both the form of the utility function and on T. For the case of log-linear utility $u(c, m) = \ln c + \alpha \ln m$, consumption will jump down (being equal to $(1 + e^{(r-\beta)T} - e^{-\beta T})^{-1} \beta/(1 + \alpha)$ times after-tax wealth, rather than $\beta/(1 + \alpha)$ times after-tax wealth). For a CRRA utility function, consumption may jump either up or down, depending on both the coefficient of risk aversion and on T. For now, I concentrate on the case of separable, log-linear utility.

With no jump in γ and a downward jump in c at $t = 0$, (18) indicates that $\dot{\gamma} > 0$ at $t = 0$. Inspection of the dynamic equations for a and b^P individually shows that $\dot{a}$ and $\dot{b}^P$ are both negative at $t = 0$, so that in $a - b$ space, the movement of the system must be above a 45-degree line from the initial steady state. (See Figure 2.1.)

The movement of the system after $t = 0$ can be found first by differentiating (18) to obtain

$$\ddot{\gamma} = \beta \dot{\gamma} - \dot{c}, \tag{20}$$

where $\ddot{\gamma}$ indicates the second derivative of γ with respect to time. Since $\dot{\gamma}$ is zero at $t = 0$ but $\dot{c}$ is negative $\ddot{\gamma}$ will be positive at $t = 0$. $\dot{\gamma}$ will therefore be positive immediately after 0. Since $\dot{c}$ is negative until T, repeating this argument implies that $\dot{\gamma} > 0$ until T, meaning the slope of the path is less than one in absolute value. With no capital controls after T, individuals can freely trade assets so that there is no jump in γ at T. Therefore the entire path is bounded from *below* by a 45-degree line, as in Figure 2.1. In words, the path is characterized by government debt decreasing at a rate greater than the rate at which individual wealth is decreasing, so that net income-producing assets are rising as a result of the increase in reserve requirements.

The importance of this result may be seen by considering the fiscal position at T as in terms of feasible expenditures from equation (9). With b^{CB} constant at T, differentiating with respect to b is equivalent to differentiating with respect to b^P. Differentiating (9) with respect to b and using the assumption that $\tau = \tau(a - b)$ we obtain

$$\frac{da}{db} = \frac{\tau' + r^*}{\tau' + r^* m_a} \tag{21}$$

where m_a is the change in m at T with respect to a_T. Since consumer maximization implies that $m_a < 1$, we have that da/db is greater than one, implying that the isoexpenditure lines are bounded by a 45-degree line from *above*.

Combined with the characteristics of the dynamic path, we find that the movement of the system is unambiguously in the direction of an improved fiscal position. To summarize, for the case of a log-linear utility function, an increase in reserve requirements prior to a capital market liberalization leads to an unambiguous improvement in the fiscal position at the date of liberalization when this change is accompanied by accommodative monetary policy. Both government indebtedness is lower (implying lower debt service) and the tax base is higher.

More generally, an unambiguous fiscal improvement and increase in the tax base depends on consumption either jumping down or staying constant at $t = 0$. If consumption takes an initial upward jump, net asset accumulation will initially fall, with its dynamics afterwards being ambiguous. In such a case, the fiscal improvement is no longer unambiguous: whether government spending can be higher at the date of liberalization will depend on how large T is. As Calvo shows in his discussion of a simplified version of this model, if fiscal policy were changed so that tax revenues were returned to consumers as lump sum transfers, rather than being used to finance government spending, consumption would necessarily jump up at $t = 0$. In either case the sign of $\dot{a}$ (corresponding to the sign of $\dot{k}$ in his model where both b and m are zero) will be negative.

It may seem strange that *net* asset accumulation rises in responses to a change that should depress saving. To understand why, one should remember first that government debt is growing less fast. Second, the increase in reserve requirements affects private asset accumulation in two main ways. The first is the initial contractionary effect on bank lending and hence wealth; the second, the dynamic effect through its effect on interest rates. The contractionary effect on lending, which figures prominently in intuitive discussions, is eliminated by accommodative monetary policy. Given no contractionary effects on capital, what is left is the decrease in interest rates received by lenders. This decrease implies that consumption will be falling over time, which we saw leads to accumulation of net assets. Alternatively, one could think of the fall in consumption being driven by the fall in individual wealth following from a lower rate of return. Hence it is the setting of policy which eliminates one of the intuitive effects of higher reserve requirements and means that the fall in consumption over time is dominant.

3.2   Restrictive monetary policy

I now consider the other polar case (still under zero inflation) of raising reserve requirements without offsetting the contractionary effects of this change by an accommodative monetary policy. With no open market operations or central bank lending of reserves we see from the balance sheet of financial intermediaries that capital accumulation is 'squeezed' from two sides. On the liability side, s falls as individuals redeem deposits in order to build up their money balances. On the asset side, the increase in j means that for a given level of deposits, loanable funds fall. Hence k falls[6] while f is unchanged (by the nature of the experiment), so that γ must jump down at $t = 0$. Looked at from the perspective of the individual's asset constraint, deposits in aggregate will fall more than m rises due to the 'multiple contraction of deposits' effect.[7]

With b constant, the fall in a implies that there is also a downward jump in γ at $t = 0$, as in Figure 2.2. This fall in economy-wide net wealth taken alone worsens the fiscal position via its effects on the tax base, and represents the key negative effect of higher reserve requirements. Whether the fiscal position is also worse at time T depends on the characteristics of the path after time 0, that is, on the sign of $\dot{\gamma}$. This will depend on the change in c (reflecting in part the downward jump in a) relative to r^* times the jump in γ itself. This will of course depend on the specific utility function.

The key role of the jump in γ (and hence of non-accommodating monetary policy) may be seen by considering dynamics for the utility function $u(c, m) = \ln c + \alpha \ln m$ considered above. The downward jump in consumption is unambiguous, the result in the previous section being

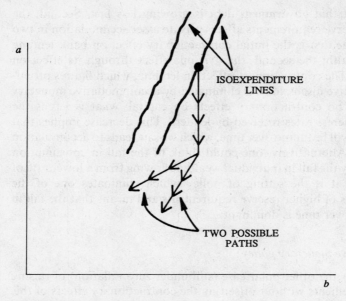

ISOEXPENDITURE
LINES

TWO POSSIBLE
PATHS

Figure 2.2   Tight monetary policy

strengthened by the downward jump in a. However, a simple calculation shows that the downward jump in c may exceed or fall short of r^* times the jump in a.[8] For α large or $(e^{(r-\beta)T} - e^{-\beta T})$ small it will fall short. (18) then indicates that $\dot{\gamma}$ will be unambiguously negative at $t = 0$. Combined with the initial downward jump in γ at $t = 0$, this means that γ and hence the tax base will be lower at the date of liberalization T, unless T is sufficiently large. This is in sharp contrast to the case of accommodative monetary policy where, for the same preferences and expectations of future tax policy, there was an unambiguous improvement in the fiscal position. Hence we see the crucial importance of accompanying monetary policy in determining whether an increase in reserve requirements leads to an improvement or deterioration in the fiscal position at the date of liberalization.

  For more general utility functions, it does not appear generally possible to calculate the magnitude of the downward jump in consumption at $t = 0$ relative to r^* times the jump in γ. A variety of paths are possible. In all cases the downward jump in γ implies a deterioration of fiscal position relative to the case of accommodative monetary policy.

  The key difference from the result in the previous section is the initial fall in economy wide wealth due to the contractionary effects of the increase in reserve requirements. To what extent this is offset over time depends on the characteristics of the response of consumption over time, reflecting the exact specification of utility. When one compares these two cases, the lesson appears to be that a policy which increases demand for bank reserves in order to exploit seigniorage while it is still available should be coupled with other aspects of monetary policy which work to avoid a 'squeeze' on capital formation.

4 Inflation policy in anticipation of capital market liberalization

I now consider how the above results would be affected for the two cases if the government had a positive rather than a zero rate of money growth. This could be interpreted in the above framework as a decision *not* to join a low-inflation monetary arrangement such as the EMS. Under the assumption of zero inflation in the rest of the world, this means there is a flexible exchange rate, implying a balanced current account. This allows us to compare the results under loose and tight monetary policy when a country has not joined the EMS to the case when it has. We shall see that in each case the freedom to choose the inflation rate will potentially improve the fiscal position, but for different reasons.

In the case of accommodative policy and a separable utility function, the dynamics of γ will be identical to the zero inflation case, as equation (18) is unaffected, meaning the economy is on the same dynamic path as before. (Note though that $\dot{f} = 0$ due to a balanced current account.) However if money demand is such that the increase in the rate of monetary growth μ^F increases the value of the term $(r + \mu^F)m$, $\dot{b}^P$ from (7) will be more negative, so that at any time $t > 0$, the economy will be farther to the left on the path in Figure 2.1. Hence, positive money growth will unambiguously improve the time T fiscal position relative to the earlier results, with the rate that maximizes seigniorage revenue giving the maximum improvement. Of course, if the utility function is not separable, different values of μ^F will affect the time path of c and hence of γ.

The separable example highlights that what is going on here is exactly the 'unpleasant monetarist arithmetic' exercise in reverse. Positive inflation improves the fiscal position at T because it implies slower growth in government debt in the transition and hence lower debt service at T. The nature of the policy experiment means this is reflected in higher g for a fixed rate of inflation (rather than lower inflation for unchanged government expenditure). In short, allowing the government to choose the inflation rate improves the fiscal position for a by now well-known reason.

The case of positive inflation under non-accommodative monetary policy is more complex. Let us assume as before that we start in a steady state with zero inflation and zero reserve requirements and then choose both j and μ^F freely at time zero. Since demand for real balances is affected by the nominal interest rate, the initial downward jump in k and hence in a will depend on the choice of μ^F. For the same change in j as in the zero inflation case, the fall in the nominal interest rate faced by individuals will be smaller, implying a smaller upward jump in money balances. This means that the initial contractionary effects of an increase in reserve requirements would be smaller. In fact it would appear possible to choose a rate of inflation at 0 such that the nominal interest rate does not jump at all, implying no jump in m. Thus the initial fall in the capital stock, which is the key to generating the potential fiscal deterioration in the tight money case, would be lower and could be absent. Therefore, not constraining the inflation rate to be zero would imply that the fiscal position would be better under a 'tight' money policy as well as under an accommodative policy, though for somewhat different reasons. In addition to the revenues from positive money growth, the initial squeeze on capital could be lessened. (Of course, the dynamic path for γ after time zero will also be affected.)

What is happening here? In the polar case described in Section 3.2 with zero inflation, monetary policy was constrained to be 'tight' in the sense of not supplying the liquidity necessary to allow individuals to increase their money balances at time 0 without a decline in investment. When the monetary authority is free in essence to choose the nominal interest rate simultaneously with the change in reserve requirements, this extra degree of freedom can mitigate the contractionary effects on investment. In the case of accommodative policy in Section 3.1, the monetary authorities offset the contractionary effects which followed the decline in interest rates faced by lenders. Here accompanying monetary policy aims for the same end not by supplying liquidity but by attempting to prevent the change in interest rates which motivated accommodation.

5   Conclusions

A number of assumptions were made in order to derive the dynamic paths. The quantitative results are therefore model-specific, which led to my characterizing them as examples. There is a payoff to this sort of exercise if the qualitative conclusions are more general, and I in fact think that some general policy conclusions can be drawn. I want to emphasize two which were suggested above.

The first general implication for policy is that choosing reserve requirements to increase revenues from money creation has implications for the dynamic paths of all assets. Focussing simply on the beneficial effects in terms of a slower growth of government debt should not divert attention from the possible detrimental effects on saving. If the fall in private asset accumulation outweighs the effect of accumulation of government debt, capital accumulation will in fact be crowded out. This means that revenues from one tax source have increased at the cost of 'destroying' another one. Even if one focusses on the narrow objective function discussed here, the government's goal is to improve its overall fiscal position, rather than simply one component of it. The details of how the fiscal position was affected in this model are less important than the general lesson of the necessity of looking at total fiscal effects.

The second policy implication should also be thought of in a general sense, rather than literally in terms of the details of the model. It is the importance of the whole set of monetary policies which are followed in determining the effects of reserve requirements on revenues. The accommodation result was meant to illustrate the need to look at the whole constellation of monetary policies and to give an example of a monetary policy which would achieve the goal of an improvement in the fiscal position, not to suggest an optimal policy. The paper should not be read as a defense of highly interventionist policies, or of having monetary policy always 'lean with the wind' in the sense of automatically supplying whatever liquid assets the economy demands. If anything, the policy message of these results is probably negative in terms of regulations which increase seigniorage revenues. In general, increasing reserve requirements to increase government revenues in the short run may well have a detrimental effect in the long run on asset accumulation, government revenue, and probably welfare as well.

NOTES

I wish to thank Costas Azariadis for numerous useful discussions, as well as Guillermo Calvo; Alberto Giovannini, Elhanan Helpman, Marco Pagano, and participants in the Penn Macro Lunch Group and at this conference for helpful comments. Guillermo Calvo also deserves thanks for pointing out a serious error in an earlier draft. Part of this paper was written during a very enjoyable stay at the Dipartimento di Scienze Economiche, Università di Bologna. Financial support from the David Horowitz Institute for Research in Developing Countries, Tel Aviv University, is gratefully acknowledged.

1 Calvo and Fernandez (1983) and Romer (1985) discuss the importance of the structure of the banking system for inflation tax revenues.
2 Fischer (1982, 1983) discusses connections between seigniorage and exchange rate regimes.
3 It is easy to show that if debt were held by foreigners, (7) would still hold.
4 I assume that there is no exchange rate change at T. A good analysis of the effect of an anticipated devaluation is given in Calvo (1988).
5 I concentrate on the case where utility is separable in c and m not because I find this a very convincing way of modelling transactions services of money, but

32   **Allan Drazen**

because it makes it possible to derive dynamic results which give some insight into more general cases.

6 Formally, with the monetary base fixed at its time 0 level (say h_0) and writing the separable utility function as $u(c) + v(m)$, one uses the relation that reserves $R = js = (j/1 - j)k$ to write the first-order condition (15) as $v_m[h_0 - (j/1 - j)k] = (1 - j)\lambda\rho$. On differentiating one finds that $dk/dj < 0$.

7 One may note that if the assumption of fixed ρ was dropped, the interest rate borrowers face would rise, so that the rate lenders face would fall by less. j would still determine the 'wedge' between the two.

8 Denoting the pre- and post-jump values of consumption by c_0 and c_+ and of net-of-tax wealth by a_0 and a_+ and using the fact that $r^* = \beta$, we seek conditions for $c_0 - c_+ < \beta a_0 - \beta a_+$. This may be shown to be implied by $(a_0 - a_+/a_+) > (\alpha/\alpha + \alpha\epsilon^2)$, where $\epsilon = e^{(r-\beta)T} - e^{-\beta T}$.

REFERENCES

Calvo, Guillermo (1988). 'Anticipated Devaluations', working paper, University of Pennsylvania, February.

(1989) 'Discussion', this volume.

Calvo, Guillermo and Roque Fernandez (1983). 'Competitive Banks and the Inflation Tax', *Economics Letters* **12**, 313–17.

Drazen, Allan (1985). 'A General Measure of Inflation Tax Revenues', *Economics Letters* **17**, 327–30.

Fischer, Stanley (1982). 'Seigniorage and the Case for a National Money', *Journal of Political Economy* **90**, 295–313.

(1983). 'Seigniorage and Fixed Exchange Rates: An Optimal Inflation Tax Analysis', in Pedro Aspe Armella, Rudiger Dornbusch, and Maury Obstfeld, editors, *Financial Policies and the World Capital Market: The Problem of Latin American Countries*, Chicago: University of Chicago Press.

Giavazzi, Francesco. (1988). 'The Exchange-Rate Question in Europe', working paper, Università di Bologna, February.

Pagano, Marco (1989). 'Discussion', this volume.

Romer, David (1985). 'Financial Intermediation, Reserve Requirements, and Inside Money: A General Equilibrium Analysis', *Journal of Monetary Economics* **16**, 175–94.

Welch, Jane (1981) editor. *The Regulation of Banks in the Member States of the EEC*, The Hague: Martinus Nijhoff.

Discussion

GUILLERMO A. CALVO

The central question raised in Drazen's paper is whether a transitory increase in the cash-deposits reserve ratio will lead to strengthening of the government's revenue position. The answer is ambiguous because the possible short-run increase in government revenue may be accompanied by a slower rate of capital accumulation, which tends to reduce revenue in the longer run.

Contrary to the previous works by Calvo and Fernandez (1983), Romer (1985) and Calvo (1985), the analysis is essentially carried out in the context of an exogenous crawling peg system (fixed exchange rates, for example), while the others allowed for a simultaneous adjustment in the rate of crawl or the rate of inflation. Furthermore, Drazen assumes that the cash-deposits ratio can be increased for a fixed length of time only, contrary to the other papers where the change in that ratio is assumed to be permanent. These strategic modelling decisions are perfectly justified, however, given that the objective is to analyze the impact of changes in the reserve ratio for a country like Italy, whose exchange rate is presently pegged to other European currencies, and is planning to fully liberalize its capital account and banking sector by 1992.

An important feature of Drazen's model is the assumption that investors and savers are completely separated, and that the investment funds are funnelled through the banking system exclusively. Thus, the imposition of a cash-deposit reserve ratio is very much like a tax on interest income. This is the mechanism through which a higher reserve ratio may result in lower future capital. Unfortunately, however, this interesting result is obscured by some of the other assumptions of the model. I find it somewhat regrettable that the proofs depend on *ad-hoc* expectations implied by the statement 'I will assume that the individual myopically anticipates that with an unchanged tax system . . . the present discounted value of tax payments will remain unchanged.'

The contractionary effect of an increase in the cash-deposit ratio can basically be illustrated in the context of a nonmonetary model with rational expectations (instead of *ad-hoc* expectations as in Drazen's paper). Consider a Ramsey-type model where net output, y, is a linear function of capital; more specifically (time subscripts are dropped for notational simplicity),

$$y = \omega + \rho k \tag{1}$$

where ω and ρ are positive constants, and k stands for the capital stock. We assume (with Drazen) that the representative individual's discount rate is also equal to ρ, and (contrary to him) that utility depends only on consumption. The latter is indicated by $u(c)$, where c is consumption, and function u is assumed to be increasing and strictly concave. As pointed out before, Drazen's reserve-ratio distortion is very similar to a tax on interest; thus, we will examine the impact of temporarily imposing a tax τ on interest. Under these assumptions, thus, the representative individual budget constraint takes the following form:

$$\dot{k} = \omega + (\rho + \tau)k + g - c \tag{2}$$

where g is lump-sum subsidies.

In order to focus on the distortionary effect of τ (and not its income effect) we will follow the tradition of public finance and assume that the tax is given back to the public in the form of lump-sum subsidies. Therefore, in equilibrium,

$$g = \tau k \tag{3}$$

Under the present assumptions, the marginal utility of wealth, λ, satisfies:

$$\lambda = u'(c) \tag{4}$$

and the Euler equation is:

$$\dot{c} = \tau u'(c)/u''(c) \tag{5}$$

which implies that c is a monotonically decreasing while τ is positive, and becomes a constant on intervals where $\tau = 0$.

By (2) and (3),

$$\dot{k} = \omega + \rho k - c \tag{6}$$

Suppose now that before time 0 we have $\tau = 0$ and the public expected $\tau = 0$ for the entire future. Thus, by (5) and (6), the only convergent solution is characterized by constant k (denoted by k^*) and constant c (denoted by c^*). Furthermore, by (6), we have

$$c^* = \omega + \rho k \tag{7}$$

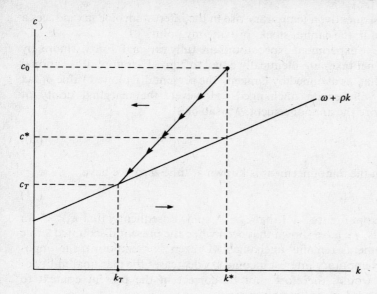

Figure 2A.1 The equilibrium path during transition

In other words, c^* and k^* are the values of c and k that would prevail at time 0 if people expected $\tau = 0$ forever.

Let us now study the impact of an announcement that $\tau > 0$ for $0 \le t < T$, for some time $T > 0$, and $\tau = 0$ for $t \ge T$. This experiment – i.e., a temporary hike in the interest income tax – corresponds to Drazen's experiment of a temporary increase of the reserve ratio. Clearly, by previous reasoning, capital after time T will remain constant and equal to k_T. Furthermore,

$$c^t = \omega + \rho k^T, \quad \text{for } t \ge T \tag{8}$$

Moreover, by (5), c declines over the interval $[0, T)$, implying that

$$c_0 > c_t, \quad \text{for all } t > 0 \tag{9}$$

Figure 2A.1 depicts the only type of path that can satisfy all of the above properties, and the condition that c be continuous with respect to time after time 0 (which in the present context can be shown to be necessary for optimality if, as usual, one constrains c to be piece-wise continuous and right-hand differentiable with respect to time). Clearly, we have that $c_0 > c^*$, capital falls monotonically until time T, and remains constant ever after. Consequently, a temporary rise in the interest income tax induces a contraction in the capital stock, proving my point.

In the above experiment expectations are fully rational. Furthermore, by definition, net taxes are identically equal to zero. Therefore, it is rational to expect that, as assumed by Drazen, 'the present discounted value of tax payments will remain unchanged.' However, the marginal utility of wealth before the announcement, λ^*, satisfies

$$\lambda^* = u'(c^*) \tag{10}$$

while when the announcement is known at time zero, we have

$$\lambda_0 = u'(c_0) \tag{11}$$

It is clear from Figure 2A.1 that $c_0 > c^*$, and consequently that $\lambda_0 < \lambda^*$. In other words, we have shown that even when the present discounted value of tax payments remains unchanged (Drazen's assumption), the imposition of a temporary interest income tax decreases the marginal utility of wealth. It would, therefore, not be correct in the present context to assume that λ does not jump at time 0.

Returning to more substantive matters, I am not sure that reserve ratios ought to be put at the centre of the discussion about what to do before 1992. This, of course, is no criticism of Drazen's analysis which is interesting in its own right. The main point is that in the transition to 1992 countries like Italy have many other policy options that could substantially increase the additional revenue necessary to substitute for the present reliance on high-powered money and government bonds. Some of these options have a long-lasting value, like an increase in regular taxes. Others are essentially transitory but may help endowing the economy with the 'right' initial conditions in 1992, like a one-time capital levy, or a partial repudiation of the domestic debt (either openly, or through an unanticipated devaluation, for example). Choosing the optimal instruments is not an easy task, but the point that I am trying to make is that reserve requirements is just one of the many possible instruments, and, as it transpires from the above partial list of options, probably not the most significant instrument from a policy point of view.

I would like to say very emphatically, however, that I find myself in complete agreement with the general thrust of the paper, which is to stress the importance of getting one's house in order and firmly bolted down in preparation for the brave new world of 1992. It would be extremely dangerous if countries got to that stage without having solved their fiscal problems. A country whose fiscal situation is incompatible with zero or German-type inflation, for example, will enter a cycle of periodic devaluations and arrhythmic inflation. Capital mobility in such a context may be so distorting that social welfare could actually become substantially lower than with capital mobility controls (see Calvo, 1987). Thus, after a period long enough for the costs of intermittent adjustments to be painfully brought home, the political winds are likely to turn against capital mobility and financial liberalization since they will be seen as the proximate causes for the uninvited misery (my Southern Cone background makes me very pessimistic about a happy ending in which the political machinery comes to its senses and fixes the root of the problem, namely, the fiscal deficit). After a costly and confusing interlude, therefore, the country may find itself back where it started. Worse even, because policies like international capital mobility and financial decontrol – which could indeed be highly beneficial in the right environment – are now likely to be politically stigmatized.

REFERENCES
Calvo, Guillermo A. (1986). 'Welfare, Banks and Capital Mobility in Steady State: The Case of Predetermined Exchange Rates', Ch. 5 in Sebastian Edwards and Liaquat Ahamed (eds), *Economic Adjustment and Exchange Rates in Developing Countries*; Chicago: University of Chicago Press for the NEBR.
  (1987). 'On the Costs of Temporary Policy', *Journal of Development Economics* **27**, 245–61.
Calvo, Guillermo A. and Roque Fernandez (1983). 'Competitive Banks and the Inflation Tax', *Economic Letters* **12**, 313–17.
Romer, David (1985). 'Financial Intermediation, Reserve Requirements, and Inside Money: A General Equilibrium Analysis', *Journal of Monetary Economics* **16**, 175–94.

MARCO PAGANO

This paper offers a rigorous positive analysis of the effects of a change in reserve requirements. Its contribution is all the more valuable because this theme, despite its potential policy relevance, has so far received modest attention from macroeconomists. My comments will be organized around three main questions. First, what are the insights that Drazen adds to the understanding that we have of this topic? Second, what policy prescriptions emerge if the objective of the government is welfare maximization, rather than revenue maximization as in Drazen? Third, what is the empirical relevance of this area of research for current policy in Italy?

1   *Drazen's contribution in perspective*

One of the lessons to be drawn from Drazen's paper is methodological. The model shows that one cannot assess the fiscal effects of a change in reserve requirements without fully specifying the saving and portfolio behaviour of the private sector and the setting of monetary policy. As often happens when the analysis is cast in a general equilibrium framework, it turns out that partial equilibrium analyses are flawed and that unambiguous results are hard to obtain. But of course this is not meant to be a criticism. Quite the reverse, the ambiguity of the results in Drazen's paper is reassuring, being shared by its main forerunner, *i.e.* Dave Romer's (1985) article. In fact, if anything, Drazen obtains sharper results, mainly because he employs two simplifying assumptions that are not in Romer's paper – an inelastic demand for loans by private investors and the absence of any non-bank financial intermediary.

On surface, the two models appear quite different. Romer uses an overlapping generations framework and concentrates on steady states, while Drazen assumes infinite-lived agents and focuses on dynamics and short-run policy analysis. However, there are some striking similarities in the general logic of the two models. In both of them, raising reserve requirements has two distinct effects, which for short I will label the 'tax effect' and the 'direct contraction' effect.

The tax effect can be understood as the effect of a tax on deposits levied at the same rate as the reserve requirement. This effect is ambiguous in sign, as it depends on what is assumed about saving, portfolio and investment behaviour. It also depends on the monetary policy setting, since the rate of inflation determines the level of nominal rates and thus the demand for money by the public.

The direct contraction effect, instead, is unambiguous. It reduces the amount of loans that banks can make out of a unit of deposits below the level produced by the tax effect alone, and can be counteracted by reducing government borrowing. In fact Romer says that 'a reserve requirement is equivalent to a combination of tax on deposit interest and a government issue of bonds' (p. 189), so that the direct contraction effect can be balanced by retiring public debt. In an overlapping generations model, in fact, retirement of government bonds frees saving for private investment and thus has an expansionary effect on capital and output. Here Drazen shows that the direct contraction effect exists also in an infinite horizon model, and that in such context it can be offset by a one-time accommodation of the implied rise in the demand for reserves, so as to keep the amount of lending unchanged.[1]

In effect, the direct contraction effect simply captures the fact that by raising reserve requirements, the government borrows from the private sector below the equilibrium interest rate. The debt retirement in Romer and the fully accommodating reserve policy in Drazen eliminate this effect with an offsetting loan from the government to the private sector.

The novelty of Drazen's paper, however, is not confined to recasting Romer's analysis in terms of an infinite horizon model, that lends itself more naturally to the study of dynamics and short-run policy changes. It also points to a new and potentially important channel through which higher reserve requirements can reduce tax revenue, by noticing that their contractionary effect on capital accumulation can lead to a smaller tax base in the future. Even though Romer had already shown that increasing reserve requirements may either lower or raise the revenue from the inflation tax, the possibility that it may reduce revenue from other taxes (*e.g.*, from the income tax) further into the future had not been taken into account. For the policy-maker, this insight by Drazen provides one more reason for caution against the widespread presumption that raising reserve requirements can increase revenue.

2   What does this suggest for optimal tax policy?

Drazen assumes throughout that the government is trying to maximize revenue. While this is not unrealistic, it is natural to ask what policy prescriptions would be obtained if the government were to maximize social welfare. Here we really face two questions: first, for a given level of revenue from seigniorage, what is the optimal combination of reserve requirements and inflation to achieve it? Second, what is the optimal combination of revenue that should be extracted from seigniorage relative to other taxes?

On the first point, the normative analysis of Freeman (1987) shows that, precisely because of the contractionary effect on capital accumulation, a government aiming at a given revenue from seigniorage should minimize reserve requirements and maximize the rate of money creation consistent with the target level of revenue. For the same reason, if the government can levy an excise tax on deposits, it should replace all seigniorage on reserves with such a tax and set the reserve requirements ratio at zero. Though obtained in an overlapping generations model like Romer's, according to Freeman these results are quite general.[2]

On the second point, *i.e.* on the optimal combination between seigniorage and other taxes, there is the burgeoning literature exemplified by Mankiw (1987) and Grilli (in this volume), that prescribes equating the marginal welfare cost of revenue from seigniorage with that from other sources. So far, these normative models have overlooked the problem that squeezing more taxes out of the private sector today may hinder its contributive power tomorrow, or – as Drazen now suggests – that raising the inflation tax today may erode the income tax base tomorrow. At a formal level, the neglect of this point arises from the joint assumption that the government has an intertemporally additive loss function and that the path of private sector income is exogenously given. At a substantive level, these models overlook the effect that the assumed tax distortions have on capital accumulation.

It is tempting then to analyze the issue raised by Drazen in a modified version of these normative models, assuming that the inflation tax reduces, via the reserve requirement channel, the rate of capital accumulation and thereby the rate of real growth of the income tax base. This exercise is meant to provide just a first line of attack on the normative issue, since a full-fledged treatment of the problem would require explicit modeling of private sector saving and portfolio behaviour as in Drazen's paper.

Suppose that the government has two controls, the income tax rate (τ) and the inflation rate (π), where 'inflation rate' is used as a short-hand for 'policy variables that raise current revenue from seigniorage (and the implied deadweight loss) but may lower the current rate of capital accumulation'. For instance, under appropriate assumptions about private sector behaviour, the reserve requirement and the rate of interest paid on reserves can be placed under this label. Thus, raising 'inflation' has three effects: raising more revenue, inducing costly distortions in the same period and affecting the future tax base by lower growth. The first two effects are the usual ones, while the third is the 'Drazen effect'.

I analyze four cases. *Case A* is the standard one, where inflation has no effect on growth, and is never constrained to take specific values. It is used just as a benchmark of analysis. In this case the government's problem is just as in Mankiw (1987):

$$\text{Min } L_0 = \int_0^\infty e^{-rt}[f(\tau_t) + h(\tau_t)]y_t\,dt, \tag{1}$$

where $f', f'', h', h'' > 0$,

s.t.

$$\dot{b}_t = rb_t + g_t - \tau_t y_t - (\pi_t + \gamma_t)kt_t, \quad \lim_{t \to \infty} b_t e^{-rt} = 0 \tag{2}$$

where $b_t =$ debt, $k =$ velocity, $g_t =$ spending, $y_t =$ real income and $\gamma_t \cong \dot{y}_t/y_t$. In *case B*, there is negative feedback from inflation to growth:

$$\dot{y}_t = \gamma(\pi_t)y_t, \tag{3}$$

where $\gamma(\pi_t) = \gamma - \alpha(\pi_t)$, $\gamma > 0$, $\alpha(0) = 0$, $\alpha' > 0$, $\alpha'' \leq 0$

so that γ is the growth rate associated with no inflation tax and that the elasticity of the inflation-sensitive component of growth, $-\alpha(\pi_t)$, is less than or equal to unity. In *case C*, I revert to the assumption that the inflation tax has no effect on growth but assume that the government is constrained to set the inflation rate at zero from time T onwards. Formally, I remove constraint (3) and add

$$\pi_t = 0, \quad \text{for } t > T. \tag{4}$$

In *case D*, both elements are present: inflation reduces growth and must be set at zero from T onwards. Thus, constraints (2), (3) and (4) are all imposed simultaneously. Cases C and D try to capture the fact that exogenous factors, such as greater integration in the EEC credit market, may eliminate revenue from seigniorage in countries like Italy. It is, in a normative framework, the same problem as that analyzed by Drazen from a positive standpoint.

Results can be summarized as follows (optimal values are superscribed in each case the corresponding letter and derivations are in the appendix):

Case A (baseline case).   As well known, in this case the optimal tax rate and inflation rate are constant, and their instantaneous marginal costs must be equated, $h'(\pi^A) = kf'(\tau^A)$. As marginal costs are increasing, this equality implies that the two rates are positively related. For instance, if permanent expenditure rises, both have to increase.

Case B (the inflation tax reduces growth, but is never constrained to be zero).   As in case A, the optimal policy entails constancy of both the tax rate and the inflation rate, and a positive relationship between the two. However, now the relationship between the two implies $h'(\pi^B) < kf'(\tau^B)$. Thus, if the tax rate is the same as in case A ($\tau^A = \tau^B$), the inflation rate will now be lower ($\pi^B < \pi^A$). If $h(\cdot)$ and $f(\cdot)$ are restricted to be quadratic, one gets the stronger result that the ratio between the inflation and the tax rate must be smaller in case B than in case A, even if the two tax rates differ ($\pi^B/\tau^B < \pi^A/\tau^A$, $\forall \tau^A, \tau^B$). In other words, the optimal policy contemplates relatively less reliance on the inflation tax and more on the income tax, reflecting the government's desire not to compromise the growth of the tax base.

Case C (the inflation tax does not affect growth, but must be zero after T).   Somewhat more surprisingly, in this case also the government must set both rates at a constant level, as long as it can. The tax rate is kept at the same value throughout, and the inflation rate until T. Up to that time, the two rates are linked by the same relationships as in case A, $h'(\pi^C) = kf'(\tau^C)$. The only difference is that, since seigniorage has been ruled out after T, the government must set both the income tax rate and the inflation rate at a level higher than in case A to pay for the same stream of permanent expenditure.

Case D (the inflation tax reduces growth, and is constrained to be zero after T). Again, the tax rate on income must be kept constant throughout, but this no longer holds for the inflation rate. If the $\gamma(\cdot)$ function is restricted to be linear, the time profile of the optimal inflation rate π_t^D is rising before T (and possibly flat at the beginning). Intuitively, this is because an increase in inflation, and the implied reduction in growth, has now different effects on the future tax base depending on its timing, since after T seigniorage will no longer be collected. It is best to concentrate reductions in growth right before T, when they will be eroding only the base of the income tax, rather than earlier on, when they would also be reducing the base of the inflation tax. Witness to this is the fact that, if $\tau^D = \tau^B$, the optimal inflation rate at time T is larger in case D than in case B $(\pi_T^D > \pi^B)$, where the government must worry also about its effects on seigniorage after T.

Moreover, at time T the relationship between the two rates is such that $h'(\pi_T^D) < kf'(\tau^D)$, so that, if $\tau^D = \tau^A = \tau^B$, in case D there is less reliance on the inflation tax than in cases A and C, where there is no feedback from inflation to growth. In the special case where $h(\cdot)$ and $f(\cdot)$ are quadratic, this implies that the ratio π_T^D/τ^D is smaller than π^A/τ^A and π^C/τ^C (even if $\tau^D \neq \tau^A \neq \tau^C$). Recalling that π_t^D/τ^D reaches its maximum for $t = T$ (for $\gamma(\cdot)$ linear), it is immediate that this ratio is smaller than π^A/τ^A and π^C/τ^C for all t. In other words, if the instantaneous loss functions are quadratic, the ratio between the inflation tax and the income tax, though increasing over time until T, should be always lower than in cases A and C.

Thus the introduction of the 'Drazen effect' in standard normative models of tax composition invalidates the rule according to which one must equate the instantaneous marginal costs of the two taxes. Due to the effect of seigniorage on growth, the inflation tax must be set below the level that equates the two instantaneous marginal costs. In the special case of quadratic loss functions, this implies a lower ratio between the inflation and the income tax rate. However, if the government expects that from some future date T onwards it will be deprived of all seigniorage revenue, it must tap revenue from this source at an increasing rate until date T.

	(1) $M/Y =$	(2) $\hat{C}/Y +$	(3) $\hat{R}/T =$	(4) $(C/Y +$	(5) $R/D \cdot$	(6) $D/Y) \cdot$	(7) $\hat{Y}$	(8) $-\hat{V} \cdot M/Y$	(9) $+ e$
1976	0.032	0.011	0.021	0.091	0.154	0.788	0.249	− 0.017	− 0.004
1977	0.034	0.010	0.024	0.085	0.155	0.800	0.213	− 0.005	− 0.005
1978	0.044	0.013	0.031	0.086	0.162	0.842	0.169	+ 0.017	− 0.010
1979	0.026	0.010	0.016	0.080	0.154	0.831	0.216	− 0.016	− 0.002
1980	0.022	0.010	0.012	0.075	0.150	0.751	0.254	− 0.022	− 0.002
1981	0.021	0.011	0.010	0.074	0.149	0.692	0.185	− 0.009	− 0.003
1982	0.022	0.008	0.014	0.071	0.149	0.698	0.172	− 0.005	− 0.003
1983	0.023	0.007	0.016	0.069	0.156	0.689	0.147	+ 0.000	− 0.003
1984	0.022	0.006	0.016	0.067	0.163	0.676	0.139	+ 0.001	− 0.003
1985	0.028	0.006	0.022	0.070	0.181	0.668	0.113	+ 0.011	− 0.005
1986	0.012	0.004	0.008	0.064	0.177	0.658	0.106	− 0.006	− 0.001
1987	0.017	0.005	0.012	0.064	0.183	0.646	0.089	+ 0.002	− 0.001

Table 2A.1 *Decomposition of M/Y in Italy, 1976–87*

M = monetary base, C = currency with the public, R = total bank reserves, D = bank deposits, Y = nominal GDP, V = velocity, e = approximation error.

Source: Banca d'Italia, *Annual Report*.

3   *Are changes in reserve requirements revenue-effective in practice?*

Let us shift the focus from welfare issues back to the revenue-effectiveness of increases in reserve requirements (that is the point considered by Drazen) but this time at the empirical level. Despite all theoretical ambiguities, one would be inclined to think that, at least to a first-order approximation, the impact effect of higher reserve requirements is an increase in the revenue from seigniorage, and possibly a considerable increase. In fact, one of the stylized facts from which Drazen moves is that over the period 1979–87 the revenue from seigniorage in Italy 'fell far less than the inflation rate' because of the increase in the marginal reserve requirement (from 15.75% to 20% in 1981 and to 25% in 1982), a fact first noted by Giavazzi (1988). This seems to suggest that reserve requirements are a powerful policy tool. In what follows, I will argue that the Italian data suggest exactly the reverse, *i.e.* that the contribution of changes in reserve requirements to the revenue from seigniorage has been quite modest.

A commonly used measure of the revenue from seigniorage is the change in the monetary base, standardized by national product ($\dot{M}/Y$). In Table 2A.1 this measure is decomposed in two different ways. First, it is broken down into two components, the growth of currency held by the public and that of bank reserves (columns 2–3), and then it is decomposed according to a simple quantity theory equation in rates of change (columns 4–9). The first breakdown confirms that indeed the growth rate of reserves has declined by less than that of currency, apparently confirming the alleged effectiveness of changes in reserve requirements. However, the second shows that the fact that since 1979 seigniorage revenue has fallen proportionately less than the inflation rate is to be attributed not merely to the behaviour of required reserves (R/D) but also to other two factors: (i) the growth rate of nominal income ($\hat{Y}$) has fallen by less than inflation, because of sustained real growth in 1984–7; (ii) velocity has decreased slightly in the 1980s, whereas it had been rising sharply at the end of the 1970s (column 8).

Moreover, the contribution of the growth in reserves is overstated by the fact that $\dot{M}/Y$ is actually a mistaken measure of revenue from seigniorage, since it does not net out the interest on reserves paid out by the Central Bank (in contrast with Drazen's definition of seigniorage revenue, that does make this adjustment). Since these interest payments are positively related to the size of required reserves, in the case at hand this mistake is, ironically, made worse by the very increase in reserve requirements in the 1980s. In Table 2A.2 I report the correct measure of seigniorage (column 1) and of the contribution of reserves growth to seigniorage revenue

	Correct measure of seigniorage (S) divided by GDP (Y)			Estimate of seigniorage with $R/D = 0.15$		Wedge between average lending rate, deposit rate and rate paid on reserves (%)		
	(1) $\frac{S}{Y} =$	(2) $\frac{\dot{C}}{Y} +$	(3) $\frac{\dot{R} - i^R R}{Y}$	(4) $\hat{S}$	(5) $S - \hat{S}$	(6) $i^l - i^d$	(7) $i^l - i^R$	(8) $(i^l - i^R)\frac{R}{D}$
1976	0.027	0.011	0.016			6.78	12.83	1.732
1977	0.028	0.010	0.018			7.27	14.03	1.866
1978	0.038	0.013	0.025			6.20	11.36	1.534
1979	0.020	0.010	0.010			5.72	10.46	1.094
1980	0.018	0.011	0.007	0.018	0.000	8.53	14.82	1.971
1981	0.016	0.011	0.005	0.016	0.000	9.00	17.39	2.295
1982	0.017	0.008	0.009	0.017	0.000	8.05	17.58	2.456
1983	0.018	0.007	0.011	0.017	0.001	7.00	15.74	2.282
1984	0.016	0.006	0.010	0.016	0.000	7.04	13.57	2.049
1985	0.022	0.006	0.016	0.020	0.002	5.85	12.01	1.958
1986	0.006	0.004	0.002	0.005	0.001	6.45	10.28	1.727
1987	0.011	0.005	0.006	0.010	0.001	5.80	7.93	1.372

Table 2A.2 *Alternative estimates of seigniorage*

i^l = lending rate, i^d = deposit rate, i^R = rate paid on reserves (averages).
Source: Banca d'Italia, *Annual Report*.

(column 3). After the correction, the contribution of the latter in the past decade appears to fall about as sharply as that of currency growth ($\dot{C}/Y$).

This is confirmed by running a counterfactual experiment in 'seigniorage accounting'. Imagine that no change in reserve requirement had occurred in 1981–2, and that the reserve–deposit ratio had remained constant at its 1980 level ($E/D = 0.15$). What would have been revenue from seigniorage, using the correct measure and assuming that all other variables took their actual values? The result of this experiment (performed using the second decomposition of Table 2A.1) is reported in columns 4–5 of Table 2A.2. The difference between actual seigniorage (S) and its estimate at constant reserve requirements ($\hat{S}$), displayed in column 5, shows that the increase in revenue that can be attributed to the increase in reserve requirements is very small: 1/10 of 1% of GDP on average!

The perverse interaction of fixed nominal rate on reserves (i^R) and increased reserve requirements (R/D) is partly to be blamed for this, as shown out most vividly by another counterfactual experiment: if R/D were to rise to 0.50 from the current value of 0.18 and all other variables stood at their 1987 values, the revenue from seigniorage would be unchanged, due to the higher interest burden. This is to be contrasted with the effectiveness of an increase in inflation: raising inflation from the current 5% to 10% would, *ceteris paribus*, increase revenue by 1% of GDP.

It is noticeable that the combination of falling inflation and a fixed rate on reserves has also swamped the impact of increased reserve requirements on the wedge between borrowing and lending rates. Rather than rising together with R/D, the implicit tax imposed by reserve requirements on each lira of loans, $(i^l - i^R)R/D$, has fallen from 2.3% in 1981 to 1.4% in 1987, due to the fall of the differential between the lending rate and the rate paid on reserves, $i^l - i^R$, that in turn reflect the spread between inflation and i^R (see Table 2A.2, columns 6–8). Thus, just as it has had a negligible impact on revenue, the increase in reserve requirements has had a negligible impact on the wedge between the rate faced by depositors and that paid by firms.

4   Conclusions

One of the results in Romer (1985) was that higher reserve requirements may not entail higher revenue from seigniorage. Drazen has now reinforced this argument by noticing that higher reserve requirements can also lower future revenue from other taxes, via their contractionary effect on capital accumulation and growth.

On welfare grounds, Freeman (1987) proved that a government wanting to raise a target level of seigniorage revenue should do so by choosing the smallest feasible reserve requirement and highest rate of inflation. In Section 2 I have instead investigated what is the optimal combination between seigniorage and other distorting taxes on the assumption that seigniorage revenue is (at least partly) increased by raising reserve requirements and that this reduces capital accumulation, as suggested by Drazen. It turns out that it is optimal to keep the inflation tax below the value that equates its instantaneous welfare cost with that of other taxes, as one should do in the absence of the 'Drazen effect'. This result holds also if at some future date the government will have to give up seigniorage as a source of revenue (although in this case it should have increasing recourse to seigniorage until the terminal date).

Finally, in the recent Italian experience increases in reserve requirements have proved rather ineffective at raising revenue for the government, especially compared with changes in inflation. Thus, positive and normative analysis seems to agree with recent experience in warning policy-makers against reliance on increases in reserve requirements as tools to increase revenue.

Appendix

A. Baseline case: Min (1) s.t. (2)
From the Hamiltonian:

$$H = e^{-rt}[f(\tau_t) + h(\pi_t)]y_t + \lambda_t[rb_t + g_t - \tau_t y_t - (\pi_t + \gamma)y_t]$$

one finds the optimality conditions:

$$f'(\tau_t) = \lambda_t e^{rt} \tag{A1}$$

$$h'(\pi_t) = \lambda_t e^{rt} k \tag{A2}$$

and the costate equation:

$$\dot{\lambda}_t = -r\lambda_t \ \diamondsuit \ \lambda_t = \lambda_0 e^{-rt} \tag{A3}$$

Using (A3), the two optimality conditions can be rewritten:

$$f'(\tau_t) = \lambda_0 \quad \forall t \tag{A1'}$$

$$h'(\pi_t) = \lambda_0 k \quad \forall t \tag{A2'}$$

so that the optimal tax and inflation rate are constant ($\tau_t = \tau^A$, $\pi_t = \pi^A$, $\forall t$), and are related by:

$$h'(\pi^A) = kf'(\tau^A) \tag{A4}$$

π^A and τ^A solve the system formed by (A.4) and the integral budget constraint:

$$b_0 = \int_0^\infty [[\tau^A + (\pi^A + \gamma)k]y_0 - g_0]e^{-(r-\gamma)t}\,dt$$

$$= \frac{[\tau^A + (\pi^A + \gamma)k]y_0 - g_0}{r - \gamma} \tag{A5}$$

where I assume spending to grow exponentially at the rate of income (to simplify notation) and impose the transversality condition $r > \gamma$.

B. Inflation tax lowers growth: Min (1) s.t. (2) and (3)   The Hamiltonian is the same as in case A, with $\gamma - \alpha(\pi_t)$ replacing γ. The optimality conditions are:

$$f'(\tau_t) = \lambda_t e^{rt} \tag{B1}$$

$$h'(\pi_t) = \{\lambda_t[1 + \gamma'(\pi_t)]k - \mu_t\gamma'(\pi_t)\}e^{rt} \tag{B2}$$

and the costate equations for b_t and y_t are respectively:

$$\dot{\lambda}_t = -r\lambda_t \tag{B3}$$

$$\dot{\mu}_t = -[f(\tau_t) + h(\pi_t)]e^{-rt}$$
$$\quad + \lambda_t[\tau_t + (\pi_t + \gamma(\pi_t))k] - \mu_t\gamma(\pi_t) \tag{B4}$$

(B1) and (B3) imply that the optimal tax rate is a constant, satisfying

$$f'(\tau^B) = \lambda_0 \tag{B1'}$$

Then suppose that $\mu_t = \mu_0 e^{-rt}$ solves (B4). Rewriting (B2) accordingly (and using (B1') and $\tau_t = \tau^B$), it is immediate that the optimal inflation rate is itself a constant $\pi_t = \pi^B$. Equations (B2) and (B4) then become:

$$h'(\pi^B) = f'(\tau^B)[1 + \gamma'(\pi^B)]k - \mu_0\gamma'(\pi^B) \tag{B2'}$$

$$f(\tau^B) - f'(\tau^B)\tau^B + h(\pi^B)$$
$$\quad - f'(\tau^B)[\pi^B + \gamma(\pi^B)]k = [r - \gamma(\pi^B)]\mu_0 \tag{B4'}$$

that jointly determine μ_0 and π^B, for any given value of τ^B.

To prove that $h'(\pi^B)/f'(\tau^B) < h'(\pi^A)/f'(\tau^A) = k$, as stated in the text, notice that, by equations (A1'), (A2'), (B1') and (B2'),

$$h'(\pi^B)/f'(\tau^B) < h'(\pi^A)/f'(\tau^A) \quad \text{iff} \quad \mu_0 < f'(\tau^B)k \tag{B5}$$

Thus let us write

$$\mu_0 < f'(\tau^B)k + \epsilon \tag{B6}$$

and show that $\epsilon < 0$. Correspondingly, (B2') can be rewritten

$$h'(\pi^B) = f'(\tau^B)k - \gamma'(\pi^B)\epsilon \tag{B7}$$

Using (B6) and (B7), after some steps equation (B4') can be rewritten as:

$$f(\tau^B) - f'(\tau^B)\tau^B + h(\pi^B) - h'(\pi^B)\pi^B$$
$$= rf'(\tau^B)k + [r - \gamma(\pi^B) + \gamma'(\pi^B)\pi^B]\epsilon \tag{B8}$$

The LHS of this expression is negative, because both $f(\cdot)$ and $h(\cdot)$ are convex functions. The first term on the RHS, $rf'(\tau^B)k$, is positive, whereas the last has the same sign as ϵ. To see why, recall that due to the transversality condition, $r > \gamma(\pi_t)$, $\forall \pi_t \Diamond r > \gamma$, and notice that $\gamma(\pi^B) - \gamma'(\pi^B)\pi^B = \gamma - \alpha(\pi^B) + \alpha'(\pi^B)\pi^B \le \gamma$ because $\alpha(\cdot)$ is concave. Thus $r - \gamma(\pi^B) + \gamma'(\pi^B)\pi^B > 0$. It follows that if $\epsilon \ge 0$, the LHS is negative and the RHS positive, which is a contradiction. Hence $\epsilon < 0$. This completes the proof.

C. Inflation must be 0 after time T: Min (1) s.t. (2) and (4)   The problem must be solved in a dynamic programming fashion, optimizing first over the interval (T, ∞) (treating b_T as predetermined), and then over the interval $(0, T)$, assuming the objective to be optimized from T onwards. Over (T, ∞) the tax rate is the only control, and must be set equal to a constant (denoted by τ''). The optimality and costate equations in fact yield:

$$f'(\tau_{T+s}) = \lambda_T \Diamond \tau_{T+s} = \tau'', \quad \forall s \tag{C1}$$

$$\lambda_{T+s} = \lambda_T e^{-rs} \quad \forall s \tag{C2}$$

Writing the integral budget constraint at time T and solving for τ'', one finds:

$$\tau'' = [b_T(r - \gamma) + g_T]/y_T = \varphi(b_T), \tag{C3}$$

where $\varphi'(b_T) = (r - \gamma)/y_T > 0$

The loss function at time 0 can now be written as the sum of two terms:

$$L_0 = \int_0^T [f(\tau_t) + h(\pi_t)]y_t e^{-rt} dt + L_T^* \tag{C4}$$

where $L_T^* = \int_T^\infty f(\tau'')e^{-rt}\,dt = f(\varphi(b_T))y_T e^{-rT}/(r-\gamma)$

is the optimized value of the loss function after T, or 'salvage value' at T.

The optimality and costate equations are the same as in case A. Thus the optimal tax rate is a constant, to be denoted by τ', that solves:

$$f'(\tau_t) + \lambda_0 = \lambda_T e^{rT} \Diamond \tau_t = \tau'' \quad \forall t < T \qquad (C5)$$

and the optimal inflation rate is also a constant π^C such that:

$$h'(\pi^C) = kf'(\tau') \qquad (C6)$$

In addition, we now have the transversality condition:

$$\lambda_T = \partial L_T^*/\partial b_T$$

$$= \frac{\partial}{\partial b_T}[f(\varphi(b_T))y_T e^{-rT}/(r-\gamma)] = f'(\tau'')e^{-rT} \qquad (C7)$$

This, together with condition (C5), shows that $\tau' = \tau'' = \tau^C$, i.e. that the tax rate must be set at the same level throughout. The only difference with case A is then that, since now $\pi_t = 0$ for $t > T$, it must be that $\tau^C > \tau^A$, $\pi^C > \pi^A$ to meet the budget constraint. To prove this, integrate (2) at time 0:

$$\tau^C - \tau^A = k\{\tau(\tau^A) - \psi(\tau^C) + [\psi(\tau^C) + \gamma]e^{-(r-\gamma)T}\} \qquad (C8)$$

where $\psi(\cdot) = h'^{-1}[f'(\cdot)]$. Assume $\tau^A \geq \tau^C \Diamond$ LHS ≤ 0. Since $\psi'(\cdot) > 0$, $\tau^A \geq \tau^C \rightarrow \psi(\tau^A) \geq \psi(\tau^C) \Diamond$ RHS > 0, that is a contradiction. Hence it must be $\tau^C > \tau^A$, and therefore $\pi^C > \pi^A$. This completes the proof.

D. Inflation lowers growth and must be 0 after T: Min (1) s.t. (2), (3) and (4)   The solution method is as in case C. After T, the results are identical. Over the interval $(0, T)$, instead, optimality conditions and costate equations are as in case B (B1–4), with the addition of the two transversality conditions:

$$\lambda_T = \partial L_T^*/\partial b_T = f'(\tau^P)e^{-rT} \qquad (D1)$$

$$\mu_T = \partial L_T^*/\partial y_T = e^{-rT}[f(\tau^P) - f'(\tau^P)\tau^P]/(r-\gamma) < 0 \qquad (D2)$$

Also in this case, then it is immediate that the tax rate is to be set at a constant level throughout (denote it by τ^P). Moreover, using (D2) to evaluate the optimality condition for π_t at $t = T$, we get

$$h'(\pi_T^P) = f'(\tau^P)[1 + \gamma'(\pi_T^P)]k$$
$$- [f(\tau^P) - f'(\tau^P)\tau^P]\gamma'(\pi_T^P)/(r-\gamma) \qquad (D3)$$

Comparing (D3) with the corresponding expressions for case A and C, i.e. (A4) and (C7), one sees that, as stated in the text, $h'(\pi_T^D)/f'(\tau^D) < h'(\pi^A)/f'(\tau^A) = h'(\pi^C)/f'(\tau^C) = k$ (notice that the last term in (D3) is negative).

Restricting $\gamma(\cdot)$ to the linear form $\gamma(\pi_t) = \gamma - \alpha\tau_t$, it can also be shown that: (i) if the tax is the same as in case B ($\tau^D = \tau^B$), inflation at T is higher in case D ($\pi_T^D > \tau^B$); (ii) π_t^D is rising before T, may be initially constant, but is never decreasing. To show (i), notice that (B2'), (B4') and (D3) imply

$$h'(\pi_T^D) - h'(\pi^B) = \alpha[h'(\pi^B)\pi^B - h(\pi^B)$$
$$+ \gamma kf'(\tau^B)]/(r - \gamma) > 0 \; \lozenge \; \pi_T^D > \pi^B \qquad (D4)$$

To show (ii), remark that, if $\gamma(\cdot)$ is restricted to be linear, the optimality conditions and the costate equation respectively specialize to:

$$h'(\pi_t) = f(\tau^D)(1 - \alpha)k + \mu_t \alpha e^{rt} \qquad (D5)$$

$$\dot{\mu}_t = e^{rt}\{[f'(\tau^D)\tau^D - f(\tau^D)] + [h'(\pi_t^D)\pi_t^D - h(\pi_t^D)]$$
$$+ f'(\tau^D)k\gamma\} - \mu_t\gamma$$
$$= -r\mu_t + e^{-rt}\{(r - \gamma)(\mu_t e^{rt} - \mu_T e^{rT})$$
$$+ [h'(\pi_t^D)\pi_t^D - h(\pi_t^D)] + f'(\tau^D)k\gamma\} \qquad (D6)$$

Since from (D5) $h'(\pi_t) - h'(\pi_T) = \alpha(\mu_t e^{rt} - \mu_T e^{rT})$, one can rewrite (D6) as:

$$\dot{\mu}_t + r\mu_t = e^{-rt}\{(r - \gamma)[h'(\pi_t) - h'(\pi_T)]/\alpha$$
$$+ [h'(\pi_t^D)\pi_t^D - h(\pi_t^D)] + f'(\tau^D)k\gamma\} \qquad (D6')$$

Then, differentiating (D5) with respect to time, one gets:

$$h''(\pi_t)\dot{\pi}_t = \alpha(\dot{\mu}_t + r\mu_t)e^{rt} = (r - \gamma)[h'(\pi_t) - h'(\pi_T)]$$
$$+ \alpha[h'(\pi_t^D)\pi_t^D - h(\pi_t^D) + f'(\tau^D)k\gamma] \qquad (D7)$$

Since $h''(\cdot) > 0$, $\dot{\pi}_t$ has the same sign as the RHS. The term $[h'(\pi_t) - h'(\pi_T)]$ is 0 when $\pi_t = \pi_T$, negative when $\pi_t < \pi_T$ and positive vice versa. The rest of the expression is positive, $\forall \pi_t$. Both terms on the RHS are increasing in π_t. It follows that $\dot{\pi}_t > 0$ at $t = T$ and also for $t \in (t', T]$, t' being the date when (D7) turns 0 ($\dot{\pi}_{t'} = 0$). Consider now (D7) at date t'' (for $t' - t'' > 0$ and small). If $\dot{\pi}_{t''} < 0$, then $\pi_{t''} > \pi_{t'}$, so that the RHS of (D7) is negative, implying a contradiction, and vice versa if $\dot{\pi}_{t''} > 0$. Hence, $\forall t \leq t'$, it must be $\dot{\pi}_t = 0$. If there is a date t' at which π_t is not growing, before t' it must be constant.

NOTES

1 Drazen allows the Central Bank to pump in currency also via an open market sale of debt, so that the fall in the deposit rate due to the higher reserve

requirements is prevented from causing a portfolio shift out of deposits and into currency. Notice that the distortion in the choice between currency and deposits induced by the higher deposit rate would arise also if the government were to raise taxes on deposits rather than reserve requirements. Thus the open market sale of debt really offsets the part of the 'tax effect' concerning the currency–deposit choice. This still leaves another part of the tax effect at work, *i.e.* the distortion in the consumption–saving choice, induced by the fall in the real rate of interest paid to lenders. It is this residual part of the tax effect that drives the model in the case with accommodating monetary policy and zero inflation.

2 He claims that they apply to any model where the real rate of return on capital is greater than the population growth rate, fiat money is real wealth and intermediated capital may serve as money (p. 311).

REFERENCES

Freeman, Scott (1987). 'Reserve Requirements and Optimal Seigniorage', *Journal of Monetary Economics* **19**, No. 2, March, 304–14.

Giavazzi, Francesco (1988). 'The Exchange Rate Question in Europe', mimeo., revised, February.

Grilli, Vittorio (1989). 'Seigniorage in Europe', chapter 3 in this volume.

Mankiw, N. Gregory (1987). 'The optimal collection of seigniorage: Theory and evidence', *Journal of Monetary Economics* **20**, No. 2, 327–41.

Romer, David (1985). 'Financial Intermediation, Reserve Requirements, and Inside Money: A General Equilibrium Analysis', *Journal of Monetary Economics* **16**, No. 2, 175–94.

3   Seigniorage in Europe

VITTORIO GRILLI

1   Introduction

One of the most debated problems in Europe today is the definition of the strategy for achieving monetary integration. The European Monetary System (EMS) was established as an intermediate step toward such unification. The EMS has produced increasing stability in exchange rates, but this success has been facilitated by the existence of widespread capital controls that have discouraged speculative activities. The process of financial liberalization which is now in progress, while certainly beneficial in other respects, could seriously undermine the solidity of the EMS. One of the main reasons for concern is the uneven status of the government finances of the member countries. Exchange rate systems like the EMS impose monetary discipline that may be too tight for countries that are struggling with large public deficits.

The close link between budget decisions and the exchange rate is analysed in Grilli (1988). There it is shown that the financing of government expenditures may be incompatible with a fixed exchange rate and that, historically, this incompatibility has been one of the main causes of exchange rate crises. According to this point of view, inflation is an essential element of an optimal taxation program. Therefore, waiving discretionary power over money supply decisions (as implied by a fixed exchange rate system) without, at the same time, surrendering sovereignty over fiscal policies, may not be a credible arrangement. Similar concerns have been expressed by others, e.g. Dornbusch (1987) and Giavazzi (1987). Dornbusch (1987) suggests that, given the probable existence of large discrepancies in seigniorage needs among the European countries, a more realistic exchange rate arrangement would be a crawling peg. In this system, the rates of depreciation would be set to meet national budgetary requirements.

Whether or not these are critical considerations is ultimately an empirical

53

issue. In particular, it is important to establish whether revenue needs have indeed affected the way in which inflation has been determined in the past, and if they are likely to be important in the future.

In order to address these issues, we first present a simple theory of seigniorage and income taxation, which is related to pioneering work by Phelps (1973), and which has been recently revived by Mankiw (1987), Poterba and Rotemberg (1987) and Grilli (1988), among others. We derive the time-series properties of seigniorage and income taxes. It is shown that, if the government behaves optimally, the tax rate and the rate of inflation should be martingale processes. Furthermore, the tax rate and the inflation rate should be cointegrated. We test these implications for ten European countries (Belgium, Denmark, France, Germany, Greece, Ireland, Italy, Netherlands, Spain, and the UK).

Next, we analyse the effects of three important elements on the results. First, we investigate the consequences of the development of financial markets on the demand for monetary base. Second, we study the constraint imposed on seigniorage policies by the existence of a fixed (semi-fixed) exchange rate system. Finally, in order to evaluate the potential future needs for revenues in general, and seigniorage in particular, we analyse the government budget situation of the ten countries by formally testing for their long-run solvency.

2   A common argument for uncommon currencies: the inflation tax[1]

2.1   A simple closed economy model of optimal seigniorage

For an exchange rate system to be reasonably stable it is necessary that the inflation rates of the participating countries do not diverge in the long run. Therefore, it is important to understand the criteria according to which monetary growth is determined in the various countries, and if they imply converging rates of inflation. Table 3.1 presents the average rates of inflation in selected sub-periods since 1950 for the ten European countries. The average rate of inflation increased in all these countries after the collapse of the Bretton Woods system. In the period of flexible exchange rates between 1971 and 1978 the rate of inflation was, on average, highest. While in the 1980s the rate of inflation has been, on average, lower than in the 1970s, the cross-country variance has been higher. Why is inflation diverging across the countries, and is this pattern likely to continue?

There are several ways of modelling the process that generates inflation. In the most popular models the authorities, following a Phillips curve-inspired policy, try to use inflation for stabilization purposes. More recently, game-theoretic applications of this idea, initiated by Barro and

	1950–70	1971–78	1979–86	1950–86
Belgium	0.03	0.08	0.05	0.05
Denmark	0.05	0.10	0.08	0.07
France	0.04	0.09	0.10	0.07
Germany	0.03	0.06	0.03	0.04
Greece	0.04	0.13	0.20	0.10
Ireland	0.04	0.14	0.11	0.08
Italy	0.04	0.14	0.17	0.10
Netherlands	0.04	0.09	0.04	0.05
Spain	0.08	0.15	0.14	0.12
UK	0.04	0.13	0.10	0.07
Mean	0.04	0.11	0.10	0.07
Standard deviation	0.014	0.032	0.054	0.026

Table 3.1 *Rates of inflation*

Gordon (1983), have pointed out that, if the authorities cannot credibly commit to time-inconsistent policies, the equilibrium will be characterized by high (sub-optimal) rates of inflation. Since the equilibrium inflation rate depends on the particular structure of the economy and on the objective function of the authorities, this approach could potentially explain cross-country differences in inflation.

A different but not necessarily alternative approach investigates the potential connection between inflation and government financing decisions. This way of looking at the problem, while not novel, has recently received renewed attention, perhaps because budgetary problems have become the central issue in the policy debate. According to this approach, the proper way of looking at inflation is from a public finance point of view. Money creation is a source of revenues (seigniorage) for the government. One important reason for inflating the economy (the most important according to this approach), is to finance the primary deficit. To understand inflation we have to analyse the behaviour of budget variables, like expenditure and other sources of revenues (taxes). Table 3.2 presents the average government expenditure-output ratios for selected periods. As was the case for inflation, expenditure has increased on average in all of the countries after 1970. Also, in the 1980s, both the average expenditure-output ratio and its cross-country variance have been higher than in the 1970s. These figures seem to be compatible with a public finance-oriented explanation of inflation. In order to construct a more formal way of testing the validity of this theory, we present a simple benchmark model,

	1950–70	1971–78	1979–86	1950–86
Belgium	0.24	0.29	0.41	0.30
Denmark	0.19	0.33	0.41	0.27
France	0.37	0.41	0.49	0.41
Germany	0.15	0.27	0.31	0.21
Greece	0.18	0.23	0.31	0.22
Ireland	0.29	0.40	0.50	0.36
Italy	0.15	0.26	0.37	0.23
Netherlands	0.25	0.30	0.39	0.29
Spain	0.12	0.21	0.29	0.19
UK	0.28	0.35	0.40	0.32
Mean	0.22	0.31	0.39	0.28
Standard deviation	0.076	0.069	0.074	0.068

Table 3.2 *Ratio of government expenditure to output*

close in spirit to the work on optimal inflation tax by Phelps (1973), which has been recently used by Mankiw (1987) and Grilli (1988).

The basic structure of the model is straightforward. The government's problem is to choose the optimal mix of distortionary taxes and deficits to finance an exogenous and stochastic stream of expenditure. Formally, the problem can be expressed as:

$$\min_{T_t, S_t} E_t \sum_{j=0}^{\infty} \left(\frac{1}{1+r}\right)^j \{c_1(T_{t+j}) + c_2(S_{t+j})\}$$

$$\text{s.t.} \sum_{j=0}^{\infty} \left(\frac{1}{1+r}\right)^j \{T_{t+j} + S_{t+j}\}$$

$$= \sum_{j=0}^{\infty} \left(\frac{1}{1+r}\right)^j G_{t+j} + (1+r)B_{t-1} \tag{1}$$

where r is the (assumed) constant real interest rate, T_t are income tax revenues (at time t), G_t are real government expenditures, B_t is real government debt, S_t is seigniorage. $c_1(\cdot)$ and $c_2(\cdot)$ are convex functions, which model the potential welfare loss associated with income taxation and inflation, respectively. The costs of income taxation are associated with its distortionary effects on labour supply and with the administrative costs of collection. The costs of raising seigniorage are related to the distortionary effects of inflation. These potentially involve both reduction in desired cash holdings (and the consequent negative effects transactions) and unwelcome redistributive effects.[2] It is assumed that the government selects T_t and S_t in order to minimize the expected present discounted value of the distortions introduced by taxation. This type of model produces the tax smoothing result obtained by Barro (1979). Taxes (both income tax and inflation) are set on the basis of permanent government expenditure, with temporary deviations from this level being financed by issuing debt.

Even if not evident from the way we formulated the problem, the optimal policy implied by (1) may not be time-consistent. As originally pointed out by Calvo (1978), the difficulty arises because inflation may be distortionary *ex-ante*, but not *ex-post*. This will be the case, for example, if the only costs associated with inflation are its negative effects on (forward-looking) money demand. *Ex-post*, i.e. after individuals made their decisions about their cash holdings, the monetary authorities may deviate from the '*ex-ante* optimal' rate of inflation, thus increasing seigniorage without inducing a reduction in cash holdings. In the rest of this paper we will be discussing the properties of the optimal policy, without explicitly addressing time-consistency issues. This simplification, however, is not crucial to the analysis. First, for some of the countries under consideration, credibility of the monetary authorities is not a serious issue. Second, as has recently been shown by Persson, Persson and Svensson (1987), there exist very simple schemes that may resolve the basic time-inconsistency problem for this class of models. Third, and most important, Poterba and Rotemberg (1987) have shown that, if the costs of inflation also involve ex-post components (as in the case of redistribution effects), the time-consistent solution has basically the same time-series properties as the one we will be discussing below.

If we make the simplifying assumption that the two cost functions are quadratic in T_t and S_t, i.e.

$$c_1(T_t) = \left(a_1 + \frac{b_1}{2}\,T_t^2\right) \tag{2}$$

$$c_2(S_t) = \left(a_2 + \frac{b_2}{2}\,S_t^2\right) \tag{3}$$

the first-order conditions of (1) imply:

$$E(T_{t+1}) = T_t \tag{4}$$

$$E(S_{t+1}) = S_t \tag{5}$$

The first implication of the theory is that income tax revenues and seigniorage should be martingale processes, independently of the process generating government expenditure. This is, of course, a result analogous to the random walk property of consumption derived by Hall (1978). Notice that the first-order conditions imply a linear relationship between seigniorage and tax revenues:

$$S_t = \frac{b_1}{b_2} T_t \qquad (6)$$

Quite intuitively, the relative importance of seigniorage in an optimal taxation package depends positively on the cost of using income taxes (b_1) and negatively on the cost of using monetization (b_2).

The model also produces a positive relationship between revenues and expenditures. By taking the expectation operator, E_t, across the budget constraint, and substituting the first order conditions:

$$E_t T_{t+j} = \frac{\lambda}{b_1} ; \quad E_t S_{t+j} = \frac{\lambda}{b_2}$$

(where λ is the Lagrange multiplier associated with the intertemporal budget constraint) we obtain:

$$T_t = \frac{b_2}{b_1 + b_2} \left[\left(\frac{r}{1+r} \right) \sum_{j=0}^{\infty} \left(\frac{1}{1+r} \right)^j E_t G_{t+j} + r B_{t-1} \right] \qquad (7)$$

$$S_t = \frac{b_1}{b_1 + b_2} \left[\left(\frac{r}{1+r} \right) \sum_{j=0}^{\infty} \left(\frac{1}{1+r} \right)^j E_t G_{t+j} + r B_{t-1} \right] \qquad (8)$$

By making explicit assumptions about the stochastic process driving expenditure, G_t, we can derive from (7) and (8) expressions for T_t and S_t which are functions of observables only. For example, under the assumption that G_t is a random walk, we obtain:

$$T_t = \frac{b_2}{b_1 + b_2} [G_t + r B_{t-1}] \qquad (9)$$

$$S_t = \frac{b_1}{b_1 + b_2} [G_t + r B_{t-1}] \qquad (10)$$

Taxes and seigniorage are constant proportions of expenditure inclusive of interest payments. If we introduce an additive random error in the theoretically exact relationships (6), the stochastic implication of this theory is that S_t and T_t must be cointegrated, with the constant of integration being a measure of the relative cost of income tax and seigniorage. A similar argument holds for the expressions (9) and (10) which imply that taxes and seigniorage must be cointegrated with government expenditure (inclusive of interest payments). Notice that, in this special case, since all shocks to G_t are perceived to be permanent, the fiscal authorities will never issue any new debt. However, the properties derived above do not depend on the assumption that G_t is a random walk. Government expenditure may follow a more general non-stationary process of the form:

$$G_t = G_{t-1} + \sum_{j=0}^{I} b_j \epsilon_{t-j}$$

and the same cointegration property would still hold.[3] In this (more general) case, government debt will have a role.

It can be argued that a more appealing way to model the distortionary effect of taxation and the choice of policy instruments is not in terms of total income tax and seigniorage, but in terms of the income tax rate and the rate of inflation. This can be done by properly respecifying the model. For example, assume that the cost functions have the form:

$$c_1(T_t) = \left(a_1 + \frac{b_1}{2}\, \tau_t^2\right) Y_t \tag{11}$$

$$c_2(S_t) = \left(a_2 + \frac{b_2}{2}\, \pi_t^2\right) Y_t \tag{12}$$

where τ_t is the (average) income tax rate and π_t is the inflation rate.

We can reformulate (1) as:

$$\min_{\tau_t, \pi_t} E_t \sum_{j=0}^{\infty} \left(\frac{1}{1+r}\right)^j \left[\left(a_1 + \frac{b_1}{2}\, \tau_{t+j}^2\right) Y_{t+j}\right.$$

$$+ \left.\left(a_2 + \frac{b_2}{2}\, \pi_{t+j}^2\right) Y_{t+j}\right]$$

$$\text{s.t.} \sum_{j=0}^{\infty} \left(\frac{1}{1+r}\right)^j [\tau_{t+j} Y_{t+j} + \pi_{t+j} m_{t+j}]$$

$$= \sum_{j=0}^{\infty} \left(\frac{1}{1+r}\right)^j G_{t+j} + (1+r) B_{t-1} \tag{13}$$

where m_t are real cash balances and we have used $\pi_t m_t$ as a measure of seigniorage.[4] If we assume that money demand is a constant fraction of output: $m_t = m y_t$ we obtain:

$$\pi_t = \frac{b_1 m}{b_2} \tau_t \tag{14}$$

This model, therefore, predicts that τ_t and π_t must be cointegrated. Also, it is approximately true that:[5]

$$\tau_t = \frac{b_2}{(b_1 m^2 + b_2)} \frac{(G_t + rB_{t-1})}{y_t} \tag{15}$$

$$\pi_t = \frac{b_1 m}{(b_1 m^2 + b_2)} \frac{(G_t + rB_{t-1})}{y_t} \tag{16}$$

The tax rate and the rate of inflation should be cointegrated with government expenditure (inclusive of interest payments) expressed as a fraction of output. Note, also, the effect of the velocity of money on seigniorage and income taxation. Countries with low velocity (high m) will find it optimal to have a relatively high rate of inflation.

As pointed out by Mankiw (1987), allowing for the velocity to be a function of inflation would not change the basic results. In particular, the positive correlation between seigniorage and taxes would still be present. Suppose, for example, that $m_t = [\alpha - (\beta/2)\pi_t] y_t$. Then, from the first-order conditions of (13) we derive:

$$\pi_t = \frac{b_1 \tau_t}{b_1 + \beta b_1 \tau_2}$$

which implies that $(d\pi_t / d\tau_t) > 0$.

2.2   Empirical evidence

Results from previous analysis.   The insight that, in an environment like the one described above, the inflation rate and the tax rate should be positively correlated, is the basic idea behind recent analyses by Mankiw (1987), and Poterba and Rotemberg (1987). Mankiw (1987) argues that the theory of optimal seigniorage performs reasonable well in explaining the behaviour of nominal interest rates and inflation in the postwar United States. His conclusion is based on the finding that the inflation rate (and the nominal interest rate) and the average tax rate are indeed positively correlated, and that the regression coefficients are significant, on the basis of the standard T-statistics. Poterba and Rotemberg (1987), on the other hand, raise some doubts about the generality of the theory. They extend Mankiw's analysis to Japan, Germany, France and the UK, and they find that a significant positive correlation is present only in the Japanese data.

A fundamental problem with both analyses is that they do not take into consideration the full range of empirical implications of the theory. They look only for a positive correlation between inflation and tax rate, but they do not inquire about their unit root and cointegration properties. More importantly, the very nature of these properties, i.e. the fact that inflation and taxes should have a unit root, may invalidate the kind of tests used in those papers. It is well known, in fact, that standard regression techniques cannot be used in presence of non-stationary variables. In general, the standard T-statistics do not have a limiting distribution and cannot be used to test the significance of regression coefficients. In this case, the proper approach is to test for the existence of cointegration among the non-stationary variables. We refer the reader to Engle and Granger (1987) for a discussion of the topic.

Our empirical analysis proceeds in two steps. First, we test whether the various measures of seigniorage and income taxes have a unit root, a necessary condition if a country is behaving according to the simple theory outlined above. Second, we test for the existence of cointegration among revenue variables and between revenues and expenditures. All the data are drawn from the International Monetary Fund International Financial Statistics, and are all in logarithms. The sample size varies across countries, and it is the longest possible in the period 1948–86. Consequently, it varies from a maximum of 38 observations (for Ireland and the UK) to a minimum of 22 (for Spain). For all the other countries it is between 30 and 35 observations. Expenditure and revenue data have been expressed in real terms using the GDP deflator of the respective country. In the Appendix we provide a more detailed description of the data sources.

Unit root tests

We conducted a variety of unit root tests, including tests proposed by Dickey and Fuller (1979), Dickey and Fuller (1981), Phillips (1987) and Phillips and Perron (1987). Since the results of the different tests were very similar, we report only the Z_α (Phillips 1987), the Z_μ and Z_τ (Phillips and Perron, 1987) tests, which are presented in Tables 3.3, 3,4 and 3.5. The basic difference between the three tests is that the Z_α test is designed for a pure autoregressive process, the Z_μ for an autoregressive process with a drift and Z_τ for an autoregressive process with a drift and time trend. The

(Phillips-Perron Z_α, Z_μ and Z_τ)

	T			τ		
	Z_α	Z_μ	Z_τ	Z_α	Z_μ	Z_τ
Belgium	0.22	− 5.03	− 6.14	− 0.35	− 0.93	− 10.83
	(<90)	(>95)	(<90)	(<90)	(<90)	(<90)
Denmark	0.19	− 0.61	− 4.08	0.18	− 0.81	− 8.86
	(<90)	(<90)	(<90)	(<90)	(<90)	(<90)
France	0.26	− 0.63	2.18	− 0.34	0.19	− 11.79
	(<90)	(<90)	(<90)	(<90)	(<90)	(<90)
Germany	0.39	− 0.82	− 8.21	− 0.43	− 0.99	− 7.19
	(<90)	(<90)	(<90)	(<90)	(<90)	(<90)
Greece	0.40	− 0.58	− 21.96	− 0.31	− 4.96	− 23.05
	(<90)	(<90)	(>95)	(<90)	(<90)	(>95)
Ireland	0.24	0.27	− 6.13	− 0.44	− 0.34	− 15.31
	(<90)	(<90)	(<90)	(<90)	(<90)	(<90)
Italy	0.21	− 0.34	− 16.62	− 0.39	0.42	− 4.49
	(<90)	(<90)	(<90)	(<90)	(<90)	(<90)
Netherlands	0.15	− 0.33	− 5.17	0.05	0.21	− 5.29
	(<90)	(<90)	(<90)	(<90)	(<90)	(<90)
Spain	0.22	− 0.85	− 3.18	− 0.44	− 0.75	− 10.37
	(<90)	(<90)	(<90)	(<90)	(<90)	(<90)
UK	0.09	− 3.68	− 33.37	0.01	− 31.38	− 31.85
	(<90)	(<90)	(>99)	(<90)	(>99)	(>99)

Table 3.3 *Unit root tests: taxes*

Notes: Z_α tests H_0: $y_t = y_{t-1} + \epsilon_t$ against H_1: $y_t = \rho y_{t-1} + \epsilon_t$; $|\rho| < 1$
Z_μ tests H_0: $y_t = y_{t-1} + \epsilon_t$ against H_1: $y_t = \alpha + \rho y_{t-1} + \epsilon_t$; $|\rho| < 1$
Z_τ tests H_0: $y_t = \alpha + y_{t-1} + \epsilon_t$ against
H_1: $y_t = \alpha + (t - T/2) + \rho y_{t-1} + \epsilon_t$; $|\rho| < 1$

The number in parenthesis indicates the confidence level with which, H_0: Unit Root, is rejected.

exact form of the null hypotheses and of the alternatives for these tests are given at the bottom of the tables.

Table 3.3 tests for the existence of a unit root in the total tax revenues and average tax rate series. The results of the same test for the total government expenditure and the expenditure/GDP ratio (g_t) series, are reported in Table 3.5. Not surprisingly, for all the countries both G_t and g_t are non-stationary in the sample periods. For Greece, the existence of a unit root in G_t is rejected against the alternative of a linear time trend at a more than 97.5% confidence level. The same general non-stationarity is true for T_t and τ_t. A notable exception is the UK, for which the average tax rate appears to be stationary.

(Phillips-Perron Z_α, Z_μ and Z_τ)

	S			π		
	Z_α	Z_μ	Z_τ	Z_α	Z_μ	Z_τ
Belgium	− 0.76	− 4.89	− 7.57	0.04	− 5.03	− 6.14
	(<90)	(<90)	(<90)	(<90)	(<90)	(<90)
Denmark	− 0.22	− 16.01	− 26.77	− 14.23	− 14.62	− 24.14
	(<90)	(>95)	(>97.5)	(>99)	(>95)	(>95)
France	− 0.94	− 11.26	− 20.31	− 0.33	− 9.57	− 17.62
	(<90)	(<90)	(<90)	(<90)	(<90)	(<90)
Germany	− 1.68	− 18.93	− 26.11	− 9.99	− 12.24	− 22.95
	(<90)	(>97.5)	(>97.5)	(>95)	(>90)	(>95)
Greece	− 1.12	− 7.30	− 15.44	− 0.39	− 2.73	− 17.60
	(<90)	(<90)	(<90)	(<90)	(<90)	(<90)
Ireland	− 7.17	− 33.04	− 35.72	− 5.63	− 29.41	− 35.06
	(>90)	(>99)	(>99)	(>90)	(>99)	(>99)
Italy	− 3.92	− 29.89	− 33.16	− 0.25	− 17.61	− 29.95
	(<90)	(>99)	(>99)	(<90)	(>97.5)	(>99)
Netherlands	− 2.25	− 41.81	− 43.09	− 36.77	− 40.53	− 43.44
	(<90)	(<99)	(>99)	(<90)	(>99)	(>99)
Spain	− 0.53	− 6.03	− 8.17	0.29	− 3.54	− 8.34
	(<90)	(<90)	(<90)	(<90)	(<90)	(<90)
UK	− 0.68	− 10.83	− 16.44	0.12	− 10.67	− 12.95
	(<90)	(<90)	(<90)	(<90)	(<90)	(<90)

Table 3.4 *Unit root tests: seigniorage*

Table 3.4 presents the same battery of tests for total seigniorage, and inflation. The unit root hypothesis for π_t is never rejected when the alternative is a pure autoregressive process. The rejection is instead possible at the 99% confidence level for Ireland, Italy and the Netherlands when the alternative includes a drift, or a drift and a time trend. At a lower confidence level, rejection is also possible for Germany, which, in a sense, confirms the result by Poterba and Rotemberg (1987). Similar results hold for S_t: rejection of non-stationarity is possible for Denmark, Ireland, Italy and the Netherlands.

Summarizing, as far as seigniorage is concerned, the evidence is somewhat mixed. Specifically, Ireland, Italy, the Netherlands, and possibly Germany and Denmark, may not be satisfying the unit root condition. The unit root implication for the income tax rate receives wider support: only the UK may be violating this condition. Finally, the assumption of unit root processes for government spending, made to derive the cointegration property between revenues and expenditure, is strongly supported by the data.

(Phillips-Perron Z_α, Z_μ and Z_τ)

	G			g		
	Z_α	Z_μ	Z_τ	Z_α	Z_μ	Z_τ
Belgium	0.23	− 0.46	− 7.81	− 0.47	− 0.12	− 5.90
	(<90)	(<90)	(<90)	(<90)	(<90)	(<90)
Denmark	0.20	− 0.55	− 3.12	0.20	− 0.62	11.52
	(<90)	(<90)	(<90)	(<90)	(<90)	(<90)
France	0.26	− 0.36	− 3.54	− 0.37	0.78	− 7.64
	(<90)	(<90)	(<90)	(<90)	(<90)	(<90)
Germany	0.39	− 0.79	− 11.56	− 0.45	− 1.15	− 7.89
	(<90)	(<90)	(<90)	(<90)	(<90)	(<90)
Greece	0.45	− 0.48	− 28.70	− 0.54	− 0.48	− 15.50
	(<90)	(<90)	(>97.5)	(<90)	(<90)	(<90)
Ireland	0.25	− 0.13	− 5.61	− 0.71	− 1.18	− 10.42
	(<90)	(<90)	(<90)	(<90)	(<90)	(<90)
Italy	0.22	0.01	− 12.84	− 0.48	0.59	− 5.33
	(<90)	(<90)	(<90)	(<90)	(<90)	(<90)
Netherlands	0.17	− 0.24	− 11.74	− 0.08	0.45	− 7.98
	(<90)	(<90)	(<90)	(<90)	(<90)	(<90)
Spain	0.25	− 0.79	− 4.32	− 0.60	− 0.41	− 11.67
	(<90)	(<90)	(<90)	(<90)	(<90)	(<90)
UK	0.12	− 0.12	− 11.65	0.07	− 0.69	− 11.46
	(<90)	(<90)	(<90)	(<90)	(<90)	(<90)

Table 3.5 *Unit root tests: expenditure*

Cointegration tests   In this section we test for the existence of cointegration between seigniorage (inflation) and expenditures, and seigniorage (inflation) and taxes. Given the results of the unit root tests, including Denmark, Ireland, Italy, Germany and the Netherlands in the analysis may not be appropriate. However, it is interesting to know whether the inflation rate and the tax rate have moved in the same direction, even if this finding may not be considered evidence that seigniorage was used in an efficient way. In fact, even if taxes are globally set at suboptimal levels, it could be the case that the relative weights of the different tax instruments are still chosen according to the above theory. For example, if a government decide, (for reasons exogenous to our model) to set taxes at levels lower than what would be necessary to satisfy its budget constraint, the inflation rate and the income tax rate could be displaying a stationary behaviour. Nonetheless, if it is using inflation for revenue purposes, it may still find it desirable to move the inflation rate and tax rate together. Moreover, the unit root tests used above, as well as the cointegration tests

(Augmented Dickey-Fuller)

	C	T	R^2	ADF
Belgium	− 2.53	1.32	0.49	2.44
	(3.63)	(5.24)		
Denmark	− 1.27	0.68	0.38	1.58
	(4.76)	(4.68)		
France	− 2.42	1.20	0.59	5.06
	(4.88)	(6.88)		
Germany	− 4.39	2.07	0.27	5.09
	(3.34)	(3.55)		
Greece	− 4.70	2.47	0.78	4.25
	(8.87)	(10.60)		
Ireland	− 5.86	2.29	0.23	4.05
	(2.82)	(3.51)		
Italy	− 10.27	2.85	0.25	3.59
	(2.52)	(3.30)		
Netherlands	− 3.23	1.66	0.09	2.34
	(2.30)	(2.10)		
Spain	− 0.96	0.94	0.74	2.68
	(2.38)	(7.70)		
UK	− 1.94	1.05	0.21	1.95
	(3.43)	(3.21)		

Table 3.6(a) *Cointegration test: total seigniorage and total taxes*

Notes: The *ADF* tests the hypothesis of no-cointegration. High values of *ADF* reject the hypothesis. Critical values for one explanatory variable are (Phillips-Ouliaris, 1987):

Confidence level:	0.01	0.025	0.05	0.075	0.10
Critical value:	3.94	3.49	3.34	3.16	3.05

that we will be using below, are all asymptotic tests. Therefore, given the small sample size, the margin of error may be bigger than the one based on asymptotic distributions.

In Tables 3.6(a) and (b) we present the results of regressing total seigniorage on total taxes, and total seigniorage on total government expenditure (inclusive of interest payments). Tables 3.7(a) and (b) present analogous results based on the inflation rate, the tax rate and the expenditure rate. Finally, Tables 3.8(a) and (b) report the results of regressing total taxes on total expenditure, and the tax rate on the expenditure rate. Following the suggestion by Engle and Granger (1987), the cointegration tests are based on the Augmented Dickey–Fuller test (ADF). The critical values of the ADF test are based on Phillips and

(Augmented Dickey-Fuller)

	C	G	R^2	ADF
Belgium	− 1.91	1.06	0.40	2.42
	(2.75)	(4.39)		
Denmark	− 1.13	0.61	0.37	1.41
	(4.67)	(4.59)		
France	− 2.35	1.17	0.58	4.72
	(4.77)	(6.78)		
Germany	− 4.17	1.95	0.23	5.10
	(3.07)	(3.27)		
Greece	− 4.16	2.17	0.77	4.07
	(8.58)	(10.48)		
Ireland	− 5.59	2.13	0.23	4.01
	(2.76)	(3.47)		
Italy	− 8.09	2.35	0.25	3.80
	(2.38)	(3.31)		
Netherlands	− 2.79	1.41	0.08	2.26
	(2.20)	(1.98)		
Spain	− 0.80	0.89	0.74	2.63
	(2.11)	(7.74)		
UK	− 2.21	1.20	0.37	2.13
	(4.92)	(4.65)		

Table 3.6(b) *Cointegration test: total seigniorage and total expenditure*

Ouliaris (1987), where they derive the asymptotic distribution of the test for a different number of right-hand variables.

   Notice first, that the positive correlations between seigniorage and taxes, seigniorage and expenditure, and taxes and expenditure are present for all the ten countries. Also, on the basis of the standard T-statistics, these correlations are very significant. The same is true for the correlations between inflation rate, tax rate, and expenditure rate. However, we should be cautious in interpreting these statistics when non-stationary variables are involved. Even if these variables moved in the same direction in the post-World War II period, the ADF test rejects the hypothesis of cointegration for several of the countries.

   On the basis of these tests, we can divide the ten countries into two groups. The countries composing the first group (Belgium, Denmark, the Netherlands, Spain and the UK), do not show evidence of cointegration in any of the regressions. However, the second group (France, Germany, Greece, Ireland and Italy), provides partial support to the theory. Given that the regression residuals for the countries for this second group are

(Augmented Dickey-Fuller)

	C	τ	R^2	ADF
Belgium	0.53	3.16	0.37	2.67
	(1.10)	(4.09)		
Denmark	− 0.39	1.46	0.44	2.65
	(2.32)	(5.27)		
France	0.55	4.45	0.40	3.96
	(1.40)	(4.69)		
Germany	− 0.25	2.02	0.04	7.09
	(0.27)	(1.59)		
Greece	2.70	5.42	0.39	2.88
	(3.19)	(4.68)		
Ireland	1.48	5.17	0.16	4.09
	(1.41)	(2.82)		
Italy	1.49	4.04	0.06	3.14
	(0.89)	(1.74)		
Netherlands	0.13	3.13	0.00	2.66
	(0.07)	(0.92)		
Spain	− 0.29	0.89	0.37	2.40
	(1.57)	(3.67)		
UK	− 0.85	0.84	0.01	1.56
	(2.20)	(1.12)		

Table 3.7(a) *Cointegration test: inflation rate and tax rate*

stationary, we can be more confident about the meaningfulness of the relationships among revenue variables and between revenue and expenditure variables. It is possible, however, that the stationarity of the residual of the seigniorage regressions for Ireland, Italy or Germany, is simply a consequence of the fact that the dependent variable is, indeed, stationary.

The evidence in this second group, even if more favourable, is not homogeneous. In general, the hypothesis of cointegration between taxes and expenditure receives less support than the cointegration between seigniorage and expenditure. The result that income taxes have not been cointegrated with expenditure is a surprising and worrying result. It can be argued, in fact, that inflation has been used for purposes other than seigniorage, and this is responsible for the lack of cointegration with expenditure. This argument, however, is much less convincing in the case of other sources of revenue. The lack of this long-run relationship between expenditure and taxes raises the question of whether the current budget policies are compatible with long-run government solvency. We will investigate this problem later on in the paper. Another characteristic that

(Augmented Dickey-Fuller)

	C	g	R^2	ADF
Belgium	− 0.49 (1.49)	1.73 (2.89)	0.21	2.60
Denmark	− 0.53 (3.72)	1.20 (5.32)	0.45	2.15
France	0.16 (0.47)	3.62 (4.39)	0.36	3.69
Germany	− 0.69 (0.73)	1.46 (1.37)	0.01	7.37
Greece	1.12 (2.34)	3.56 (4.98)	0.43	3.04
Ireland	0.50 (0.68)	4.21 (2.72)	0.15	4.05
Italy	0.52 (0.54)	3.08 (2.06)	0.10	3.61
Netherlands	− 0.54 (0.42)	1.93 (0.85)	0.00	2.44
Spain	− 0.38 (2.28)	0.79 (3.61)	0.36	2.30
UK	0.47 (1.65)	3.49 (6.16)	0.51	2.55

Table 3.7(b) *Cointegration test: inflation and expenditure rate*

emerges from the analysis is that the regressions based on total seigniorage receive more support than ones based on the rate of inflation. This is particularly true for Greece and Italy.

Once again, the empirical evidence is mixed. For some countries, seigniorage has been an important revenue instrument, while, for others, there was no consistent inflation tax policy. These results are a cause for concern because they indicate that there exists a lack of homogeneity in the role of monetary policies among European countries. This is a potential source of conflict, especially in forming a common exchange rate policy.

These conclusions are based on a simple benchmark model. In the following section we point out the most important simplifications and discuss the possible implications of these hypotheses.

3   Extensions of the model

3.1   Variability in velocity and in the cost function

The above analysis assumed, in common with Mankiw (1987), that velocity is fixed over time. Changes in velocity, however, might affect the

(Augmented Dickey-Fuller)

	C	G	R^2	ADF
Belgium	0.27	0.88	0.98	2.07
	(3.81)	(35.34)		
Denmark	0.19	0.90	0.99	3.00
	(7.71)	(65.35)		
France	0.05	0.98	0.99	1.87
	(1.55)	(87.20)		
Germany	− 0.01	1.00	0.99	3.41
	(0.31)	(60.59)		
Greece	0.22	0.88	0.99	1.62
	(7.77)	(77.92)		
Ireland	0.11	0.94	0.99	3.38
	(2.29)	(65.71)		
Italy	0.80	0.82	0.99	1.78
	(9.96)	(48.88)		
Netherlands	0.19	0.89	0.99	0.21
	(7.10)	(60.68)		
Spain	0.18	0.94	0.99	0.78
	(3.14)	(53.22)		
UK	0.36	0.79	0.79	2.86
	(3.01)	(11.56)		

Table 3.8(a) *Cointegration test: total taxes and total expenditure*

desirability of seigniorage as a source of revenue. In general, in fact, it is optimal to have a higher level of seigniorage in periods of low velocity. Ignoring these movements in velocity may introduce bias in the estimates. For example, increases in seigniorage induced by increases in expenditure might have been offset by decreases induced by increases in velocity. In equation (14), for example, this is equivalent to a decrease in m.

As Table 3.9 shows, important changes in velocity occurred during the period under investigation. Two distinct patterns emerge. A first group of countries (Belgium, Denmark, France, the Netherlands and the UK) has experienced a pronounced decrease in the ratios of monetary base to output. We believe that this tendency is the consequence of the innovations in the financial markets that greatly reduced the use of monetary base in transactions in the last 30 years. The other group (composed of Germany, Greece, Ireland, Italy and Spain), does not show the same negative trend. On the contrary, Spain and Greece exhibit, if anything, a positive trend.

What is interesting is the almost identical composition of these two

(Augmented Dickey-Fuller)

	C	g	R^2	ADF
Belgium	− 0.26	0.66	0.91	2.72
	(12.11)	(17.00)		
Denmark	− 0.10	0.81	0.97	3.01
	(6.60)	(32.34)		
France	− 0.09	0.81	0.92	2.43
	(5.33)	(19.20)		
Germany	− 0.04	0.97	0.96	3.42
	(1.52)	(28.79)		
Greece	− 0.32	0.61	0.92	3.86
	(14.96)	(18.81)		
Ireland	− 0.19	0.82	0.94	3.46
	(11.79)	(24.30)		
Italy	− 0.32	0.63	0.91	1.38
	(13.59)	(17.05)		
Netherlands	− 0.20	0.64	0.89	3.43
	(9.73)	(16.93)		
Spain	− 0.10	0.89	0.98	0.86
	(4.19)	(28.68)		
UK	− 0.28	0.44	0.14	3.10
	(3.35)	(2.63)		

Table 3.8(b) *Cointegration test: tax rate and expenditure rate*

	1950	1958	1968	1978	1986
Belgium	26.7	23.1	17.6	11.8	8.1
Denmark	11.6	10.7	8.4	3.8	4.7
France	16.9	15.1	13.6	7.2	6.1
Germany	11.8	11.7	10.1	11.2	9.4
Greece	8.8[a]	11.6	18.2	18.4	18.2
Ireland	15.9	14.4	16.8	15.3	10.2
Italy	—	16.5	16.5	21.8	15.4
Netherlands	17.3	15.1	10.3	6.6	7.6
Spain	14.5[b]	13.3	12.3	12.1	19.8
UK	13.5	10.9	9.4	6.7	4.2

Table 3.9 *Ratio of monetary base to GDP (%)*
[a]This number corresponds to Greece 1953.
[b]This number corresponds to Spain 1952.

groups and the groups based on the cointegration results. With the exception of France, the countries that experienced a strong positive trend in velocity are also the ones for which the cointegration properties are absent. Similarly, the countries for which the evidence of cointegration was stronger, are also the ones (with the exception of Spain) in which the ratio of monetary base and output remained relatively high.

It is likely that the increase in velocity has induced a shift in the seigniorage policies of those countries, with inflation tax losing much of its importance. In addition to the recent developments in the financial markets, other factors contributed to the diverse behaviour of velocity among the European countries. Giavazzi (1987) suggests that government policies, by altering the reserve requirements of the commercial banks, had a major impact on the demand for monetary base. In fact, Greece, Spain, Italy and Germany are the countries that, in 1986, had the highest reserves-to-deposit ratios.[6] These differences in reserve requirements are possible, at the moment, because of the existence of capital controls which reduce the international competition among commercial banks. The unification of the European capital markets, however, will require the harmonization of these regulations. At that point, the use of seigniorage will be greatly compromised. Another strong hypothesis that is used to obtain the relationship between seigniorage and taxes like (6) or (14), is that the cost functions $c_1(\cdot)$ and $c_2(\cdot)$ have been assumed to be constant over time. While it is difficult to model the way in which these cost functions may have changed, we cannot rule out this possibility. By inducing shifts between the use of seigniorage and the use of income taxation, the occurrence of changes in the relative costs of the two tax instruments tends to reduce the significance of the (positive) relationship linking them. Moreover, if the process driving the relative cost (e.g. b_1/b_2 in equation (6)) has a unit root, then by estimating it with a constant we will be introducing a non-stationary component in the residual. This will lead to a failure to detect cointegration between seigniorage and income tax revenues. A similar argument applies to equation (14) with the addition that velocity $(1/m)$ might also have been a unit root process.

3.2 Seigniorage vs. fixed exchange rates

In our basic mode, we implicitly assumed that the monetary authorities were potentially free to choose any level of seigniorage.

This approach, however, fails to consider a crucial element in the monetization decisions, i.e. the exchange rate regime. In fact, a fixed exchange rate system imposes serious constraints on the ability of governments independently to set the level of inflation. Given that a country values a stable exchange rate, it may be willing to suffer the cost of a suboptimal use of the inflation tax. These are important considerations since most of the observations in our data set refer to periods of fixed or controlled exchange rates: Bretton Woods first and the EMS later on.

A simple way to model this idea is to introduce into the government loss function an additional term which penalizes the variance of inflation (around the mean level of the system or around the level of a leader country). We may think of this as the costs associated with devaluations and switches to flexible exchange rates and with the resulting increase in volatility of the real exchange rate. We can rewrite the fiscal authority problem as:

$$
\begin{aligned}
\min_{\tau_t, \pi_t} E_t \sum_{j=0}^{\infty} \left(\frac{1}{1+r}\right)^j & \left[\left(a_1 + \frac{b_1}{2}\, \pi_{t+j}\right) Y_{t+j} \right. \\
& + \left(a_2 + \frac{b_2}{2}\, \pi_{t+j}^2\right) Y_{t+j} \\
& \left. + \frac{b_3}{2}\, (\pi_{t+j} - \pi_{t+j}^*)^2\, Y_{t+j} \right] \\
\text{s.t.} \sum_{j=0}^{\infty} \left(\frac{1}{1+r}\right)^j & \{\tau_{t+j} Y_{t+j} + \pi_{t+j} m Y_{t+j}\} \\
= \sum_{j=0}^{\infty} & \left(\frac{1}{1+r}\right)^j G_{t+j} + (1+r) B_{t-1}
\end{aligned} \tag{17}
$$

where π_t^* is the inflation rate in the leader country in the system (e.g. US before 1971 and Germany after 1979). From the first-order conditions, it is easily obtained:

$$
\pi_t = \frac{b_1 m}{b_2 + b_3}\, \tau_t + \frac{b_3}{b_2 + b_3}\, \pi_t^*
$$

The larger the cost of deviating from π_t^*, the smaller the correlation between π_t and τ_t. In the limiting case of $b_3 \to \infty$: $\pi_t = \pi_t^*$. It is clear that unless b_3 is very small, we may introduce a serious bias if we omit π_t from the regression.

Table 3.10 reports the results of adding the inflation rate of the leader country as an explanatory variable. π_t^* was chosen to be the US inflation rate up to 1971, except for Ireland where UK inflation was used for the whole sample. After 1971, π_t^* was switched to be the German inflation rate, except for Greece and Spain for which US inflation rate was still used. Also, it is important to verify that, for the US, the inflation rate has a unit root. If US inflation were stationary, we would not have any hope of inducing stationarity in the residuals by adding it as a regressor. Tests analogous to the one performed in the previous sections could not reject

(Augmented Dickey-Fuller)

	C	τ	π^*	R^2	ADF
Belgium	0.85	2.10	0.67	0.52	2.85
	(1.96)	(2.78)	(3.05)		
Denmark	0.12	0.88	0.56	0.59	2.61
	(0.60)	(3.11)	(3.62)		
France	0.80	3.37	0.46	0.50	3.65
	(2.19)	(3.57)	(2.78)		
Germany	− 5.65	− 7.81	1.86	0.24	5.27
	(2.82)	(2.24)	(3.00)		
Greece	3.05	4.78	0.54	0.42	3.14
	(3.57)	(3.99)	(1.60)		
Ireland	2.68	3.43	1.61	0.33	3.97
	(2.66)	(1.99)	(3.21)		
Italy	2.74	3.84	0.94	0.06	3.54
	(1.29)	(1.65)	(0.96)		
Netherlands	0.94	0.14	1.63	0.00	2.63
	(0.51)	(0.03)	(2.13)		
Spain	− 0.68	1.23	− 0.46	0.50	1.73
	(2.98)	(4.80)	(2.47)		
UK	− 1.13	− 0.28	0.31	0.51	3.63
	(4.09)	(0.50)	(6.01)		

Table 3.10 *Cointegration test: exchange rate constraint*
Critical values for one explanatory variable are (Phillips-Ouliaris, 1987):

Confidence level:	0.01	0.025	0.05	0.075	0.10
Critical value:	4.35	4.01	3.77	3.59	3.47

the unit root hypothesis. Cointegration is accepted for France, Germany, Ireland, Italy and the UK, suggesting that, for these countries, the exchange rate system may have been a serious constraint to the seigniorage policies. In this respect, the experience of Germany and the UK is very revealing. In both cases, the positive correlation between seigniorage and taxes disappears. This can be interpreted as an indication of the priority of exchange rate policies over seigniorage policies in these two countries.

4   Is Mr Ponzi really dead? Solvency and fiscal reforms

Suppose that, regardless of the results obtained in the previous sections, we believe that seigniorage has not, at least since the 1950s, played any significant role in the conduct of monetary policies in Europe. Could we then conclude that seigniorage is not a serious threat to exchange rate stability and to the existence of the EMS? A problem with this point of view is that it neglects to consider the current status of the various governments' finances in the Community. Many economists believe that several of the countries in our sample are not following fiscal policies which are sustainable in the long run. Sooner or later these countries will have to undertake budget adjustments which may well involve resorting to seigniorage revenues. While it is true that inflation does not need to be part of a fiscal reform, the existence of domestic political constraints on the use of alternative sources of revenues may make seigniorage indispensable.

In this section we present results of econometric tests designed to determine whether the idea that some European countries are following potentially insolvent fiscal policies, is indeed founded.

Consider the government budget constraint at time $t + 1$:

$$B_{t+1} = (1 + r)B_t + G_{t+1} - R_{t+1} \tag{18}$$

where R_{t+1} are total revenues (i.e. taxes plus seigniorage). Taking the expectations at time t, and by recursive substitutions, we obtain:

$$B_t = - E_t \sum_{j=0}^{\infty} \left(\frac{1}{1 + r} \right)^j [G_{t+j} - R_{t+j}]$$

$$+ \lim_{j \to \infty} E_t \left(\frac{1}{1 + r} \right)^j B_{t+j} \tag{19}$$

In order for the budget constraint to hold, it must be true that:

$$\lim_{j \to \infty} E_t \left(\frac{1}{1 + r} \right)^j B_{t+j} = 0 \tag{20}$$

This is the usual condition which says that the stock of debt cannot increase faster than the government borrowing rate. Condition (20) implies, as noted by McCallum (1984), and Hamilton and Flavin (1986), that a constant deficit *inclusive of interest payments* is consistent with intertemporal solvency. In this case, in fact:

$$B_{t+j} = (j + t)K + B_0 \tag{21}$$

where K is the constant size of the deficit, so that condition (20) is satisfied. Hamilton and Flavin (1986) test the intertemporal budget constraint for the US in the period 1962–84. Using a deterministic bubble test of the kind proposed by Flood and Garber (1980), they conclude that the US 'government budget historically has been balanced in expected present value terms' (p. 809).

More recently, Trehan and Walsh (1987) have employed a similar test, closer in spirit to the ones employed in the previous sections of this paper. The intuition behind this test is quite simple. The condition of a constant

	Z_α	Z_μ
Belgium	0.83	− 0.50
	(<90)	(<90)
Denmark	− 6.62	− 6.67
	(<90)	(<90)
France	0.64	− 0.61
	(<90)	(<90)
Germany	− 8.47	− 9.78
	(<90)	(<90)
Greece	1.34	− 1.46
	(<90)	(<90)
Ireland	1.03	− 0.47
	(<90)	(<90)
Italy	0.56	− 2.20
	(<90)	(<90)
Netherlands	− 1.12	− 2.16
	(<90)	(<90)
Spain	− 2.34	0.36
	(<90)	(<90)
UK	− 22.33	− 22.25
	(>99)	(>99)

Table 3.11 *Solvency constraint: deficit inclusive of interest payments*

deficit (inclusive of interest payments) is extended in a stochastic environment to the one of the deficit being a stationary variable. More specifically, suppose that the vector $z_t = (G_t R_t)$ follows a process given by:

$$(1 - L)z_t = \alpha + A(L)\epsilon_t \tag{22}$$

where L is the lag operator, α is a vector of constants, $A(L)$ is a 2×2 matrix of polynomials in L, and ϵ_t is a vector of white noise innovations. The process (22) implies that, consistent with our data, G_t and R_t must be differenced once in order to induce stationarity. Under this condition, Trehan and Walsh (1987) show that the necessary and sufficient condition for the budget to be intertemporally balanced is that the first difference of the stock of debt, i.e. the deficit inclusive of interest payments, is stationary. They also test this condition for the US, on a longer sample than Hamilton and Flavin (1986), and they reach the same conclusion.

Table 3.11 presents the unit root tests for the deficits of the ten European countries. The non-stationarity of the deficit is rejected only for the UK and, at a lower level of confidence, for Germany and possibly Denmark. For the other countries, this analysis suggests that the current budget policies will have to be revised if intertemporal balance has to be guaranteed. Even if, given the small sample size, these results should be interpreted with caution, they definitely indicate that for some of these countries the temptation to repudiate their European commitments, even by reintroducing controls on the capital markets or by abandoning the defence of their exchange rate parity, may become very strong.

5   Conclusions and Policy Implications

In this chapter, based on the experience of ten European countries, we tried to understand the relevance of seigniorage revenues in the recent past, and speculate about their importance in the near future. A first conclusion is that the members of the European Community differ widely in the way they manage monetary policies. At a first level of approximation, we divided the countries into two groups. For the first group, composed of Belgium, Denmark, the Netherlands, Spain and the UK, we could not identify a consistent seigniorage policy. However, for the countries of the second group (France, Ireland, Italy, Germany and Greece), seigniorage appears to have been an important component of their financing policies. This lack of consensus about the role of monetary policies is a potential source of conflict in designing common exchange rate policies.

A formal analysis of the current status of the finances of the governments of the ten European countries revealed that several of them are now following budget policies that are potentially incompatible with their long-run solvency. This also represents a major obstacle toward monetary unification on exchange rate stability. Member countries will be faced with quite different needs for revenues and eliminating a (politically) flexible instrument like seigniorage may result in an unstable situation. This problem is likely to become more acute in the near future since, with the dismantling of capital controls, other forms of taxation which instrinsically depended on the segmentation of capital markets, will have to disappear. In the periods of social conflict which are likely to characterize times of fiscal reforms, the temptation to resort to seigniorage and thus either reintroduce capital controls or abandon the exchange rate parity, may become very strong.

What is going to be the future of the exchange rate system in Europe? In what direction should we move? One possibility is the return to a free float. Recent experience, however, has generated widespread scepticism about the desirability of such an arrangement. There exists a fear that movements of the nominal exchange rate are dominated by speculative bubbles, and thus that they may induce market responses that are unrelated to economic fundamentals. It is contended that a higher exchange rate variability may also induce inefficiencies in the allocation of resources. McKinnon (1988), for example, argues that in a world where markets are highly incomplete, forward markets alone cannot provide sufficient insurance against exchange rate risk, especially for long-term irreversible investments. But, more fundamentally, a return to a free float is in contradiction with the goal of a European monetary unification.

Another extreme possibility is the switch to an irrevocable fixed exchange rate system. At the moment, however, there do not seem to exist the proper conditions for a tightening of the EMS bands and for the implementation of a strictly fixed exchange rate system. During the next few years, the top priority of several member countries will be the correction of their public finances. This will probably involve major adjustments in their fiscal and monetary policies. What should be avoided is forcing a country out of the EMS because it imposed constraints that were too rigid to be compatible with its domestic policies.

Practicable fiscal adjustments may require several realignments in the exchange rate parities. This, however, need not imply the end of the EMS. What is important is that these realignments occur without major speculative activities which may interfere with a smooth process of integration. A way to guarantee the flexible management of the EMS, even in the absence of capital controls, has been suggested by Grilli and Alesina (1987). This would involve the expansion of the inter-country credit facilities and the formal commitment to a large short-term loans to central banks who come under the danger of a speculative attack.

Appendix

The data are from the International Monetary Fund IFS tape:

(1)	Monetary Base	line 14
(2)	Government Revenues[a]	line 81
(3)	Government Expenditure[a]	line 82
(4)	Nominal GNP	line 99A
(5)	Real GNP	line 99A.P
(6)	Nominal GDP	line 99B
(7)	Real GDP	line 99B.P
(8)	Price Level	line (4)/(5) or (6)/(7)

[a]French data, not available from the IFS, are from the OECD National Accounts, Income and Outlay Transactions of General Government.

NOTES

I would like to thank for helpful discussions Alberto Giovannini, Gabriel de Kock, Guillermo Mondino and Guido Tabellini. Financial support from the National Science Foundation and the Council for West European Studies is gratefully acknowledged
1 The title of this section was inspired by the title of Mundell (1973).
2 Even if not done here, it is possible to derive these type of cost function from more fully specified general equilibrium models. See Grilli (1988).

3 See Trehan and Walsh (1987) for a formal derivation.
4 Different measures of seigniorage can be found in the literature. The most common are the inflation rate multiplied by real cash balances, the rate of growth of monetary base multiplied by real cash balances, and the nominal interest rate multiplied by real cash balances. Drazen (1985) provides a general measure of seigniorage which produces most of the popular measures as special cases.
5 Equations are not exactly true since, in general, $\mathrm{Cov}(\tau_t, y_t)$ and $\mathrm{Cov}(\pi_t, Y_t)$ are not zero.
6 See Giavazzi (1987).

REFERENCES

Barro, R. (1979) 'On the Determination of Public Debt,' *Journal of Political Economy* **87**, 940–71.

Barro, R. and D. Gordon (1983) 'A Positive Theory of Monetary Policy in a Natural Rate Model,' *Journal of Political Economy* **91**, 589–610.

Calvo, G. (1978). 'On the Time Consistency of Optimal Policy in a Monetary Economy', *Econometrica* **46**, 1411–28.

Dickey, D. and W. Fuller (1979) 'Distribution of the Estimators for Autoregressive Time Series with a Unit Root,' *Journal of the American Statistical Association* **74**, 427–31.

    (1981) 'Likelihood Ratio Statistics for Autoregressive Time Series with a Unit Root,' *Econometrica* **49**, 1057–72.

Dornbusch, R. (1987). 'The EMS, The Dollar and the Yen', unpublished manuscript.

Drazen, A. (1985). 'A General Measure of Inflation Tax Revenues', *Economic Letters* **17**, 327–30.

Engle, R.F. and C.W.J. Granger (1987). 'Co-integration and Error Correction: Representation, Estimation and Testing', *Econometrica* **55**, 251–276.

Flood, R. and P. Garber (1980). 'Market Fundamentals Versus Price Level Bubbles: The First Tests', *Journal of Political Economy* **87**, 745–70.

Giavazzi, F. (1987). 'The Exchange-Rate Question in Europe', unpublished manuscript.

Grilli, V. (1988). 'Fiscal Policies and the Dollar/Pound Exchange Rate: 1870–1894', NBER Working Paper no. 2482.

Grilli, V. and A. Alesina (1987). 'Avoiding Speculative Attacks on EMS Currencies: A Proposal'. Economic Growth Center Discussion paper No. 547.

Hall, R. (1978) Stochastic Implications of the Life Cycle-Permanent Income Hypothesis: Theory and Evidence,' *Journal of Political Economy* **86**, 971–87.

Hamilton, J. and M. Flavin (1986). 'On the Limitation of Government Borrowing: A Framework for Empirical Testing', *American Economic Review* **76**, 809–19.

Mankiw, N.G. (1987). 'The Optimal Collection of Seigniorage: Theory and Evidence', *Journal of Monetary Economics* **20**, 327–41.

McCallum, B. (1984). 'Are Bond-Financed Deficits Inflationary? A Ricardian Analysis', *Journal of Political Economy* **92**, 123–35.

McKinnon, R. (1988). 'Monetary and Exchange Rate Policies for International Financial Stability: A Proposal'. *Journal of Economic Perspectives* **2**, 83–100.

Mundell, R. (1973). 'Uncommon Arguments for Common Currencies', in H. Johnson and A. Swoboda (eds.), *The Economics of Common Currencies*, George Allen and Unwin.

Persson, M., T. Persson and L. Svensson (1987). 'Time Consistency of Fiscal and Monetary Policy', *Econometrica* **55**, 1419–31.

Phelps, E. (1973). 'Inflation in the Theory of Public Finance', *Swedish Journal of Economics* **75**, 67–82.

Phillips, P.C.B. (1987). 'Time Series Regression With a Unit Root', *Econometrica* **55**, 277–301.

Phillips, P.C.B. and P. Perron (1987). 'Testing for a Unit Root in the Time Series Regression', CFDP n. 795, Yale University.

Phillips, P.C.B. and S. Ouliaris (1987). 'Asymptotic Properties of Residual Based Tests for Cointegration', CFDP n. 847, Yale University.

Poterba, J. and J. Rotemberg (1987). 'Inflation and Taxation With Maximizing Governments', unpublished manuscript.

Trehan, B. and C. Walsh (1987). 'Common Trends, The Government's Budget Constraint and Revenue Smoothing', unpublished manuscript.

Discussion

RUDIGER DORNBUSCH

Grilli's paper is an ambitious attempt to draw out and test the implications of seigniorage theory. He explores the theory in three directions: the full econometric implications of the intertemporally optimal public finance model, observations on seigniorage when velocity is changing and lastly the question of exchange rate regimes in countries where the hypothesis of solvency of the fiscal regime can be questioned.

Consider first the implications of the public finance model.[1] The government, in an intertemporal optimization model, has to select a path of taxes and inflation and debt issue, given the spending path, which finances the budget. The solution is to finance transitory spending fluctuations by debt, but to respond to permanent changes by variations in the tax and inflation rates. Specifically, in this model the tax rate and the inflation rates will be proportional and, to avoid intertemporal distortions, their path is flat.

In this approach the work could hardly be done more thoroughly. Grilli rightly notes and emphasizes that simply establishing a positive correlation between inflation and the tax share, as done in some earlier work, does not exploit the full implications of the theory. The theory, taken all the way, predicts proportionality between the tax rate and the rate of inflation. This suggests cointegration tests as a possible means of checking

whether the European experience supports the predictions of the public
finance model. Grilli tests for the restrictions implied by the theory and
finds that the evidence, in half the cases, does not support the theory. That
must lead one to ask whether the theory is, in fact, very interesting and
whether it is tested in the best way.

The equilibrium approach to macroeconomics has as its basic premises
that economic agents, and their agent which is the government, use
information efficiently, they maximize and they are not unemployed
except when paid to be so. In this setting inflation is used as part of an
efficient public finance system (in the absence of non-distortionary
instruments such as the proverbial head tax). The government 'sets' the
inflation rate along with marginal tax rates on other activities so as to
optimally finance the targeted level of outlays. Of course this view strikes
many as preposterous. For many observers the government is desperately
at work, at large costs in terms of output and employment, to fight
inflation. By assumption the equilibrium model rules out inflation as a
coordination problem – say an oil price increase that is poorly digested –
and sees it rather as a conscious choice of taxation. It is interesting then to
ask why the oil price shocks were so inflationary in Europe? Why did the
government not resort to the usual rule of financing transitory shocks by
debt creation?

I do not want to argue that seigniorage considerations are irrelevant. A
government that chooses an exchange rate regime that implies a very low
average rate of inflation must recognize the revenue implications. But it is
a vast step from there to believe that Britain's 28% inflation rate in 1975
(see Figure 3A.1) was chosen optimally. If public finance was part of the
issue, it certainly also was the least concern. In fact, the slightest attempt
to correlate in annual data seigniorage and inflation shows exceptionally
poor results. Much of the effort therefore in establishing cointegration
results between taxes, spending and inflation may be misdirected from the
outset. A serious model of inflation cannot possibly assume that the
government 'sets' inflation. Moreover, as the work of Sargent (1983) and
Sargent and Wallace (1981) documents, changes in the monetary strategy
may have serious implications for public finance over and above the
revenue loss. Real interest rates may rise (because the policy is not
believed) and unemployment can increase vastly. Table 3A.1 shows data
for Ireland that can be viewed in this perspective.

Another difficulty with Grilli's analysis concerns the precise implications
of the theory. The use of quadratic cost functions is surely *ad hoc*. There is
no model of the microeconomic foundations of money even suggestively
offered. The point is critical because for welfare costs (unlike for macroeconomics) microfoundations of money *do* matter. It certainly is to be

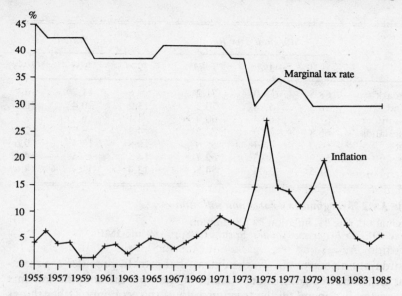

Figure 3A.1   UK inflation and marginal tax rate, 1955–85

	1970–81	1982–87
Real interest (% p.a.)	− 2.9	6.7
Real GNP growth	3.8	− 0.1
Seigniorage (% of GNP)	1.95	0.73
Unemployment (% of labour force)	7.20	15.7
Debt/GNP	73.5	117.2

Table 3A.1 *Ireland: growth, seigniorage and real interest rates (per cent, period average)*
Source: Dornbusch (1988b).

expected that there are cross-effects in the welfare costs of income taxation and taxation of money. This would certainly be the case if labour and money were substitutes in production or if leisure time had to be given up to manage cash at lower average levels. If one does take the welfare cost arguments seriously these become the dominant issues. Of course, it may be difficult to test a really serious microeconomic model of the welfare costs, but that surely does not make the case for testing a poorer version.

I would also note that the public finance of seigniorage involves not only

	Marginal Tax Rate			Inflation		
	1979	1981	1983	1979	1981	1983
Denmark	68.5	69.0	71.2	9.6	11.7	6.9
Ireland	55.5	57.8	70.2	13.2	20.4	10.5
Germany	61.1	60.5	60.9	4.1	6.3	3.3
Netherlands	66.8	69.0	73.5	4.2	6.7	2.8
France	66.9	66.7	68.8	10.8	13.4	9.6
Italy	56.3	59.5	62.7	14.8	19.5	14.6
UK	51.5	53.4	54.5	13.4	11.9	4.6

Table 3A.2 *Marginal tax rates and inflation*
Marginal tax rate %; inflation % per annum.
Source: OECD *Economic Studies*, Spring 1988, p. 189 and IMF.

inflation but also growth. To the extent that growth provides a government with revenue from money creation the optimal tax-inflation mix must certainly depend on the trend growth of the economy. Other things equal, the lower the trend growth rate the higher the optimal rate of inflation. This point is not recognized in the theory or the empirical implication of the Grilli model.

There is another respect in which the theory could be implemented with a sharper edge. In the relevant theory, the welfare cost will depend on the *marginal* rates of taxation, not on tax shares in GNP. But the testing is done as if there were no difference between average and marginal. Suppose one did look at marginal rates. Figure 3A.1 shows the case for the UK. The tax rate shown there is the standard rate (kindly supplied by James Poterba) which applied to most wage earners. It is apparent to the naked eye that proportionality between inflation and the tax rate does not hold. Given the vast divergence between average and marginal rates, I suppose that the same pattern holds in most European countries.

Some indication of the likely finding is given in Table 3A.2. This shows marginal tax rates on a single worker and inflation rates for three years. It is apparent to the naked eye that the hypothesized positive correlation between inflation and tax rates is simply not present.

As more recent data become available, covering the return to near-German levels of inflation in Europe, the divergence between marginal tax rates (and average spending shares and tax shares) and the inflation rate will become more and more striking. Marginal tax rates have increased sharply from their levels of the 1960s but inflation is back to the level of the 1960s. There is no conceivable sense in which the proportionality hypothesis of taxation, spending and inflation will go through. And the more high real interest rates and debt accumulation make it difficult to bring down the spending share the more it becomes apparent (as in Ireland, for example) that policy makers have gone the wrong way. They have disinflated too furiously, forgetting about the budget implications.

The cost of inflation in the Grilli model comes entirely from the implied tax on the use of money and the resulting distortion in the allocation of resources. But surely inflation in the 1970s had another effect: in the presence of long-term debt it was a powerful instrument to reduce the real value of existing claims. These benefits (resulting from the exercise of time-inconsistent policies) were once-and-for-all gains; with the reduced importance of long-term debt (partly as a result of these policies, partly as a result of the shortening of maturities which follows in the aftermath of such an experience when long-term debt becomes a lemon) the marginal cost of inflation is sharply higher. This would suggest that the optimal use of inflation, including now the use of surprise inflation, is a function of the structure of existing debt. In the context of the oil price shocks debt-income ratios declined due to negative real interest rates. This might be interpreted as an emergency measure where the government sacrifices massively on reputation as a means of financing an unusually large shock in part by reneging on its liability. But Grilli does not pick up this track.

The more the debt is short-term or denominated in foreign exchange, the smaller the incentive for inflation policy. Moreover, when tax brackets are not fully indexed inflation helps raise the marginal tax rate without the need for political action. If it is politically costly to raise tax rates than inflation has a beneficial side effect here, too. Both the debt and the tax-rate raising effects of inflation are not recognized in this study even though their importance in some instances may dominate the seigniorage issue.

Grilli rightly makes the point that some European countries are pursuing budget policies that are on a collision course with solvency. I am not sure that the assumption of a time-invariant process, which he estimates, makes much sense. It is in the very nature of budget troubles that a poor regime is chosen and then, to correct the course, a period of austerity follows. But what are the implications of this apparent lack of solvency on the current course? The answer is presumably to have work fare, spending cuts, increased efficiency in the public sector and a tax reform which, US style, broadens the base and reduces marginal tax rates. It is doubtful that inflation or repudiation will be the answer in Europe.

NOTE

1 For an older tradition of the seigniorage literature see Mundell (1971, 1972), including a monetary theory of colonialism.

REFERENCES

Dornbusch, R. (1988a). 'Money and Finance in European Integration' in European Free Trade Area Association, *Money and Finance in European Integration*, Geneva.
 (1988b). 'Ireland's Failed Stabilization', mimeo, Massachusetts Institute of Technology.
Giavazzi, F. (1987). 'The Exchange Rate Question in Europe', mimeo, University of Bologna.
Mundell, R.A. (1971). *Monetary Theory*, Pacific Palisades: Goodyear.
 (1972). 'The Optimum Balance of Payments Deficit', in E. Claassen and P. Salin (eds.), *Stabilization Policy in Interdependent Economies*, Amsterdam: North-Holland.
Sargent, T. (1983). 'Stopping Moderate Inflation: The Methods of Poincare and Thatcher' in R. Dornbusch and M. Simonsen (eds.), *Inflation, Debt and Indexation*, MIT Press.
Sargent, T. and N. Wallace (1981). 'Some Unpleasant Monetarist Arithmetic', Federal Reserve Bank of Minneapolis, *Quarterly Review* 1, 1–17.
Spaventa, L. (1987). 'The Growth of Public Debt: Sustainability, Fiscal Rules, and Monetary Policy', *IMF Staff Papers*, June.

LUIGI SPAVENTA

There are many ingredients in Grilli's very interesting paper. He views inflation as a source of revenue for the government, in the tradition of the literature on seigniorage. He uses a model *à la* Mankiw (1987), where minimization of a loss function, which accounts for rising marginal costs of both inflation and distortionary taxation, subject to the budget constraint, yields positive seigniorage, a direct relationship between the latter and the tax rate, and a dependence of both on revenue requirements. He then uses unit root tests and cointegration tests to examine the empirical relevance of his model for a number of countries. In discussing how changes in velocity affect the results, Grilli, along with Giavazzi (1987), emphasizes the role of reserve requirements for the use of seigniorage. He also models the effects of the constraints on money creation imposed by fixed exchange rates. By means of empirical tests Grilli shows that the fiscal policies of some European countries do not meet the solvency requirement. Finally he points to the contradictions that may arise between tighter EMS monetary discipline and capital markets liberalization, on the one hand, and the need for some countries to rely on seigniorage in order to finance deficits, on the other.

I very much agree with the spirit of Grilli's paper: the public finance approach to inflation is important and the policy problem he raises are

Total change 1974–1983	+ 11.27
Due to:	
– rise in real incomes	+ 2.27
– discretionary changes	– 5.44
– fiscal drag due to inflation	+ 14.44

Table 3B.1 *Direct taxes as a share of labour income in Italian industry (%)*
Source: CER (1984).

very relevant. I shall not discuss the econometric tests presented in the paper. I shall instead confine my comments to the specification of the model from which he obtains the results he tests for and from which he draws his policy conclusions. There are at least three points which, I think, ought to be clarified before even proceeding to econometric tests.

In the model, the positive relationship between the inflation rate and the tax rate is the result of a rational decision of cost-minimizing policy makers facing an intertemporal budget constraint. For the authorities money creation and taxation are alternative means of financing: both are optimally used because both have rising marginal costs.

Consider now a system where income taxation is progressive and tax rates are not indexed. In such system there will be an intrinsic complementarity between the ratio of taxes to income and the inflation rate, which does not stem from cost minimization: the higher the inflation rate, the higher the *real* tax rate owing to the fact that the average tax bracket rises with nominal income. Higher inflation provides the government with the bonus of higher tax revenues which are obtained without having to submit discretionary measures to Parliament. The importance of this fiscal drag as a source of revenues is examined by Giavazzi and Spaventa (1988). Table 3B.1 reports some striking data for a high inflation period in Italy. No doubt, the direct effects of inflationary financing of the budget were less relevant than its indirect effects through rising tax revenues. It is of course possible that the authorities optimize taking the structure of the tax system into account. But with progressive income taxation, once they have decided on inflation, they have also decided on taxation; and they may even be forced to propose discretionary tax *rebates* if the inflation-induced increase in tax revenues is too high. With proportional taxation, on the other hand, there would be no intrinsic link between inflation and tax revenues, and the inflation rate and the tax rate would be two independent policy variables: then, but only then, could a test showing a positive relationship between the inflation rate and the tax rate be taken as convincing evidence for the model used by Grilli. This is particularly true

	to GDP		to monetary base		to deposits
	Monetary bases	M2	Total reserves	Compulsory reserves	Compulsory reserves
1976–80	− 2.7	− 6.9	+ 3.6	+ 2.4	− 0.3
1980–85	− 0.3	− 6.8	+ 4.1	+ 5.7	+ 3.1
1980–87	− 1.1	− 8.8	+ 4.5	+ 8.4	+ 4.1

Table 3B.2 *Italy: changes in ratios, 1980–87 (%)*

Note: For the period 1980–87, new national accounts.
Source: Bank of Italy Report.

when tests cover, for each country, a span of almost 40 years, when there have been important changes in the structure of the tax system, and comparisons are made for different countries with very different tax systems.

My next two points concern the measure of the source of revenue due to inflation and the extension of the model to allow for the effects of reserve requirements on the tax base of seigniorage. In Grilli (as in most other models) the inflationary revenue in the budget constraint is measured simply as the inflation rate times the ratio of monetary base to GDP; it is then argued that, as the latter ratio depends also on reserve requirements, lower reserve requirements caused by deregulation would reduce the possibility of extracting seigniorage.

Once reserve requirements appear in the picture, however, they should be modelled explicitly as a separate policy instrument, along with the inflation rate and the tax rate. Introducing the compulsory reserve ratio in the budget identity is straightforward, but from then on things are far more difficult.[1] A model of the kind used by Grilli is ill suited for the purpose, as it is not clear how reserve requirements can find a separate place in the loss function: subsuming them under a generic inflation variable[2] defeats the very purpose of the analysis, which ought to be that of determining simultaneously the optimal value of the three policy instruments – the inflation rate, the tax rate *and* the inflation tax base. What must be recognised is that consideration of reserve ratios requires the explicit consideration of deposits as another asset along with money. This is done by Drazen (1988), where however deposits serve no transaction purposes. A richer specification of asset demand functions, as in Romer (1985) (and even simpler exercises of partial equilibrium analysis) show that, while reserve requirements are an important component of an optimal plan, their relationship with seigniorage is ambiguous and that drawing policy conclusions on their role from a model where the inflation tax base is treated as an exogenous variable is not legitimate.

In the medium run the demand for deposits depends of course on financial innovations, and hence on the degree of development of the country's financial structure. Table 3B.2 shows, for Italy, that increases in reserve requirements cannot offset the effects of a declining trend in the demand for deposits.

My third point concerns the definition of seigniorage in the budget constraint. In an open economy with fixed or quasi-fixed exchange rates monetary financing of the budget and total money creation may and usually do differ. Drazen (1988, but see also 1985) takes this into account and provides a very precise measure of seigniorage. In the budget constraint, only money growth 'above that required to manage the exchange rate' should be considered. I add that stringent assumptions are needed to make the latter coincide with the inflation rate, which is an argument of the loss function. Under fixed rates, on the other hand, the proceeds from foreign exchange reserves should be included in the seigniorage to the extent to which they are returned to the Treasury; but they do not coincide with the flow of money creation currently used to acquire reserves.

This may be a minor point, but it is certainly relevant for a country like Germany, where the central bank financing of the Treasury (properly defined as 'seigniorage' in the Bundesbank Bulletin) is but a tiny fraction of total central bank money creation.

Finally there is perhaps unexploited potential in the model used by Grilli. Taxes and inflation depend positively on the level of expenditure *inclusive* of interest payments. Hence they depend on the level of outstanding debt, which, as in all tax-smoothing models, is an unexplained variable. This allows to establish an interesting intertemporal link between past debt accumulation and current inflation, or between current debt accumulation and future inflation. We would thus expect to find a relationship between levels of debt and inflation over the long run.

NOTES

1 The issue is discussed in Spaventa (1988).
2 As Pagano (1988) does.

REFERENCES

CER – CentroEuropa Ricerche (1984). *Rapporto* n. 1, Roma.
Drazen, Alan (1985). 'A general measure of inflation tax revenues', *Economic Letters* 17, 327–30.
   (1988). 'Monetary policy, capital controls, and seigniorage in an open economy'. This volume.
Giavazzi, Francesco (1987). 'The exchange rate question in Europe', mimeo.
Giavazzi, Francesco and Luigi Spaventa (1989). 'Italy: an unconventional story?', *Economic Policy*. The real effects of Inflation and Disinflation.

Mankiw, N. Gregory (1987). 'The optimal collection of seigniorage', *Journal of Monetary Economics* **20**, 327–41.

Pagano, Marco (1988). Discussion of Drazen, this volume.

Romer, David (1985). 'Financial intermediation, reserve requirements and inside money: A general equilibrium analysis', *Journal of Monetary Economics* **16**, 175–94.

Spaventa, Luigi (1988). 'Seigniorage: Old and new policy issues', *European Economic Review*, forthcoming.

Overview of chapters 2 and 3

MICHAEL BRUNO

Being somewhat of an outsider to this particular literature I found the two papers very interesting in terms of the theoretical questions that are raised in them. Given the policy context of this conference, however, I will concentrate my few comments on the policy-relevant issues as they appear to me rather than on first-order conditions or econometrics.

Two questions come to mind in the context of the optimal seigniorage revenue literature based on Barro-Phelps, recently tested by Mankiw for the US and now extended by Grilli to the European scene. The first question is whether inflation rates are actually chosen in practice so as to maximize or optimize seigniorage revenue. In the US context, according to the recent Mankiw study, the answer appears to be positive. In the European context, according to Grilli's present study, the answer seems more doubtful. My second question relates to the quantitative importance of seigniorage revenue in general, whether optimally determined or not.

I have serious doubts on both questions, at least in the context of industrial or semi-industrialized countries. The most relevant extreme examples I can think of are recent cases of very high chronic inflation. In my own country, Israel, seigniorage revenue was more or less constant at only 2% of GDP (or 4% of total revenue) while inflation was going up from 10 to 50 and to 500% per annum. The recent figures for other very high inflation countries like Argentina, Brazil or Mexico, are not substantially different. The bulk of finance even in such high inflation cases comes from taxes, as well as domestic and foreign borrowing. The only cases in the recent history of the industrial world in which seigniorage really became important are the explosive hyperinflations of the 1920s; e.g., in Germany at the height of the 1923 pre-stabilisation phase seigniorage briefly became almost the only source of revenue, with taxes virtually wiped out. In a more recent hyperinflation, that of Bolivia, the share was, I believe, 50%. But these are irrelevant extremes. Taking the more 'modest' high inflation countries, which were governments running such high inflation rates, which can be shown empirically to go substantially beyond the 'optimum' point (the elasticity of demand for money going above unity)? The answer is that governments mess up their policies for a variety of reasons that have very little to do with seigniorage revenue – they are forced into fiscal and monetary accommodation in the face of external shocks and battles over internal shares, and there may be other co-ordination failures, all of which lead to higher inflation. It may be a Nash-equilibrium but certainly not a Pareto-optimum.

The last empirical point to make in this context is one that has already been mentioned by a number of discussants. Inflation affects the budget on both the revenue and the expenditure side in many different ways which may be quantitiatively more important than the seigniorage element. Luigi Spaventa has mentioned the fiscal drag of tax revenue on wage income and Rudi Dornbusch has mentioned the endogenous debt element. As against that there is the Tanzi effect which recent experience in my own country has shown to be important not only on the revenue side. Inflation helps individual government agencies to avoid strict central budgeting discipline (through financial manipulation). During sharp disinflation the disappearance of this flexibility has proved to be a very important source of one-time real expenditure cuts.

I will now turn to the policy issues that may be raised in relation to Drazen's very interesting paper. While I am in sympathy with the study as a thought experiment I have a problem with the practical implication of the way the questions are set up. Choosing a positive inflation rate until the day the country joins the common financial market implies an extreme flexibility in the ability to switch in and out of inflation as a way of life. This runs counter to past experience in such countries. The experiment also assumes that the tax base is independent of the inflation rate itself (cf. our earlier remark about the importance of Tanzi-type effects, etc.). Finally, it is hard to think favourably of the experiment in which a country first opens up for capital flows and only later stabilizes prices and the exchange rate (think of all the poor policy experience of Latin American countries, in this respect, during the 1970s). Somehow I would think of an individual country (such as Italy) joining the EMS and at a later stage opening up for free capital flows as a way of imposing rules on itself as a substitute for policy discretion. One government is capable of doing what any other government can do if only circumstances force it to do so. Just as joining the EMS was probably a way of imposing relative price and wage discipline on itself, the threat of 1992 may make Italy adjust its fiscal policy in time in a way in which it might otherwise not bring itself to do.

EDMUND S. PHELPS

I am fascinated that my 1973 paper on optimal inflation from a public finance viewpoint has apparently become a reference for thinking about inflation and a source of some controversy. I must admit that it never occurred to me when working on it that governments might in fact tend to choose the optimum inflation rate, so that the model was not only prescriptive but descriptive as well.

Having been asked to comment on this development, I have to say, at the risk of seeming ungrateful, that optimal inflation needs to be considered from a wider perspective. Such a wider view was precisely the subject of my (1972) book, *Inflation Policy and Unemployment Theory*, which contained the public-finance viewpoint and more. The (1973) paper was a further (and more technical) elaboration of a portion of the book.

The beginning of the optimal inflation discussion was 1963. Previously a number of Chicago economists, notably Bailey (1956), Cagan and Friedman, wrote of the costs of inflation but did not have the concept of the optimum rate, let alone a model of it. In (1963), Alvin Marty wrote of the 'satiety' level of real cash balances, which entailed deflation in the absence of interest on money, and independently of him Paul Samuelson and I, with some exchange, also developed the notion of what I called 'full liquidity'. From this liquidity angle, the optimum algebraic inflation rate makes the nominal interest rate just low enough that no paycheck or dividend recipient has an incentive to go out-of-and-back-into money between pay-days in view of the transaction costs of doing so. Oddly enough, however, a somewhat crude reformulation by Milton Friedman several years later became the standard reference and now receives the credit.[1] (Friedman, 1969; Phelps, 1965.)

Looking at inflation from a wider perspective, though, one sees drawbacks to full liquidity as the goal of inflation policy. One of these, obviously, is the cost of reaching such a target when initially the economy is acclimated to a moderate or higher rate of inflation. A theme of my book on inflation policy (and a 1967 paper) is that the deflation rate necessary for full liquidity is overly ambitious if, although the policy planner looks beyond the present, 'future utility' is discounted relative to present utility in the intertemporal optimization. Then the planner would not optimally keep the economy in the vice of a recession until liquidity was full to the brim. Moderation in all things and, in particular, *modified* full liquidity.

There seems to me no analogue to this point in the recent analyses of Grilli (1989) and Mankiw (1987). The reason is tied up with the rational expectations premise in the latter work. There, a sharp drop of inflation would be entirely expected and the decreases in seigniorage and in the cost of seigniorage would be entirely immediate. Hence, to take a convenient example in which there are no disturbances and the stock of public debt will be constant if an optimal policy is followed, the tax rate and the rate of tax on liquidity will both jump immediately to their optimum stationary-state values. (In my 1973 analysis the latter tax rate is shown to be the nominal interest rate; see Drazen, 1985.) But this was not so in my way of looking at the matter: some important *costs* of a sudden inflation reduction, such as an increase of unemployment, are front-loaded onto the *present*, while much of the *benefit*, which results from the reduced price of liquidity, will not be realized until the *future* when the populace has *learned* by painful experience to expect lower inflation (so that interest rates will be correspondingly lower).

Another drawback to full liquidity is pointed to in the argument for 'stability through inflation' put forward by William Vickrey (1954), and taken up in my 1973 book. Vickrey had argued in his famous 1954 Kurihara volume paper that inflation was better in that it put the economy on a steeper part of its demand-for-money curve (and hence a steeper part of its *LM* curve) so that output and employment were better cushioned against the feared Keynesian shocks to investor and entrepreneur confidence. A low-inflation economy would be whiplashed by attempted swings of investors in and out of earning assets. Neither Vickrey nor I seem to have asked whether increased inflation would enhance stability if the shocks were predominantly *LM* shocks rather than *IS* shocks. To analyze that question one would want to figure out whether it is better to take as given the lateral fluctuations of the *LM* curve, in which case stability is indeed reduced by steepness in the *LM* curve, or to take as given the vertical fluctuations of that curve, in which case stability is again increased by steepness.

In the past two decades, fluctuations in the expected rate of inflation appear to have been an important disturbance and that is an *IS* disturbance, of course. On the other hand, we would not have undergone so many exercises in disinflation had the average rate of inflation been lower. I would conclude that stability is only an argument for mild, politically supportable inflation, like the 5% inflation rate per annum suggested in my 1972 book. At the very least, though, stability strongly argues against the positive deflation rate that would normally be necessary (especially in these days of high real rates of interest) for full liquidity and perhaps even for modified full liquidity. I conclude that the *ideal* liquidity level is less than full.

Today these drawbacks to full liquidity are completely neglected and largely unknown. The focus of attention is entirely on the case for – and the case against – inflation as an optimal tax. I argued the case for a positive inflation tax in my 1972 book, section 6.4.2. The first argument proceeded from the premise that liquidity appears in the utility function along with leisure and real consumption expenditure, and I reasoned that liquidity should not be spared from being taxed – especially if the demand for money is highly interest inelastic. The second argument portrayed liquidity as a means of production, entering the production function and contributing to the production of taxable income. Here I pointed out that to show the optimality of a positive tax on liquidity it would be necessary to show that substituting a certain inflation tax for some part of an income tax would induce an increase of employment, owing to some mechanism of 'differential substitutability' – the term I used for the net effect on untaxed leisure (hence on employment) of the resulting change in relative prices. The third argument flowed from the point that there are positive collection costs in raising revenue through the ordinary taxes on income and sales. This public finance case for higher inflation than would otherwise be optimal seems to have been broadly accepted by Mankiw and Grilli, and by many others.

Now a criticism of this public-finance case has been mounted by Kent Kimbrough (1986), Robert Lucas (1986), and others. In their view, the premise that liquidity appears in the utility function is without foundation, in which case my first argument seems to be in trouble. They maintain that liquidity belongs only in the production function. If so, as I recognized in my second argument, the case for an inflation tax (leaving aside collection costs) will depend on differential substitutability. However, Lucas proceeds to exhibit a model, one that is a variation on the cash-in-advance model, in which there is no differential substitutability: raising the inflation rate, total tax revenue constant, does not succeed in reducing leisure or increasing labour supply so as to reduce the dead-weight burden of taxation. This is a significant finding. One hopes that it will not still the discussion of the inflation tax, however, since there is more to be said, as I am going to try to show.

Let us recapitulate. In view of the stability point, we want *ideal* liquidity, not *full* liquidity. And we want *modified* ideal liquidity, not the ideal level, in view of the one-time cost of boosting the level. So the question is whether the optimal inflation rate is still higher, whatever its algebraic sign, in view of the public-finance arguments.

The first issue is whether liquidity appears, large or small, in the utility function. It seems possible that the services of liquidity are not just a kind of capital good or kind in intermediate good the taxation of which would constitute double taxation. Could not liquidity be a good *per se*, reminiscent of the proverbial New Yorker who says that he values knowing he could avail himself of its opportunities if he wanted to? Also, some cash balances are held for transactions in the shadow, or underground, economy, so it is not true that liquidity already bears implicitly the right burden of taxation as a result of the income and exise tax systems.

But suppose it were true that liquidity belongs only in the production function in the sense that all its benefits to holders are fully reflected in real taxable income. There are many models in this vein, not all of them available in full (or indeed any) detail, and the cash-in-advance model is just one of them. A neglected point, with which my 1972 discussion began, is this: if, with *lump-sum* taxes available, the optimum nominal interest rate would be some positive i^* in excess of the minimum supportable level, because stability and time preference considerations make the modified ideal liquidity level less than the full-liquidity level, the introduction of an *income* tax rate t by which to raise the government revenue would drive the after-tax interest rate, $(1 - t)i$, below i^* at the same inflation rate, thus effectively injecting a subsidy to liquidity; hence a higher inflation rate would be appropriate in order to push the price of liquidity, $(1 - t)i$, back up in the direction of i^* (whether or not it is optimal to drive it exactly to i^*). The cash-in-advance model does not exhibit this 'subsidy' to liquidity from income taxation because it portrays the velocity of money as a constant, independent of the opportunity cost of liquidity. Let me recall also the point, the third argument in the book, that there are collection costs in raising revenue by means of income and sales taxes, so that higher inflation would produce cost savings in the government budget. Finally, there is the point, also in the book, that *if* relying more on inflation-tax revenue, hence less on other distortionary taxes, would on balance increase employment – the employment level corresponding to, say, the natural rate of unemployment, if we adopt that hypothesis for convenience – then, there being too little employment owing to tax distortions, the result is a welfare gain. It is an empirical question, the answer to which we do not know, but I made the 'sporting guess' that employment would in fact increase. The important contribution to this subject by Allan Drazen (1979) shows that in an intertemporal model what matters is not just the net increase of labour supply but also the net decrease of consumption demand. The more sanguine 'supply side' advocates would say here that a revised tax mix with lower marginal income tax rates would encourage better tax compliance and thus promote a self-enforced reduction of consumer demand.

I conclude that the public-finance case for inflation, on which Grilli and earlier Mankiw have built, is solid enough. A wider framework would build also on the stability case and the time-preference case for moderate inflation.

NOTES
1 The existence of a monetary equilibrium in which the real rates of return to money and capital are exactly equal is not clear if (as seems necessary to motivate holding positive average cash balances) there are transaction costs of moving from money to capital and back again.

REFERENCES
Bailey, Martin J. (1956). 'The Welfare Cost of Inflationary Finance', *Journal of Political Economy*, April, reprinted in K.J. Arrow and T. Scitovsky, eds., *Readings in Welfare Economics*, Chicago: Irwin (1969).
Drazen, Allan (1979). 'The Optimal Rate of Inflation Revisited', *Journal of Monetary Economics*, April.
Friedman, Milton (1969). 'The Optimum Quantity of Money', in M. Friedman, ed., *The Optimum Quantity of Money and Other Essays*, Chicago: Aldine.
Grilli, Vittorio (1989). 'Seigniorage in Europe', this volume.
Kimbrough, Kent (1986). 'The Optimum Quantity of Money Rule in the Theory of Public Finance', *Journal of Monetary Economics*.
Lucas, Robert E. Jr (1986). 'Principles of Fiscal and Monetary Policy', *Journal of Monetary Economics*.
Mankiw, N. Gregory (1987). 'The Optimal Collection of Seigniorage: Theory and Evidence', *Journal of Monetary Economics*.
Marty, Alvin L. (1961). 'Money in a Theory of Finance', *Journal of Political Economy*, February.
Phelps, Edmund S. (1965). 'Anticipated Inflation and Economic Welfare', *Journal of Political Economy*, February.
    (1972). *Inflation Policy and Unemployment Theory*, New York: W.W. Norton.
    (1973). 'Inflation in the Theory of Public Finance', *Swedish Journal of Economics*, March.
Samuelson, Paul A. (1963). 'D.H. Robertson (1890–1963)', *Quarterly Journal of Economics*, November.
Vickrey, William S. (1954). 'Stability through Inflation', in K.K. Kurihara, ed., *Post-Keynesian Economics*, New Brunswick, N.J.: Rutgers University Press.

4 Factor flexibility, uncertainty and exchange rate regimes

GIUSEPPE BERTOLA

Early contributions to the theory of 'Optimal Currency Areas' focused on the different efficacy of stabilization policy in different nominal exchange rate regimes, and on the relevance of imperfect factor mobility to the economy's ability to respond to disturbances in the presence of nominal rigidities (Mundell, 1961; McKinnon, 1963). The debate on the desirability of fixed exchange rates has since focused on stabilization policy, disregarding the microeconomics of factor reallocation.

Issues of factor mobility have been studied in the real trade literature but, in most cases, under certainty. Recent advances in the microeconomic theory of costly reallocation under uncertainty have shown that the degree of uncertainty about the future, as well as the size of adjustment costs, is an important determinant of the propensity to reallocate resources in response to disturbances. The more uncertain is their environment, the greater should be the reluctance of rational economic agents to undertake adjustments that may *ex-post* be regretted.

In order to provide new theoretical foundations to the old arguments for and against nominal exchange rate stability, these partial-equilibrium insights would have to be combined with a better understanding of the sources of macroeconomic instability and of the stabilizing role of monetary policy in different exchange rate regimes. Any analysis of stabilization policy presupposed instability in the environment and should, consequently, take explicit account of uncertainty. This paper takes a first step towards this new area of research. It briefly surveys the theoretical links between nominal exchange rate regimes and macroeconomic stability, describes the new insights on the importance of uncertainty for reallocation decisions, and reviews the relationship between microeconomic agents' dynamic optimization problems and the stability of the macroeconomic environment.

Section 1 summarizes the relevance of imperfect factor mobility to the early arguments about the optimal size of currency areas. The main points

95

made in this early work are still intuitively valid, but their formal analysis needs to be updated on two levels. On the one hand the original treatment is based on outdated (though probably not yet satisfactorily replaced) monetary theory, and on a simplified view of the role of economic policy. On the other, it neglects issues of dynamics and uncertainty, which are essential for a proper treatment of 'factor mobility'.

Section 2 surveys theoretical and empirical results on real effects of different nominal exchange rate regimes, and in particular on stabilization of economic activity. Rigorous theoretical work has not been able, as yet, to provide uncontroversial answers; some fruitful directions for future research are easy to identify, but are quite difficult to pursue. Empirical evidence suggests that uncertainty about real exchange rates is lower in a fixed exchange rates regime.

Section 3 reviews recent advances of the theory of costly adjustment under uncertainty and gives an intuitive interpretation of the results. Section 4 argues that the insights provided by explicit consideration of uncertainty should be useful in the study of factor mobility and macro-economic stability, and proposes a simple formal model. Section 5 concludes.

1   Factor mobility and optimal currency areas

The seminal contributions to the theory of optimal currency areas focused on factor mobility as the main determinant of the scope of monetary unification. Mundell (1961) argued that, if factors of production are immobile, downward rigidity of nominal prices would in general make exchange rate flexibility preferable. A real shock, such as a shift in demand, causes disequilibrium in the goods and labour markets if prices and/or wages are rigid: under flexible exchange rates, movements of nominal exchange rates can alter relative prices and eliminate excesses of supply or of demand. Under fixed exchange rates, instead, excess supply (unemployment) and excess demand (inflation) are unavoidable – unless factors can move out of the excess supply region and into the excess demand one. Based on this reasoning, Mundell argued that exchange rates should be flexible among areas subject to different real shocks (i.e. among 'regions' rather than nations). Rigidity of the nominal price of different products would not matter at all if all pairs of products that may need a change in relative prices had prices denominated in different currencies, with exchange rates so flexible as to obtain any needed variation of relative prices. While this extreme form of exchange rate flexibility would repro-duce the flexible-price allocation, it would also eliminate the economic role of money: if prices of different products were all quoted in terms of different currencies, with flexible conversion rates, the economy would effectively be working on a barter basis.

Little would be lost in terms of stability, however, if exchange rates were fixed among areas between which factors are easily movable, or which are subject to perfectly correlated real shocks. Given that monetary exchange is more efficient than barter, in Mundell's (1961) view an optimally-sized area of exchange rate fixity can in principle be defined, and is characterized by a high degree of internal factor mobility and/or by its homogeneity as to the impact of real disturbances.

McKinnon (1963) pointed out that factors of production are often not only geographically immobile, but immobile across sectors in the same region as well. Some industries produce nontradable goods and services: if factors are immobile between the tradable and nontradable sectors, the optimality of fixed exchange rates has to be judged on the basis of the degree of openness of the economy. From the point of view of a small country that takes tradables' prices as given, fixed exchange rates imply that the value of money is fixed in terms of tradable goods, while flexible exchange rates imply that the value of money is fixed in terms of nontradables. If money is to be useful as a store of value, the former system is best for a country (or a region) whose consumption basket consists mostly of tradables, since its residents will then be able to use the national money as a store of value and will not need to invest abroad to protect their purchasing power in terms of tradables; but flexible exchange rates are better for a relatively closed economy whose residents consume mostly nontradables. Once again, between these extremes some optimally-sized area should exist, for which a common currency of fixed exchange rates are preferable to complete flexibility. More generally, it should be possible to construct an argument along McKinnon's (1963) lines whenever nominal contracts are prevalent, and currency substitution or denomination of contracts in foreign currency is ruled out *a priori* or deemed undesirable.

After Mundell's and McKinnon's seminal contributions, in the 1960s and 1970s the debate on the optimal size of currency areas was extended to more general issues. Effectiveness and feasibility of stabilization policy still were the main concern of most authors in this literature (comprehensively surveyed by Tower and Willett, 1976). In particular, authors were concerned with the shape of unemployment-inflation tradeoffs available to policy makers under flexible or fixed exchange rates. Factor mobility was neglected by most authors for the sake of simplicity, as many other facets of the problem were brought into view: for example Kenen (1969) noted the important role of a single currency for administrative purposes, as it eases the coordination of fiscal policy in regions more or less severely hit by a downturn of activity. Cooper (1976) stressed the relevance of factor mobility to determination of the size of integrated regions, from the point of view of the effectiveness of economic policy in a wider acception than simple stabilization policy, tackling the issues of the provision of public goods and of income distribution and considering the implications of custom unions rather than of common currency arrangements.

Factor mobility and the desirability of fixed exchange rates are both very active areas of current research. But the link between the two that was central to the early optimal currency areas contributions appears to be lost.

Research on 'optimal' currency areas is still mostly concerned with the constraints that fixed exchange rates impose on economic policy. Arguments for and against currency unions are not based on the simple unemployment-inflation tradeoff described by the Phillips curve, which has not survived the rational expectations revolution. The Phillips curve has been replaced in international monetary models by its direct descendants, namely, the game-theoretic models of monetary policy introduced by Barro and Gordon (1983), and the concerns for authorities' reputation deriving from such models (see for example Giavazzi and Pagano, 1988, for an application to the European Monetary System).

Like most of the older models surveyed by Tower and Willett (1976), current treatments of exchange rate arrangements neglect the microeconomics of production and factor mobility. Factor mobility has instead been extensively studied in the framework of structural adjustments to exogenous shocks, disregarding, however, the source of the shocks and the possibility of stabilization. The following section discusses current theoretical views and empirical evidence on the links between stabilization policies, exchange rate regimes and macroeconomic stability.

2   Nominal exchange rate regimes, stabilization and uncertainty: theoretical models and empirical work

Fixing nominal exchange rates does affect the real allocation of resources, and is not unconsequential in reality. There would otherwise be no reason for theoretical and political debate on exchange rate arrangements. Characterizing the real effects of the nominal exchange rate regime is, however, quite difficult in both theoretical and empirical work.

In the simple Keynesian model that underlay Mundell's (1961) treatment of optimal currency areas, the relevance of nominal exchange rate regimes was ascribed to the different leeway of monetary policy. The assumed downward rigidity of nominal (in terms of home currency) prices and wages ensured efficacy of monetary policy, which could be used to fine-tune the level of economic activity in the face of disturbances. Under flexible exchange rates many instruments (many monies, rather than one) would be available to offset different sources of disturbances, with the implication that better stabilization would be achievable as flexibility of many monetary aggregates counteracted the rigidity of many nominal price levels.

The rational expectations approach to macroeconomics has questioned the rationality of the sort of price rigidity postulated in Keynesian models, and has thrown doubt on the efficacy of monetary policy. The literature on exchange rate determination has split into two approaches, that Stockman (1987) labels the 'equilibrium' and 'disequilibrium' ones.

Disequilibrium models (as in Dornbusch, 1976) adopt the maintained assumption that nominal prices are sticky. In the short run, adjustment in the goods market is assumed to occur mostly through quantities, while prices adjust slowly to differences between desired supply and demand. Changes in the quantity of nominal money then have real effects, though only in the short run. Assuming that flexible exchange rates adjust continuously to clear financial and monetary markets, nominal disturbances produce 'overshooting' of the nominal exchange rate beyond its long-run equilibrium level: changes in money supply have large effects on real exchange rates, and on output, in the short run.

Recent disequilibrium models do try and rationalize, to some extent, the rigidity of nominal prices in the short run. (In Dornbusch, 1980, Taylor's model of overlapping wage contracts is adapted to an international setting. Microeconomic rationales for wage contracts and other forms of low price flexibility, based on microeconomic costs of changing prices, are reviewed in Blanchard and Fischer, 1988.) Price rigidity is necessary to ensure that manipulation of monetary aggregates has effects on the level of activity, at least as long as capacity constraints do not become binding. As shown by Fischer (1977) and others, stabilization of economic activity is desirable even in a rational-expectations framework if some prices or wages in the economy cannot – because of contractual arrangements – immediately be changed in response to shocks to preferences or technology.

The 'disequilibrium' framework then preserves an important role for monetary policy, similar to its role in Mundell's static Keynesian model. In a dynamic sticky-prices model fixed exchange rates might increase the variability of activity levels, as they reduce the monetary authorities' freedom of action when inflationary shocks in one country occur together with deflationary shocks in another. Countries subject to highly correlated shocks are, once again, good candidate members of a currency area.

Conversely, equilibrium models of exchange rate determination rule out price rigidity, assume that markets always clear, and are based on, rational microeconomic optimization. Providing rigorous micro foundations for the role of money in a maximization framework is difficult. Stockman (1980), Helpman and Razin (1982) and others adopt cash-in-advance constraints for goods transactions, and choose the timing of transactions in assets so as to obtain that money be held in equilibrium, possibly with variable velocity of circulation. In these models, the real equilibrium may not depend on the monetary regime if markets are complete in the Arrow-Debreu sense (or if there is no uncertainty): *ex-ante* arrangements allow agents to *ex-post* neutralize the effects of all variations in nominal money supplies, because all transactions can be made contingent on the realization of monetary as well as real uncertainty.

The constraints imposed by analytical tractability produce a trade-off between theoretical rigour and realistic complexity in these models. Stockman and Svensson (1987) provide the first, complex model of exchange rate determination in a general equilibrium setting, taking explicit account of investment and uncertainty. Svensson and van Wijnbergen (1986) propose instead a model that combines elements of the equilibrium literature (perfectly pooled equilibrium, i.e. agents of all countries trade assets so as to share equally all risks, and cash-in-advance constraints to model the role of money) with the disequilibrium assumption that prices be set before all relevant information is known, with *ex-post* excess supply or excess demand.

Stockman (1983) takes the alternate route of including real money balances in the agents' utility functions, rather than imposing cash-in-advance constraints, to model the economic role of money. A detailed study of equilibrium in a two-period model allows him to conclude that very stringent conditions are needed to obtain invariance of real allocations and prices to the nominal exchange rate regime: in general, monetary shocks will affect real exchange rates and real allocations – although in the framework of equilibrium exchange rate theories, which do not allow for nominal rigidities, willful manipulation of monetary supplies can never improve on the equilibrium allocation produced by a competitive market. Whether they affect real allocations or not, changes in monetary aggregates are 'disturbances'.

Some very strong empirical evidence is available on the different variability of real exchange rates in different exchange rate regimes. Stockman (1983) finds that the variability of real exchange rates is significantly higher whenever nominal exchange rates are flexible, and Dornbusch and Giovannini (1988) and Giovannini (1987) present further evidence that real exchange rates are less stable in a regime of flexible nominal exchange rates.

However, it is not immediate that the environment should *overall* be more stable when real exchange rates fluctuate less. If real variables are determined by market equilibrium, more stability in one real variable (the exchange rate) would indeed imply less stability of the whole economic system. But in a disequilibrium system it may well be the case that other variables, such as activity levels and interest rates, are less stable although real exchange rates fluctuate less. Tower and Willett (1976), following Mundell (1961), noted that fixity of nominal rates could imply less leeway for stabilizing monetary policy, and therefore wider fluctuations of interest rates and economic activity.

It is not easy to verify empirically whether nominal (and real) exchange rate stability contributes to stability of activity levels, because the different intensity of macroeconomic disturbances (such as oil shocks) in different periods is difficult to control for. Baxter and Stockman (1988) attempt to find effects of the exchange rate regime on the cyclical behaviour of output and consumption in many countries: they find, however, that such differences are hardly significant or of ambiguous sign.

Taylor (1988), using empirical results on the degree of price stickiness and on the shape of behavioural relationships in the major industrial countries, conducts simulations to compare the performance of monetary policy rules under fixed and flexible exchange rate regimes. In a dynamic, rational-expectations framework stabilization policies have to be modeled in the form of feedback rules (e.g. interest rate rules), declared in advance and therefore known to the agents. Given some degree of price stickiness, such rules can succeed in stabilizing the economy.

Unfortunately, no clear answer emerges from the exercise, as Taylor's results depend crucially on the treatment of the shocks in the uncovered interest-parity equation:

$$e_{t+1} = e_t + (r_t - r_t^*) + \epsilon_t \tag{1}$$

where e_t denotes the logarithm of the nominal exchange rate between a pair of currencies and r_t and r_t^* are the interest rates on loans, denominated in the two currencies, with one-period term. The variance of the innovation ϵ_t has been large throughout the flexible exchange rates period. If this high variability is considered endogenous to the flexible exchange rates system (deriving for example from changing risk premia), it can be assumed away under fixed exchange rates; prices and output are then more stable under fixed than under flexible exchange rates, and this is Taylor's conclusion. But if the variability of ϵ_t in (1) is assumed to be as large under fixed rates as it has historically been under flexible rates, monetary policy has to produce large fluctuations in interest rates, outputs and prices if nominal exchange rates are to be stablized. The latter situation is very much in line with Mundell's view, that fixed rates would in general destabilize output as monetary policy could not counteract 'natural' shocks as effectively as under flexible rates.

A common, if puzzling, conclusion can be drawn from both Taylor's and Baxter and Stockman's empirical work: although nominal exchange rates fluctuate much more than price levels in a flexible exchange rates regimes, it is difficult to pinpoint the effects of the resulting real exchange rate variability on the macroeconomic performance of countries under different exchange rate regimes.

On the basis of casual empiricism, as well as of the formal empirical evidence presented for example by Dornbusch and Giovannini (1988) and Giovannini (1987), price stickiness (and incomplete capital markets) are realistic features of real-life economic systems. Price stickiness rationalizes at a theoretical level the efficacy and usefulness of monetary policy, and should be taken into account when analyzing the opportunity of fixing exchange rates on the basis of policy arguments.

If prices do not move to clear markets, quantities will: and the possibility of shifting factors out of excess supply regions or sectors into excess demand ones will, in general, improve welfare, as argued by Mundell (1961). A joint formal and dynamic treatment of price stickiness and costly quantity adjustments would be necessary to make the point more precise. The micro foundations of sticky-price 'disequilibrium' models, however, are not so detailed as to allow a straightforward analysis of factor mobility issues. Not only are sticky prices usually assumed without microeconomic rationalization, but the mechanics of disequilibrium transactions are most often left in the background in international macroeconomic models, which usually rule out any form of rationing and assume perfectly elastic supply in the relevant range. The production side of such models is sketchy or nonexistent: capacity, or output, are taken as given, with no allowance for investment decisions (the most formal disequilibrium model, that proposed by Svensson and van Wijnbergen, 1986, assumes equally-sized countries and exogenous, random potential output in each country).

Supply, however, cannot *always* be perfectly elastic if costly factor reallocation and other forms of investment are to be explicitly modeled: if prices do not always react to market disturbances, in a dynamic model rationing will occur at least part of the time. Costs of changing prices and costs of changing quantities (capacity) should be jointly modeled in future work: this will be made all the more difficult by want of a satisfactory model of rationing.

3   Costly adjustment under uncertainty: the basic insights

Turning now to the second topic suggested by Mundell (1961), let us consider *dynamic* models of factor reallocation *under uncertainty*.

The dynamic reaction of economic systems to exogenous shocks has been extensively studied in nonmonetary models (see for example Mussa, 1974, 1978; Gavin, 1988; Dixit, 1987a; Krugman, 1988b). In reality, resources are neither completely immobile nor perfectly mobile: for most factors, mobility between regions and sectors is possible but costly. Mussa (1974, 1978), Gavin (1988), and others propose models of dynamic adjustment under certainty. If the cost of moving one unit is modeled as an increasing function of the speed of adjustment, along the adjustment path to an unexpected and unrepeatable shock differences in incomes of the same factor in different uses are *slowly* eliminated. The speed of adjustment is chosen so as to continuously maintain equality between the difference in returns and the marginal adjustment cost, and therefore decreases as returns converge asymptotically. These models are important advances over static, one-period analyses of mobility, and throw light on some short-run characteristics of the adjustment process.[1] They are, however, not quite adequate for the study of the stabilization policy issues underlying the debate on nominal exchange rate regimes, as they neglect *ongoing uncertainty*: in these models every shock is assumed to be unexpected, and perceived as unrepeatable, by the economic agents. To model the usefulness of stabilization policies, one should realistically assume that shocks may occur sequentially, with different sign and intensity, and that agents are aware of such uncertainty in their environment.

Explicit consideration of uncertainty (as in Dixit, 1987b; Krugman, 1988b) provides important insights into the responsiveness of an economic system, and of factor reallocations in particular, to exogenous shocks. Recent work on adjustment under uncertainty was spurred by observation of the puzzling (at least to some) behaviour of US trade flows during the 1980s. Swings in the dollar exchange rate appeared to produce insignificant, delayed, or even perverse effects on prices and quantities of US imports. In particular, the descent of the dollar from its peak value was not reflected in the dollar price of American imports.

The models in Baldwin and Krugman (1986), Dixit (1987a), and Krugman (1988a) rationalize these facts by assuming that entry into a (foreign) market entails a one-time cost, which is *ex-post* sunk. If the real exchange rate fluctuates randomly – so that presence in a market generates uncertain profits – firms will exercise caution in both entry and exit decisions. Given the possibility of adverse shocks, it will not be optimal to pay the entry cost unless the exchange rate is very favourable; conversely, the exchange rate will have to be very unfavourable to induce firms to exit the market, as established firms are aware that the now sunk entry cost will have to be paid again if re-entry is desired in the future.

In such models, export supply is relatively insensitive to exchange rate changes as long as entry or exit are not triggered; this can explain the quasi-constancy of prices and quantities of imports in the face of the large dollar devaluations of the past four years. Large shocks, which do trigger entry, can have very long-lasting consequences.

Costly reallocation of resources in response to terms-of-trade or real exchange rate shocks can be analyzed along the same lines. Dixit (1987a) shows that reallocation of resources out of a sector experiencing a random decline in the price of its products should, if costly, be undertaken only if the profitability of the resources in their alternative use is very much larger than that in their present use plus the reallocation cost. Krugman (1988b) shows how the solution depends on persistence and size of the shocks to relative prices.

In this class of models, the size of shocks needed to trigger adjustment increases in the degree of ongoing uncertainty. This can be understood on the basis of analogies to well established results in option pricing theory. In financial markets, the holder of a call option has the right to buy (and the holder of a put option has the right to sell) a specified asset, such as a unit of stock or of currency, at a prespecified price. In the case of 'European' options, such right has to be exercised on a prespecified *expiration date*, while holders of 'American' options can choose not only whether, but when to exercise them, at any time up to the expiration date. Options are valuable to rational agents, as they give the right, but not the obligation, to perform the transaction. A rational agent will only exercise options if it is profitable to do so – i.e. when the value of the asset that can be purchased exceeds the price agreed upon at the time the option contract is signed. An option's value is then the (properly discounted) expected gain from optimal exercise. By arbitrage, this value will also be the cost of purchasing the option in an efficient financial market.

A basic insight from option pricing theory is that increased uncertainty about the future value of the *underlying* asset – the asset which the option entitles to purchase at the prespecified price – will *increase* the option's value, all else being equal. Consider an option to buy one share at time T, paying a fixed price P. Denote S_T the value of the share at the expiration of the option. Being rational, you know that you will exercise the option (and realize a profit of $S_T - P$) only if $S_T > P$; if $S_T < P$, it would be cheaper to buy the share on the market at T than to exercise the option. Higher uncertainty about S_T increases the probability of very high *and* of very low values, as the probability mass is spread further away from the centre of the distribution (see Figure 4.1). While this makes it more likely that large profits will be obtainable by exercising the option, it does not symmetrically increase the probability of large losses. Since exercise is voluntary,

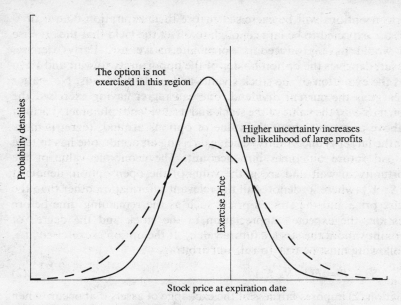

Figure 4.1 The value of an option

once the cost of obtaining the option is sunk, no further losses can occur. It follows that a European option's value – and its price – are higher when uncertainty is higher.

Higher uncertainty also increases the value of American options, which can be exercised at any time *up to* their expiration date. Since the value of such options is not simply given by the expected, discounted payoff to the holder at a *given* point in time, the simple argument above is not sufficient to prove the result. In general, both the size of the profit from exercising the option, and the time at which such profit can be obtained, have to be considered in computing the expected discounted payoff. But the basic intuition is the same. As long as exercise is voluntary, only good outcomes have to be taken into account in computing the option's value – bad outcomes induce the holder *not* to exercise the option, and the payoff is zero independently of exactly how bad the outcome is. As uncertainty increases, and probability mass is spread towards extreme values, only the increased probability attached to large, early profits matters.

Early exercise of an American call option cannot be optimal unless the underlying asset pays dividends to its owner.[2] If the option is exercised before expiration, the yield that the amount of the exercise price would (if not paid) produce in alternative uses is forsaken, without any offsetting advantage. If the underlying stock does pay dividends to its owner then

American options will be exercised before their expiration date if dividends are expected to be large enough to offset the yield that the exercise price would have produced in some alternative use. Early exercise, however, deprives the option holder of the opportunity to wait and learn about the evolution of the stock's value and of its dividends. No matter how large is the current dividend, one can regret having exercised the option if *ex-post* the value of the stock and its dividends plummet. Turning the above argument about the value of options around, regret is more likely the larger is uncertainty: when exercising an option one has to take only bad future outcomes into account. The economic value of the opportunity to wait and see is the value of the open option; denote it $F(P, S_t, X_t)$ (where X_t denotes all the relevant information other than the exercise price and the stock's price, such as the remaining time before expiration, the expected appreciation of the stock and the degree of uncertainty about the stock's future value). If the option is exercised at τ, the following must be true to rule out arbitrage:

$$S_\tau - P = F(P, S_\tau, X_\tau) \tag{2}$$

Equation (2) imposes fairness of the exchange of assets that occurs when the option is exercised: the option's holder obtains S in exchange for P, the out-of-pocket price, *plus* his renouncing the opportunity of exercising the option later – which is worth F to him and to any other rational agent. An individual purchasing the option at τ would immediately gain $S_\tau - P$, and the price $F(\cdot)$ he pays must equal this gain.

From (2), and from the positive relationship between uncertainty and option value, the difference between the stock's value and the price paid for it at exercise is larger if uncertainty about the future is larger. In a more uncertain environment, a larger current value of the underlying stock is required for the option to be exercised: in this sense, rational agents are induced to exercise options *with caution* if uncertainty is large.

Factor mobility can be formalized in terms of 'real' options, options that arise in natural optimization problems rather than being artificially created in financial markets. Consider an economic agent who is in a position to change location or occupation, paying a fixed cost. The present discounted value to her of her income in the present location is a human capital asset, which can be exchanged, paying an exercise price, with an asset defined as the present value of earnings in the alternative location, plus the option to migrate again. In terms of option pricing theory, the underlying stock is then the difference between one's discounted expected lifetime earnings in two different locations: if the option is ever exercised, it must be the case that not only is the stock paying positive dividends, i.e. that earnings are currently higher at the alternative location than at the present one, but that the difference is higher the higher is uncertainty about future differentials. Once again, larger uncertainty implies more reluctance to act – less factor mobility, in this framework.

Although the qualitative effects of uncertainty on relocation decisions is most easily understood in terms of the option evaluation arguments sketched above, Dixit (1987a) and Bertola (1987) find that the solution of costly adjustment problems can be based on traditional dynamic programming methods as well as on marginal option pricing. From the point of view of dynamic optimization, the reluctance to adjust derives from the awareness on the part of the decision maker that future costly adjustments are possible under uncertainty, and will be made more or less probable by current adjustment decisions. In terms of factor mobility decisions, use of dynamic programming makes it possible to solve for the dynamic equilibrium of relocation 'markets'; atomistic decision makers endowed with rational expectations take into account the possibility of future mobility decisions by others. The higher is uncertainty about future earnings in different locations or sectors (i.e. the more likely are further changes of the differential in either direction), the more reluctant an individual should be to move – both because she is aware that migrating back will be costly if the wage differential changes sign, and because even larger earnings differentials will induce migration by others, reducing (through externalities) the income available to her in the new location.

4   Factor mobility, stabilization and uncertainty

The previous section argues that factor mobility is, to some extent, endogenous to the workings of the economic system, as it depends on the degree of ongoing uncertainty perceived by the agents: when large fluctuations are likely, factor reallocations will not be easily triggered by differences in returns; conversely, much smaller differentials will suffice to trigger adjustment in a stable environment.

No general equilibrium model incorporating these insights has yet been produced. Dixit (1987a) solves for the dynamic equilibrium of an industry, taking as exogenously given the stochastic behavior of forcing factors (the real exchange rate, in his model); similarly, Dixit (1987b) and Krugman (1988b) derive the dynamics of competitive intersectoral factor reallocation taking changes in relative prices or in capital flows as given.

It is at least conceivable that a general equilibrium model could be set up and solved in a competitive framework. If all markets are assumed to be perfectly competitive, one can set up the reallocation problem as the solution to a central planner's optimization problem, and perfect competition would ensure that the price signals taken as given by all agents correctly decentralize the planner's command optimum. Such a framework, however, would hardly be appropriate to study exchange rate flexibility issues: market imperfections (and in particular nominal rigidities and capital-market imperfections) are needed to analyze monetary policy. The same imperfections that make the problem interesting also make solution of general equilibrium models extremely difficult.

We can, however, argue at an intuitive level about the role of 'endogenous' factor mobility in a dynamic version of Mundell's informal model. Assume that stability both of relative incomes and of exchange rates is valued by the planner in charge of choosing a policy regime, and that monetary policy can stabilize incomes but is hampered in that role by limits imposed to exchange rate variability. The social planner is then faced by a trade-off relationship between exchange rate and income stability, with a shape determined, among other things, by the degree of factor mobility.

In this framework, relative incomes in regions where different currencies circulate are more variable the more stable are exchange rates, to imply lower factor mobility:[3] fixed exchange rates themselves reduce the promptness of those supply adjustments which, with inflexible prices, could decrease the income fluctuations imposed by fixed exchange rates and price stickiness. This affects the shape of the trade-off between income and exchange rate uncertainty, and should be taken into account when reconsidering the Mundell (1961) arguments. The remainder of this section sketches a simple *ad-hoc* formal model based on these ideas.

Consider a small region in a dynamic endowment economy: homogeneous, infinitesimal agents with total measure N_t are located in the region at time t, and enjoy instantaneous utility proportional to the log of their per capita income $y_t = Y_t/N_t \cdot Y_t$, total income in the region at time t, follows a stochastic process whose form and parameters (to be specified below) are known to the agents, who take it as given. For given N, per capita income of residents in the region fluctuates randomly. Agents are infinitely lived and value the expected stream of income, discounted at rate δ: the state of the system is summarized by y_t, and we define the value of remaining in the region as

$$V(y_t) = E_t \int_t^\infty e^{-\delta(\tau - t)} \log(y_\tau)\, d\tau$$

$$= \int_t^\infty e^{-\delta(\tau - t)} E_t\{\log(Y_\tau) - \log(N_\tau)\}\, d\tau \qquad (3)$$

It is possible, but costly, for the residents to move into and out of the region if they find it profitable to do so. The process followed by $\{N_t\}$ given $\{Y_t\}$, hence by y_t and $V(y_t)$, has then to be endogenously determined.

Assume, for simplicity, that the value of residing outside the region under consideration is constant and equal to $\bar{V}$, and let the cost of relocating one unit of population (in either direction) be denoted by k. If the decision to relocate is left to the individuals, a dynamic competitive equilibrium of this simple economy must be such that

$$\bar{V} - k \leq V(y_t) \leq \bar{V} + k \tag{4}$$

at all times t: at the margin, individuals will relocate when the value of what is given up equals the value of what is obtained. For movements *out of* the region, what is given up is the stream of income for a continuing resident, $V(y_t)$, plus the relocation cost k; what is obtained is a stream of income with value $\bar{V}$. In a dynamic, competitive equilibrium, 'arbitrage' will ensure that this swap of assets occurs whenever it is (even only marginally) profitable – hence the first inequality. In the symmetric case of a movement *into* the region, agents give up $\bar{V}$ and the relocation cost k to obtain $V(y_t)$, and the second inequality follows.

To explicitly solve for the optimal relocation decision and for $\{Y_t\}$, assume that the logarithm of total income in the region, $\log(Y_t)$, would spontaneously evolve through time according to the stochastic differential

$$d[\log(Y_t)] = \sigma dW_t \tag{5}$$

where dW_t is the increment of a Wiener process.[4] Equation (5) defines the simplest suitable stochastic process, the continuous-time equivalent of a logarithmic random walk.

Under this assumption, the state of the system is at all times completely described by the current value of y_t, and relocation decisions take a simple form: to satisfy equation (4), $\{N_t\}$ decreases only when $\log(y_t)$ equals a lower bound l, and increases only when $\log(y_t)$ equals an upper bound u, so as to obtain that

$$e^l \leq y_t \leq e^u \tag{6}$$

The logarithm of y_t then follows a *regulated* Brownian motion process, in the sense of Harrison (1985). To compute the values of l and u corresponding to a given σ, δ and k, it is necessary to find the functional form of the discounted expectation in equation (3). Adapting results from Harrison (1985), the Appendix shows that if $\{\eta_t\}$ is a regulated Brownian motion process with zero drift and standard deviation σ, then

$$f(\eta; u, l) = \frac{1}{\delta}[\eta + A(u, l)e^{\eta \Phi} + B(u, l)e^{-\eta \Phi}] \tag{7}$$

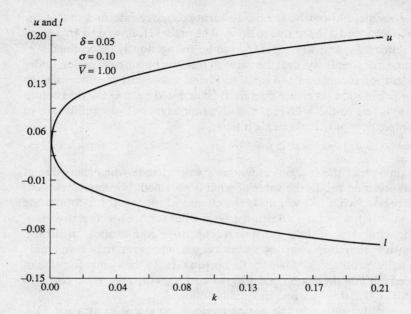

Figure 4.2   Adjustment cost and income fluctuations

where $\Phi = \sqrt{\dfrac{2\delta}{\sigma^2}}$, and $A(u, l)$ and $B(u, l)$ are defined in the Appendix.

Inserting (7) into (4), we obtain two nonlinear equations which can be numerically solved for u and l:

$$\bar{V} - k = \frac{1}{\delta}(l + A e^{l\Phi} + B e^{-l\Phi}) \tag{8}$$

$$\frac{1}{\delta}(u + A e^{u\Phi} + B u^{-u\Phi}) = \bar{V} + k \tag{9}$$

If $k = 0$, the system of nonlinear equations collapses to a single equation, and it is apparent that $u = l$ (it can be shown, by taking the appropriate limits of A and B, that in this case the common value of the two boundaries equals $\delta\bar{V}$): perfect 'factor mobility' ensures complete stability of per capita income.

If $\sigma = 0$, then $y_\tau = y_t$ for all $\tau > t$, and $V(y_t) = \log(y_t)/\delta$. The critical boundaries for $\log(y_t)$ are $l = \delta(\bar{V} - k)$ and $u = \delta(\bar{V} + k)$. Relocation is undertaken only if the certain discounted stream of additional utility offsets the equally certain and immediate mobility cost (for example, exit from the region requires $\log(y_t)/\delta \leq \bar{V} - k$).

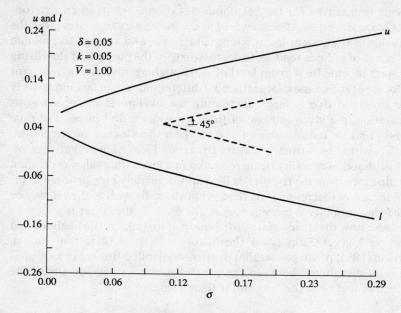

Figure 4.3   Uncertainty and income fluctuations

In general, the willingness of agents to relocate in response to a given income differential depends on both k and σ. Given the assumed absence of drift in the region's total income, u and l, the values of $\log(y_t)$ that trigger mobility into and out of the region, are equidistant from $\delta \bar{V}$ for any values of k and σ.

In Figure 4.2 u and l are plotted against the unit relocation cost for a given value of σ. As noted above, per capita income is perfectly stable at $\delta \bar{V}$ if $k = 0$, and becomes progressively more unstable as k increases. Note, however, that the widening of the bands is very pronounced for low values of k, but becomes shallower as k increases: in the presence of substantial uncertainty ($\sigma = 0.10$ in Figure 4.2), agents are reluctant to pay even very small adjustment costs and are willing to bear wide fluctuations in per capita income (once again, the rationale for this is simple: in the presence of large uncertainty, even very large deviations of y_t can be swept away in a short time, and it is worth it to wait and see whether this will happen rather than paying the relocation cost).

Figure 4.3 plots u and l against σ, the standard deviation per unit time of $\log (y_t)$ in the absence of mobility, for given k. It is apparent from Figure 4.3, in accord with the arguments of the previous section, that mobility is only triggered by large income differentials if uncertainty is large.

Having thus solved for the behaviour of rational agents in an environment characterized by a given level of uncertainty, we can now explore the behaviour of the system for different values of σ, and attempt to evaluate the efficacy of policies tending to decrease σ with the purpose of stabilizing per capita income for a given level of σ. Though agents become reluctant to relocate as σ increases, larger income differentials are in fact more likely to be observed if σ is large, increasing the likelihood of spontaneous stabilization in a given interval of time. Consider a unit interval of time $[t, t+1]$ and an initial value of $y_t \in [l, u]$: in the absence of relocation, $\log(y_{t+1})$ would be normally distributed around $\log(y_t)$, with variance σ^2. The likelihood of mobility being triggered in a given interval of time, for a given distance from the triggers, is then approximately proportional to σ:[5] if u (l) increases (decreases) less than proportionally with σ, then it may be argued that mobility is more frequent, for given k, the larger is σ.

Consider now the steady state distribution of $\log(y_t)$, i.e. the likelihood of observing $\log(y_T) \in d\log(y)$ if the history of $\{y_t; t \le T\}$ is not known. Harrison (1985, p. 90) proves that driftless controlled Brownian motion is uniformly distributed between the control barriers in steady state. The variance of $\log(y_t)$ in the long run is then, using

$$u - \delta\bar{V} = \delta\bar{V} - l$$

$$\text{avar}[\log(y)] = \int_l^u (x - \delta\bar{V})^2 dx = \frac{(u - \delta\bar{V})}{3} \tag{10}$$

and the steady state standard deviation of $\log(y_t)$ is proportional to $(u - \delta\bar{V})$.

Suppose now that it is desirable to stabilize per capita income, and that it is possible to choose a regime that would imply a lower σ, thus stabilizing the exogenous process for Y_t defined in equation (5), but would also impose costs of a different nature: for example the government might pursue a more active monetary policy to stabilize income with costs due to the consequently higher variability of exchange rates and interest rates (or in general to money becoming 'less useful' as in Mundell, 1961). The choice of σ should then be based on

$$\text{Max}_{\sigma} \{f[\sqrt{\text{avar}[\log(y)]}] - c(\sigma^{-1})\} \tag{11}$$

where the increasing and concave function $f(\cdot)$ expresses the preference for lower variability of per capita income in steady state, and the increasing function $c(\cdot)$ indexes the costs associated with policy rules tending to decrease the natural variability of total income in the region.

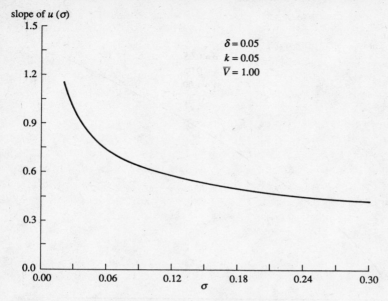

slope of $u(\sigma)$

$\delta = 0.05$
$k = 0.05$
$\overline{V} = 1.00$

Figure 4.4 Uncertainty and change in readiness to adjust

The model provides a framework in which to reevaluate Mundell (1961)'s arguments on the desirability of flexible exchange rates (and of a free hand in stabilization policy) in the presence of imperfect factor mobility. Equation (11) takes a pragmatic attitude towards the theoretical issues explored in Section 2 above, taking it for granted that, at a cost, income can be stabilized by adoption of flexible exchange rates. If there are mobility costs, lower variability of Y_t does imply strictly lower variability of $\log(y_t)$ (whose steady state standard deviation is proportional to $(u - l)$: see Figure 4.3). The shape of the tradeoff, however, depends on the slope of $\sqrt{\mathrm{avar}[\log(y)]}$ as a function of σ. The relationship between the two is not linear, because of endogenous factor mobility. Recall from equation (10) that $\sqrt{\mathrm{avar}[\log(y)]}$ is proportional to $(u - \delta\overline{V})$: in Figure 4.3, straight lines with 45° inclination are drawn to help evaluate the slope of $u(\sigma)$ and $l(\sigma)$. In Figure 4.4 the slope of the $u(\sigma)$ function of Figure 4.3 is plotted against σ, and in Figure 4.5 $(u - \delta\overline{V})/\sqrt{3}$, the asymptotic standard deviation of per capita income, is plotted as a function of σ.

The increased reluctance to move in an uncertain environment produces, so to speak, *increasing returns to stabilization policies* for a given cost of mobility k. In a fully specified model this phenomenon would, given the policy preference functions $f(\cdot)$ and $c(\cdot)$ and the technological mobility parameter k, tilt the balance towards adoption of flexible exchange rates.

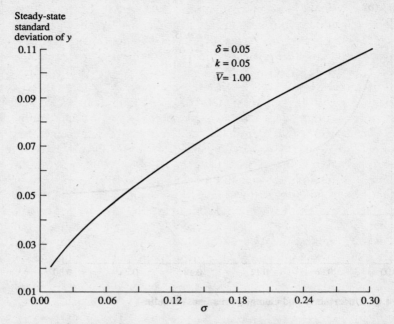

Figure 4.5   **Trade-off between stabilization of aggregate income and stability of per capita income**

5   Concluding comments

International economists have to be concerned with mobility – of goods and of factors of production – across locations. If everything were perfectly and instantaneously mobile, there would be no reason to study the interaction of separate national economies, as there would be only one, global economy. One of the reasons for distinguishing goods according to the nation in which they are produced, and factors according to the nation in which they produce, is that different currencies are used for monetary exchange in different countries.

International macroeconomists are specially concerned with a very special price, the exchange rate between two currencies. The exchange rate is special among prices not only because its variations are equivalent to simultaneous variations in thousands of relative (real) prices of goods and factors, but also because, being the relative prices of fiat monies, the nominal exchange rate can be manipulated by monetary authorities, and be fixed if it is deemed opportune to do so.

The twin concern of the international economist – with mobility on the one hand, and with the importance of monies and of their relative price on the other – was addressed jointly twenty-five years ago by the debate on the optimal size of 'currency areas'. The study of the theory of factor reallocation and that of the monetary theory of stabilization and exchange rates have since gone separate ways. No integration of the two issues has yet been attempted.

This paper reviews the relevant theoretical and empirical issues, and proposed a new facet of the problem: when dealing with stabilization policies, we should take uncertainty explicitly into account; since the relocation decisions of microeconomic agents are very much affected by the perceived degree of uncertainty, factor mobility is partly endogenous to the choice of nominal exchange rate regime as long as this choice has effects on the variability of real variables.

Future research will have to undertake the important and difficult task of combining in a single model, the well established economic theory of factor reallocation and the more informal and shaky treatments of the sources of nominal rigidities and of the role of money. The importance of the exchange rate regime for monetary policy, and the high degree of uncertainty experienced during the past fifteen years in the international economy, should give high priority to this effort.

Appendix

A Brownian motion process with zero drift, regulated at u and l, can be written as

$$\eta_t = \xi_t + L_t - U_t$$

where $\{\xi_t\}$ is Brownian motion process with stochastic differential $d\xi_t = \sigma dW_t$, $\{U_t\}$ and $\{L_t\}$ are increasing and continuous processes, $\{L_t\}$ only increases when $\eta_t = l$, and $\{U_t\}$ only increases when $\eta_t = u$. We are interested in finding

$$f(\eta_0) = E_0\left\{\int_0^\infty e^{-\delta\nu}\eta_\nu d\nu\right\} \tag{A1}$$

By Ito's lemma, noting that $\{U_t\}$ and $\{L_t\}$ have finite variation and using the properties of U_t and L_t above,

$$df(\eta_t) = \frac{\sigma^2}{2}f''(\eta_t)dt + \sigma f'(\eta_t)dW_t + f'(l)dL_t - f'(u)dU_t$$

Applying the Integration By Parts formula found in Harrison (1985, p. 73) to $\{f(\eta_t)e^{-\delta t}\}$, obtain

$$e^{-\delta t} f(\eta_t) = f(\eta_0) + \int_0^t e^{-\delta v} \left[\frac{\sigma^2}{2} f''(\eta_v) - \delta f(\eta_v) \right] dv$$

$$+ \int_0^t e^{-\delta v} \sigma f'(\eta_v) dW_t + f'(l) \int_0^t e^{-\delta v} dD_v$$

$$- f'(u) \int_0^t e^{-\delta v} dU_v \tag{A2}$$

Take the expectation at time 0 of (A2), noting that

$$E_0 \int_0^t e^{-\delta v} \sigma f'(\eta_v) dW_t = 0$$

and let $t \to \infty$, so that the left hand side vanishes since $f(\eta_t)$ is bounded between l and u. The result is

$$0 = f(\eta_0) + E_0 \left\{ \int_t^\infty e^{-\delta v} \left[\frac{\sigma^2}{2} f''(\eta_v) - \delta f(\eta_v) \right] dv \right\}$$

$$+ E_0 \left\{ f'(l) \int_0^t e^{-\delta v} dD_v - f'(u) \int_0^t e^{-\delta v} dU_v \right\} \tag{A3}$$

Comparing (A1) with (A3), we find that the function $f(\cdot)$ defined in (A1) must be such that

$$\frac{\sigma^2}{2} f''(\eta_v) - \delta f(\eta) = - \eta_v \tag{A4}$$

$$f'(l) = 0 \tag{A5}$$

$$f'(u) = 0 \tag{A6}$$

The solution to differential equation (A3) is

$$f(\eta) = \frac{1}{\delta} [\eta + A e^{\eta \Phi} + B e^{-\eta \Phi}] \tag{A7}$$

where we define $\Phi \equiv \sqrt{(2\delta/\sigma^2)}$, and A and B are constants of integration determined by the boundary conditions (A5) and (A6):

$$A \quad \frac{e^{-l\Phi} - e^{-u\Phi}}{\Phi[e^{(l-u)\Phi} - e^{-(l-u)\Phi}]}$$

$$B \quad \frac{e^{l\Phi} - e^{u\Phi}}{\Phi[e^{(l-u)\Phi} - e^{-(l-u)\Phi}]}$$

NOTES

I am indebted to the discussants for their comments. Thanks to Alberto Giovannini for suggesting the topic; writing this paper has been quite a learning experience. Of course, responsibility for any errors and shortcomings of the paper is mine.

1 Mussa (1984) shows that the apparent disequilibrium in the aftermath of a shock is really welfare-maximizing in the absence of market imperfection, although it can be improved upon by government intervention if, for example, wages are imperfectly flexible.
2 An American put option may be optimally exercised before expiration – see Merton (1973) – even in the absence of dividends: if the price of the underlying asset becomes low enough, it is a good idea to sell it for the present price and lock in the profits, which may vanish if the option is kept open.
3 In the sense that larger differentials would be needed before factors are induced to move but, as argued below, not in the sense that movements of factors would be less frequent or of smaller size in a more unstable system: larger differentials are needed to trigger adjustment, but such differentials will be observed more frequently in the presence of more uncertainty.
4 $\{W_t\} = \{W_0 + \int_0^t dW_\tau\}$ is a process with normally distributed, zero-mean increments, whose variance is proportional to the length of the time interval over which the increment is measured (the integral is an Ito integral; see Malliaris and Brock, 1982, for an introduction to stochastic calculus).
5 Only approximately, since sample paths of the driving Brownian motion $\{\sigma W_t\}$ which in the absence of control would exit $[l, u]$ but re-enter before one unit of time is elapsed increase the per-time unit probability of control over what would be implied by the cumulative normal function.

REFERENCES

Baldwin, Richard and Paul R. Krugman (1986). 'Persistent Trade Effects of Large Exchange Rate Shocks', NBER working paper.
Barro, Robert and David Gordon (1983). 'A Positive Theory of Monetary Policy in a Natural Rate Model', *Journal of Political Economy* **91**, 589–610.
Baxter, Marianne and Alan C. Stockman (1988). 'Business Cycles and the Exchange Rate System: Some International Evidence', mimeo, University of Rochester.
Bertola, Giuseppe (1987). 'Irreversible Investment', mimeo, M.I.T.
Blanchard, Olivier J. and Stanley Fischer (1988). *Macroeconomics*, M.I.T. Press (forthcoming).
Cooper, Richard N. (1976). 'Worldwide Regional Integration: Is There an Optimal Size of the Intergated Area?', in F. Machlup (ed.), *Economic Integration: Worldwide, Regional, Sectional*; New York: St. Martin's.
Dixit, Avinash (1987a). 'Hysteresis, Import Penetration, and Exchange Rate Passthrough', mimeo, Princeton University.
  (1987b). 'Intersectoral Capital Reallocation under Price Uncertainty', mimeo, Princeton University.
Dornbusch, Rudiger (1976). 'Expectations and Exchange Rate Dynamics', *Journal of Political Economy* **84**, 1161–76.
  (1980). *Open Economy Macroeconomics*, Basic Books.

Dornbusch, Rudiger and Alberto Giovannini (1988). 'Monetary Policy in the Open Economy', forthcoming in *Handbook of Monetary Economics*, North Holland.

Fischer, Stanley (1977). 'Long Term Contracts, Rational Expectations, and the Optimal Money Supply Rule', *Journal of Political Economy* **85**, 163–90.

Gavin, Michael K. (1988). 'Structural Adjustment to a Terms of Trade Disturbance: The Real Exchange Rate, Stock Prices and the Current Account', mimeo, Columbia University.

Giavazzi, Francesco and Marco Pagano (1988). 'The Advantage of Tying One's Hands: EMS Discipline and Central Bank Credibility', *European Economic Review*.

Giovannini, Alberto (1987). 'Prices and Exchange Rates: What Theory Needs to Explain', mimeo, Columbia University.

Harrison, J. Michael (1985). *Brownian Motion and Stochastic Flow Systems*, John Wiley and Sons.

Helpman, Elhanan and Assaf Razin (1982). 'A Comparison of Exchange Rate Regimes in the Presence of Imperfect Capital Markets', *International Economic Review* **23**, 365–88.

Kenen, Peter B. (1969). 'The Theory of Optimum Currency Areas: An Eclectic View', in R.A. Mundell and A.K. Swoboda (eds.): *Monetary Problems of the International Economy*, University of Chicago Press.

Krugman, Paul (1988a). *Exchange Rate Instability*, The Robbins Memorial Lectures, M.I.T. Press.

  (1988b). 'Deindustrialization, Reindustrialization, and the Real Exchange Rate', mimeo 1988.

Malliaris, Anastasios G., and William A. Brock (1982). *Stochastic Methods in Economics and Finance*, North-Holland.

McKinnon, Ronald I. (1963). 'Optimum Currency Areas', *American Economic Review* **53**, 717–25.

Merton, Robert C. (1973). 'Theory of Rational Option Pricing', *Bell Journal of Economics* **4**, 141–83.

Mundell, Robert A. (1961). 'A Theory of Optimum Currency Areas', *American Economic Review* **51**, 651–67.

Mussa, Michael (1974). 'Tariffs and the Distribution of Income: The Importance of Factor Specificity, Substitutability, and Intensity in the Short Run and Long Run', *Journal of Political Economy* **82**, 1191–1203.

  (1978). 'Dynamic Adjustment in the Heckscher-Ohlin-Samuelson Model', *Journal of Political Economy* **86**, 775–91.

Stockman, Alan C. (1980). 'A Theory of Exchange Rate Determination', *Journal of Political Economy* **88**, 673–98.

  (1983). 'Real Exchange Rates under Alternative Nominal Exchange-Rate Systems', *Journal of International Money and Finance* **2**, 147–66.

  (1987). 'The Equilibrium Approach to Exchange Rates', *Economic Review* (Federal Reserve Bank of Richmond) March/April 1987, 12–30.

Stockman, Alan C. and Lars E.O. Svensson (1987). 'Capital Flows, Investment and Exchange Rates', *Journal of Monetary Economics* **19**, 171–202.

Svensson, Lars E.O. and Sweder van Wijnbergen (1986). 'International Transmission of Monetary Policy', Institute for International Economic Studies Seminar Paper No. 362.

Taylor, John B. (1988). 'Should the International Monetary System Be Based on

Fixed or Flexible Exchange Rates?', Chapter 7 of 'International Monetary Policy Rules: An Econometric Evaluation', mimeographed, Stanford University.

Tower, E. and T. Willett (1976). *The Theory of Optimal Currency Areas and Exchange Rate Flexibility*, International Finance Section, Princeton.

Discussion

WILLIAM H. BRANSON

This paper presents an interesting exploration of the connections between recent work on factor flexibility under certainty and the older literature on optimum currency areas. The research on factor flexibility, much of it done by Bertola, models the agent facing the choice between remaining in his current occupation or location or moving to another, with income in both uncertain and with fixed moving costs. In this case, the expected income differential that induces movement must exceed the fixed moving cost by an amount that is related to the probability that the agent may want to reverse the movement in the future. This amount can be modelled as the price of an option to move. In this framework, the pattern of movement exhibits hysteresis. Within a range of expected income differentials, there is no movement, and the width of this range depends positively on the degree of uncertainty. Thus an increase in income uncertainty reduces factor mobility, and feeds back on itself, further increasing uncertainty. Since the criterion for an optimum currency area introduced by Mundell was factor mobility within, but not between, areas, it seems reasonable that the new results on factor flexibility could put the literature on optimum currency areas on a better footing. Bertola explores this possibility without coming yet to a clear conclusion.

Section 1 of the paper provides a brief review of the literature on optimum currency areas, concentrating on the role of factor mobility. Section 2 discusses the effect of the choice of nominal exchange rate regime on the variability of real exchange rates and various forms of real activity. The point is made that real exchange rates were more variable during the period when nominal rates were floating. But more emphasis should be put on the possibility that this was because the environment external to the exchange rate system was more variable then. The discussion of the effects of variability of real exchange rates is inconclusive. In some cases variable real rates stabilize output. Mention might have been made here of several of the papers in Marston (1988). Section 3 on costly adjustment under uncertainty provides a nice review of the recent work by Bertola and others applying the theory of option pricing to the decision to adjust, and the resulting hysteretic pattern of adjustment. The important point that more uncertainty makes the rational agent more reluctant to adjust to a given disturbance is made clearly. The marginal product of waiting for more information rises with increasing uncertainty.

The connection between factor flexibility and the choice of exchange rate regime is made in Section 4. The discussion is not as clear as it might be because it is cast in the context of a monetary authority trying to stabilize real income with a limit on exchange rate flexibility. The discussion would be clearer, and more relevant to the current European situation, if monetary policy were dedicated to controlling the nominal exchange rate, and fiscal policy were stabilizing income. I will outline the logic of the point, starting from Bertola's case. In his example, monetary policy is attempting to stabilize income but is hampered by limits to exchange rate movements. The reader should recall that in the Mundell-Fleming model the exchange rate is the principal channel through which monetary policy influences output. In this case, with stochastic relative disturbances between two areas, increased exchange rate stability increases income variability. Since factors are less mobile between the two areas the more variable is income, more stable exchange rates reduce factor mobility. This, in turn, increases income variability. So more flexible exchange rates would reduce income variability, and with increasing returns due to the effect on factor mobility.

The general point could be put more clearly by observing that any policies that stabilize income make factors more mobile, thus making it easier to stabilize income. The choice of monetary policy as the instrument to stabilize income in Bertola's example biases the results toward exchange rate flexibility. A better example would be to use monetary policy to stabilize the exchange rate, and fiscal policy to stabilize income. Then, in the Mundell-Fleming model, stability of the exchange rate makes fiscal policy more effective. This will increase factor mobility, and make it even easier to stabilize income. In this case the increasing returns to stabilization come from exchange rate stability. This seems more relevant for the EMS and the EC of 1992. With monetary policy tied down by the EMS, adjustment is left to factor mobility and fiscal policy. From Bertola's analysis, we see that stabilizing fiscal policy will generate increasing returns as it increases factor mobility within the area.

The importance of the availability of fiscal policy as an instrument to stabilize income was emphasized in a slightly different context by Peter Kenen (1969), referenced by Bertola. Kenen pointed out that in the face of relative real disturbances in the US, the federal fiscal system makes fiscal transfers automatically between the affected areas. When New England is booming and Texas is in a recession, tax payments rise and unemployment benefits and welfare claims fall in New England and the opposite in Texas. The fiscal transfer is made automatically, without a negotiation between the governments of New England and Texas. In fact, the federal fiscal system communicates directly with the affected individuals in the two areas, without going through the intermediation of the state governments. This automaticity of the federal fiscal transfer mechanism led Kenen to add an integrated fiscal system at the area level to the set of criteria for an optimal currency area.

As Europe approaches 1992 with the EMS expanding and capital mobility rapidly increasing, limited mobility of labour between states, compared to the US, and the virtual non-existence of a fiscal system at the Community level make it seem likely that given relative real disturbances will generate more instability in real incomes than otherwise, and more than within the US. And following Bertola's analysis, this will reduce labour mobility, further destabilizing real incomes. This could lead to political resistance to further integration of the EC and perhaps to some disintegration. Thus problems of labour immobility and fiscal inflexibility, and their Bertola interactions, deserve prominence on the Community's research and policy agendas.

REFERENCES

Marston, Richard C. (ed.) (1988). *Misalignment of Exchange Rates: Effects on Trade and Industry*. University of Chicago Press.

FIORELLA PADOA SCHIOPPA

This paper revisits the old theory of the optimal currency area, which stresses its ability to combine the macro argument on stabilization policy with the micro argument on factor reallocation. While, over the past decade, the two aspects have been studied separately in international monetary economics and in the trade literature respectively, Bertola tries to reintroduce a more integrated, and updated, analysis. Notably, he proposes to adopt a more modern view on the stabilization properties of different exchange rate regimes under the assumption of rational expectations and at the same time to examine the effects of uncertainty on costly factor reallocation. Thus, Bertola's purpose is very ambitious, possibly too ambitious to expect to be fully successful in his first essay on this subject.

With this aim, Bertola applies option pricing theory to the costly and risky decisions about human-non-human capital mobility, precisely as he has done before, by analogy, with irreversible investments and labour demand in the presence of hiring and firing costs (see Bentolila and Bertola, 1987). More than in his previous research, in the present extension to the market for migration, Bertola's partial equilibrium approach seems keen but somehow inadequate, because it cannot leave scope for externalities. Ignored by the single emigrant, these, however, are extremely important both for the country of origin, possibly because of a brain-drain problem, and for the destination country, as stressed by the literature based on the so-called MacDougall-Kemp model.

The most attractive feature of Bertola's combined treatment of stabilization and factor reallocation consists in proving that the rate of factor mobility is endogenous and optimally selected according to many elements, some of which are essentially macro – like the degree of uncertainty about forcing variables – others essentially micro – like adjustment costs. Consequently, if the level of uncertainty associated with two different exchange rate regimes is not the same, one is not authorized to compare their stabilization properties taking the level of factor mobility as a common exogenous datum. This is a behavioural parameter endogenously determined, among other things, by the exchange-rate policy.

One might question, however, the importance of this particular case of the well known Lucas critique addressed to the old optimal currency area theory. More generally, one might wonder whether Bertola's revisiting of the related literature – from Mundell (1961) to Tower and Willett (1976), through McKinnon (1963) and Kenen (1969) – though analytically very interesting, constitutes a leap forward in the understanding of today's subject: 'Monetary Regimes and Monetary Institutions. Issues and Perspectives in *Europe*' (the italics are mine).

On the first issue, it seems to me that Bertola could have at least mentioned another behavioural, policy-determined parameter, which is crucial for the updating of the optimal currency area argument in the European context. Flood and Marion (1982) have shown that, in assessing the consequences of alternative exchange rate regimes, the degree of indexation cannot be considered exogenous. As every European statesman knows by now, the rate of real wage rigidity has weakened in the high-risk countries after entering into the EMS. A common explanation for this phenomenon is based on the idea that the EMS marks an important self-disciplining device.

On the whole, the problem of real rigidities is totally ignored in Bertola's contribution, while he accounts for nominal rigidities in discussing the two approaches to exchange rate determination, split between the so-called 'equilibrium' and 'disequilibrium' analyses. This forgetting real rigidities appears particularly surprising in the European setting where, as indicated by Sachs (1979) long ago, rigidities are, unlike in the US, more real than nominal. Neither can it be considered a deliberate choice motivated by the consideration that real wage rigidities imply ineffectiveness of monetary policy in every exchange rate regime. This cannot be the case in Bertola's paper because, by the same reasoning, he should also have neglected the 'equilibrium' approach to the exchange rate which, on the contrary, he discusses at length. Indeed, as pointed out for example in Marston's survey (1985), the policy implications of full indexation and of full wage and price flexibility under rational expectations are very close from many viewpoints. In particular, 'full indexation prevents the exchange rate from affecting domestic output at all . . . Full indexation results in output varying to the same extent under flexible rates and fixed rates. With such indexation, therefore, the choice between regimes must be made not on the basis of output behaviour but on other grounds' (pp. 906–7).

More generally, I feel that in updating the old theory of the optimal currency area in the European perspective, Bertola should have reformulated some of the crucial hypotheses of that analysis which currently appear more controversial. I will simply mention two of them. According to one of these, the optimal currency area is defined without any consideration for strategic interactions, threats, games and coalitions between the players. That this assumption proves unsuitable for understanding the prerequisites for the creation of a currency area, such as the European one *in fieri*, was already pointed out more than ten years ago by Richard Cooper. In his *Worldwide Regional Integration: Is There an Optimal Size of the Integrated Area?* republished in his *Essays in World Economics* (1986), one reads (p. 133):

> Even when factor mobility is not present, one hears charges of 'unfair' competition from a country that pursues practices somewhat different from one's own. Economic stabilization and income redistribution have become more difficult for countries to achieve acting alone. On all these grounds, therefore, an argument can be made for increasing the size of jurisdictions – for forming regional groupings out of nations. The European Economic Community is one response to these pressures. The motivations behind the formation of the Community are many, and are

mainly political, but at their root was a perception that European nations acting along one by one would have a diminishing influence in the course of world events and hence even on their own welfare; thus, they joined together to pool their influence and to try to restore some autonomy to their evolution.

To be frank, it seems that this kind of argument based on strategic considerations, though intensively studied and intuitively appealing to common sense, is not yet complete. Indeed, it is not easy to demonstrate in general the existence and the dimension of the welfare gain obtained by transforming many small open economies, which are followers in the international market, into one large economy monopolistically competitive with the rest of the world. Moreover, as this currency area would at best be a second-best solution, naming it optimal would only be acceptable if it were possible to prove that a deadweight loss is in any case inevitable. Admittedly, for the time being, this subject deserves a deeper exploration to understand the desirability and 'optimality' of European integration.

In my opinion, the relevance for the European perspective of the original optimal currency area theory is also questioned with respect to a second hypothesis, namely full employment. This assumption, maintained ever since Mundell (1963) and subsequently integrated by the Phillips Curve only with reference to the short-run dynamics (see Tower and Willett, 1976), is implicitly accepted by Bertola, who does not even mention it.

It is no coincidence that this literature dried up after the first oil shock, because, on the one hand, that event marked the end (more permanently in Europe) of the belief that full employment is a steady phenomenon with only some cyclical disturbance; and, on the other hand, that hypothesis is very important to establish the connections, within the original approach of the optimal currency area, between stabilization and factor reallocation. This is clear in Mundell's words, reprinted in his *International Economics* (1968).

> Consider a simple model of two entities (regions or countries), initially in full employment and balance-of-payments equilibrium and see what happens when this equilibrium is disturbed by a shift of demand from the goods of entity B to the goods of entity A. Assume that money wages and prices cannot be reduced in the short run without causing unemployment, and that monetary authorities act to prevent inflation. Suppose first that the entities are countries with national currencies. The shift of demand from B to A causes unemployment in B and inflationary pressure in A (p. 178) . . . Unemployment could be avoided . . . if central banks agreed that the burden of international adjustment should fall on surplus countries which would then inflate until unemployment in deficit countries is eliminated . . . But a currency area of either type cannot prevent both unemployment and inflation (p. 179).

Indeed – Mundell concludes – this is not an optimum currency area, where

> optimality is defined in terms of the ability to stabilize national employ-
> ment and price levels . . . The optimum currency area is the region
> defined in terms of internal factor mobility and external factor immobi-
> lity (p. 182).

However, if owing to structural rigidities, permanent unemployment
becomes a more convincing hypothesis on which to base a modern optimal
currency area argument, the link between stabilization and factor reallocation needs to be re-examined because it does not necessarily hold in the
same traditional way. This point may be further clarified through a
convenient example drawn from European experience. Europe embraces
regions with unemployment due to insufficient capacity – classical
unemployment, to quote Malinvaud's (1978) terminology, for instance in
the Mediterranean area – and regions where unemployment and excess
capacity are demand-constrained – so-called Keynesian unemployment,
for example in some Northern European areas. Following Mundell's
lines, let us label the latter as entity A and the former as B, and let us
suppose that, at given prices and wages, a disturbance occurs shifting the
final demand from B to A. In this event, unlike under the full employment
assumption, factor mobility is not necessary to stabilize the price and
output levels. Indeed, the shock is helpful in reabsorbing at least part of
the original disequilibrium, in raising overall employment at fixed
exchange rates and constant relative (and absolute) prices.

In a sense, one might argue that this is an 'optimal' currency area,
because, in the presence of limited factor mobility and wage and price
rigidity, consumers tend to spill over from entities (B) where they are
rationed, to entities (A) where there is a notional excess supply: substitution in consumption partly replaces substitution in production. No doubt,
perfect factor mobility would generally be useful. But it is not always
needed to optimally absorb a shock within a currency area with
unemployment. It might rather be more necessary in the absence of
disturbances, because the original disequilibrium could be to some extent
a consequence of regional and sectoral mismatch.

Mismatch and imperfect factor mobility are certainly connected, but the
connections are far from obvious. Interesting enough, mismatch, which has
always existed not only in Europe but also in established currency areas such
as the US (see Burda, 1988), is now clearly rising everywhere, as documented
in the Chelwood Gate Conference (1988). Meanwhile, the interregional
mobility of labour and capital, illustrated by the number of emigrants or the
foreign investment units, is also growing (see Ruffin, 1984). Indeed, labour
mobility and migration do not necessarily lead to a mismatch reduction and
may even imply a mismatch increase (as hinted by Lilien, 1982).

REFERENCES

Bentolila, S. and G. Bertola (1988). 'Firing Costs and Labour Demand: How Bad is Eurosclerosis?', CNR Working Paper, Rome, June.

Burda, M.C. (1988). 'Is Mismatch Really The Problem? Some Estimates Of An Aggregate Disequilibrium Model With US Data', mimeo, Conference on European Unemployment, Chelwood Gate, May.

Cooper, R.N. (1986). 'Worldwide Regional Integration: Is There an Optimal Size of the Integrated Area?', in *Economic Policy in An Interdependent World. Essays in World Economics*, Cambridge, Mass., The M.I.T. Press.

Flood, R.P. and N.P. Marion (1982). 'The Transmission of Disturbances Under Alternative Exchange-Rate Regimes With Optimal Indexing', *The Quarterly Journal of Economics* 47, February, pp. 43–66.

Kenen, P.B. (1969). 'The Theory of Optimum Currency Areas: An Eclectic View', in R.A. Mundell and A.K. Swoboda (eds.), *Monetary Problems of the International Economy*. Chicago, University of Chicago Press.

Lilien, D.M. (1982). 'Sectoral Shifts and Cyclical Unemployment', *Journal of Political Economy* 90, August, pp. 777–93.

Malinvaud, E. (1978). *The Theory of Unemployment Reconsidered*, Oxford, Basil Blackwell.

Marston, R.C. (1985). 'Stabilization Policies in Open Economies', in R.W. Jones and P.B. Kenen (eds.), *Handbook of International Economics*, Vol. II, Amsterdam, Elsevier Science Publishers, pp. 859–917.

McKinnon, R.J. (1963). 'Optimum Currency Areas', *The American Economic Review* 53, September, pp. 717–25.

Mundell, R.A. (1968). 'A Theory of Optimum Currency Areas', in *International Economics*, New York, MacMillan Company.

Ruffin, R.J. (1984). 'International Factor Movements', in R.W. Jones and P.B. Kenen (eds.), *Handbook of International Economics*, Vol. I, Amsterdam, Elsevier Science Publishers, pp. 237–88.

Sachs, J.D. (1979). 'Wages, Profits and Macroeconomic Adjustment: A Comparative Study', in *Brookings Papers on Economic Activity* 2, pp. 269–333.

Tower, E. and T.D. Willett (1976). *The Theory of Optimum Currency Areas and Exchange-Rate Flexibility*, Princeton University, Special Papers in International Economics, No. 11, May.

ALAN C. STOCKMAN

Giuseppe Bertola has provided us with a paper full of intriguing suggestions for research on the differences between economic behaviour under alternative exchange rate systems. The main theme of his paper is that uncertainty in the presence of costly factor reallocation affects economic behaviour. If the degree of economic uncertainty or the form in which it manifests itself differ across alternative exchange rate systems, then investment, factor allocations, and allocative decisions will also differ.

The irreversible (or reversible only with a cost) nature of many allocative decisions is an important feature that has received only limited attention. Bertola has recently made an important contribution to this literature in his dissertation on irreversible investment. This paper applies some insights from that work to macroeconomic issues connected with alternative exchange-rate systems. This is a difficult step because it requires leaving the framework of partial-equilibrium models and encountering the difficulties of general equilibrium. But a general equilibrium framework is essential to address the macroeconomic problems associated with alternative exchange-rate systems.

Bertola's paper does not quite go all the way to a general equilibrium model. As I will explain below, this makes me reluctant to adopt his conclusion that 'in a fully specified model, this phenomenon would . . . tilt the balance towards adoption of flexible exchange rates.' However, this paper points the way for additional research that could end up yielding that conclusion. Before discussing the formal model, I want to comment on some other parts of the paper that I think are important.

The paper summarizes the contributions of Mundell and McKinnon to the theory of optimal currency areas. There is a tradeoff between (i) permitting exchange rate changes to reduce the costs of disequilibrium associated with sluggish nominal price adjustment in the presence of real shocks, and (ii) keeping the exchange rate fixed with a common currency to achieve the benefits of using a single money for all transactions. Bertola tries to relate these arguments to the degree of factor mobility to motivate his subsequent model. But, with sluggish nominal price adjustment, a real disturbance (as Mundell emphasized) can lead to disequilibrium regardless of the degree of factor mobility. Factor immobility only makes the production possibility frontier more convex (lowers elasticities of supply) and therefore raises the *magnitude* of the disequilibrium.

The paper makes a good case for using models with microeconomic foundations, and with explicit uncertainty, to examine issues of alternative exchange rate systems. In fact, uncertainty is important in even a more general context than the paper emphasizes. Suppose that some exogenous variable (such as productivity) is uncertain. If there were complete markets, then the economic effects of high realizations of productivity differ radically from the effects of a rise in productivity in a model that ignores the uncertainty. Essentially, financial markets permit analysis of the wealth effects of a rise in productivity in a model that ignores the uncertainty. The wealth effects of uncertainty can be traded in financial markets and allocated optimally across states of nature, so substitution effects of high realizations become relatively more important in models when models explicitly include uncertainty. When financial markets are more limited, which is obviously the realistic case, agents have incentives to alter *other* real allocative decisions in order to help reduce risks. So the explicit recognition of uncertainty in economic models produces different results for labour supply, capital utilization, investment, consumption and savings, inventories, factor allocations, the composition of production, and so on. The magnitude of these effects depends on the degree of risk-aversion (and the amount of uncertainty): the effects are larger when people are more risk-averse. A key insight from Bertola's work is that, when there are fixed costs of reallocations, uncertainty has real effects similar to these *even when agents are risk-neutral*.

Decisions under uncertainty can always be thought of as involving the exercise of options. Bertola's work has shown that this is a particularly useful way to think of these decisions when there are fixed costs. As in standard option-pricing theory, options have greater value when there is more uncertainty. Similarly, the right to move to a different location or engage in some other action becomes more valuable with greater uncertainty. When there are fixed costs of taking an action, the expected benefit from the action must exceed that cost before the action is taken. The greater the uncertainty about the future, the more likely one would want to reverse in the future any action taken today. But the reversal would involve a fixed cost. So the greater the uncertainty, the more reluctant will be a decision-maker to act in response to any *given size change* in circumstances. I have emphasized the qualifier in the last sentence because it is important: there is a second effect that works in precisely the *opposite* direction. Greater uncertainty follows from a higher standard deviation of exogenous shocks. But a higher standard deviation of these shocks implies that *realizations of the shocks will tend to be larger* in absolute value. Larger shocks (in absolute value) tend to *reduce* the reluctance to act. This effect opposes the increased reluctance to act from greater uncertainty. The figures in the paper (such as Figure 4.4) indicate that, unless the standard deviation of shocks is quite small, an increase in the standard deviation of shocks *raises* the likelihood that the action will be taken.

The microeconomics involved in these issues is technically difficult, but basically straightforward. The macroeconomics are more elusive. It is clear that some sources of uncertainty can be attributed to nature (such as productivity) and others to government actions (such as changes in tax rates). One can treat these variables as exogenous in a general equilibrium model and, with increases in uncertainty about future tax rates, derive aggregate consequences from the decision problems of individuals in general equilibrium. When the uncertainty in the individual's decision problem involves endogenous variables such as prices, the endogeneity and general equilibrium aspects of the problem make it more difficult. The stochastic behaviour of variables such as prices cannot simply be assumed: it must be consistent with general equilibrium in the model. When the problem involves monetary variables, nominal prices, and exchange-rate systems, the issues become even more elusive. In addition to the general-equilibrium problems just mentioned, the model must take a stand on the way that nominal and real variables interact. Moreover, the interaction must be one that can be modeled at a microeconomic level in order to address the effects of uncertainty on decision problems and the general-equilibrium consistency issue.

Bertola presents a model in which he assumes that the standard deviation of aggregate real income can be reduced under flexible exchange rates (or some other policy), but only at a cost (introduced in equation (11)). His view is that this is a 'pragmatic attitude' toward the issue. As he notes (and see Baxter and Stockman, 1988), there is little evidence that the variance of real output, or any other macroeconomic or international-trade quantity, is affected substantially by the exchange rate system. (Real exchange-rate variability, though, is clearly affected.) That is not to say that the system does not have *some* real effects. One possibility is that these may be mainly distributional and have small aggregative consequences. This would square some of the existing evidence with the valid argument that *something* real probably differs across exchange rate systems or people wouldn't be so concerned about them. Alternatively, there may be macroeconomic effects that existing empirical studies have for some reason failed to isolate.

The model in the paper does not derive the effects of alternative exchange-rate systems from the decision problems it studies. Rather, it assumes that a system of flexible exchange rates reduces the variance of aggregate real income. It also assumes that there is a cost to reducing this variance. The conclusion that a more complete model along these lines would favour a system of flexible exchange rates is based on the functional forms in the model: as the variance of real income is reduced more and more, the benefits rise faster than the costs. Whether this conclusion continues to hold up in a deeper model seems to me to depend on some very difficult issues in monetary theory, such as those involving the benefits to using a single currency, or to having pegged exchange rates and avoiding the costs of calculating conversions of prices from one money to another, and so on. In addition, there are the usual issues associated with the non-neutralities of money. If a flexible exchange rate system can stabilize real income, it must be because of some sluggish nominal price adjustment, some externalities, or similar 'market imperfections'. But these would affect the decision problems of agents. They would affect and possibly alter the conclusions about responses to disturbances in a world of uncertainty and adjustment costs. It would be useful to incorporate these features explicitly into the model from the outset. A rigorous investigation of these issues would be quite difficult and perhaps not tractable analytically. In some of Bertola's other work, he uses numerical methods to study properties of similar models. It seems to me that further research along these lines is worth undertaking. It would be useful first to study an economy without sluggish nominal prices or externalities as a benchmark case. Then menu costs or other similar features could be added to the model and the model calibrated, as many 'real business cycle' models have been recently, to try to match features of the data for macroeconomic behaviour under alternative exchange-rate systems. The implied research agenda looks promising, and Bertola deserves great credit for his initial work along these lines.

REFERENCES

Baxter, Marianne and Alan C. Stockman (1988). 'Business Cycles and the Exchange Rate Regime: An Empirical Investigation'. NBER Working Paper No. 2689, August.

5 Management of a common currency

ALESSANDRA CASELLA and
JONATHAN FEINSTEIN

1 Introduction

The possibility of European monetary integration has been frequently
discussed in the past few decades; see for example the volumes edited by
Fratianni and Peeters (1979), Johnson and Swoboda (1973), Salin (1984),
and Masera and Triffin (1984). Much of the debate derives from the theory
of optimum currency areas originally proposed by Mundell (1961) and
extended by McKinnon (1963) (see also a useful recent discussion in
Wood, 1986). More generally, Fischer (1983) provides an enlightening
commentary on the problems involved. While interesting issues have
emerged, the literature has remained informal, with few attempts to
provide a systematic foundation on which to base arguments for and
against common currency.

  Our purpose in writing this paper is to present a formal two-country
general equilibrium framework in which the question of alternative
monetary systems can be addressed, in the spirit of Helpman (1981) and
Helpman and Razin (1982). We are especially interested in contrasting
three monetary regimes, flexible exchange rates, a common currency
issued autonomously by both countries, and a common currency whose
management is delegated to a jointly controlled central bank. Flexible
exchange rates are the appropriate reference case, since they will prevail
whenever either country deviates from the common currency agreement.
We keep our model very simple, especially in that we assume complete
information and consider only the case of two countries. As an added
simplification we summarize each country's welfare in terms of a single
representative citizen. The citizen possesses a parametric utility function
which depends on both the home and foreign goods, which are different,
and on the home country government's provision of a public good. Money
is needed to help finance the public good, which alternatively can be
financed through lump-sum taxation.

131

Broadly stated, we find that establishing a common currency area is difficult, because each country views such a system as a means of exploiting the other. These pervasive free rider problems tend to reduce both countries' welfares, often below that which they achieve under flexible exchange rates. Of course, these difficulties are of the same nature as those studied in the literature on international policy coordination, from Hamada (1976) onwards.

More specifically, when the two countries maintain a common currency which each can print, the free rider problem leads to an equilibrium that is strictly dominated by the flexible exchange rate case. In our model this result is always true, but more generally it will be true when governments weigh the utility of future generations sufficiently. We argue, therefore, that such a regime is not enforceable, since both countries would have an incentive to deviate by issuing a national currency. This first result suggests that the organization of a jointly controlled central bank is crucial for a common currency, and we devote much of the paper to this case. Unfortunately, even here coordination is difficult. When the countries maintain control over taxation the central bank is unable to improve over the flexible exchange rate system: each country uses its tax policy to manipulate the Bank, hoping thereby to strengthen its position vis-à-vis the other, but in the process attenuating Bank effectiveness. With no taxes, the Bank can improve welfare. However, its policies naturally favour the bigger country, and to encourage the smaller country to participate requires giving that country a disproportionately large representation in the Bank's objective function. Such an arrangment seems to us difficult to support politically, though we believe further research in this area would be very useful.

As mentioned, the model is very simple and we do not claim these results to be general. Nonetheless, the incentive effects which arise are likely to be important in evaluating a variety of suggestions for monetary integration. Our results also suggest that considerably more attention should be addressed to the specific organizational features of a jointly controlled central bank. In particular the following seem relevant: the mechanism design literature; the application of Groves' mechanisms as a way for the central bank to coordinate countries' fiscal interventions; and the political forces lying behind the Bank's charter and decision-making body.

2   Model specification

The world is comprised of two countries, Red and Blue (R and B). Each period, citizens of each country are born with a fixed endowment of their respective good; Red are born with θ, Blue with $(2 - \theta)$. When young, the citizens sell their endowment on a competitive market in their home country. When old, they spend the proceeds from their previous period's sales on purchases of both the domestic and the foreign good; they then return home, consume, and exit the economy.[1] All transactions happen through money.

In addition to a private goods, the consumers' utility depends on the provision of a public good (as in Kehoe, 1987). While demand for the public good might be independent of events in the private sector (for example military spending), we prefer to think of it as directly related to the trading process itself. Thus for example the Red and Blue markets may be situated on the border between the two countries; to arrive at the markets consumers travel on roads maintained by their respective governments. If the roads are in poor condition, purchased goods depreciate substantially before consumption is possible.

More formally,

$$U_{Rt} = 0.5\log(C_{RRt}) + 0.5\log(C_{BRt})$$

$$U_{Bt} = 0.5\log(C_{BBt}) + 0.5\log(C_{RBt})$$

C_{ijt} denotes consumption of good i by a citizen of country j in time period t, and for each period t

$$C_{RR} = \Gamma_R^r R_R \quad C_{BR} = \Gamma_R^r B_R \quad r > 0$$

$$C_{BB} = \Gamma_B^b B_B \quad C_{RB} = \Gamma_B^b R_B \quad b > 0$$

with R_j (B_j) being the quantity of good R (B) purchased by a citizen of country j during t, and Γ_j representing provision of the public good by the government of country j in the period.

The government supplies the public good by collecting resources from the private sector. This can be done wither in the form of direct lump-sum taxation of the citizens' endowments (denoted $T_j, j = R, B$), or through the expenditure of fiat money on the domestic market ($M_j, j = R, B$).[2] For each period we define

$$\Gamma_j = T_j + m_j$$

where

$$m_j = M_j/p_j$$

with p_j the nominal price on market j.

Depending on the monetary regime between the two countries, we can solve for the equilibrium prices on the private markets as a function of the governments' policies. This results in country-specific indirect utility functions, which the governments in turn maximize over the variables T_j and M_j.

The interest of this simple model rests precisely in the interaction between the two governments' policies. Each country's welfare function depends on foreign choices of taxes and money, and lack of cooperation leads to suboptimal equilibrium.

In the next sections we study different forms of monetary (and fiscal) linkages between the countries; we are interested in which types of linkages lead to effective coordination of the governments' actions and achieve the highest welfare outcomes. We focus on three possible regimes: flexible exchange rates, a common fiat currency printed autonomously by the two governments, and delegation of monetary policy to a common central bank.[3]

3   Flexible exchange rates

Each country issues its own currency which must be used on the local market. Exchange rates are perfectly flexible and there are no transactions costs.

In period t the red consumer maximizes

$$U_{rt} = r\log(\Gamma_{Rt}) + 0.5\log(R_{Rt}) + 0.5\log(B_{Rt}) \tag{1R}$$

subject to the budget constraint

$$p_{Rt}R_{Rt} + e_t p_{Bt}B_{Rt} = p_{R(t-1)}(R_{R(t-1)} + R_{B(t-1)} + m_{R(t-1)}) \tag{2R}$$

where e_t is the exchange rate (defined as units of Red Currency required in exchange for one unit of Blue Currency), $p_{R(t-1)}$ is the nominal price on the Red market last period, and m_{Rt} is the real money spent by the Red government on the Red market. (The left-hand-side of equation $(2R)$ gives the nominal income earned by a red consumer through the previous period sale of his endowment.)

Similarly a Blue consumer maximizes

$$U_{bt} = b\log(\Gamma_{Bt}) + 0.5\log(R_{Bt}) + 0.5\log(R_{Bt}) \tag{1B}$$

subject to

$$e_t p_{Bt}B_{Bt} + p_{Rt}R_{Bt} = e_t p_{B(t-1)}(B_{B(t-1)} + B_{R(t-1)} + m_{B(t-1)}) \tag{2B}$$

Equilibrium conditions on the two markets are

$$\theta - T_{Rt} = R_{Rt} + R_{Bt} + m_{Rt} \tag{3R}$$

$$2 - \theta - T_{Bt} = B_{Bt} + B_{Rt} + m_{Bt} \tag{3B}$$

(where recall that θ and $2 - \theta$ are the initial endowments), leading to the demand functions

$$R_{Rt} = \frac{p_{R(t-1)}(\theta - T_{R(t-1)})}{2p_{Rt}}$$

$$B_{Rt} = \frac{p_{R(t-1)}(\theta - T_{R(t-1)})}{2p_{Rt}} \cdot \frac{p_{Rt}}{e_t p_{Bt}}$$

$$B_{Bt} = \frac{p_{B(t-1)}(2 - \theta - T_{B(t-1)})}{2p_{Bt}}$$

$$R_{Bt} = \frac{p_{B(t-1)}(2 - \theta - T_{B(t-1)})}{2p_{Bt}} \cdot \frac{e_t p_{Bt}}{p_{Rt}} \tag{4}$$

Substituting these demands in $(3R)$ and $(3B)$ determines the market clearing price

$$p_t = \frac{p_{Rt}}{e_t p_{Bt}} = \frac{2 - \theta - \Gamma_{Bt}}{\theta - \Gamma_{Rt}} \tag{5}$$

and the equilibrium relationship between the two inflation rates:

$$1 = \frac{2 - \theta - T_{B(t-1)}}{2(1 + \pi_{Bt})(2 - \theta - \Gamma_{Bt})} + \frac{\theta - T_{R(t-1)}}{2(1 + \pi_{Rt})(\theta - \Gamma_{Rt})} \tag{6}$$

where $(1 + \pi_{jt}) = p_{jt(t-1)}$.

Equilibrium on the Red Currency market requires that the nominal amount spent last period (by Red and Blue consumers and the Red government) equal the nominal private demand for Red currency this period:[4]

$$p_{Rt}R_{Bt} + p_{Rt}R_{Rt} = p_{R(t-1)}(m_{R(t-1)} + R_{R(t-1)} + R_{B(t-1)}) \tag{7}$$

With the budget constraint $(2R)$ this implies

$$p_{Rt}R_{Bt} = e_t p_{Bt}B_{Rt} \tag{8}$$

the equality of cross currency nominal demands. Substituting from the expressions for the equilibrium price (5) and the demand functions we obtain

$$\frac{1 + \pi_{Rt}}{1 + \pi_{Bt}} = \frac{\theta - T_{R(t-1)}}{2 - \theta - T_{B(t-1)}} \cdot \frac{2 - \theta - \Gamma_{Bt}}{\theta - \Gamma_{Rt}} \tag{9}$$

Finally, (9) and (6) can be solved for the two inflation rates:

$$1 + \pi_{Rt} = \frac{\theta - T_{R(t-1)}}{\theta - \Gamma_{Rt}} \qquad 1 + \pi_{Bt} = \frac{2 - \theta - T_{B(t-1)}}{2 - \theta - \Gamma_{Bt}} \qquad (10)$$

Demands for the Red and Blue goods are then given by

$$R_{Rt} = R_{Bt} = (\theta - \Gamma_{Rt})/2 \qquad (11R)$$

and

$$B_{Bt} = B_{Rt} = (2 - \theta - \Gamma_{Bt})/2 \qquad (11B)$$

and the utility functions can be written

$$U_{Rt} = r\log(\Gamma_{Rt}) + 0.5\log(\theta - \Gamma_{Rt}) \\ + 0.5\log(2 - \theta - \Gamma_{Bt}) - \log(2) \qquad (12R)$$

$$U_{Bt} = b\log(\Gamma_{Bt}) + 0.5\log(2 - \theta - \Gamma_{Bt}) \\ + 0.5\log(\theta - \Gamma_{Rt}) - \log(2) \qquad (12B)$$

Each government chooses the path $\{T_{jt, m_{jt}}\}$ that maximizes the discounted sum of its citizens' utilities:

$$\max_{\{T_{jt}, m_{jt}\}} W_j = \sum_{t=0}^{\infty} \delta^t U_{jt}$$

where δ is the discount rate reflecting the length of the governments' horizon.

The interaction between the governments may therefore be formulated as a dynamic game, possessing multiple equilibria. Since instantaneous utilities only depend on contemporaneous policy variables (i.e. $U_{jt} = U_{jt}(T_{jt}, m_{jt})$), we can easily solve for one possible equilibrium of this game: the 'static' equilibrium in which dynamic interactions are neglected, reducing the dynamic case to a sequence of repetitions of the 'one-shot' (single period) game. The static solution is a perfect equilibrium of the full dynamic game.

Maximization of U_{Rt} over Γ_{Rt} and U_{Bt} over Γ_{Bt} yields optimal expenditure policies, which are constant over time:

$$\Gamma_R^* = \frac{2r\theta}{1 + 2r} \qquad \Gamma_B^* = \frac{2b(2 - \theta)}{1 + 2b} \qquad (13)$$

Two points are noteworthy. First, whether a country's public good is financed by taxes or by fiat money is irrelevant. An increase in the proportion financed by money increases inflation, while leading at the

	European statistics		Parameter values	
	1984 GDP (billion (ECUs)	1984 government share (%)	Size θ	Government share r
Belgium	96.9	17.4	(1.0 equal)	$\frac{1}{4}$ (20%)
Denmark	68.7	25.9	1.25 (1.67 to 1)	$\frac{1}{2}$ (33%)
West Germany	783.8	13.6	1.50 (3 to 1)	1 (50%)
Greece	42.7	19.0		
Spain	198.5	12.3		
France	623.3	16.4		
Ireland	22.2	19.0		
Italy	445.3	19.4		
Luxembourg	4.4	15.7		
Netherlands	157.9	16.8		
Portugal	24.4	—		
United Kingdom	540.3	21.9		

Table 5.1 *Calibration of model parameters*

Source: Eurostat: Basic Statistics of the European Community. Luxembourg: Office for Official Publications of the European Communities, 1987.

same time to a proportionate depreciation of the exchange rate. Thus the higher nominal wealth of the country's citizens does not translate into a higher share of world resources. Second, the governments' decisions are independent of one another, even though each country's citizens' utility depends on the other country's policy; this finding is special to the simple Cobb–Douglas utility form we have specified.

Since each government neglects the effect of its public expenditure on the other country's welfare, the non-cooperative Nash equilibrium we have derived is not Pareto optimal. In fact, the two countries spend too large a fraction of their resources on the public good. The intuition is straightforward. An increase in government expenditure reduces the supply of goods for private consumption. While residents are compensated by the additional supply of the public good, foreigners, in our model, do not benefit from it in any way. A central planner, maximizing the sum of the two countries' welfare ($U_{Rt} + U_{Bt}$), would set

$$\Gamma_R^* = \frac{r\theta}{1 + r} \quad \Gamma_B^* = \frac{b(2 - \theta)}{1 + b}$$

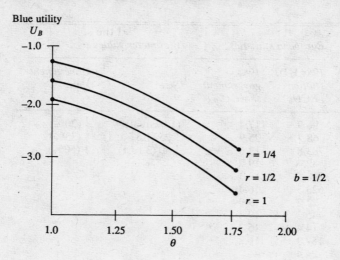

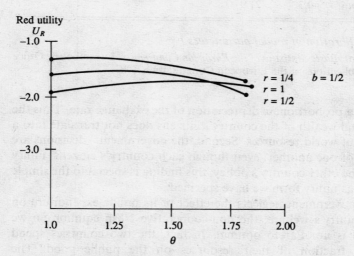

Figure 5.1   Utilities under flexible exchange rates

3.1   Simulation methodology

Each of the models presented has been simulated over a range of parameter values. We concentrate on variation in two parameters: θ, which measures the relative size of Red as opposed to Blue; and r (with b fixed) which measures Red's relative desire for the public good (the size of the public sector). To calibrate these parameters, consider the left-hand side of Table 5.1, which lists the European countries which are members of the EEC, together with their GDP (in ECU units) and the share of GDP devoted to government. The right-hand side of Table 5.1 depicts the ranges of θ, r, and b chosen. The variable θ ranges from 1.0 (equal size) through 1.25 and 1.50 to 1.75 (7 to 1 size differential), while b is fixed at $\frac{1}{2}$ (government's share is then one-third) and r ranges over $\frac{1}{4}$, $\frac{1}{2}$, and 1.

3.2   Simulation of flexible exchange rate regime

Figure 5.1 illustrates Red and Blue utility under flexible exchange rates as a function of the relative endowment (θ), for different values of r (Red's need for the public good). As θ increases, the share of world resources owned by the Blue country falls, and so does Blue welfare. As the weight of the public good in Red utility, r, increases, so does the intervention of the Red government in the Red market. This implies a decrease in the proportion of Red goods available for private consumption, and therefore a loss of utility for Blue nationals.

In the Red country, an increase in θ increases national wealth, but reduces relative world supply of the Blue good. The two effects tend to counteract each other, the first dominating for θ close to one and the second becoming progressively more important, until Red utility begins to fall for θ approximately larger than 1.5. The relevance of this second effect is smaller, as expected, when the public good plays a larger role in utility (r higher).

4   A common currency printed by both countries[5]

Suppose now that the two countries use the same currency, and that each country maintains a central bank and can print as much of the currency as it likes. This seems the natural setting for the case of perfectly subsitutable currencies studied in the literature (see for example Kareken and Wallace, 1981)[6] and is to be distinguished from the case of a common currency printed by a joint central bank.

Derivation of the demand functions is identical to the flexible exchange rate case with e_t set equal to 1 for all t. Substitution of (4) in the two goods markets' equilibrium conditions yields the equilibrium relative price:

$$p_t = \frac{p_{Rt}}{p_{Bt}} = \frac{2 - \theta - \Gamma_{Bt}}{\theta - \Gamma_{Rt}}$$

and inflation rates:

$$1 - \pi_{Rt} = (1/2) \left[\frac{\theta - T_{R(t-1)}}{\theta - \Gamma_{Rt}} \right.$$

$$\left. + \frac{(\theta - \Gamma_{R(t-1)})(2 - \theta - T_{B(t-1)})}{(\theta - \Gamma_{Rt})(2 - \theta - \Gamma_{B(t-1)})} \right] \quad (14R)$$

$$1 - \pi_{Bt} = (1/2) \left[\frac{2 - \theta - T_{B(t-1)}}{2 - \theta - \Gamma_{Bt}} \right.$$

$$\left. + \frac{(2 - \theta - \Gamma_{B(t-1)})(\theta - T_{R(t-1)})}{(2 - \theta - \Gamma_{Bt})(\theta - \Gamma_{R(t-1)})} \right] \quad (14B)$$

Demands can then be written

$$R_{Rt} = (\theta - \Gamma_{Rt})(\theta - T_{R(t-1)})(2 - \theta - \Gamma_{B(t-1)}) \cdot \Delta_t \quad (15)$$

$$B_{Rt} = (2 - \theta - \Gamma_{Bt})(\theta - T_{R(t-1)})(2 - \theta - \Gamma_{B(t-1)}) \cdot \Delta_t$$

$$B_{Bt} = (2 - \theta - \Gamma_{Bt})(\theta - \Gamma_{R(t-1)})(2 - \theta - T_{B(t-1)}) \cdot \Delta_t$$

$$R_{Bt} = (\theta - \Gamma_{Rt})(\theta - \Gamma_{R(t-1)})(2 - \theta - T_{B(t-1)}) \cdot \Delta_t$$

where

$$\Delta_t = \frac{1}{(2 - \theta - T_{B(t-1)})(\theta - \Gamma_{R(t-1)}) + (2 - \theta - \Gamma_{B(t-1)})(\theta - T_{R(t-1)})}$$

Instantaneous utilities are given by

$$U_{Rt} = r\log(\Gamma_{Rt}) + \log(\theta - T_{R(t-1)})$$
$$+ 0.5\log(\theta - \Gamma_{Rt}) + \log(2 - \theta - T_{B(t-1)})$$
$$+ 0.5\log(2 - \theta - \Gamma_{Bt}) + \log(\Delta_t) \quad (16R)$$

$$U_{Bt} = b\log(\Gamma_{Bt}) + \log(2 - \theta - T_{B(t-1)})$$
$$+ 0.5\log(2 - \theta - \Gamma_{Bt}) + \log(\theta - T_{R(t-1)})$$
$$+ 0.5\log(\theta - \Gamma_{Rt}) + \log(\Delta_t) \quad (16B)$$

The utility of a consumer at time t now depends both on contemporaneous and last-period government policies. However, the problem is greatly simplified by the additively separable form of the utility function. At time t, a government maximizing the present discounted sum of its citizens' utilities can isolate the terms depending on its period t policies. Redefining this sum as the government payoff of the 'one-shot' game, the repetition of the static solution yields once more a perfect equilibrium for the dynamic problem, in which each period's policy is independent of the previous period choice.

Taking into consideration only the relevant terms, the Red government will act as time t so as to maximize the expression

$$r\log(\Gamma_{Rt}) + 0.5\log(\theta - \Gamma_{Rt})$$
$$+ \delta[\log(\theta - T_{Rt}) + \log(\Delta_{t+1})] \tag{17R}$$

subject to the constraint $\Gamma_{Rt} = m_{Rt} + T_{Bt}$. Similarly, the Blue government maximises

$$b\log(\Gamma_{Bt}) + 0.5\log(2 - \theta - T_{Bt})$$
$$+ \delta[\log(2 - \theta - T_{Rt}) + \log(\Delta_{t+1})] \tag{17B}$$

subject to $\Gamma_{Bt} = m_{Bt} + T_{Bt}$.

In contrast to the flexible exchange rate regime, the policy mix between money and taxes is now relevant to welfare. The first important observation is that, in this framework, the optimal level of taxes is zero in both countries. Collecting revenues through seigniorage has a positive effect on the relative wealth of nationals next period, because the world inflation rate rises less than proportionately. Since this is not true for taxes, all government expenditure will be completely financed by fiat money.

In fact the expressions (17R) and (17B) can be written

$$r\log(\Gamma_{Rt}) + 0.5\log(\theta - \Gamma_{Rt})$$
$$- \delta\log\left[(2 - \theta - \Gamma_{Bt}) + \frac{(2 - \theta - T_{Bt})}{(\theta - T_{Rt})}(\theta - \Gamma_{Rt})\right]$$

$$b\log(\Gamma_{Bt}) + 0.5\log(2 - \theta - \Gamma_{Bt})$$
$$- \delta\log\left[(\theta - \Gamma_{Rt}) + \frac{(\theta - T_{Rt})}{(2 - \theta - T_{Bt})}(2 - \theta - \Gamma_{Bt})\right]$$

For given Γ_{Bt} and Γ_{Rt} each function is strictly decreasing in domestic taxes.

Setting $T_{Bt} = T_{Rt} = 0$ for all t, the governments' problems may be rephrased as:

$$\max_{m_{Rt}} r\log(m_{Rt}) + 0.5\log(\theta - m_{Rt})$$
$$+ \delta[\log(\theta) - \log[\theta(2 - \theta - m_{Bt})$$
$$+ (2 - \theta)(\theta - m_{Rt})]] \tag{18}$$

$$\max_{m_B} b\log(m_B) + 0.5\log(2 - \theta - m_{Bt})$$
$$+ \delta[\log(2 - \theta) - \log[(2 - \theta)(\theta - m_{Rt})$$
$$+ \theta(2 - \theta - m_{Bt})]]$$

with m_{Rt} and m_{Bt} each restricted to the unit interval.

The nature of the solution depends on the value of δ (the length of the governments' horizon). If δ is equal to zero (the governments do not consider future generations' utilities), then optimal policy is identical to the flexible exchange rate considered above.

$$m_{Rt} = \frac{2r\theta}{1 + 2r}$$

$$m_{Bt} = \frac{2b(2 - \theta)}{1 + 2b}$$

utilities are also equal to the flexible exchange rate case. However, as δ increases (as the governments give more weight to future generations' utilities), the optimum amount of money becomes larger since its only partial effect on world inflation allows each government to increase the purchasing power of its future citizens. At the same time, utilities become lower, as the Nash equilibrium yields ever higher world inflation. Eventually, for δ equal to one (the governments care equally about current and future generations), this monetary regime fails to possess a Nash equilibrium: for any amount of currency issued by the foreign government, the home government desires to supply more.

In the simple case $\theta = 2 - \theta = 1$, the first-order conditions associated with optimization problems (18) are:

$$\frac{r}{m_{Rt}} = \frac{1}{2(1 - m_{Rt})} + \frac{\delta}{(2 - m_{Bt} - m_{Rt})} = 0$$

$$\frac{b}{m_{Bt}} = \frac{1}{2(1 - m_{Bt})} + \frac{\delta}{(2 - m_{Bt} - m_{Rt})} = 0$$

If $\delta = 1$ and $r = b = 0.5$, these expressions can be further simplified:

$$m_{Rt} = \frac{m_{Bt} - 2}{2m_{Bt} - 3} \tag{19}$$

$$m_{Bt} = \frac{m_{Rt} - 2}{2m_{Rt} - 3}$$

Examination of the equations (19) demonstrates that the two reaction functions do not intersect within the relevant range $[0, 1] \times [0, 1]$.

For different values of δ, we were unable to obtain a simple closed-form solution, and we checked our intuition with numerical simulations. The results of the simulations, confirming the expected outcome, are depicted in Figure 5.2. The conclusion does not depend on the symmetry of this

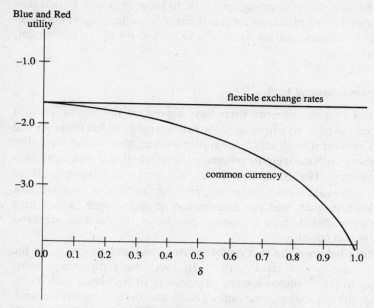

Figure 5.2 Common currency, national central banks: utilities as a function of the discount rate ($\theta = 1.0$, $r = b = 0.5$)

simple example. Different endowments ($\theta \neq 1$) or different needs for the public good ($r \neq b$) did not alter the qualitative nature of our result.[7]

The important point established by this exercise is that, at least in our model, independent printing of a common currency by national central banks is strictly dominated by the flexible exchange rate regime, and is not, therefore, a viable institutional arrangement. Each country has an incentive to deviate, printing a new currency and requiring its exclusive use on the domestic markets.

The source of this result lies in two effects. The first one relates to the distortion caused by non-cooperation between the two governments in the flexible exchange rate regime. In our model, the two public sectors in a Nash equilibrium with national currencies are too large. The second effect is the free-rider problem connected with the shift to a common money. If δ is different from zero, such a shift implies an ever higher level of spending by the governments (this is quite general, and does not depend on our specific assumptions). When the two effects are added, the result, of course, is that the institution of a common currency exacerbates the already present distortion and leads to a decrease in welfare. While our result remains true in models in which flexible exchange rates achieve the first-best, in a more general setting the welfare comparison would depend on δ. We believe that it is always possible to identify a $\delta^* < 1$ such that welfare under flexible exchange rates is inferior to welfare under common currency and national central banks if and only if $\delta < \delta^*$. In our model, $\delta^* = 0$.

5   A common central bank

Suppose now that the two countries have agreed on the institution of a common central bank to whom decisions concerning the fiat currency are deferred. The central bank acts to maximize the weighted sum of the utility of its members, with the weights reflecting the proportional representation of each country. The Bank determines the paths over time of three quantities, aggregate world money supply, the fraction of that amount spent on each market, and the distribution of seigniorage (which may differ from the distribution of money purchases on the two markets) between the two countries.

Competition between the two countries now emerges indirectly, in the struggle to manipulate Bank policy. In fact, the setup bears some relationship to the 'common agency' framework of Bernheim and Whinston (1986), although we assume that all Bank actions are observable, and, as an initial simple example, that full information about each country's parameters is common knowledge. We also, for the time being, assume that the weight of each country in aggregate welfare is proportional to the size of its endowment ('proportional representation'); we may think of these weights as the countries' relative bargaining powers. While this arrangement is *ad hoc*, it is a reasonable reference point on which further extensions can be built.

The central bank maximizes

$$\sum_{t=0}^{\infty} \delta^t [\theta Y_{Rt} + (2 - \theta) U_{Bt}]$$

with respect to $\{s_{Rt}, s_{Bt}, m_{Rt}, m_{Bt}\}$ and the constraints that $s_{Rt} + s_{Bt}$ equal $m_{Rt} + m_{Bt} = m_t$, and that m_{Rt} not exceed θ and m_{Bt} not exceed $2 - \theta$. Here s_{it} are seigniorage revenues distributed to country i in period t and m_{it} is the real amount of fiat currency spent on market i during t.

In general, the two countries can supplement Bank action with their own fiscal and monetary interventions. However, as the earlier analysis showed, in the case of common currency, free and independent issuing of money by the two governments results in lower welfare. This remains true when the governments' decisions coexist with a central bank.[8]

More interesting, and relevant, is the case in which each government retains its right to collect taxes from its nationals, while monetary policy is fully delegated to the central bank. Quite surprisingly, it is possible to prove that in this regime it is optimal for the central bank to set new money issues to zero. The two countries will completely finance themselves through taxes, and will achieve exactly the same welfare as in the flexible exchange rate case.

The intuition is as follows. For any positive amount of real money injected into the domestic market, an increase in taxes implies a reduction in the availability of the domestic good in the private sector, and hence a rise in its relative price (relative to the other country's good). This requires a higher level of nominal money from the Bank to achieve the same real money injection, thereby increasing nationals' relative wealth.

In other words, if m_R and m_B are positive, each government chooses a level of expenditure that is larger than in the flexible exchange rate case, in the effort to exploit central bank policy for its own purposes. In equilibrium, this implies a welfare loss. If instead m_R and m_B are both set to zero by the central bank, it is easy to show (by comparing equations (16) and (12)) that the current problem is identical to the flexible exchange rate case.

Slightly more formally, the conclusion follows from proving that, for any m_{jt}, the marginal utility of taxes in country j is higher in the common currency regime than in the flexible exchange case. Substituting the demand functions given in (4), we obtain the discounted sum of the citizens' utility,

$$\frac{dW_j}{dT_{jt}} = \frac{d(j\log \Gamma_{jt})}{dT_{jt}} + 0.5\frac{d(\log X_{jjt})}{dT_{jt}} + 0.5\frac{d(\log X_{ijt})}{dT_{jt}}$$

$$+ \delta\left[0.5\frac{d(\log X_{jj(t+1)})}{dT_{jt}} + 0.5\frac{d(\log X_{ij(t+1)})}{dT_{jt}}\right]$$

which may be evaluated as

$$\frac{dW_j}{dT_{jt}} = \frac{j}{m_{jt} + T_{jt}} - \frac{d(\log(1 + \pi_{jt}))}{dT_{jt}}$$

$$- 0.5\frac{d(\log(\theta_j - m_{jt} - T_{jt}))}{dT_{jt}} + \delta\left[\frac{d(\log(\theta_j - T_{jt}))}{dT_{jt}}\right.$$

$$\left. - \frac{d(\log(1 + \pi_{j(t+1)}))}{dT_{jt}}\right] \tag{20}$$

In the flexible exchange rate regime, π_{jt} is given by equation (10); in the common currency regime by equation (14). Examination of these equations demonstrates that

$$\frac{d(\log(1 + \pi_{jt}))}{dT_{jt}}$$

is the same in both, whereas

$$\frac{d(\log(1 + \pi_{j(t+1)}))}{dT_{jt}}$$

is larger in the flexible exchange rate regime for all m_{it} different from zero. Since all other terms in equation (20) are the same across the two regimes, the result follows.[9]

In our model, if the governments retain their fiscal powers, not only is the central bank incapable of improving coordination between the two countries, but in addition any action it takes serves only to introduce incentives driving the countries further away from a first-best outcome. Once again, the unqualified strength of this result depends on the specific assumptions of the model (the direction of the distortion in the flexible exchange rate regime; the lump-sum character of the taxes and their effect on the terms of trade). The point we want to stress is general, however, and, we believe, important: the presence of a common currency, even under the control of a central planner, is the source of additional potential distortions. In a world which is not Pareto optimal, the final outcome would then depend on second-best types of arguments.

Consider now the extreme case in which the two governments are not allowed to collect taxes. The only resources available for the supply of the public good are, in each country, those distributed as seigniorage by the central bank.

Since the central bank maximizes weighted aggregate social welfare, its choices will clearly constitute a first-best arrangement in this case; what is less clear is how the countries' weights translate into individual country utility, particularly as compared with the earlier monetary regimes.

The instantaneous utilities U_{Rt} and U_{Bt} are given by equation (16), setting T_{Rt} and T_{Bt} to zero. They are rewritten here for convenience:

$$U_{Rt} = r\log(s_{Rt}) + 0.5\log(2 - m_{Bt}) + \tag{16R}$$
$$\log(\theta) + \log(2 - \theta - m_{B(t-1)}) + 0.5\log(\theta - m_{Rt}) + \log(\Delta_t)$$

$$U_{bt} = b\log(s_{Bt}) + 0.5\log(2 - \theta - m_{Bt}) + \tag{16B}$$
$$\log(2 - \theta) + \log(\theta - m_{R(t-1)}) + 0.5\log(\theta - m_{Rt}) + \log(\Delta_t)$$

where

$$\Delta_t = \frac{1}{(2 - \theta)(\theta - m_{R(t-1)}) + (2 - \theta - m_{B(t-1)})\theta}$$

As above, the central bank maximizes the weighted sum of discounted utilities.

If $\theta = 2 - \theta = 1$, the optimal choice for the central bank is characterized by the following equations:

$$s_{Bt} = \frac{b}{r + b} m_t$$

$$m_{Bt} = \frac{m_t}{2}$$

$$m_t = \frac{2(r + b)}{r + b + 2}$$

(Note that δ does not enter these expressions.) The total amount of money is spent on the two markets in equal proportions, while the division of seigniorage is determined by the relative need for the public good.

For $\theta \neq 1$ (and $\delta \neq 0$), we have not been able to obtain a closed-form solution, and we present the results of numerical simulations. In Figure 5.3 the welfare of the two countries is depicted as a function of the relative size of the endowments and of the weight of the public good in Red utility (for $\delta = 0.9^{10}$). As θ increases, the Blue country becomes poorer and has less influence on the decisions of the central bank. As expected, its utility declines. The Blue country's utility is also lower the higher is r, since a higher r implies a proportionally lower Blue share in the division of seigniorage. This second effect becomes more important the larger is θ.

As in the flexible exchange rate case, the Red utility increases with θ, until the negative effect of the Blue good's scarcity starts to dominate the positive impact of larger national wealth and larger bargaining power. The relative importance of the negative effect (scarcity of the Blue good) is lower the larger is the weight of the public good in Red utility, since a larger r gives added relevance to Red's increased bargaining power in the sharing of seigniorage revenues.

6   Welfare comparisons

It is now possible to compare utility levels across different monetary regimes, as functions of the parameters. Since the common currency –

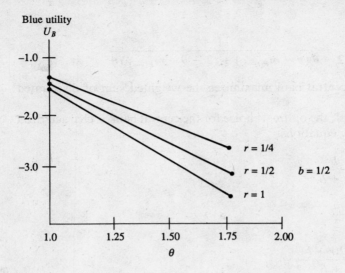

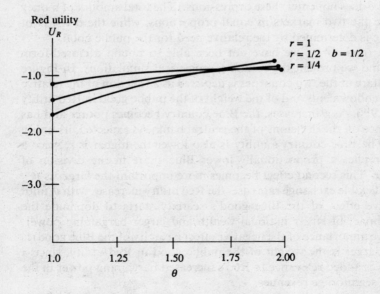

Figure 5.3   Utilities under a central bank (money only)
($\delta = 0.9$)

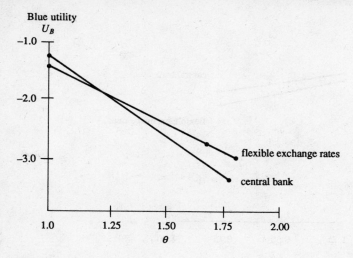

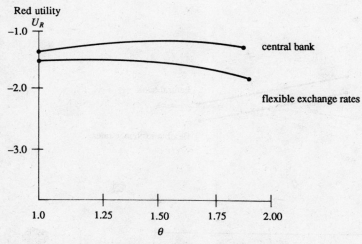

Figure 5.4 **Comparison of utilities under flexible exchange rates and a central bank**
$(\delta = 0.9, r = b = 0.5)$

national central banks arrangement is strictly dominated by the flexible
exchange rate case, we have already argued that such a regime cannot be
sustained in our model. In addition, we have proved that when the
countries agree on a common currency and a common central bank, but
retain fiscal powers, the equilibrium reduces identically to the one
characterizing flexible exchange rates. The interesting comparison is
therefore between the latter regime and the case in which, with a common

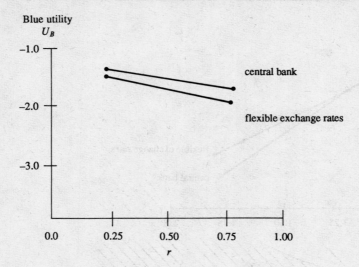

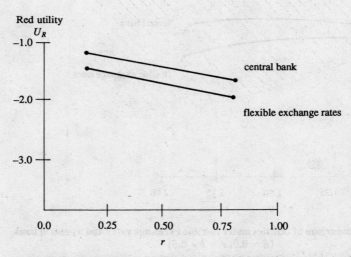

Figure 5.5   Comparison of utilities under flexible exchange rates and a central bank: dependence on need for the public good
$$(\delta = 0.9, b = 0.5, \theta = 1.0)$$

currency, the financing of the public good is entirely deferred to the common central bank.

In Figure 5.4, the welfares of the two countries under the two regimes are drawn as a function of θ, the relative endowment of Red. When θ is

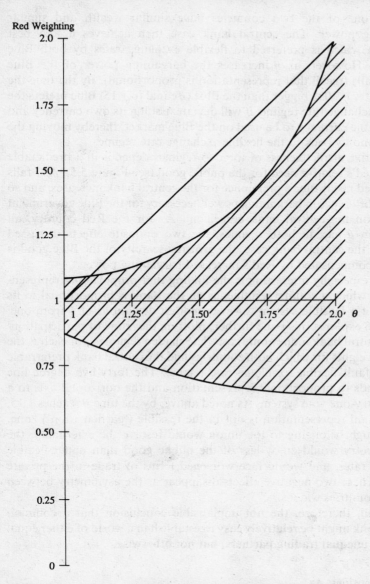

Figure 5.6   Zone of participation: central bank (money only)
$$(\delta = 0.9, \, r = b = 0.5)$$

close to one of the two countries have similar wealth and similar bargaining power. The central bank case then achieves a first best allocation which is preferred to flexible exchange rates by both Blue and Red. However, as θ increases the bargaining power of the Blue country falls (recall that representation is proportional). By the time the Red country is 30% bigger than the Blue (θ equal to 1.15) Blue prefers the flexible exchange rate regime: it will deviate, issuing its own currency and requiring the currency to be used on the Blue market, thereby moving the world economy back to the flexible exchange rate regime.

The relative attractiveness of the two regimes depends in a predictable way on Red's relative need for the public good (see Figure 5.5). As r falls (diminished need) Blue's preference for the central bank increases, and so does the difference in bargaining power necessary for the Blue government to abandon the central bank agreement. As for the Red country, an increase in θ has, in both regimes, the two opposite effects discussed above. In the central bank case, the growing scarcity of the Blue good is partially compensated by Red's increased bargaining power.

What is especially interesting is the finding that proportional representation, in which a country's influence on the Bank is proportional to its size, is not a feasible system for even modest deviations of θ from one. Figure 5.6 explores this issue further, plotting the 'zone of participation' for the central bank money only case. The shaded region is, for each θ, the range of weights for which both countries find the central bank preferrable to the default flexible exchange rate regime. The forty-five degree line corresponds to proportional representation and the horizontal axis to a one country-one vote system. As noted above, by the time θ reaches 1.15, proportional representation is not in the feasible ('participation') zone. Even though belonging to the union would resolve the externality, the small country would enjoy less of the public good than under flexible exchange rates, and would face worsened terms of trade in the private market. These two negative effects disappear as the asymmetry between the two countries widens.

We reach, therefore, the not implausible conclusion that a common central bank might be relatively easy to establish in a world of either equal or highly unequal trading partners, but not otherwise.

7   Extensions

We believe the model presented here could be usefully extended in several directions. First, we could investigate more fully the mechanism design problem facing the two countries in the creation of an 'optimal' central bank. Since the sharing of power is crucial to the willingness of countries to participate, devising an appropriate system of representation seems to be a crucial issue.

Second, the extension of our model to a multi-country world would be nontrivial. The incentives to join or abandon the union, and the choice of policy, presumably held in common by all members, towards outsiders are example of important questions that would require analysis.

Third, we can study optimal policy in a world of uncertainty. What we specifically have in mind is a situation where the Red country knows r and the Blue b, but neither country knows the other; by assumption the central bank observes neither r nor b, and must solicit each from the respective countries, designing incentives which ensure these are reported truthfully. We would guess that it will be difficult for the central bank to do better in this case than in the perfect information example we have presented.

Finally, there is a more fundamental point that needs to be addressed. While the model we built can be used to study the potential for policy coordination in different monetary regimes, it does not address an important aspect of the current European debate. Specifically, nowhere does it demonstrate (derive endogenously) a need amongst the countries for a common currency, and more generally, common institutions, such as common financial and bank laws. This problem is general and very important. Welfare improving trade between agents requires efficient communication, and this requirement becomes more crucial as the economy grows, with technology becoming more sophisticated and fields of specialization narrower. Traders who 'speak a different language' will not only suffer transactions costs, but will increasingly lose opportunities and information. Eventually, they might remain confined to a secluded, low-productivity corner of a global market. We are currently developing analyses which address these points.[11]

NOTES

We thank participants in the conference, and especially our discussants Torsten Persson and Guido Tabellini for helpful comments.
1 Simple technical assumptions can give rise to the described sequence of transactions. Suppose, for example, that each good comes in a specific variety and each consumer has specific preferences. Then a competitive market will be needed to provide optimal matching.
2 The solution presented assumes that lump-sum taxes are collected in the first period of consumers' lives. However, the result is identical if agents are taxed when old on the monetary revenues of their first-period sales. In this formulation governments are prohibited from purchasing goods on the foreign market, and of course they can only tax their own nationals.
3 For completeness, we have also solved the model for the case in which the two countries use the same currency, but this is supplied monopolistically by one of

the two. Imagine that the Red currency is needed for transactions on both markets. We write here this solution as a future reference, for comparison with results obtained later in the text. The Red government alone can print the currency, and spends it on the Red market to finance the public good. It can be proved that the Red government will never resort to direct taxation. The two instantaneous utility functions are then:

$$U_R = r\log(m_{Rt}) + 0.5\log(\theta - m_{Rt}) + \log(\theta)$$
$$- 0.5\log(2 - \theta - T_{Bt}) - \log(2\theta - m_{R(t-1)}) \qquad (1AR)$$

$$U_B = b\log(T_{Bt}) + 0.5\log(2 - \theta - T_{Bt}) + \log(\theta - m_{R(t-1)})$$
$$- 0.5\log(\theta - m_{Rt}) - \log(2\theta - m_{R(t-1)}) \qquad (1AB)$$

Maximization of $\sum_{t=0}^{\infty} \delta^t U_{Rt}$ with respect to m_{Rt} gives the condition

$$m_{Rt}^2(\delta - r - 1/2) = \theta m_{Rt}(\delta - 3r - 1) + 2\theta^2 r \qquad (2A)$$

while the Blue government will set T_{Bt} to

$$T_{Bt} = \frac{2b(2 - \theta)}{1 + 2b}$$

The welfare of the two countries can then be derived as a function of the parameters θ, δ, b and r. As a reference, for comparison with results in the text, when $r = b = 0.5$ and $\delta = 0.9$, we have for θ equal to one:

$$U_R = -1.39 \qquad U_B = -2.6$$

and for θ equal to 1.5:

$$U_R = -1.33 \qquad U_B = -3.06$$

The general result is that the Red country does better than in any other regime, while the Blue country does worse.

4 We assume no government intervention in the foreign exchange market.
5 While it is clear that a better equilibrium can be reached through coordination of financing decisions, there is no reason why we should expect this to occur automatically, or even just more easily, in a world with a unique currency. The shift to such a regime requires justifications that are outside the model presented. As usual, the simplest justification is transactions costs. Think, for example, of a scaling down of utility when consumers purchase on the foreign market, spending time and effort to understand the workings of a foreign currency system. This point is further discussed in the Extensions section of this paper. For an interesting approach to transactions costs in the context of optimum currency areas, see Mundell (in Johnson and Swoboda, 1973, Chapter 7).
6 If there are two distinct currencies, perfect substitutability requires the highly unlikely existence of fixed exchange rate regime with zero probability of revision.
7 Two points are worth mentioning. (1) While the dependence of optimal policy on the government's horizon is well-known in the literature (see Alesina and Tabellini, 1987), our model is somewhat special since it focuses on the strategic interaction between the two countries (and not between two successive national governments) when a common currency is used. This explains why our

conclusion (a myopic government inflating less than a forward-looking one) is in contradiction to previous results. Of course, it would be interesting to extend the analysis to a model taking both effects into consideration. (2) Strictly speaking, the maximization problem is not well defined for $\delta = 1$ (since the objective function is a non-converging infinite sum). We should then rewrite the problem as the maximization of a time average, which we believe would give the same result. This is a minor technical point.

8 It is presumably possible to design a tax scheme such that the two countries are taxed by the central bank on their additional printing of the common currency, and these tax revenues are then redistributed. It is crucial that each country not receive back what was withdrawn from it in taxes. In fact, in accordance with the Groves' mechanism solution to the free rider problem in public finance, it might be sensible to study an agreement in which the taxes collected from one government are distributed to the other. The tax rates would then depend on the inflation rate. We would like to develop this point further.

9 More precisely, our result is obtained by assuming that the central bank acts as a Stackelberg leader with respect to the national governments. The conclusion is sensitive to the equilibrium concept we use.

10 When θ is different from 1, the solution seems to depend on δ, but only slightly. We have simulated the model for values of δ ranging from 0.5 to 1, obtaining substantially the same result.

11 See Casella and Feinstein (1988).

REFERENCES

Alesina, Alberto and Guido Tabellini (1987). 'A Positive Theory of Fiscal Deficits and Government Debt in a Democracy', NBER Working Paper No. 2308.

Bernheim, D. and M. Whinston (1986). 'Common Agency', *Econometrica*, Vol. 54.

Casella, Alessandra and Jonathan Feinstein (1988). 'Notes on Language and Communication in a Model of Economic Development', and 'Extension to the Economy of Symbols and Confusion', mimeos.

Fischer, Stanley (1983). 'The SDR and the IMF: Toward a World Central Bank?', in *International Money and Credit: The Policy Roles*, ed. by George von Furstenberg, Washington D.C.: International Monetary Fund.

Fratianni, M. and T. Peeters (ed.) (1979). *One Money for Europe*. New York: Praeger.

Hamada, Koichi (1976). 'A Strategic Analysis of Monetary Interdependence', *Journal of Political Economy*, Vol. 84.

Helpman, Elhanan (1981). 'An Exploration in the Theory of Exchange Rate Regimes', *Journal of Political Economy*, Vol. 89.

Helpman, Elhanan and Assaf Razin (1982). 'Dynamics of a Floating Exchange Rate Regime', *Journal of Political Economy*, Vol. 90.

Johnson, Harry G. and Alexander Swoboda (ed.) (1973). *The Economics of Common Currencies*. London: George Allen and Unwin.

Kareken, John and Neil Wallace (1981). 'On the Indeterminacy of Equilibrium Exchange Rates', *Quarterly Journal of Economics*, Vol. 96.

Kehoe, Patrick (1987). 'Coordination of Fiscal Policies in a World Economy', *Journal of Monetary Economics*, Vol. 19.

Masera, R. and R. Triffin (eds.) (1984). *Europe's Money*, New York: Oxford University Press.

McKinnon, Ronald (1963). 'Optimum Currency Area', *American Economic Review*, Vol. 53.

Mundell, Robert A. (1961). 'A Theory of Optimum Currency Areas', *American Economic Review*, Vol. 51.

Salin, Pascal (ed.) (1984). *Currency Competition and Monetary Union*. The Hague: Martinus Nijhoff.

Wood, Geoffrey E. (1986). 'European Monetary Integration? A Review Essay', *Journal of Monetary Economics*, Vol. 18.

Discussion

TORSTEN PERSSON

I will devote the first part of my discussion to some general comments on methodology and on the new issues in the paper. Then I will turn to more specific comments, trying to interpret the main results and to discuss their robustness.

1   Methodology

I like this paper for its choice of modeling strategy. The authors view the relative attractiveness of alternative exchange rate arrangements, not as a partial problem of foreign exchange markets, but as a general problem of optimal macroeconomic policy design. Following that approach, they determine policies endogenously and address explicitly the sources of policy conflict. A general equilibrium model, which is admittedly simple but has appropriate microeconomic foundations, is the framework of analysis. The model is riddled with only a few distortions and non-neutralities. These features serve to highlight the role of the alternative institutions *per se*. They also allow the authors to rely on a well-specified welfare criterion when comparing the different monetary arrangements. I wish this type of methodology was much more common in the literature on alternative exchange rate systems.

2   Issues

I also like the paper for the new issues that it raises. Most of the literature focuses on monetary policy only and views fixed exchange rates as restricting the scope of policy. Here too, the regime when the common central bank has a monopoly of issuing money restricts monetary policy. But the authors show how this regime instead adds new incentives and more scope for fiscal policy. This insight, which is not common in the literature, indeed drives many of the results. Another new issue is how differences in countries' economic size help shape the incentives for and against cooperation. To analyse differences in size is interesting and highly relevant for today's debate in Europe. Most of the literature simply assumes these kinds of asymmetries away for analytical convenience.

The authors' model is very simple. Simplicity is a virtue, since it yields strong and understandable results. But it also raises questions about robustness and relevance. It is the inevitable job of the discussants to discuss such questions. To avoid repetition, I will not address the questions raised by Guido Tabellini in his discussion, but I agree with his points.

3   What is going on?

The policy conflicts that appear in the model are all due to international redistribution. Under floating rates, higher government spending on public goods in one country yields excess demand for home private goods and turns the terms of trade in the country's favour. This mechanism is well known from the trade literature. Basically, the policy equilibrium under floating is like an optimal tariff-type equilibrium with retaliation. As a result of the negative externality, there is oversupply of public goods in both countries.

In the regime with a common currency but where each country retains the right to issue money, expanding the money supply makes the foreign country bear part of the inflation tax. This leads to non-existence of equilibrium. When the countries give up the right to issue money to the common central bank, they can only control government spending (financed by lump-sum taxes). But higher government spending drives up the common inflation rate and this accentuates the oversupply of public goods relative to floating.

4   Is a common currency always worse?

We have seen that the redistribution mechanism added in the common-currency regime pulls in the same direction as the redistribution mechanism present in the floating regime. But this need not be the case. Suppose there was instead undersupply of public goods in the policy equilibrium under floating. This might happen – with a minor change in the model – if public goods would expand supply rather than demand for private goods. Or – with a major change in the model – if fiscal policy would have locomotive effects in the presence of underemployment. (Locomotive effects have indeed been frequently discussed in the European policy debate.) In either set-up, an incentive to increase government spending under a common currency would presumably be a good thing. This argument suggests that the negative results regarding the desirability of a common currency may not be robust. A more general way to pose the counterargument rests on 'the theory of the second-best': with one distortion already in place, adding another does not necessarily make things worse.

5   More on public finance

Making further reference to public finance, the model relies on one strong and unrealistic assumption: neither direct taxation nor indirect taxation via inflation imposes any excess burdens (ignoring the international externalities). Thus the 'cost of public funds' is equal to the marginal utility of private consumption. Suppose, more realistically, that both sources of revenue were distortionary. This would modify some of the strong results and raise some new issues. First, the presently undetermined combination of taxes and inflation to finance any given level of spending would be determined by the usual condition that the distortion on the last dollar of revenue be equated across tax bases. Second, the distortions associated with inflation would lead to a well-defined Nash equilibrium in the regime where individual countries can issue the common currency. Third, there would be an additional cost of a common currency. The common inflation rate would drive each country away from the combination of taxes and inflation that minimizes the overall excess burden (cf. above). Fourth, distortionary means of raising revenue would introduce well known credibility problems of optimal monetary policy, by giving incentives for surprise inflation. Among the many extensions one can always suggest, adding these public finance aspects to the analysis in the present paper seems to me both feasible and relevant.

GUIDO TABELLINI

This paper focuses on a very interesting question: namely, what are the fiscal repercussions of alternative monetary regimes? This question is both important and relatively new. It may seem surprising, but in the large literature on international policy coordination very few papers have addressed this issue, at least in a rigorous way.

In order to answer this question, the paper defines a monetary regime as a set of 'rules of the game' within which policy is chosen. Alternative regimes are then evaluated by comparing social welfare in the equilibrium corresponding to each regime.

Since the contribution of the paper is to analyse these issues within a general equilibrium model, many of my comments are on the model itself. Towards the end I suggest some more general remarks on the topic of the paper.

1   The model

The analysis is carried out by means of an overlapping generations model. The model specification implies that, in the first two monetary regimes under consideration, the policy game reduces to a repeated static game. This simplifies the analysis a lot. However, this specification is achieved at the price of some special assumptions.

Thus, even though the analysis is very competently and rigorously carried out, I think that the main points of the paper could have been derived from a simpler framework. In particular, I would have traded off less generality in the infinite-horizon structure in exchange for more simplicity and more generality in other aspects of the model. For instance, with only some minor changes, I think that the main results of the paper could be derived from the following two-period structure. In the first period, agents are born and pay taxes. They cannot store their endowment, but they can sell it (against money) to an agency of the government (or to an intermediary) who can store it. In the second period, the consumers spend their money to buy back this commodity(ies) from the government agency and consume it. The government can also bid for the good(s) with newly printed money.

In my opinion such a structure would not involve any important loss of generality compared to the overlapping generations model analysed in the paper, but it would be much simpler and more transparent. In particular, it would be easier to see that the results of the paper are driven by two key features of the economic environment. Namely: The presence of (i) a *real* international externality associated with public spending in each country; and (ii) a *nominal* international externality, that arises in some monetary regimes and not in others, and that depends on what proportion of public spending is financed by seigniorage rather than explicit taxation.

The real externality is due to a standard terms of trade effect: more domestic public spending increases the world demand for domestic output, and hence drives up its price relative to that of foreign output. As Torsten Persson has pointed out in his comments, in this respect the model is analogous to a tariff game. Since he has already discussed this aspect of the model, I limit my comments to the nominal externality.

2   The nominal externality

Under the assumptions of the model, this externality is operative only in the regimes with a common currency. In such regimes, printing money raises the price level and hence devalues the money held by foreigners. Thus, with a common currency but in the absence of full monetary cooperation, both countries have an incentive to overexpand the money supply, so as to collect some inflation tax from foreigners.

This result is very intuitive. However, I doubt that it has strong implications for the issue of regime choice, since the model specification is 'biased' in favour of the flexible rate regime, and against the common currency regime, in two respects.

First, in the flexible exchange rate regime, foreigners cannot hold domestic nominal assets (and vice versa for domestic citizens). If this restriction were relaxed, then the incentive to overinflate would also be present in the flexible exchange rate regime, and the welfare comparisons would be ambiguous.

Second, it is not clear that every kind of common currency regime would distort the monetary policy incentives in the way implied by this paper. For instance, consider a fixed exchange rate regime. There a unilateral monetary expansion would lead to patterns of redistribution between countries that depend critically on how exactly the exchange rate intervention rules are designed: thus, a fixed exchange rate regime could have an inflation bias, a deflation bias, or no bias at all, depending on the specific form of the intervention rules.

More generally, every model contains a choice of what to focus on. Here, much of the focus is on the terms of trade effect of government spending. I think that the authors are right in emphasizing the spending implications of alternative monetary policy arrangements. However, I am not sure that the terms of trade effect deserves all this emphasis, and perhaps a one-good model would not have involved a big loss of generality. Where instead there is still scope for enriching the set up is, I think, in the analysis of the monetary externality. In particular, by allowing some international portfolio choice to occur, both in the form of currency substitution and amongst interest-earning assets; and by considering alternative kinds of common currency regimes, sustained by different monetary policy and exchange rate intervention rules. If the authors plan to carry this line of research further in the future, then these would be natural extensions to consider.

3   Concluding remarks

Finally, let me mention another dimension along which to evaluate alternative international monetary regimes, that is not discussed in the paper. International agreements can provide a commitment technology. Here this issue does not appear because: (a) there is no lack of policy instruments: hence, there is no time-inconsistency of policy: and (b) the government is assumed to be a social planner; hence, there is no domestic political distortion. In general, these two conditions would be violated. In that case, international monetary policy agreements might increase government credibility, or might act as a disciplinary device to correct a political market failure. I believe that these issues play a crucial role in the current debate concerning European monetary integration, as Giavazzi, Giovannini and Pagano, amongst others, have recently argued in various papers on the EMS.

 Despite some of the critical comments raised in the previous pages, I found this an extremely interesting and thought provoking paper, that raised several novel issues in a rigorous and original way. I hope that the authors will carry this line of research further in the future.

6 The tastes of European central bankers

CARLO CARRARO

1 Introduction

In most theoretical analyses of alternative monetary regimes, it is not possible to derive clear-cut conclusions on the decision-makers' welfare under different institutional setting and 'rules of the game', without assuming knowledge of their objective functions. For example, international cooperation between two countries can be counterproductive, if some other countries do not join the cooperative agreement; a precise evaluation of the profitability of international cooperation can thus be provided only if policymakers' preferences and the structure of the economic system can accurately be estimated. Moreover, in the absence of binding agreements, international cooperation can only be sustained by the other policymakers' threat to revert to non-cooperation, if one policymaker deviates from the cooperative strategy at a given stage of the policy game. The sustainability of cooperation thus depends on the players' discount rates, on their policy targets and their preferences over these targets.

It is often argued, for example, that gains from cooperation are larger if the policymakers in the two countries have very different targets. Very different targets, however, imply a greater incentive to deviate from the cooperative strategy. A final evaluation of the sustainability of cooperation can thus be provided only after having determined the parameters of the policymakers' objective functions.

It is therefore crucial to estimate these parameters in order to understand whether international cooperation is productive and, if so, whether it can be a stable regime.

Other examples of the importance of determining the preferences of policymakers can be found in the analysis of domestic coordination of fiscal and monetary policy (e.g. Carraro, 1988), and in the comparison between different exchange-rate regimes (see Giavazzi and Giovannini, 1988).

162

This paper addresses the issue of estimating the tastes of different interacting policymakers, both from a theoretical and an empirical viewpoint.

On the theoretical side, we provide the solution of an *inverse dynamic game*, and we derive the mathematical conditions for the solution of the problem to be well-defined, i.e. for the weighting matrices of the policymakers' objective functions to be positive semidefinite. Then, from the solution of the inverse dynamic game, we derive estimation both the *ranking* over different policy targets and the *desired values* for these targets. Identifiability conditions are also provided.

On the empirical side, we first estimate a state-space form multi-country model in which eight players are supposed to interact. In each country, the central bank and the government set their instruments in order to achieve their desired values with respect to three targets: output growth, inflation and trade balance relative to GDP. Four countries are simultaneously considered: Britain, France, Germany, and Italy. We assume that the central bank and the government share the same objective function in Britain and France. The Italian and German central banks are instead supposed to be independent: they thus take the government policy as given. Nash strategies are also played by all policymakers with respect to foreign policymakers.

We determine the tastes of the central bankers under two possible regimes: in the first, central banks set the money stock and exchange rates are flexible; in the second regime, Germany sets its money stock, and the other countries set their exchange rates with respect to the Deutsche Mark.

In order to derive explicit estimators for the policymakers' preferences, we assume their objective functions to be quadratic and the model to be linear. Quarterly data from 1979: 1 to 1986: 4 are used. By using numerically simulated residuals, we will be able to compute both consistent estimates of the tastes of European central bankers, and the relative standard errors, thus making possible hypothesis testing on the estimated parameters.

With respect to previous work (e.g. Oudiz and Sachs, 1984), the main improvements are: (i) a dynamic, intertemporal, framework is explicitly considered; (ii) desired values are estimated instead of being exogenously given; (iii) policymakers' discount factors are introduced among the parameters of the objective function, and are then estimated – this is crucial information with respect to the sustainability of cooperation; (iv) standard errors of the estimated parameters are computed.

The structure of the paper is as follows: the next section outlines the scope of this research, and shows what information can be useful to evaluate the profitability and sustainability of international policy coordination.

The ambiguity of simple approaches to this problem is emphasized. Section 3 presents the econometric methodology that will be used,
in Section 4, to estimate the tastes of European central bankers. Section 3
presents the main mathematical and econometric results: more specific
issues related to the solution of an inverse dynamic optimization problem
are discussed in the Appendix. Section 4 presents the model, discusses the
main assumptions introduced to solve the game, and shows the policymakers' estimated objective functions. The (revealed) preferences of
European central bankers will then be compared and analysed. Section 5
tries to evaluate the relevance and the implications of the information
derived from the previous econometric estimates.

2   Conflicting targets and cooperation

It was argued in the introduction that knowledge of policymakers' preferences is necessary for a correct evaluation of the profitability and the
sustainability of international policy coordination. When discussing the
issue of a European central bank, the problem of policy coordination is
certainly relevant. The tasks that a European central bank must accom-
plish certainly include the coordination of countries' monetary policies.
The birth of a European central bank can thus be facilitated if coordinated policies benefit all countries, and if rules can be set such that
coordination can be sustained as an equilibrium outcome of the game
taking place among central bankers. This is why this paper aims at
computing the best possible estimates of the tastes of European central
bankers.

Before proceeding to the econometric analysis, however, we would like
to point out some ambiguities that can emerge if the information derived
from the estimation of central bankers' preferences is not carefully uti-
lized. A couple of examples are now proposed, thus postponing the
general analysis to the next sections.

Let us suppose that an N-player non-cooperative, one-stage static game
describes the interactions among the European central bankers and the
constraints they face. Suppose that: (i) a Nash equilibrium of this game
exists; (ii) the Nash outcome is not Pareto optimal. Cooperative strategies
can therefore benefit all players, if all players cooperate. However, each
player has an incentive to deviate from cooperation, whenever the other
players cooperate. Cooperative strategies are therefore unstable, i.e. they
are not equilibrium strategies.

Suppose now that the game is repeated T times. Then, under suitable
conditions, there exist equilibrium (trigger) strategies that can sustain the
cooperative outcome at (almost) all stages of the game.[1] If T is infinite,

then a sufficient condition for cooperation to be the equilibrium outcome
at all stages of the game is (see Friedman, 1971):

$$\beta_i \geq (P^{d_i} - P^{c_i})/(P^{d_i} - P^{o_i}) \quad i = 1 \ldots N \tag{1}$$

where P_i denotes player i's payoff function, P^{o_i} is player i's Nash payoff,
P^{c_i} is the payoff in the presence of cooperation, and P^{d_i} is player i's best
payoff when he deviates from cooperation, whereas the other players do
cooperate; β_i is player i's discount factor.

Equation (1) can also be written as:

$$1 \geq \beta_i \geq ID_i/(ID_i + GC_i) \equiv \mu_i \quad i = 1 \ldots N \tag{2}$$

where $ID_i = P^{d_i} - P^{c_i} \geq 0$ is player i's Incentive to Deviate from cooperation, and $GC_i = P^{c_i} - P^{o_i} \geq 0$ is player i's Gain from Cooperation
(relatively to the Nash payoff).

Notice that coordinated policies benefit all players if GC_i is positive for
all $i = 1 \ldots N$, and can be sustained as an equilibrium of the repeated
game if (2) is satisfied for all $i = 1 \ldots N$. It is thus important to derive the
relationship between (2) and players' preferences.

The question to be answered is the following: are conditions (2) more
easily satisfied when players' preferences become more similar, i.e. when
desired values, or/and weights assigned to policy targets, are closer?

If the answer were positive, this paper could provide precise information
on the incentive to establish a European central bank. We show however
that the answer is ambiguous, and that a deeper analysis is needed.

It is often argued that both the incentive to deviate from cooperation ID_i,
and the benefit from cooperation GC_i become smaller when players'
preferences get closer.[2] In this section, it is argued that this is not always
true, and that, even when both ID_i and GC_i decrease as preferences get
closer, more similar tastes do not always mean easier cooperation, i.e.
conditions (2) may not be more easily satisfied.

Let us consider first the second part of this proposition. We can re-phrase
it in the following way:

Proposition 1: *If both the incentive to deviate and the gain from cooperation
become smaller when players' preferences get closer, and the discount factor
does not change, cooperation can more easily be sustained if and only if the
relative change of the incentive to deviate is larger (in absolute value) than
the relative change of the gain from cooperation.*

Proof. For the sake of simplicity, we consider only two players (e.g. two
central bankers). Let the preferences of the first player be described by a
vector θ that contains both weights and desired values. The second player
(starred) has preferences θ^*. Let $\beta \geq \mu \equiv ID/(ID + GC)$ and
$\beta^* \geq \mu^* \equiv ID^*/(ID^* + GC^*)$ be the two sufficient conditions for the

sustainability of the cooperative outcome. If discount factors are fixed, cooperation becomes more likely if μ and μ^* decrease as preferences get closer. Differentiating μ, with respect to $\theta - \theta^*$, we get:

$$\partial\mu/\partial(\theta - \theta^*) = [GC(\partial ID/\partial(\theta - \theta^*)) \\ - ID(\partial GC/\partial(\theta - \theta^*))]/(ID + GC)^2 \qquad (3)$$

If both ID and GC decrease as θ and θ^* get closer, then $GC(\partial ID/\partial(\theta - \theta^*)) \geq 0$ and $ID(\partial GC/\partial(\theta - \theta^*)) \geq 0$. The global effect on μ is therefore ambiguous. It is easy to see that the right hand side of (3) is positive, i.e. μ decreases as $\theta - \theta^*$ is smaller, if:

$$(\partial ID/\partial(\theta - \theta^*))/ID > (\partial GC/\partial(\theta - \theta^*))/GC \qquad (4)$$

that is, if the relative change of the incentive to deviate is larger than the relative change of the gain from cooperation. A similar result holds for μ^*, thus proving the proposition.

It is not possible to provide general conditions for (4) to be satisfied. In general, it will depend on the form of the player's payoff function and on the value of its parameters before the change of preferences.

However, in order to provide some geometric examples of the effect that closer preferences have on the sustainability of cooperation, we re-write μ as $\mu = 1/(1 + GC/ID)$. Hence $\partial\mu/\partial(GC/ID) < 0$. Furthermore, we can write:

$$\partial\mu/\partial(\theta - \theta^*) = [\partial\mu/\partial(GC/ID)][\partial(GC/ID)/\partial(\theta - \theta^*)]$$

Therefore, μ decreases as $\theta - \theta^*$ becomes smaller, if GC/ID increases as preferences get closer. This is just another way of interpreting Proposition 1.

This simple result can be used to provide some counterexamples to the intuition that similar preferences make cooperation easier. Consider first Figure 6.1 in which players' preferences are circular. Players' decision variable are, respectively, m and m^* (e.g. the money stocks). A and A^* denote players' bliss points before preferences change; B and B^* are bliss points after the change. Notice that different bliss points do not necessarily mean that the parameters of the two players' payoff functions are different. However, we assume that the difference between bliss points is also due to different tastes. C_1 denotes the cooperative equilibrium before, and C_2 after, the change of preferences. The distances $N_i E_i$, and $N_i E_i^*$, $i = 1, 2$, represent gains from cooperation; $E_i D_i$, and $E_i^* D_i^*$, $i = 1, 2$, represent incentives to deviate. Suppose the change of preferences is such that bliss points get closer, but preferences remain circular (only desired values change). The figure shows that the gain from cooperation and the incentive to deviate decrease for both players. However, the ratio

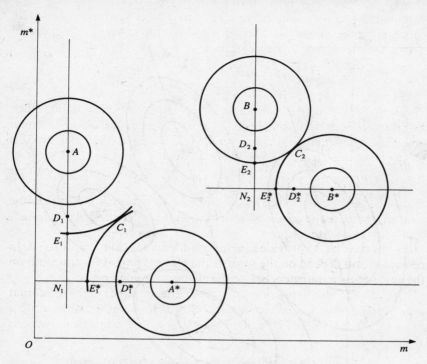

Figure 6.1   The sustainability of cooperation (circular preferences)

GC^*/ID^* grows as we move from the game represented on the left to the game represented on the right, i.e. as preferences get closer. The starred player is therefore more likely to sustain cooperation (low discounting is less crucial). In contrast, the ratio GC/ID decreases, so that cooperation becomes more difficult for the other player. It is thus impossible to conclude that closer preferences make cooperation easier.

   Another example is represented in Figure 6.2. Preferences are still quadratic, but a change of his own instrument affects player i's payoff more than change of the other player's instrument. This is consistent with the normal form of most international policy games (e.g. Sachs, 1983; Cooper, 1985). We still assume that the change of preferences is such that the two bliss points get closer and that indifference curves do not change. By measuring on the player's reaction function the distance between N, E, and D before and after the change of preferences, it is possible to see that GC/ID is equal to GC^*/ID^* before the change occurs. After the change of preferences, both ratios decrease, thus making cooperation more difficult to sustain (lower discount rates become necessary). Furthermore, GC/ID

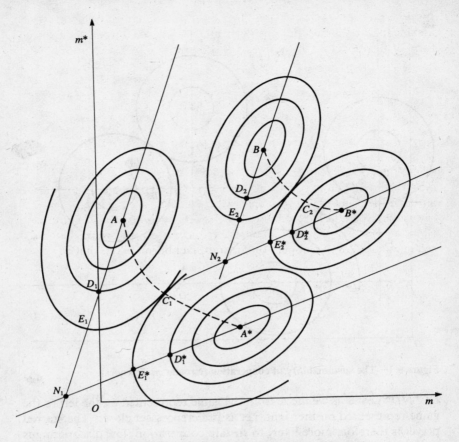

Figure 6.2   The sustainability of cooperation (elliptical preferences)

decreases more than GC^*/ID^*. The first player is thus more likely to deviate from cooperation. This second example shows that more similar preferences can be counterproductive, if discount factors do not increase accordingly.

We now turn to the second proposition, that is:

Proposition 2: *The distance between player's bliss points can increase when their preferences become more similar. Hence, closer preferences can imply a larger incentive to deviate and a larger gain from cooperation.*

Proof. To prove this proposition we simply need an example. Suppose the world economy is described by the two-country model analysed by Henderson and Canzoneri (1987) and discussed in Giavazzi and Giovannini (1988) and Carraro and Giavazzi (1988). The two countries are supposed to be symmetric: only their preferences may be different. If we assume that foreign output positively affects national output, the reduced form of the model is the following (see Carraro and Giavazzi, 1988):

$$y = (\alpha - 1)(w - m) + \epsilon y^* \qquad \epsilon < 1, \quad \alpha < 1$$

$$y^* = (\alpha - 1)(w^* - m^*) + \epsilon y$$

$$q = \alpha m + (1 - \alpha)w + \theta[(m - m^*) - (w - w^*)]$$

$$q^* = \alpha m^* + (1 - \alpha)w^* + \theta[(m^* - m) - (w^* - w)]$$

where y denotes (the log of) output, q is (the log of) consumer price index, m is (the log of) money stock and w is (the log of) nominal wage. Starred variables denote foreign variables. All parameters are positive.

In order to simplify the analysis we suppose nominal wages are fixed ($w = \log W = 0$). We thus obtain the reduced form of the model analysed in Sachs (1983), Cooper (1985), and Blackburn (1987), that is:

$$y = a_1 m + a_2 m^*$$

$$a_1 = (1 - a)/(1 - \epsilon^2) > a_2 = \epsilon(1 - \alpha)/(1 - \epsilon^2)$$

$$y^* = a_1 m^* + a_2 m$$

$$q = b_1 m - b_2 m^* \qquad b_1 = (\alpha + \theta) > b_2 = \theta$$

$$q^* = b_1 m^* - b_2 m$$

Suppose the two central banks have the following quadratic objective functions:

$$p = - \sigma(y - k)^2 - (q - h)^2$$

$$p^* = - \sigma^*(y^* - k^*)^2 - (q^* - h^*)^2$$

where $\sigma \neq \sigma^*$, $k \neq k^*$ and $h \neq h^*$.

Let us compute the players' bliss points. For the home country, we have:

$$m = (b_2 k + a_2 h)/\tau \qquad m^* = (b_1 k - a_1 h)/\tau$$

where $\tau = b_1 a_2 + a_1 b_2$. The foreign country's bliss point is:

$$m = (b_1 k^* - a_1 h^*)/\tau \qquad m^* = (b_2 k^* + a_2 h^*)/\tau$$

The geometric distance between the two bliss points is given by:

$$d_1 = \sqrt{[(x + z)^2 + (x + w)^2]}$$

where

$$x = (1/\tau)[(b_2 - b_1)k + (a_1 + a_2)h]$$

$$z = (1/\tau)[b_1(k - k^*) + a_1(h^* - h)]$$
$$w = (1/\tau)[- b_2(k - k^*) + a_2(h^* - h)]$$

Suppose now that the foreign central bank changes its preferences in such a way that $k^* = k$ and $h^* = h$. Countries have now the same preferences. Then, the distance between the two players' bliss points becomes:

$$d_2 = x\sqrt{2}$$

Is d_2 small than d_1? There is no unambiguous answer to this question, and we can have $d_2 > d_2$, i.e. closer preferences increase the distance between bliss points, thus increasing both the gain from cooperation and the incentive to deviate. A simple example is the case in which, before the change of preferences, we have $h = h^* = 0$, and $k < k^*$. Then $|z| - |w| = (1/\tau)(b_1 - b_2)(k - k^*) < 0$ and $d_2 > d_1$. This proves the proposition.

The two propositions that we have just proved aim at clarifying the meaning of the results presented in the next sections. We have shown that the information provided by the knowledge of central bankers' preferences does not necessarily provide precise indications on the possibility that cooperative outcomes be sustained by players' strategies. Closer preferences do not necessarily imply either a lower conflict among countries, or larger gains from cooperation, or a greater incentive to sustain cooperative policies. What we need is therefore a two-stage analysis. In the first stage, central bankers' preferences must be estimated and tested. In the second stage, using the estimated preferences, the game among central bankers must explicitly be solved, in order to compute the actual gains from cooperation and the incentives to deviate. This paper solves the first stage problems, and estimates the tastes of central bankers. The second stage analysis will be provided in a sequel.

Notice, however, that one unambiguous piece of information is provided. As previously stated, we estimate central bankers' discount factors. This is one of the crucial variables determining the sustainability of coordinated outcomes (see the left hand side of equation (2)). If the discount factor is low (i.e. the discount rate is high), players are revealed to be myopic, and coordination is not likely to be achieved. The emergence of international institutions, such as a European central bank, thus heavily depends on the farsightedness of all policymakers involved in the unification process.

In the next section, we present the theoretical framework that is used to estimate the tastes of European central bankers. Since the game will be assumed to be dynamic, the previous analysis can be used as a logical guideline. Its message remains indeed unchanged, even if the mathematics becomes much more complicated (see Currie and Levine, 1987; Backus and Driffill, 1987; and Dockner and Neck, 1987).

3   An inverse dynamic Nash game

Let us first present the structure of the dynamic game that is assumed to describe the behaviour of the government and of the central bank of N interacting countries.

The multi-country economic system is represented by the following state space model:

$$y_t = Az_{t-1} + \sum_{i=1}^{N} \sum_{j=M,F} B_{ij}x_{ijt} + Cw_t + b + u_t \tag{5}$$

$$y_{it} = H_i z_t \qquad i = 1 \dots N; \; j = M, F \tag{6}$$

where z_t is the $(n \times 1)$ state vector at time t that contains all variables that are necessary to define the starting point of the dynamic evolution from one period to another (the state vector is also called the memory of the system in engineering). The $(k_j \times 1)$ vector x_{ijt} denotes player j's policy instruments in country i at time t. Players can be the monetary authority (denoted by M) and the fiscal authority (denoted by F). The number of instruments does not depend on the player's country. The $(h \times 1)$ vector w_t denotes exogenous variables that affect the economic system, whereas b is an $(n \times 1)$ vector of constants and u_t is an $(n \times 1)$ vector of random disturbances that we assume to be independently and identically distributed with zero mean and variance equal to Ω. $A, B_{ij}, i = 1 \dots N, J = M, F$, and C are matrices of constant parameters. The $(m_i \times 1)$ vector y_{it} denotes the policy targets in country i. We assume that the government and the central bank of a given country have the same policy targets, even if they may have different desired values for these targets. The relationship between policy targets and state variables is provide by the matrix $H_i, i = 1 \dots N$.

Each policymaker's objective (loss) function is described by the following equation:

$$V_{ij} = E\left\{ \sum_{t=1}^{T} (\beta_{ij})^{t-1}[(y_{it} - a_{ij})' K_{ij}(y_{it} - a_{ij}) + x'_{ijt}Q_{ij}x_{ijt}] \right\}$$

$$= E\left\{ \sum_{t=1}^{T} (\beta_{ij})^{t-1}[(z_t - \alpha_{ij})' \Phi_{ij}(z_t - \alpha_{ij}) + x'_{ijt}Q_{ij}x_{ijt}] \right\}$$

$$i = 1 \dots N; \quad j = M, F \tag{7}$$

where $a_{ij} = H_i \alpha_{ij}$ and $\Phi_{ij} = H_i' K_{ij} H_i$. Furthermore, T denotes the policy horizon, β_{ij} is the discount factor and a_{ij} is the vector of desired values for the target variables contained in y_{it}. Because this vector is assumed to be time-invariant, target variables must be expressed as rates of change or ratios, and no change of regime is allowed for. The matrix K_{ij} represents the policymaker's preferences over different policy targets. These preferences are also assumed to be time invariant (at least in the sample period).[3] The matrix Q_{ij} represents the cost of changing the value of policy instruments. We assume that policy variables can also be expressed as rates of change or ratios. Both K_{ij} and Q_{ij} are positive semidefinite, that is each policymaker aims at minimizing the (loss) function (7).

Furthermore, we assume the $(n \times 1)$ vector z_0, that denotes the starting value for the dynamic system, to be given.

The 'rules of the game' are the following. Each policymaker minimizes the intertemporal loss function (7) with respect to his own policy variables, given the dynamics of the system and the policy strategy of the other policymakers. The solution of this problem is computed by backward recursion, i.e. the resulting equilibrium is subgame perfect. This equilibrium of the dynamic game is known as feedback Nash equilibrium.

It has been shown by Tu and Papavasillopoulos (1985) that the linear-quadratic framework of the game allows us to introduce the certainty equivalence principle for computing the optimal feedback rule. Hence, the optimal policy strategy adopted by each policymaker is defined by:

$$x_{ijt} = G_{ij} z_{t-1} + g_{ij} \qquad i = 1 \ldots N; \quad j = M, F \tag{8}$$

where we have assumed T large enough to ensure the convergence of the feedback matrices G_{ijt} and g_{ijt} to constant matrices G_{ij} and g_{ij} (see Chow, 1975; Carraro, 1985a).

The matrices G_{ij} and g_{ij} that solve the feedback Nash optimization problem are defined by the following equations (Kydland, 1975; Chow, 1981; Murata, 1982):[4]

$$(Q_{ij} + B_{ij}' S_{ij} B_{ij}) G_{ij} = - B_{ij}' S_{ij} (A + B_{ih} G_{ij} +$$

$$\sum_{s=1}^{N} \sum_{q=M,F} B_{sq} G_{sq} \Bigg) \tag{9}$$

$$j, h = M, F \qquad h \neq j; \qquad i, s = 1 \ldots N, \quad s \neq i$$

$$S_{ij} = \Phi_{ij} + \beta_{ij} (P' S_{ij} P + G_{ij}' Q_{ij} G_{ij}) \tag{10}$$

$$P = A + \sum_{i=1}^{N} \sum_{j=M,F} B_{ij} G_{ij} \tag{11}$$

$$Q_{ij} g_{ij} + B'_{ij} S_{ij} p = B'_{ij} s_{ij} \tag{12}$$

$$p = b + \sum_{i=1}^{N} \sum_{j=M,F} B_{ij} g_{ij} \tag{13}$$

$$s_{ij} - \Phi_{ij} \alpha_{ij} = \beta_{ij} P' \left(s_{ij} - S_{ij}(b + B_{ih} g_{ih} + \sum_{s=1}^{N} \sum_{q=M,F} B_{sq} g_{sq} \right) \tag{14}$$

$$j, h = M, F \qquad j \neq h; \qquad i, s = 1 \dots N, \quad i \neq s$$

where all equations hold for $i = 1 \dots N$ and $j = M, F$.

This is the feedback Nash solution of the dynamic game.

The inverse game, in contrast, aims at determining positive semidefinite matrices K_{ij} and Q_{ij}, and vectors a_{ij}, given the dynamics of the system (5), (6) and the optimal feedback rules (8). We now derive the equations which determine K_{ij}, Q_{ij} and a_{ij}. The conditions for K_{ij} and Q_{ij} to be symmetric and positive semidefinite are discussed in the Appendix.

In order to compute K_{ij} and Q_{ij}, we re-write (9) as

$$B'_{ij} S_{ij} P = - Q_{ij} G_{ij}$$

By vectorizing this matrix equation and (10), we have:

$$(P' \otimes B'_{ij}) \operatorname{vec}(S_{ij}) = - (G'_i \otimes I) \operatorname{vec}(Q_{ij}) \tag{15}$$

$$[I - \beta_{ij}(P' \otimes P')] \operatorname{vec}(S_{ij})$$
$$= \operatorname{vec}(\Phi_{ij}) + \beta_{ij}(G'_{ij} \otimes G'_{ij}) \operatorname{vec}(Q_{ij}) \tag{16}$$

Let k^*_{ij} be a vector that contains the unknown elements of the matrices K_{ij} and Q_{ij}, and let θ_{ij} be a known selection matrix which maps the elements of k^*_{ij} into the corresponding elements of Φ_{ij} and Q_{ij}, that is $\theta_{ij} k^*_{ij} = [\operatorname{vec}(\Phi_{ij})' \operatorname{vec}(Q_{ij})']'$. Then, solving (16) with respect to $\operatorname{vec}(S_{ij})$ and assuming the invertibility of $[I - \beta_{ij}(P' \otimes P')]$, we have:

$$[R_{ij} | (\beta_{ij} R_{ij}(G'_{ij} \otimes G'_{ij}) + (G'_{ij} \otimes I))] \theta_{ij} k^*_{ij} = 0 \tag{17}$$

where

$$R_{ij} = (P' \otimes B'_{ij})[I - \beta_{ij}(P' \otimes P')]^{-1}$$

By solving this system, we obtain the values of the weighting matrices K_{ij} and Q_{ij}. However, the system is homogeneous, so that we can only estimate the relative weight that each policymaker assigns to his targets.

Furthermore, if we consider the discount factor β_{ij} among the parameters to be estimated, the matrix equation described by (17) becomes highly non-linear, and cannot explicitly be solved with respect to β_{ij} and k_{ij}^{**}, where $k_{ij}^{**} \equiv (k_{ij2}^*/k_{ij1}^* \ldots k_{ijq}^*/k_{ij1}^*)$, $q = m_i(m_i + 1)/2 + k_j(k_j + 1)/2$, and where the policymaker's preferences have been normalized with respect to the first element of the vector k_{ij}^*.

Let us therefore fix β_{ij} equal to a given initial value β_{ij}^*. Denoting the first column of the matrix

$$D_{ij}^* = [R_{ij} | (\beta_{ij}^* R_{ij}(G_{ij}' \otimes G_{ij}') + (G_{ij}' \otimes I))] \, \theta_{ij}$$

by d_{ij} and the remaining columns by D_{ij}, we can write (17) as:

$$d_{ij} + D_{ij} k_{ij}^{**} = 0 \tag{18}$$

The policymaker's relative preferences over his policy targets are therefore determined by the following equation:

$$k_{ij}^{**} = - (D'_{ij} D_{ij})^{-1} D'_{ij} d_{ij} \qquad i = 1 \ldots N; \quad j = M, F \tag{19}$$

where the identification condition is that the columns of D_{ij} must be linearly independent. The order condition is

$$nk_j \geq m_i(m_i + 1)/2 + k_j(k_j + 1)/2 - 1,$$
$$i = 1 \ldots N; \quad j = M, F$$

The vector a_{ij} that contains the policymaker's desired values can be obtained in the following way. First, we compute Φ_{ij} from the value of K_{ij} obtained from (19) (assuming $k_{ij1}^* = 1$), and S_{ij} from equation (17). Then, using (14) to solve for s_{ij} and substituting into (12), we have:

$$B_{ij}'(I - \beta_{ij}^* P')^{-1} \Phi_{ij} \alpha_{ij} = \delta_{ij} \tag{20}$$

where $\delta_{ij} = Q_{ij} g_{ij} + B_{ij}'[\beta_{ij}^*(I - \beta_{ij}^* P')^{-1} P' S_{ij}(p - B_{ij} g_{ij}) + S_{ij} p]$.

Let Γ_{ij} be a known selection matrix that maps the unknown elements of a_{ij} into α_{ij}, that is $\Gamma_{ij} a_{ij} = \alpha_{ij}$. Denoting the matrix $B_{ij}'(I - \beta_{ij}^* P')^{-1} \Phi_{ij} \Gamma_{ij}$ by π_{ij}, the desired values for the policy targets that the policymaker tries to achieve are:

$$a_{ij} = (\pi_{ij}' \pi_{ij})^{-1} \pi_{ij}' \delta_{ij} \qquad i = 1 \ldots N; \quad j = M, F \tag{20}$$

where the identification condition is that the columns of the $(k_j \times m_i)$ matrix π_{ij} be linearly independent. Notice that a necessary condition is $k_j \geq m_i$, i.e. the number of instruments used by player j must be greater or equal than the number of targets that he tries to achieve (this order condition coincides with Tinbergen's rule).

The next step is to compute a revised estimate of the discount factor β_{ij}.

Solving (14) with respect to $\beta_{ij}(S_{ij}p - s_{ij})$ and substituting this value into (13), we get:

$$B'_{ij}(P')^{-1}(\Phi_{ij}\alpha_{ij} - s_{ij}) + \beta_{ij}B'_{ij}S_{ij}B_{ij}g_{ij} = -\beta_{ij}Q_{ij}g_{ij} \qquad (22)$$

From (10) we obtain $\Phi_{ij} = S_{ij} - \beta_{ij}(P' S_{ij} P + G'_{ij} Q_{ij} G_{ij})$. Substituting this expression into (20) and using (9), yields:

$$\beta_{ij}[(I - (G_{ij}P^{-1}B_{ij})')Q_{ij}G_{ij}\alpha_{ij} \\ + (Q_{ij} + B'_{ij}S_{ij}B_{ij})g_{ij}] = (P^{-1}B_{ij})'(s_{ij} - S_{ij}\alpha_{ij}) \qquad (23)$$

If we re-write this system of linear equations as $\beta_{ij}\phi_{ij} = \sigma_{ij}$ (identities are obvious), we can revise the prior value of β_{ij} by using the following estimator:

$$\beta^*_{ij} = \left(\sum_{h=1}^{k_j} \sigma_{ijh}\right) \Big/ \left(\sum_{h=1}^{k_j} \phi_{ijh}\right) \qquad (24)$$

Given this new value of β_{ij}, new estimates of K_{ij}, Q_{ij}, and a_{ij} can be obtained by using (19). This algorithm must be iterated until convergence. Using standard results on two-stage regressions (e.g. Magnus, 1978), the resulting estimates can be shown to be consistent. The matrices containing the estimates of the policymaker's preferences are also positive semidefinite, if the conditions provided in the Appendix are satisfied.

From the above solution of the inverse dynamic game, we can thus derive the following two-stage econometric algorithm, which allows us to compute consistent estimates of the parameters of the policymakers' objective function:

Step 1: obtain consistent estimates of the matrices A, B_{ij}, b, G_{ij}, g_{ij}, $i = 1 \ldots N$, $j = M, F$; the appropriate technique can be OLS if the state space system is derived from the estimation of a reduced form model (see Preston and Wall, 1973; Sarris, 1973) or a system identification technique if the state space system is estimated directly (see Aoki, 1987);

Step 2: use (19), (21) and (24) to obtain consistent estimates of the parameters which define the policymaker's preferences. Because the restrictions, provided in the Appendix, for the policymaker's estimated loss function to be convex, cannot easily be imposed, an inequality constrained estimator can be used to estimate K_{ij}, Q_{ij}, β_{ij}, $i = 1 \ldots N$, $j = M, F$. In this case, consistency of the estimates can be shown by combining Magnus's (1978) results with those provided in Liew (1976).[5]

A further problem concerns the non-linearity of the estimators defined by (19), (21) and (24) with respect to the matrices estimated in the first step of the algorithm. It is thus impossible to derive the covariance matrix of the estimated preferences from the error covariance matrix of A, B_{ij}, b, G_{ij},

g_{ij}, $i = 1 \ldots N$, $j = M$, F. In order to solve this problem we propose to use the bootstrap method. We thus add the following step:

Step 3: compute the residuals from the estimation of the dynamic system (5), (6), and use these residuals to estimate the empirical distribution function of u_t. Then, generate numerically simulated random variables u_t^*, $t = 1 \ldots T$, according to the estimated distribution function. Simulated residuals are then used to obtain a new simulated vector y_{it}^*, $i = 1 \ldots N$, $t = 1 \ldots T$. This allows us to compute new estimates of A, B_{ij}, b, G_{ij}, g_{ij}, $i = 1 \ldots N$, $j = M$, F (step 1), from which new values of K_{ij}, Q_{ij}, β_{ij} and a_{ij} can be determined (step 2). Then iterate these three steps.

After NR replications of this algorithm, we approximate the distribution of the nonlinear estimator of K_{ij}, Q_{ij}, β_{ij} and a_{ij} with the empirical distribution function of the NR estimates obtained by using the bootstrap method. We thus have consistent estimates of the policymaker's preferences and a numerically simulated covariance matrix for these estimates. Standard errors for the parameters defining policymaker's tastes can thus be computed and hypothesis testing can be performed.

4   Estimation and testing of central bankers' preferences

In order to apply the methodology presented in the previous section, we need a careful specification of the economic model and an appropriate selection of target and policy variables. Model selection procedures are however constrained by the limited number of observations required to make the assumption of constant preferences plausible. We therefore used a number of *a priori* assumptions on the structure of the economic model. Furthermore, other crucial assumptions are related to the possibility of solving the inverse dynamic game, the identification conditions previously derived, and the positive semidefiniteness of the weighting matrices. The list is the following:

(i) we assume policymakers' preferences to be time-invariant in the period 1979:1–1986:4. This (sample) period is characterized by the introduction of EMS and by a certain consistency of all countries' economic policy over time.[6]

(ii) only four countries have been considered: Britain, France, Germany, and Italy. Interactions among these four countries are assumed to capture the relevant dynamics of the European economic system;

(iii) in each country only two decision-makers are taken into account: the government and the central bank. The behaviour of the other players is assumed to be represented by the dynamics of the system (5), (6). This is equivalent to saying that the government and the central bank act as Stackelberg leaders in their own country. All time-inconsistency problems inside the country are assumed to be ruled out by the existence of some reputation mechanism;

(iv) all governments and central banks are assumed to play feedback Nash strategies with respect to decision-makers in different countries. Hence, international policy coordination is asssumed not to have taken place in the sample period. The central banks in Britain and France are not supposed to be independent decision-makers. The government and the central bank in these two countries are thus assumed to share the same objective function, and are aggregated into one player. In contrast, the central banks in Germany and Italy are assumed to be independent players, and to play Nash strategies also with respect to their respective governments;

(v) each government controls two policy instruments: national public expenditure and tax revenue (relatively to GDP). Each central bank controls the national money stock (or the exchange rate) and the structure of interest rates (defined by a weighted average of interest rates in each country). Whenever control variables cannot directly be controlled by the relative policymaker, we assume that there exist intermediate targets that can appropriately be controlled. In each country, the targets that are assumed to be pursued by the two national decision-makers are: output growth, inflation and the trade balance.[7] All players can have different desired values for these targets;

(vi) two regimes have been analysed. In the first one, all central banks control the money stock and exchange-rates are floating. In the second regime, exchange-rates are managed, i.e. the German central bank controls its money stock, whereas the other central banks control their exchange-rate vis-à-vis the Deutsche Mark;

(vii) all policymakers are assumed to discount the future at a constant discount rate. Different players can have different discount rates;

(viii) the structure of the economic system is adequately captured by a linear state space model in which no restriction has been imposed on the interactions among different countries. This is to say that no structural model has been estimated. Economic theory enters into the model only through the selection of the set of economic variables, and through the partition of this set into target and policy variables.[8] Unobservable variables (e.g. expectations) have been solved with respect to observables and have then been substituted into the dynamic system;

(ix) policymakers' preferences can be adequately described by a quadratic function of the distance between the actual values of the policy targets and the policymaker's desired values; the quadratic loss function can be considered as a local approximation to the true objective function of the policymaker (see Rustem *et al*. 1978). Under this interpretation, the policymaker's revealed preferences must be considered as local preferences over the feasible values of his targets. Feasibility is defined by the constraints provided by the dynamic economic systems, and by the other policymakers' decisions. Therefore, the policymaker's estimated trade-offs (the vector k_{ij}^{**} of the previous section) represent local rates of substitution between targets;

(x) cross-preferences among different target variables or control variables are ruled out. This is equivalent to assuming that, if two targets (e.g. output and inflation) move simultaneously towards the policymaker's desired values, the change of welfare is the sum of the two changes of welfare induced by the independent changes of the target variables. Formally, this implies that the matrices K_{ij} and Q_{ij} are diagonal. This assumption gives us clearer conclusions on the ranking among targets, and allows us to use the inequality constrained estimator technique (see below);

(xi) as the order condition $(k_j \geq m_i)$ for the identification of the vector of desired values is not satisfied for the Italian and German central banks and governments (each has two instruments and three targets), we assume the second element of the vector a_{iM}, i = Italy and Germany, and the third element of the vector a_{iG}, i = Italy and Germany, equal to zero. In other words, we assume that central banks aim at achieving zero inflation, whereas the respective governments aim at achieving an equilibrium trade balance. A similar assumption is not necessary for Britain and France, because we have aggregated the central bank and the government. The British and French aggregated policymakers thus have four instruments and three targets.

(xii) for the sake of increasing the efficiency of our estimates, we also assume that all policymakers can freely move their policy instruments. Hence, all matrices Q_{ij} have been set to zero.

(xiii) finally, all policymakers are assumed to share the same view of the world (they all model interdependencies in the same way), and to use the same data set and estimation method. In other words, there is common knowledge with respect to the estimated system dynamics and all actual policy decisions;

Given the above assumptions, we estimated (5) and (6) by using an OLS technique and the state space form proposed by Sarris (1973) (see Carraro, 1985a). Matrix H_i, $i = 1 \ldots N$, in (6), is a known selection matrix, and was not estimated. Quarterly data from 1979:1 to 1986:4 were used. The vector y_{it} contains the annual per cent rate of change of real gross domestic product, the annual per cent rate of change of the consumer price index, and the ratio between annual trade balance and gross domestic product. In the first regime, the monetary instruments are the annual per cent rate of change of money stock ($M1$), and a weighted average of national interest rates (both as intermediate targets). In the second regime, the money stock is replaced by the national exchange rate with respect to the Deutsche mark, if the country is Britain, France, or Italy; if the country is Germany, monetary instruments remain unchanged. Fiscal instruments are the ratio between annual public expenditure and GDP, and the ratio between annual tax revenue and GDP.

After having estimated the matrices A, B_{ij}, b, G_{ij}, g_{ij}, $i = 1 \ldots N$, $j = M, F$, we used (19) and (21) to estimate each policymaker's preferences, and (24) to estimate the relative discount factors. Because the positive semidefiniteness restrictions described in the Appendix could not be imposed during the first step of the estimation algorithm, we assumed the matrices K_{ij} and Q_{ij} to be diagonal. This implies that the positive semidefiniteness of K_{ij} and Q_{ij} can be written as $(K_{ij})_{hh} \geq 0$ and $(Q_{ij})_{ss} \geq 0$, $h = 1, \ldots m_i$, $s = 1 \ldots k_j$, where $(K_{ij})_{hh}$ and $(Q_{ij})_{ss}$ denote diagonal elements of K_{ij} and Q_{ij} respectively. The inequality constrained least squares estimator proposed by Liew (1976) can thus be applied to (18), instead of the estimator (19). In this way, the resulting values of K_{ij} and Q_{ij} are all non-negative. A similar procedure has been used to impose the restriction that β_{ij} must be greater than zero and less than one. No restriction has obviously been imposed on the estimation of the policymaker's desired values.

We iterated this algorithm 30 times, by using numerically generated residuals to obtain new values of y_{it}, $t = 1 \ldots T$, $i = 1 \ldots N$ (see Section 3). We could thus compute a numerically simulated covariance matrix for the estimated policymaker's preferences.[9]

The results obtained from these computations are presented in Tables 6.1–6.10. Numbers between brackets denote standard errors. A star indicates parameters significantly different from zero at the 5% significance level. Moreover, dy denotes output growth, dp denotes inflation, and tb denotes the ratio between trade balance and GDP. Desired values for dy and dp are expressed as per cent annual rates of change. Desired values for db are expressed as one thousand times the desired ratio between annual trade balance and GDP. Policymakers' preferences have been normalized as discussed in Section 3: the weight assigned to the output target has thus been constrained to be one. In other words, the estimated value for the policymaker's ranking over his targets represents the ratio between the weight assigned to a given target and the weight assigned to output growth.

Table 6.1 shows the mean historical values of the policy target variables in the sample period and their standard errors. These values are reported

	Output growth	Inflation	Relative trade balance
Britain	1.92	9.77	− 1.73
	(4.04)	(5.82)	(1.81)
France	2.32	9.38*	− 0.83
	(1.54)	(3.28)	(0.79)
Germany	2.15	3.53	2.40*
	(1.83)	(1.87)	(1.19)
Italy	2.56)	14.46*	− 1.88
	(2.16)	(4.76)	(1.41)

Table 6.1 *Mean historical values of target variables*

to compare the estimated desired values with actual values, in order to understand whether actual policies have been successful. Furthermore, actual standard errors give us the possibility of evaluating the estimated standard errors for the policymakers' desired values.

Tables 6.2 and 6.3 contain the estimated parameters of British policymakers under the assumptions of floating and managed exchange rates. Output growth is the most relevant target. If we assume that in the sample period the monetary regime is characterized by managed exchange rates, we have that inflation is also a relevant policy target. The weight assigned to the trade balance is not significantly different from zero at standard significance levels. The desired values are consistent: the British policymakers want to achieve a relevant growth of the economy associated with zero inflation and equilibrium trade balance.

	Floating exchange rates	Managed exchange rates
	Central bank and Government	Central bank and Government
dy	1.0	1.0
dp	0.00	0.11*
	(0.01)	(0.05)
tb	0.01	0.16
	(0.02)	(0.13)

Table 6.2 *Britain: estimated relative ranking among policy targets*

	Floating exchange rates Central bank and Government	Managed exchange rates Central bank and Government
dy	6.83*	8.80*
	(2.89)	(2.47)
dp	− 8.90	− 3.47
	(7.81)	(2.12)
tb	− 78.31	11.49
	(94.06)	(16.96)

Table 6.3 *Britain: estimated desired values for policy targets*

	Floating exchange rates Central bank and Government	Managed exchange rates Central bank and Government
dy	1.0	1.0
dp	0.12*	0.08
	(0.06)	(0.14)
tb	0.05	0.23*
	(0.19)	(0.12)

Table 6.4 *France: estimated relative ranking among policy targets*

	Floating exchange rates Central bank and Government	Managed exchange rates Central bank and Government
dy	8.86*	3.39*
	(3.39)	(1.25)
dp	1.02	7.66
	(0.87)	(9.31)
tb	− 0.03	1.31
	(0.12)	(8.49)

Table 6.5 *France: estimated desired values for policy targets*

	Floating exchange rates		Managed exchange rates	
	Central bank	Government	Central bank	Government
dy	1.0	1.0	1.0	1.0
dp	0.03	0.11	0.00	0.00
	(0.06)	(0.46)	(0.00)	(0.00)
tb	0.00	0.01	0.05	0.04*
	(0.00)	(0.01)	(0.06)	(0.01)

Table 6.6 *Germany: estimated relative ranking among policy targets*

	Floating exchange rates		Managed exchange rates	
	Central bank	Government	Central bank	Government
dy	11.29*	10.05*	7.65*	11.02*
	(1.38)	(4.39)	(3.47)	(3.87)
dp	0.00	0.01	0.00	0.00
		(0.41)		(0.00)
tb	0.26	0.00	2.92*	0.00
	(3.14)		(1.42)	

Table 6.7 *Germany: estimated desired values for policy targets*

Tables 6.4 and 6.5 contain the parameters describing the preferences of French policymakers. Again, output growth is the more relevant target. Trade balance is the second target under managed exchange rates. If instead we assume floating exchange rates, the second target becomes inflation. The estimated desired values indicate that France, like Britain, tried to associate output growth with no inflation and equilibrium trade balance.

Tables 6.6 and 6.7 show German policymakers' preferences. In Germany, the central bank and the government assign quite similar weights to their targets, giving output growth the largest weight. Only under managed exchange rates is the weight that the government assigns to the trade balance significantly different from zero. Moreover, desired values are not much different and look similar in the two regimes. Notice that both policymakers want to achieve output growth and zero inflation. In the managed exchange rates regime, the central bank aims at a trade surplus.

	Floating exchange rates		Managed exchange rates	
	Central bank	Government	Central bank	Government
dy	1.0	1.0	1.0	1.0
dp	0.04	0.06	0.01	0.02
	(0.06)	(0.07)	(0.02)	(0.03)
tb	0.00	0.03	0.00	0.00
	(0.00)	(0.04)	(0.00)	(0.00)

Table 6.8 *Italy: estimated relative ranking among policy targets*

	Floating exchange rates		Managed exchange rates	
	Central bank	Government	Central bank	Government
dy	6.77*	7.21*	8.52*	11.92*
	(1.45)	(1.38)	(1.25)	(5.53)
dp	0.00	1.89	0.00	2.41
		(5.03)		(3.89)
tb	0.00	0.00	0.00	0.00
	(0.00)		(0.00)	

Table 6.9 *Italy: estimated desired values for policy targets*

Finally, Tables 6.8 and 6.9 contain the estimated preferences of Italian policymakers. Output growth is the only relevant target, and the central bank and the government assign similar weights to their targets. The desired values however show that the government's policy tried to achieve a larger output growth.

Before examining the relationship between the above results and the problem of international policy coordination, we want to emphasize two aspects of our estimates of the tastes of European policymakers. First, the estimates under the assumption of managed exchange rates seem to provide better results than those obtained by assuming floating exchange rates. This is consistent with our prior on the role of the EMS. Second, the central bank and the government in Germany and Italy have very similar tastes. This might suggest that monetary and fiscal policy in these two countries have actually been coordinated (we recall that policies in Britain and France are assumed to be coordinated because their central banks are not independent).

	Floating exchange rates		Managed exchange rates	
	Central bank	Government	Central bank	Government
Britain	0.39*		0.29*	
	(0.19)		(0.13)	
France	0.48*		0.61*	
	(0.16)		(0.21)	
Germany	0.06	0.30*	0.41*	0.42*
	(0.12)	(0.07)	(0.24)	(0.07)
Italy	0.34	0.14	0.31*	0.49*
	(0.34)	(0.15)	(0.16)	(0.02)

Table 6.10 *Estimated discount factors*

Let us consider now the problem of policy coordination. First of all, the fact that national policies are in general coordinated is likely to have positive effects on the profitability of international coordination of economic policies (see Levine, 1987). Secondly, all countries rank their targets in a similar way, and this is also likely to make coordination much easier, but not necessarily more sustainable (see Section 2). Therefore, we want to evaluate the sustainability of coordinated strategies. Crucial information is provided by policymakers' discount factors. It is well known that the higher the discount factor, the lower the probability that players deviate from the cooperative agreement. Estimates of European policymakers' discount factors are presented in Table 6.10.

Notice that in the managed exchange-rates regime all discount factors are significantly different from zero. The largest discount factor is 0.61, and most values are in a neighbour of 0.4. Hence, no country seems likely to carry out long-run policies.

These results indicate that European countries are too myopic for cooperation to be actually implemented. Coordinated strategies are unlikely to be sustainable, unless gains from cooperation are much larger than the incentive to deviate once all the other policymakers cooperate.

5   Conclusions

The following stylized conclusions can be derived from the previous results. European central bankers share several common characteristics: first, they all heavily discount the future, thus making cooperative outcomes difficult to sustain. In other words, the incentive to deviate probably overcomes the discounted benefits from cooperation. Secondly, all central bankers rank their targets in a similar way, and this is likely to make coordination among monetary policies much easier. Moreover, the countries that we analysed have fairly similar desired values for their own policy targets. Thirdly, national monetary and fiscal authorities have similar preferences; this makes possible international monetary cooperation even without achieving the international coordination of fiscal policies.

These remarks lead us to conclude that coordinated policies could be achieved if players were less myopic, and were able to appropriately evaluate the long-run gains that cooperation is likely to provide.

A good example is the constitution of a European central bank. Such an institution cannot emerge if countries keep comparing short-run scenarios. Cooperation requires policymakers to be much more forward-looking than they are at present.

Finally, and more important, our estimates of central bankers' tastes constitute the starting point for a precise analysis of the profitability and sustainability of cooperation. This analysis can only be performed by simulating the dynamic game that takes place among the European countries under alternative assumptions on the exchange-rate regimes, on the policymakers' strategies, on their national and international agreements. These simulations, however, can provide reliable information only if they are performed starting from a reliable estimation of all policymakers' objective functions. This is why our results could be relevant. Our estimates make it possible to evaluate the gains from cooperation and its sustainability in a dynamic framework, without resorting to excessive *ad-hoc* assumptions on the policymakers' preferences.[10] The examples proposed in Section 2 make this numerical, dynamic, analysis even more important.

Appendix

In this Appendix, we show under what conditions on the system matrices A, B_{ij}, b and on the feedback matrices G_{ij}, g_{ij}, is the solution of the inverse dynamic game well-defined; that is, it provides weighting matrices K_{ij} and Q_{ij} that are both symmetric and positive semidefinite. The proof of this result extends to inverse dynamic games some results that have been shown by Jameson and Kreindler (1973) and Carraro (1985a) in a control-theoretic framework.

From (5), we have:

$$B'_{ij}S_{ij}P = - Q_{ij}G_{ij} \qquad i = 1 \dots N; \quad j = M, F$$

We first prove under what conditions Q_{ij} is positive semidefinite. Then we analyse the positive semidefiniteness of K_{ij}. The following theorem can be proved:

Theorem 1: Consider the closed-loop linear system (1), (2) and (4)–(10). It is possible to construct a performance index (3) with $K_{ij} = K'_{ij}$ and $Q_{ij} = Q'_{ij} \geq 0$ that satisfies (4)–(10) such that $S_{ij} = S'_{ij} > 0$ and the absolute minimum $V^*_{ij} > 0$ is attained if:

(i) $G_{ij} P^{-1} B_{ij}$ has k_j linearly independent eigenvectors; (ii) all eigenvalues of $G_{ij} P^{-1} B_{ij}$ are non-positive; and (iii) rank $(G_{ij}) = k_{ij}$

Proof. By inverting P, we have:

$$B'_{ij} S_{ij} = - Q_{ij} F_{ij} \qquad F_{ij} = G_{ij} P^{-1}$$

that is, we obtain the same equation that was used by Jameson and Kreindler (1973) to show under what conditions an inverse control problem yields a symmetric and positive definite matrix Q_{ij}, and that was used by Carraro (1985a) to provide conditions for Q_{ij} to be positive semidefinite. We can therefore directly apply Carraro's (1985a) results, by simply substituting his matrices G, S, Q_2 and D, with matrices B_{ij}, S_{ij}, Q_{ij} and F_{ij}, respectively. In particular, the proof of Theorem 7 in Carraro (1985a) is also the proof of this theorem.

We must now add conditions for K_{ij} to be symmetric and positive semidefinite. These conditions are provided by the following theorem:

Theorem 2: Given conditions for Q_{ij} to be positive semidefinite and for S_{ij} to be positive definite, it is possible to construct a performance index (3) with $K_{ij} \geq 0$ for all z_0 and T, if and only if the eigenvalues of $R_{ij} = \beta_{ij}(P' S_{ij} P + G'_{ij} Q_{ij} G_{ij})$ in the metric of S_{ij} are less than or equal to one.

Proof. Assume $\beta_{ij} > 0$. From (6), we have:

$$H'_i K_{ij} H_i = S_{ij} - \beta_{ij}(P' S_{ij} P + G'_{ij} Q_{ij} G_{ij})$$

Notice that $S_{ij} > 0$ and $Q_{ij} \geq 0$ imply $P' S_{ij} P > 0$ (because rank $(P) = n$) and $G_{ij} Q_{ij} G_{ij} \geq 0$. hence, $R_{ij} > 0$. Then, we can apply proposition 64 in Dhrymes (1978) to the matrix difference $S_{ij} - R_{ij}$. This shows that $H'_i K_{ij} H_i$ is positive semidefinite if and only if the eigenvalues of R_{ij} in the metric of S_{ij} are less than or equal to one. By definition, $H'_i K_{ij} H_i \geq 0$ is equivalent to $x' H'_i K_{ij} H_i x \geq 0$ for all $(1 \times n)$ vectors x. Let us define a vector $z = H_i x$. Then we have $z' K_{ij} z \geq 0$ for all vectors z. This shows that K_{ij} is positive semidefinite. Finally, if $\beta_{ij} = 0$, we have $H'_i K_{ij} H_i = S_{ij} > 0$, which implies that K_{ij} is positive definite.

The conditions provided by Theorems 1 and 2 are however difficult to check after having estimated the matrices A, B_{ij}, b and G_{ij}, g_{ij}. It is even more difficult to impose these conditions during the estimation process that provides consistent estimates of A, B_{ij}, b and G_{ij}, g_{ij}. This is why we made use of the simplified procedure presented in Section 3.

NOTES

The author is grateful to Paolo Vidaich for superb research assistance, and to Francesco Giavazzi, Alberto Giovannini and John Flemming for many useful comments. Paolo Vidaich is also the author of the computer program that solves the inverse dynamic Nash game.

1 A detailed analysis of this type of strategies can be found in Benoit and Krishna (1985), Friedman (1986), Fudenberg and Maskin (1986) and Abreu (1988). Appropriate trigger strategies can be shown to exist for infinite and infinite repeated games, both with complete and incomplete information.

2 This statement can be re-phrased in the following way: very different preferences imply that gains from cooperation are large and that the incentive to deviate from cooperation is also large.

3 Were the sample period such that a_{ij} and K_{ij} cannot be assumed to be time invariant, it would not be possible to estimate the parameters of the policymakers' objective function. Furthermore, the parameters of the policymaker's reaction function would also be time-varying.

4 In the following, we assume $C = 0$ in order to simplify the exposition.

5 This problem has been discussed in Carraro (1985b) in the case of time-varying parameter models with unknown covariance matrices.

6 Because of the unexpected socialist victory in 1981, France is probably the only exception, even if the socialist experiment did not last more than a year.

7 Data sources are the following: OECD Main Economic Indicators provided data for consumer price index, trade balance, the money stock ($M1$), and the exchange-rate vis-à-vis Deutsche Mark in all countries; the same source provided data for gross domestic products in Britain, Germany and Italy and for the official discount rate in France, Germany, and Italy. We used OECD data for the British official discount rate from 1977:1 to 1981:2, then we used the British interbank rate (OECD source). Public expenditure, tax revenue, long term government bond yields in all countries, and French GDP, were provided by the IMF.

8 The advantages of estimating a state space (or a reduced form) dynamic econometric model are well explained in Sims (1980, 1982). The disadvantage is that appropriate theoretic restrictions could improve the efficiency of the estimates. However, because of the international nature of the model, the risk of misspecification was too high with respect to the benefit of the increased efficiency provided by structural restrictions.

9 The computer program that estimates the system and feedback matrices, solves the inverse dynamic game, computes the inequality constrained estimator and then simulates the residuals for the next iteration is a Gauss program which was run on an AT IBM personal computer (hard disk and mathematical co-processor are required). One iteration of the algorithm takes one hour on the average. The two complete runs (corresponding to the two regimes) took 75 hours of running time.

10 There exist several papers that aim at evaluating gains from cooperation by numerically simulating the game among different policymakers. Examples are

Oudiz and Sachs (1984), Hughes Hallett (1987), and Currie, Levine and Vidalis (1987). In all these papers, some of (or all) the parameters of the policymakers' objective functions are exogenously given.

REFERENCES

Abreu (1988). 'On the Theory of Infinitely Repeated Games with Discounting', *Econometrica* **56**, 383–96.
Aoki, M. (1987). *State Space Modelling of Time Series*, Springer Verlag, Berlin.
Backus, D. and J. Driffill, (1987). 'The Consistency of Optimal Policy in Stochastic Rational Expectations Models', mimeo.
Benoit, J.P. and V. Krishna, (1985). 'Finitely Repeated Games', *Econometrica* **53**, 905–22.
Blackburn, K. (1987). 'International Policy Games in a Simple Macroeconomic Model with Incomplete Information: some Problems of Credibility, Secrecy and Cooperation', *Ricerche Economiche* **41**.
Carraro, C. (1985a). 'The Implicit Objective Function of Italian Macroeconomic Policy', in 'New Methods for Macroeconomic Policy Analysis', Ph.D. Dissertation, Ch. 2, Princeton University. *Economic Modelling* **3**, 1988.
    (1985b). 'Regression and Kalman Filter Methods for Time-Varying Parameter Models', in 'New Methods for Macroeconomic Policy Analysis', Ph.D. Disseration, Ch. 1, Princeton University. *Ricerche Economiche* **1**, 1988.
    (1988). 'Strategic Sequential Interaction between Monetary and Fiscal Policy', prepared for the Econometric Society European Meeting, Bologna, 1988.
Carraro, C. and F. Giavazzi, (1988). 'Can International Policy Cooperation Really Be Counterproductive?', CEPR Discussion Paper No. 258.
Chow, G.C. (1975). *Analysis and Control of Dynamic Economic Models*, Wiley, New York.
Chow, G.C. (1981). *Econometric Analysis by Control Methods*, Wiley, New York.
Cooper, R.N. (1985). 'Economic Interdependence and Coordination of Economic Policy', in R. Jones, and P. Kenen, (eds), *Handbook of International Economics*, vol. 2, North Holland, Amsterdam.
Currie, D. and P. Levine, (1987). 'Credibility and Time-Inconsistency in a Stochastic World', CEPR Discussion Paper No. 94.
Currie, D., P. Levine, and N. Vidalis, (1987). 'International Cooperation and Reputation in an Empirical Two-Bloc Model', CEPR Discussion Paper No. 198.
Dhrymes, P.J. (1978). *Mathematics for Econometrics*, Springer Verlag, Berlin.
Dockner, E. and R. Neck, (1987). 'Can the Gains from International Cooperation Be Secured without Policy Cooperation?', *Ricerche Economiche* **4**, 1988.
Friedman, J. (1971). 'A Noncooperative Equilibrium for Supergames', *Review of Economic Studies* **38**, 1–12.
Friedman, J. (1986). *Game Theory with Applications to Economics*, Oxford University Press, Oxford.
Fudenberg, D. and E. Maskin, (1968). 'The Folk Theorem in Repeated Games with Discounting and Incomplete Information', *Econometrica* **54**, 533–54.
Giavazzi, F. and A. Giovannini, (1989). *Limiting Exchange-Rate Flexibility: The Experience of the European Monetary System*, MIT Press.

Henderson, D.W. and M.B. Canzoneri, (1987). 'Is Sovereign Policymaking Bad?', NBER Conference on the European Monetary System.

Hughes Hallett, A. (1987). 'How Robust Are the Gains from Policy Coordination to Variations in the Model and Objectives', *Ricerche Economiche*, 41.

Kydland, F. (1975). 'Noncooperative and Dominant Player Solutions in Discrete Dynamic Games', *International Economic Review* **16**, 321–35.

Jameson, A. and E. Kreindler, (1973). 'Inverse Problem of Linear Optimal Control', *SIAM Journal of Control* **1**, 1–19.

Levine, P. (1987). 'Three Themes from Game Theory and International Macro-economic Policy Formation', *Ricerche Economiche* 41.

Liew, C.K. (1976). 'Inequality Constrained Least Squares Estimation', *Journal of the American Statistical Association* **71**, 746–51.

Magnus, J.R. (1978). 'Maximum Likelihood Estimation of the GLS Model with Unknown Parameters in the Disturbance Covariance Matrix', *Journal of Econometrics* **7**, 281–312.

Murata, Y. (1982). *Optimal Control Methods for Linear Discrete Time Economic Systems*, Springer Verlag, Berlin.

Oudiz, G. and J. Sachs, (1984). 'Macroeconomic Policy Coordination among the Industrial Economies', *Brookings Papers on Economic Activity*, 1–64.

Preston, A.J. and Wall, K.D. (1973). 'An Extended Identification Problem for State Space Representations of Econometric Models', PREM Discussion Paper No. 16, Imperial College, London.

Rustem, B., Velupillai, K. and Westcott, J.H. (1978). 'Respecifying the Weighting Matrix of a Quadratic Objective Function', *Automatica* **14**, 567–82.

Sachs, J. (1983). 'International Policy Coordination in a Dynamic Macro-economic Model', NBER working paper No. 1166.

Sarris, A.H. (1973). 'A Minimum State Space Representation of Econometric Models', NBER Report No. W0003.

Sims, C.A. (1980). 'Macroeconomics and Reality', *Econometrica* **48**, 1–47.

Sims, C.A. (1982). 'Policy Analysis with Econometric Models', *Brookings Papers on Economic Activity*, 107–64.

Tu, M. and G.P. Papavasillopoulos, (1985). 'On the Informational Properties of the Nash Solution of LQG Dynamic Games', *IEEE Transactions on Automatic Control* **30**, 377–85.

Discussion

JOHN S. FLEMMING

The title of this paper does not do justice to the author's achievement. Not only has he advanced the techniques for inverting a dynamic game to extract preferences, he has also extended the analysis of the relations between policy makers' preferences, impatience and the sustainability of international policy cooperation. The paper brings these two strands together in a practical illustration.

Unfortunately both the technical achievement, and particularly its implementation, require stringent assumptions which also constrain one's confidence in the quantitative results. The qualitative conclusion that decision makers' myopia is the major obstacle to cooperation, is, however, all too plausible.

The procedure involves assuming that between 1979 and 1986 the central banks and finance ministries of the four countries (implicitly) used quadratic policy optimization techniques while playing a non-cooperative Nash game. This is despite the number of international meetings with agendas including cooperation.

The problems with ordinary policy optimization exercises on a macro-econometric model are (i) to find appropriate arguments for the objective function and (ii) to find a functional form which is both plausible and tractable. Tractability points towards the quadratic even though it implies a 'bliss point' contrary to the usual assumption of non-satiation. One solution to this problem is to interpret the exercise as one of smoothing or stabilizing the development of the economy around some essentially arbitrary target path. A second one in positive policy optimization is to iterate between the parameters of the objective function and the projected outcomes until the ultimate policy maker is content with the prospect and the technician has parameters he can use in subsequent minor *local* adjustments.

That is to say it may be possible to implement locally plausible marginal rates of substitution by using a globally implausible objective function. The author refers to this view; but although it seems that it might be possible to present the local rates of substitution between target variables – about which we have some intuition – what we are in fact given is the co-ordinates of the questionable bliss points.

As far as the arguments of the objective function are concerned I could question their ultimate welfare significance – but they are no worse than in most such exercises where, for example, people often try to maximize employment (given output) which (ceteris paribus) I would want to minimize.

Consistency in policy preferences is assumed in each country across the sample period despite changes of government, including the election of Kohl, Mitterrand and Thatcher. I actually agree that the UK turning point can as plausibly be put in 1976 as 1979 – but the assumption is strong.

No specification is given to the structure of the economic model beyond that implied by the selection of variables. Although the procedure does not imply a set of identical national models it does assume that all eight (six) policy players' beliefs are summarized by the same global model. This is hard to reconcile with what we know of the divergence of both professional and political beliefs.

I have some difficulty in interpreting the two regimes we are offered; monetary targetry and DM exchange rate targeting. Should not one be right and the other wrong? The UK has moved between the two modes of operation which might invalidate results assuming that either was consistently pursued. I would have thought the EMS exchange rate regime was the dominant one (and it does seem to produce the better results) but in that context exchange rate realignments are explicitly not unilateral, which is inconsistent with the assignment of the exchange rate to individual central banks and the assumption that the sample period was one of non-cooperation.

ALBERTO GIOVANNINI

This paper represents an interesting investigation in an important yet quite unexplored field: the empirical analysis of monetary policies and of monetary regimes. The analysis of central banks' policies has traditionally been carried out by postulating specific reaction functions of monetary authorities, and interpreting the coefficients of such reaction functions in terms of the relevant economic model. Examples of this approach are in the papers by Dutton (1984) and Pippenger (1984) on the pre-war gold standard, by Eigengreen, Watson and Grossman (1985) on the interwar years, and by Marston (1980), Obstfeld (1983) and Neumann (1984) on the post-World War Two period.

The use of behavioural equations in empirical analysis, however, is plagued with a number of problems that make the interpretation of reduced form coefficients extremely difficult, and unreliable. As Lucas (1976) pointed out, the coefficients of reduced form equations are complicated functions of structural parameters (like the parameters of central bankers' objective functions) and of the stochastic properties of the economic environment of central banks: hence they do not lend themselves to straightforward interpretation. These observations have led, in the past years, to the development of a large and important body of techniques designed to bridge the gap between stochastic economic models and their econometric specification and testing.[11] These techniques have been applied extensively in empirical work in macroeconomics, but not in the empirical analysis of monetary policy in open economies.[2] This paper presents a welcome exception to that rule.

In the rest of this note I will concentrate, except for one minor comment on the specification of the model, on Carraro's estimation procedure.

To help the exposition, I repeat and summarize Carraro's basic strategy. Authorities (central bankers and fiscal authorities) maximize quadratic objective functions (7) subject to a set of linear constraints (5) and (6). This produces a system of linear equations, which includes the first-order conditions for the maximization problem of the authorities and the state-space representation for the state variables (5) and (6). The solution of this system produces a set of reduced-form equations (8) describing the optimal policy strategies of the government authorities.[3]

Carraro estimates equations (5) and (6) (in reality, equation (6) is solved for y and substituted into (5), which is then estimated), and (8). Then he solves the inverse problem of finding the parameters of the objective functions, the scalars βs, the matrices Ks and the vectors as, given the reduced-form of the system. Finally he applies Monte Carlo techniques to compute the standard errors of these parameters. My comments on this procedure are listed below.

First, Carraro assumes that policymakers can behave as Stackelberg leaders with respect to private agents. This assumption allows him to bypass all the issues raised by the incentives that policymakers have to renege on *ex-ante* optimal plans. The econometric aspects of dynamic games where the expectations of the private agents play an important role are still little explored. A tractable solution to the problem of the specification and estimation of time-consistent dynamic games is presented by Sargent (1987): Sargent suggests computing first-order condition of the governments' objective functions by taking the values of the future policy instruments as given. This solution is justified by the assumption that a government at time t cannot affect the behaviour of future governments.

The second observation on Carraro's methodology regards parameter estimation. The feedback equations (8) are identities, since there are no stochastic components in the vector z. Hence these equations could not be estimated, without some explicit assumptions about the regression error. One such assumption, rather common in the estimation of models of this type, is that some of the state variables, which agents can fully observe, are unobserved by the econometrician. Productivity and demand disturbances, velocity shocks, portfolio shocks, and so on, are good candidates for these disturbances.

Finally, the method of estimating unrestricted reduced form equations and then recovering structural parameters has two important drawbacks. First, the solution of the inverse problem after the estimation of the reduced form equations, rather than jointly with the estimation of reduced forms, is bound to produce inefficient estimates of the structural parameters, since all the information contained in the structure of the game is not exploited. A standard way to estimate structural parameters, alternative to the method proposed by Carraro, would be to compute a reduced form of the system directly from the authorities' first-order conditions (7) and the laws of motion (5) and (6). This procedure would involve assuming the presence of those unobservable shocks I mentioned above. The reduced form, a highly nonlinear function of the structural parameters, could then be used to estimate the structural parameters by maximum likelihood. This alternative method has the added great advantage of allowing a test of the restriction imposed by the model: the second – and more troublesome – drawback of Carraro's procedure is that, by construction, it prevents testing of the model.

While I suspect that the calculation of the reduced form equation as a function of the structural parameters is computationally less burdensome than the solution of the inverse problem, it is still possible that its estimation with maximum likelihood will prove too expensive, even with modern supercomputers. An alternative, limited information estimator would in this case be based on the first-order condition of policymakers, obtained from equations (7). This estimator is still likely to be more efficient than the one used by Carraro, and still allows testing of the model. Tests of the restrictions imposed by the model are based on the orthogonality of the estimated disturbances to all instruments (information available). Since these instruments usually exceed the number of parameters to be estimated, the restrictions can be estimated: see Hansen (1987) for a description of the large-sample properties of the appropriate test statistic.

The loss of efficiency implicit in Carraro's estimation method is apparent in the standard errors of the structural parameters, all obtained via Monte Carlo simulations: only a small fraction of those parameters is insignificantly different from zero. This occurs despite the very high t statistics of the unrestricted, reduced form estimates which are not reported in the paper, but were shown to me by the author. In most equations they all exceed 2, and average around 3.

NOTES

1 See the essays collected in Lucas and Sargent (1981) and in particular the papers by Hansen and Sargent for an illustration of these techniques.

2 In Giovannini (1986) I further discuss these issues and test propositions about central banks' operations during the gold standard by applying the more recent approach.
3 Notice that (8) is not a set of reaction functions, since policy strategies are expressed as function of the state variables only.

REFERENCES

Dutton, J. (1984). 'The Bank of England and the Rules of the Game Under the International Gold Standard: New Evidence', in M.D. Bordo and A.J. Schwartz, eds., *A Retrospective on the Classical Gold Standard*, Chicago: University of Chicago Press.

Eichengreen, B., M.W. Watson and R.S. Grossman (1985). 'Bank Rate Policy Under the Interwar Gold Standard: A Dynamic Probit Model', *Economic Journal* **95**, September.

Giovannini, A. (1986). 'Rules of the Game During the International Gold Standard: England and Germany', *Journal of International Money and Finance* **5**, 467–83.

Lucas, R.E., Jr. (1976). 'Econometric Policy Evaluation: A Critique', in *Carnegie–Rochester Conference Series on Public Policy* **1**, 19–46.

Lucas, R.E., Jr. and T.J. Sargent (1981). *Rational Expectations and Econometric Practice*, Minneapolis: University of Minnesota Press.

Marston, R.C. (1980). 'Cross Country Evidence of Sterilization, Reserve Currencies, and Foreign Exchange Intervention', *Journal of International Economics* **10**, 63–78.

Neumann, M.J. (1984). 'Intervention in the Mark/Dollar Market: The Authorities' Reaction Function', *Journal of International Money and Finance* **3**, 223–39.

Obstfeld, M. (1983). 'Exchange Rates, Inflation, and the Sterilization Problem', *European Economic Review* **21**, 161–89.

Pippenger, J. (1984). 'Bank of England Operations 1893–1913', in M.D. Bordo and A.J. Schwartz, eds., *A Retrospective on the Classical Gold Standard*, Chicago: University of Chicago Press.

Sargent, T.J. (1987). *Macroeconomic Theory*, 2nd Edition, New York: Academic Press.

7 The costs and benefits of a European currency

DANIEL COHEN

1 Introduction

What should one fear or hope from a supranational currency in Europe? That it will offer a means to enhance the collective rationality of European economic policies, or that it will restrict the sovereignty of each national government? That it will help to smooth balance-of-payments disequilibria, or give a blank cheque to profligate governments? These are some of the questions that occur to every policymaker when considering whether or not to support the monetary unification of Europe.

History, it is true, does not plead in its favour. As reviewed in Hamada (1985), examples of supranational monetary integration are rare and usually short-lived (while trade agreements are numerous and long-lasting). In the post-World War II era, the failure of the Allies to agree upon Keynes's plan for world monetary integration and the later demise of the ephemeral European Payments Union are vivid illustrations of the difficulties involved. In this paper, however, it will be argued that both Keynes's plan and the EPU were misconceived and should not be regarded as omens of failure for European monetary integration.

In Section 2, I seek to demonstrate that Keynes's plan rested on a confusion between the management of the deficit countries' budget constraint and the issue of macroeconomic policy coordination. The following section draws the lessons of this for European monetary union. Section 4 reviews the likely effects of monetary integration on economic policies. The conclusion offers a few practical remarks on the transition path to a European monetary union.

2. Keynes's bancor and its intellectual legacy

2.1 Keynes's bancor

No one knows, and no one wants to know, the balance of payments of Massachusetts or Indiana. Whatever disequilibria may occur there are

195

either financed through saving from elsewhere when out-of-state savers find it profitable to do so, or restored to equilibrium when they do not. From the observation of such a harmonious functioning of the domestic economy, Keynes sought to reconstruct the postwar monetary order on a world currency, bancor, which he thought would mimic at the world level the functioning of domestic currencies.

Keynes was anxious to avoid a world-scale repetition of the deflationary mechanism he had analysed in the 1930s. In that process, demand insufficiency dragged supply into a downward spiral, with the end result that production ceased for lack of buyers. In terms of an international economy, the spiral can be interpreted as follows: a country with a balance-of-payments deficit is forced to cut its expenditures, whereas a country running a surplus is *not* obliged to increase them.

This asymmetry forces a deflationist bias on world trade – a bias that adversely affects surplus and deficit countries alike and that could be evaded, according to Keynes, through a single world currency. In Keynes's view, bancor would be created by a world central bank as a means of financing deficit countries and would be used as a reserve instrument by the surplus countries. Thus it would be up to the *surplus* countries to restore balance-of-payments equilibrium by spending their reserves whenever they wished to do so. While the system was liable to impart an inflationist bias to international trade, the author of the *General Theory* regarded such a risk as infinitely preferable to the opposite bias.

2.2   Keynes's fallacy

Taken literally, however, the Keynesian system was more than inflation-prone. It was unworkable. Indeed, how could it enforce the budget constraint to which every country is necessarily subjected – and in the absence of which the only optimal strategy for a country would be infinite indebtedness?

The utopian nature of the Keynesian scheme stemmed from a confusion between two dimensions of the external constraint. The first consists of a budget constraint forced on nations. This can take different forms depending on the system in force, but it always comes down to preventing a country from spending more than it earns. The second dimension pertains to the macroeconomic interaction between countries, a mechanism that, as Keynes himself pointed out, may lead to an inefficient downward spiral. While the second dimension can be overcome by macroeconomic coordination of government policies, the first dimension can be circumvented only in exceptional circumstances: in an acute crisis, or for reasons of international solidarity, a foreign-debt moratorium can or must sometimes be granted to a country. But these exceptions cannot serve as the basis for a permanent working rule. The Keynesian plan, in the literal description we have provided, is therefore unworkable unless it also spells out the precise limits to the bancor creation that deficit countries will be entitled to initiate.

The Americans were obviously not misled by a scheme designed to oblige them to grant automatic credit to deficit countries. As the Marshall Plan was to prove, the Americans were not hostile to the notion of financing the rest of the world. Rather, they were against being forced to do so through the sole mechanism of the system.

2.3 The European Payments Union

The difficulties inherent in the Keynesian scheme were subsequently illustrated by the European Payments Union (EPU) set up in the 1950s. In order to restore multilateral trade in Europe and save the continent's scarce dollar reserves, the Europeans created a mechanism that had all the appearances of a mini-Keynesian system. A European unit of account was created, to be used by central banks for settling their transactions. A generous overdraft system was allowed, enhancing the already liberal provisions of the Marshall Plan.

Very soon, however, the balance-of-payments disequilibria polarized into a persistent pattern. West Germany, heavily in deficit in 1950, moved into a lasting surplus, whereas France and the United Kingdom accumulated deficits. By 1958, the quotas allowing payment in European units of account were exceeded and, at the margin, these countries' intra-European payments were being made in gold or dollars.

The problems of the EPU are vivid proof of the problems I described in the Keynesian system. How, by whom and according to what principles was the balance-of-payments equilibrium of a deficit country to be restored? The EPU's only solution to these questions was to disband. External convertibility of European currencies was reinstated in December 1958. Gold, *de jure*, and the dollar, *de facto*, became the instruments of intra-European settlements.

3. Supranational national currency and regional disequilibria

3.1 Supranational monetary targets

To avoid repeating the mistakes of Keynes's plan and of the EPU, it is essential that monetary policy – whatever the entity in charge of it – should be conducted *independently* of regional disequilibria. Money supply should be set for the zone as a whole, and it should be left to financial intermediation to allocate it regionally. While the independence of the European central bankers – specifically, the composition of its board and the length of board member tenure – is negotiable, no national strings must be attached to its modus operandi other than of a technical nature, such as those involved in the Federal Reserve Board System.

If such a European central bank were created, how would regional balance-of-payments disequilibria be solved in practice? In order to answer this question, we must distinguish between two dimensions of the problem: first, the implications of regional balance-of-payments disequilibria triggered by *private* excess or insufficient net saving; second, the implications of public disequilibria.

3.2   Private disequilibria

Private agents, depending on their investment opportunities and their income, may generate regional balance-of-payments disequilibria when, in the aggregate, they cause their region to accumulate or decumulate claims on the rest of the world. *A priori*, there is no reason to worry about these disequilibria: savings should go to where the investment opportunities are, and their origin should not be a matter of concern.

Not all international monetary systems, though, can sustain these disequilibria. As a prime example, one may argue that the weakness of the Bretton Woods system was first revealed by such disequilibria in the early 1960s. At that time, the US trade and current accounts were still in surplus. However, the balance of capital outflows was negative, reflecting private American firms' investments abroad. It is surprising that this process, which today would be greeted with enthusiasm, should have been one of the causes of the system's collapse. No one would find it unusual that Parisian firms should borrow to set up subsidiaries in Brittany, if Brittany seemed to them a good place to sell or produce. Similarly, from an ordinary economic point of view, it makes sense that US firms – which, in the 1960s, still had large productivity reserves – should have invested in Europe, making their capital available to the European labour market and less expensive products available to consumers.

The reason why these apparently positive developments brought on the crisis of the international monetary system lies at the core of the Bretton Woods system's weakness. In order to invest abroad, US firms borrowed domestically, turned their dollars into European currencies and then turned these currencies into capital. Yet, to the extent that their current account surpluses were inadequate to match their capital accumulation abroad, US foreign investment had to be financed by European savings. If these were insufficient, three things could happen:

(1) *Inflation*: In order to avoid curbing domestic credit, the European central banks could refrain from sterilizing the money creation triggered by US investment.
(2) *Domestic contraction*: European central banks could sterilize the inflow of US dollars. Economically, this would mean financing US investments through European savings by crowding out European investments.
(3) *A restriction on US investments*: this was implemented by the Kennedy-Johnson administration through various measures (first 'voluntary,' then compulsory regulation of capital outflows).

A combination of these three solutions was attempted, but eventually the European countries chose to avoid the dilemma of (1) or (2) by allowing their currencies to float against the dollar so as to let them appreciate up to the point when (3) would occur.

A world currency would have avoided these tensions. By accepting a collectively determined worldwide rate of inflation, Europe would have followed a combination of (2) and (3): to the extent of their comparative 'know-how' advantage, US firms would have crowded out European firms, whereas to the extent of their 'inside' knowledge of European labour and customer markets, at least some European firms would have managed to compete with their US counterparts. The crisis of the Bretton Woods system hinged on the fact that the European central banks were left to solve the dilemma themselves and national pressure kept them from sterilizing the inflow of dollars at the expense of their residents' demand for credit.

3.3   Public disequilibria

While a supranational currency would certainly help to avoid the pressures generated by national currencies in the allocation of private investment, it would just as surely exacerbate the tensions involved in public deficit financing. Indeed, a supranational currency forces each government to give up a crucial instrument: the privilege of issuing legal tender. Let us review the benefits afforded by this privilege. When the government issues legal tender, any claim on the state denominated in the national currency is by definition a risk-free asset (naturally, without nominal risk). Countries, such as Panama and Liberia, that do not have a currency of their own are vulnerable to insolvency. If the government finds no more purchasers for its new loans, and if its revenues no longer cover its expenditures, the country will be technically bankrupt. It will no longer be able to honour its commitments, will have to declare a debt moratorium and will be dependent on an agreement with its creditors to renew its borrowing.

A government that is free to issue the currency in which its debt is denominated can always meet its earlier commitments. Implicitly, it collects a seigniorage tax, which can clearly be interpreted as a fiscal instrument. An additional – but not identical – benefit is the facility for devaluing older nominal debt through inflation. The moment the inflation rate exceeds the expectations implicit in the definition of the nominal interest rate, the state levies a tax that can be regarded as a wealth tax.

Let us pursue the analogy. Is it a good thing for a government to wield a fiscal instrument such as inflation that allows it to levy a wealth tax? The answer to this question calls for an analysis of what economic theorists call the 'time-inconsistency' of optimal economic policy. This notion has been elucidated in particular by Kydland and Prescott (1977). By way of illustration, let us consider the example of patents on inventions. It is economically inefficient to charge royalties on a patent. Once discovered, an invention should be a public good. However, the law protects patents because they are the guarantee to *future* inventors that their discoveries will not be expropriated. The time-inconsistency of economic policy choices becomes obvious: economic policy would like to abolish existing patents but is prevented from doing so by future patents. This paradigm applies with special force to the taxation of capital. The expropriation of capital is economically good (it dispossesses only *rentiers* and creates no economic distortion) but is rarely employed because it discourages investment (that is, the creation of future capital). These examples show the importance and implications of the 'reputation' effects sought by government in fiscal matters. They also apply to the struggle against inflation. It is always good to trigger inflation 'by surprise,' but if it sparks an expectation of further inflation, the benefits may be lost. Does this mean that the advantage of being able to create money can turn into a disadvantage – if governments want to be able to precommit themselves to not devaluing their debt? The preceding analysis would tend to suggest such a possibility, but we should like to indicate why we regard it as unlikely. To start with, let us examine the following phenomenon: with very few exceptions, governments never issue indexed debt. Now such indexation would be the way to protect the state's creditors from the risk that inflation would expropriate their assets. Isn't it a paradox to witness governments strenuously attempting to convince private agents that they will control inflation and yet depriving themselves of an instrument (indexed debt) that would certainly enhance the credibility of their aims?

For us, the key to the paradox is as follows: economic fluctuations of small magnitude around a mean value make inflation an inconvenience, and governments might choose to issue indexed debt if they were convinced that the variance of the uncertainty would remain narrow. There are, however, a certain number of events with a low probability of occurrence but tragic consequences. Wars are a typical example. With respect to such events, governments will want to preserve the option of brutally devaluing their debt if required. If it were possible to compile an exhaustive list of all these events, economic theory would recommend that the government issue 'contingent' securities as defined by Arrow and Debreu, that is, government bonds stipulating, for instance: 'In case of war, devalue your claims by 30%; in case of victory, revalue government bonds by 25%; in case of defeat, cancel sovereign debt.' Of course, it is totally improbable that such a list could ever be drawn up, but governments have a powerful substitute in inflation and the devaluing of public debt that it allows. Without searching for extremes such as wars, there naturally exist intermediate events against which inflation – that is, the possibility of inflation – affords protection. The first oil crisis is a recent example. Japan, whose performance wins it first prize here, absorbed the first oil shock with the aid of a 25% inflation rate in 1975, promptly followed by a return to an average level of less than 5%. This description of the merits of inflation gives fairly sweeping arbitrary powers to governments. The earlier discussion of time-inconsistency emphasizes the fact that inflation is an efficient instrument if the government can convince private agents that it will not be used subsequently and that it is a response exclusively to crises of a particular kind.

As crises of a 'particular kind' cannot be itemized, an element of uncertainty persists. This, in our view, is a major issue in government strategy, notably from a political standpoint. In other words, one of the objectives of policy is to agree with private agents on an *implicit* list of exceptional events that call for exceptional measures. The list is certainly impossible to establish – otherwise, the problem would have been solved. It can be said, however, that a key function of governments is to insure society against itself, but in unstated terms. In case of drought, raise a national solidarity tax, but not in case of bankruptcy – or vice-versa. Accelerate inflation in wartime, but not during an oil crisis – or vice-versa. The spectrum of political parties can be easily characterized by their different answers to the queston: 'What exceptional event would you regard as calling for exceptional government action?'

Let us summarize the benefits associated with the privilege of issuing legal tender. It procures the government a tax revenue that theoretically protects it from insolvency when sovereign debt is issued in that currency.

The tax has two components. First, the seigniorage tax: every user who keeps a central bank note in his wallet pays a tax to his government. Second, and perhaps more important, money creation allows the government to devalue its debt through inflation. Such a levy resembles a capital tax and shares its ambiguities. From the point of view of taxation, the expropriation of *rentiers* is a good thing, but only provided private agents can be persuaded that the measure will not be repeated. Similarly, inflation is a complex instrument to manage. Faced with events such as war or, perhaps, an oil crisis, it certainly remains a favourite with governments.

A supranational currency, provided it is free from regional idiosyncracies – as I emphasized it should be – would stop governments from using monetary creation as a response to their idiosyncratic shocks. To that extent, it certainly entails a loss of flexibility. However, we ought to keep in mind that aggregate shocks – that is, those common to the member regions – could be in principle offset by the European central bank. Also, the seigniorage tax collected through high-powered money creation would be redistributed to the system's members.

4   Cooperative policy arguments in favour of the ECU

This section reviews the benefits that a single currency would bring as a means to enhance the collective rationality of the economic policies implemented in each different country. I will begin with the arguments derived from the literature on exchange-rate regions (fixed or flexible rates) and conclude with a few remarks on fiscal policy.

4.1   *Against the inefficiency of fixed-exchange rate systems*

A fixed-exchange rate system is not to be confused with a single-currency system, as it preserves the multiplicity of central banks. If these cooperate explicitly and commit themselves to an identical monetary policy, they can, in theory, behave as if their currencies formed a single entity. If, however, they do not cooperate, each central bank will treat its neighbours' policies as a given over which it can exercise only an indirect influence. Let us assume, for example, that one of the central banks would like to rebuild its reserves. It will raise its interest rates (slightly) to attract capital. If there is no explicit cooperation with the other central banks, this unilateral increase will doubtless trigger a rise in the other countries' interest rates. The first country will therefore have to put up its interest rates still further if it wishes to attract capital, and this may result in a cumulative escalation. By the end of the process, it is likely that the first country, which was seeking to stimulate capital inflows, will succeed in preserving an interest-rate differential in its favour, but this will have been achieved at the price of a totally inefficient chain reaction. As an example, let us look at how the gold standard functioned in the nineteenth century.

Let us consider the two statements:

(1) The Bank of England forced its interest rate on all other countries:
(2) The Bank of England had few reserves and defended sterling by means of its interest-rate policy.

These two propositions seem contradictory: if all increases in British interest rates were matched by increases elsewhere, (1), how could the Bank of England defend sterling with interest rates, (2)? The only way to reconcile the two statements is to admit – as Lindert argues – that rises in interest rates, even if applied by all countries, were favourable to sterling because it was a more 'solvent' currency than the others. The example is a good illustration of the inefficiency of rate determination in a fixed-exchange system and in the absence of central bank policy coordination. To secure an inflow of capital, the Bank of England had to weaken the position of the other central banks by raising *all* interest rates. A coordinated policy would have led to a rise in the rates of the capital-seeking country *alone*.

A single currency avoids this inefficiency. By definition, it imposes a common monetary policy on all the countries belonging to the monetary union. In view of this argument, would it not suffice to restore a fixed-exchange system and coordinate member states' economic policies? On the face of it, this proposal may seem economically indistinguishable from the creation of a single currency. It does, however, introduce the possibility of reviewing the parity between currencies. This possibility can be interpreted as an advantage and a drawback: an advantage, in that it introduces a degree of freedom in the system; a drawback, in that the review facility can induce speculative crises leading to the system's collapse. Let us take the example of the franc zone. Its history and mode of operation qualify it as a full-fledged monetary union. However, the zone's African currencies suffer from an uncorrectable overvaluation. A devaluation would undermine the system's credibility, but no member can claim to be sheltered from one: any rumour and accompanying specu-lation can precipitate it. Conversely, some French regions are no doubt overvalued relative to others: wages there are perhaps too high with respect to productivity, and the regions are losing their inhabitants. Adjustments occur, through human and capital migration if need be, but the devaluation of, say, the 'franc of Lorraine' is not an alternative. Thus stated, the situation may seem regrettable, and it might indeed be more desirable to review currency parities than to force entire regions to lose their population. But the economic content of a real devaluation is no different, in this example, from a change in the real wages of the ailing region with respect to the other regions. This point is no doubt more relevant here than the parity-review facility. In any case, we believe the notion of devaluing the 'franc of Lorraine' is less worrying for the European countries belonging to a monetary union than for the distortions introduced at regional level. Indeed, we shall argue below that a monetary union can and must be accompanied by greater autonomy in fiscal matters – which is not (or is still hardly) the case for regions. As a conclusion, albeit provisional, to this section, we therefore believe that a single currency is certainly preferable to a fixed-exchange rates system without coordination, and doubtless superior to a fixed-exchange rates system with coordination if fiscal policy is sufficiently flexible.

4.2   Against the inefficiency of a flexible exchange rates system

A flexible exchange rates system frees central banks from the inefficiency we observed in a fixed-exchange rates system. The need to rebuild reserves is theoretically non-existent, and any change in the monetary policy of the rest of the world can, in principle, be absorbed by a shift in the exchange rate. If all prices are perfectly flexible and agents act solely in response to a change in relative prices (a change that in certain cases may be perfectly expected), a flexible-exchange rates system can protect the monetary policy of one country from that of another.

Such arguments were invoked by monetarists at a very early date in support of flexible rates. Let us immediately point out a possible misunderstanding as to the meaning of this plea. Even assuming flexible prices, floating exchange rates do not protect a country against 'real' swings in other economies. Flexible rates theoretically enable a country to be isolated from inflationary changes, but not from fluctuations in economic activity or from any variation in relative prices. This is a crucial point, whose misinterpretation may explain the disappointment of some observers with the actual track record of floating rates. Let us examine this aspect in greater detail. Let us consider, for example, an international economy whose players are perfectly rational and whose currency is a perfectly transparent medium. If we include a few additional assumptions, such an economy may be 'currency-neutral': it is a 'real' economy where only relative prices and real values count. But, because of this, any economic expansion in one country alters the equilibrium of its neighbours directly or indirectly via relative prices; any fall in real wages in one country increases its competitiveness and affects foreign trade; any change in real interest rates generates capital movements and shifts the saving equilibrium. We can see, therefore, that flexible exchange rates are hardly a miracle cure for eliminating economic interdependence; they can serve only to avert the threat of spreading inflation.

If the prices of goods adjust perfectly, flexible rates are no doubt suitable; but, in essence, if we assume a 'neutral' currency, there is little point in discussing exchange rate systems. On the other hand, if we admit with Dornbusch (1976) that merchandise prices are less volatile than financial-asset prices – a hypothesis that is virtually irrefutable from an empirical standpoint – the efficiency of flexible rates is no longer guaranteed. To substantiate this, let us examine the following problem. Domestic price formation is determined by the price and wage inertia specific to every economy and by the exchange rate, whose variations are a key component of domestic prices – directly via the price of imported goods, indirectly via competition with the rest of the world. All national monetary policies are therefore crucially dependent on how exchange rates move. Let us take the case where a central bank wants to implement a disinflation program. A sharp fall in money creation may create an overadjustment (Dornbusch) whose effects are no doubt fairly undesirable. But a sensible procedure for controlling disinflation policy can be based on the exchange rate response. By aiming for a certain rise in the exchange rate, the central bank facilitates its drive against high prices: the spectacular results obtained by the United States in this area, despite a monetary policy less restrictive than originally announced, are certainly due in part to the dollar's overvaluation. Now the influence of the exchange rate on the conduct of monetary policy creates an externality of international relations that introduces an inefficiency of flexible rates. If two central banks are both trying to revalue their currencies to fight inflation, the equilibrium they eventually reach will cancel out their respective efforts, but after two unduly restrictive attempts to create an appreciation. This is, in a sense, a dual inefficiency of the type we examined in connection with fixed rates. Here, it is the exchange rate and not the interest rate that central banks vainly attempt to drive up for their own benefit. History also provides an example of the same process in the opposite direction, the well-known 'beggar-my-neighbour' policy, whereby each country sought competitive devaluations against its trading partners. Such inefficiency is a further argument for monetary policy cooperation. A single currency, however, is not necessarily the most suitable solution. Cooperation will dispense countries from having to embark on a useless spiral of overvaluation – or overdepreciation, as the case may be – but it should also enable any country to devalue its domestic debt, if it so wishes.

It is hardly debatable, though, that a single European currency would allow economic policy coordination – in the limited sense defined above – between Europe as a whole and the United States. At present, each European country taken singly may rightly regard itself as too 'small' to alter the international monetary and financial equilibrium. In response to the rise in the dollar and in American interest rates, each country will tend to follow the crowd by raising its own interest rates to limit the depreciation of its currency. The exchange-rate and interest-rate inefficiencies therefore combine to make the international financial equilibrium utterly inefficient. A single European currency would certainly provide a powerful instrument for remedying this situation. It would allow the Europeans to negotiate with the Americans on ways to avoid a repetition of the dollar's overadjustment in recent years.

One of the consequences of such a change would also be to diversify dollar claims and debts in respect of the ECU. A very sharp trend of this kind occurred during the 1970s, when the D-mark coming into strong demand at a time when the dollar was regarded as a weak currency. Readers may recall the many reservations voiced by the German monetary authorities at the time. The internationalization of the D-mark was felt to be a destabilizing factor, as it made the German currency vulnerable to international investors' portfolio shifts. The present American experience shows that there are not only disadvantages in possessing a currency that is in international demand. In the same position, Europe would be able to borrow in a currency that it had the power to issue. This is no small advantage, as the developing countries are realizing today. Technically, the ECU's preeminence would enable Europe to levy an international seigniorage tax. It would also endow Europe with a valuable instrument for regulating the value of its debt in accordance with the Arrow-Debreu model described in Section 3.3.

4.3   *For a greater transparency of fiscal policies*

I have argued above in Section 3.3 that a single currency is likely to make public finances harder to manage. Raising taxes and curbing public expenditures are costly and lengthy processes, both economically and politically. Renouncing monetary creation may therefore appear as a devastating loss. While such fears are warranted to some extent, I would like to argue here that they may be overstated.

To begin with, the political and economic difficulties of adjusting fiscal policies are partly endogenous. As I have argued elsewhere (Cohen, 1988), fiscal policies are less likely than monetary policies to respond to disturbances, *in part* because monetary policies have a beggar-my-neighbour component that makes them more palatable: exchange rate manipulation.

Governments tend to view this component as a way of exporting their problems. In the case of worldwide shocks, this perception is mistaken – since each government tries to do the same thing – and gives rise to the inefficiencies described in the preceding section. Inasmuch as it prevents governments from exporting their troubles, a single currency is therefore likely to make fiscal policy more active than before.

  The second and related aspect of a single currency is that it will make governments' budget constraints more transparent. In the present multi-currency system, a government whose finances are perceived to be in trouble spills over its difficulties on the exchange market. In a supranational currency system, direct rationing or a risk premium on national debt would stop those problems from contaminating the rest of the economy. This is not to say that fiscal and monetary policy instruments can, in practice, be substituted for one another. Indeed, I believe that abandoning monetary policy is a *cost*. My point is simply that monetary union will create a need for additional fiscal policy and that the union, in itself, will not hinder it. A practical conclusion to be drawn from these remarks is the following: the abolition of borders within Europe, if it were to paralyze the countries with above-average rates of VAT, could prove to be an objective incompatible with monetary unification.

5   Conclusions: the phases of European monetary integration

A European monetary union is *technically* easy to implement. It would only be necessary to adopt the European Currency Unit (ECU) parities of the former national currencies; to merge the European central banks into a European Monetary Fund (EMF); to give private agents one month to exchange old notes for new ones; and to decide that the seigniorage tax collected by the EMF, through note issues and the requirement for commercial banks to set up reserves, will be redistributed to each country's government in proportion to its GDP.

  The Germans are not yet in favour of a European monetary union. Why? They should not be afraid of having to finance the deficit of other governments, for nothing would oblige them to do so – provided, of course, that the errors of bancor and the EPU are avoided and the independence of the European central bank is preserved. The financial markets are already sufficiently integrated for such consequences of a monetary union on real interest rates to be negligible. Moreover, the ECU's parity against the dollar should be less volatile than the D-Mark parity, a development that ought to rejoice rather than disappoint West Germany.

The source of German misgivings lies elsewhere. The Germans fear that the monetary union would lack the Bundesbank's credibility as defender of a solid currency. Conversely, the other European countries fear – that is, ought to fear – the persistence of an inflation differential between themselves and West Germany, causing other European prices to be excessive relative to German prices. These two apprehensions – and they are legitimate – call for a *transition period*.

A transition period could effectively serve to overcome German reservations, as it would make it possible to harmonize the legal status of the European central banks and to give them the same independence as the Bundesbank vis-à-vis their governments. As an immediate consequence, this equal status should greatly facilitate European monetary cooperation. At the same time, the regulation of commercial banks, notably as regards the establishment of reserves, could also be gradually unified.

The transition period should also be put to use to reduce the risks that an ill-chosen initial parity could entail for one of the participants. This could be achieved by a greater use of the ECU as unit of account and means of settlement, as European prices and costs would be easier to compare in a single numéraire. Governments could help by allowing an anticipated use of the ECU (cheques and notes) for national transactions and agreeing to mobilize ECU-denominated commercial paper by means of slightly attractive interest rates.

The transition period could last from three to five years. Some unilateral initiatives may occur, such as the change in status of the European central banks. But the success of the transition period depends on setting a deadline (1 January 199?) that would pressure private agents into adapting their expectations. West Germany, therefore, cannot delay indefinitely its acceptance of the single-currency principle.

To overcome any remaining German objections, one could imagine a European monetary and financial system designed both not to alienate any of the various participants and to reassure the Germans about the EMF's monetary policy. The arrangement might be the following. Just as the Director of the IMF is traditionally a European and the President of the World Bank an American, so the European monetary system could rest on a set of twin institutions: an issuing body, whose President would be known for his monetary conservatism (say, a German); and a financing institution (an enlarged European Investment Bank), whose Director could draw on budget resources provided in advance to help finance any disequilibria that might arise. This proposal, as we can see, would make it possible to achieve a synthesis between the ideas of Keynes and those of White.

REFERENCES

Cohen, D. (1988). 'Monetary and Fiscal Policy in an Open Economy with or without International Coordination,' forthcoming in Papers and Proceedings, *European Economic Review*.

Dornbusch, R. (1976). 'Expectations and Exchange Rate Dynamics,' *Journal of Political Economy*.

Hamada, K. (1985). *The Political Economy of Interdependence*, Cambridge, Mass, MIT Press.

Kydland, F. and E. Prescott (1977). 'Rules Rather than Discretion: The Inconsistency of Optimal Plans,' *Journal of Political Economy*.

Discussion

ALBERTO ALESINA

The organizers of this conference assigned a very difficult task to Daniel Cohen: he had to assess the desirability and the feasibility of a European Central Bank (ECB) with a European currency. Daniel Cohen faced a choice in writing this paper. He could have written a long essay with dozens of references, evaluating every argument for and against the ECB in a well balanced way and conclude, as economists often do, that the answer is 'it depends!' The alternative, which Daniel Cohen has chosen was to write an agile and sharp paper, dealing briefly and squarely with several issues, and conclude rather strongly on one side. Cohen followed the second strategy and concludes enthusiastically in favour of the ECB. He should be praised for writing a sharp and though provoking paper, in which he 'takes no prisoners': he has clear and strong views about this issue.

I do not intend to argue against the basic conclusion in favour of the ECB, which may very well be correct; however, I do not think that the paper provides sufficient arguments in favour of this conclusion. My impression is that several issues are not addressed deeply and extensively enough, and as a result, the paper is not as convincing as it could have been.

I will concentrate my comments on the three parts of the paper which, I believe, should have received more attention: (1) the relationship between monetary and fiscal policy coordination; (2) the issue of disagreements between member countries; and (3) the institutional arrangements for the European Central Bank.

1. Monetary integration and fiscal integration

The paper correctly argues that the creation of a single currency makes public finances 'harder to manage', particularly for the 'soft money' countries. However, Cohen claims that the cost of this loss of flexibility is 'overstated' and that the political and economic difficulties associated with the fiscal adjustments are not too worrisome.

In a recent paper on this subject, Dornbusch (1988) takes a rather different view. He argues that the recent disinflation of 'soft currencies' has gone too far and too fast, and is partly (or largely) responsible for the significant deterioration in the fiscal position of countries such as Italy, Spain, Ireland, Greece and Portugal. Even the fiscal revenue from money creation strictly defined (seigniorage) has not been trivial for these countries, as pointed out by Dornbusch (1988), and by Grilli in this volume. Second, the high inflation had some additional fiscal effects associated with devaluation of nominally denominated debt. Finally, by giving up completely capital controls, high debt countries also lose the possibility of levying higher than average wealth taxes. (This is clearly true for income taxes too, but perhaps labour is less mobile than capital.)

In summary, I would have been ready to be convinced by Cohen's argument that monetary unification does not imply prohibitive fiscal costs, but I would have liked to see a bit more evidence in support of this conclusion, since this is a crucial point. In fact, suppose that Cohen is too optimistic and Dornbusch is right, and suppose that currency unification proceeds too quickly. If the politico-economic costs of the required fiscal adjustments are too high, some countries may have to abandon the union after it is formed. This would be a major political setback and failure which should be carefully avoided.

The paper also argues that the monetary unification would make fiscal policy more 'transparent', and therefore it is desirable. This may be quite right, but again, I doubt that the paper has proven the point that this 'desire' is realistic in the short-medium run.

2. The 'optimal monetary policy'

The paper reads as if 'the' optimal monetary policy exists, and as if everybody would agree to follow it provided that various time inconsistency problems were solved by tying everybody's hands with the European currency. I do not think that this is the case. Economists and, more importantly, policymakers, disagree on monetary policy issues because (1) they believe in different economic theories or models; (2) they have different objective functions. For instance, how to respond to 'aggregate shocks' is certainly a point on which disagreement between members of the union is likely to emerge. More generally, the definition of what is the optimal monetary rule for Europe would certainly be a matter of discussion between members. For instance, Socialist and Conservative governments have in the past often shown rather different preferences on monetary policy in particular, and macroeconomic policies in general. The existence of conflicts of interests does not imply that a commonly agreed monetary policy is unattainable or undesirable. However, one needs to know what 'institutions' such as voting rules, bargaining rules, agenda setting rules, etc. are adopted to achieve the agreement. The paper does not make much progress on these issues since the problem is not even acknowledged. The author implies that since there cannot be any disagreement on the optimal monetary policy, the only problem is how to tie everybody's hand to follow the optimal (German?) policy. I believe that things are not so simple, and this leads me to the last issue I want to address.

3.   Institutional aspects

The paper provides rather little information on the possible institutional structure of the ECB. Only three points are briefly addressed:

(1) The ECB should have an issuing body headed by a 'monetary conservative', possibly German, and a financing institution (presumably more 'liberal').
(2) The ECB should be independent.
(3) Seigniorage revenues should be distributed in proportion to national products of member countries.

None of these points is uncontroversial, and I would have liked to see more discussion of each of them. For instance, on the last point, one may argue that different countries may face different contingencies, and that this rule may be occasionally abandoned. The question is when, under what conditions the rule is abandoned, and who makes this decision. This issue is closely related to the second point regarding the independence of the ECB. The superiority of independent Central Banks is not a dogma. Arguments in favour and against have been put forward (see Alesina, 1988, for a brief survey). It may also make a big difference which political body (executive or legislative) has the power to supervise monetary policy. In addition, very few Central Banks have proven to be truly independent in practice. Several authors (Woolley, 1984; Stein, 1985) convincingly claim that even the relatively independent and powerful Federal Reserve has been influenced by various administrations. Finally, on the issue of choosing a 'conservative' as the chairperson of the ECB the question is who decides 'how' conservative. That is, what body and with what voting rules would choose the European Central Bankers and (possibly) the Board of Directors?

The design of efficient monetary institutions is a subject with which policymakers, economists, and political scientists are still struggling even at the national level. Even less is known and thought about in a supranational context. A large research agenda is open on this point, and perhaps reality is moving faster than research.

In summary, I want to emphasize that this was a very difficult paper to write. As expected, Daniel Cohen could not solve every problem, but his paper serves the very useful purpose of fixing ideas and stimulating the reader to proceed further in this important area.

REFERENCES

Alesina, A. (1988). 'Macroeconomics and Politics', *NBER Macroeconomics Annual 1988*, forthcoming.
Dornbusch, R. (1988). 'Money and Finance in European Integration', *European Free Trade Association*, Geneva (January).
Stein, H. (1985). *Presidential Economics*, Simon and Shuster, New York.
Woolley, J. (1984). *Monetary Politics*, Cambridge University Press, Cambridge, U.K.

CHARLES WYPLOSZ

While public discussion of a European Monetary Union (EMU) is proceeding quickly, the lack of a proper theoretical framework hampers a dispassionate approach. In this broad ranging paper Daniel Cohen is leaning in favour of the EMU. In building up his case, he must be commended for engaging squarely a wide variety of issues. In the end, I doubt that the case has been made. Rather than engaging in the debate itself though, I limit my comments to three issues which all require further analysis: (1) is the EMS zone an optimal currency area?; (2) does the planned 1992 completion of the single European market imply the coming of age of the EMU?; (3) if we are to move eventually to the EMU, how should we tackle its institutional design?

1.   Is the EMS zone an optimal currency area?

In the traditional Mundell-McKinnon approach to optimal currency areas, a key ingredient is the degree of factor mobility. There is no serious debate that labour mobility within Europe is very limited, and will remain so for decades at least. After centuries of internal wars, the coming together of the EEC so soon after World War II is a historical breakthrough. Labour mobility however is an altogether different challenge. For the time being, on this criterion, the EMS zone is not an optimal currency area.

The other approach to the issue links up with the literature of fixed versus flexible exchange rates. This literature, taking factor (mainly labour) immobility as given, focuses instead on the channels of transmission of disturbances. In the present case, a rough rule of thumb would be as follows. If most disturbances are external to the EMS zone and affect the member countries symmetrically, a fixed exchange rate is desirable, largely because of the inefficiency described by Daniel Cohen. If, on the other side, most disturbances are country-specific, with prices and wages sticky, a flexible exchange rate is preferable. In principle this is an empirical issue, complicated by the fact that what we ought to consider are expected future, not past, disturbances, of which we know nothing *a priori*. Yet, some inference may follow from the observation that the EEC is relatively closed vis à vis the rest of the world and its member countries quite open to each other.[1] As a result, it is conceivable that the most significant disturbances are likely to be those which originate within the EEC: it is hard to envision European-wide disturbances dominating country-specific shocks. On that criterion too, the EEC (or the EMS) does not appear to be an ideal case for a currency area.

The latest approach to the issue of monetary unification centres around the issue of credibility and the particular role of the Bundesbank as lending its reputation to the other European central banks. Of course the question is, why cannot countries achieve credibility through national institutional reform? As Daniel Cohen discusses such a possible reform, namely the issuing of indexed public debt, he correctly notes that one reason why such instruments are rarely supplied is the small probability of large disturbances for which surprise inflation would be an appropriate policy response. This can be turned as an argument against the EMU: adjustable exchange rates may well be needed for such contingencies.

2.   Do we need an EMU by 1992?

It is sometimes mistakenly believed that the removal of the last barriers to trade requires monetary unification. The argument is based upon the implications of trade in financial services and the resulting integration of capital markets. As national financial centres compete directly with each other, crises in anticipation of exchange rate realignments may rise to unknown proportions. Indeed, 1992 will potentially magnify strains within the EMS. On one hand, increased openness to trade may make exchange rate adjustments more needed if country-specific disturbances occur. On the other hand, such adjustments may be much harder to organize smoothly. The correct implication, in my view, is not that the EMU becomes more desirable (indeed how to correct for asymmetric shocks?) but that EMS reform is unavoidable. The only argument for the EMU is that tighter integration of European economies will make costlier the uncoordinated response to external disturbances. But that is the argument already discussed in Section 2.

3. Institutional design: a research agenda

The case for or against the EMU is not complete until we know what institutions are envisioned. There is little experience to draw upon: instances of sovereign countries giving up their central banks are rare. The French franc zone is one little studied case (see de Macedo, 1983). The Latin European Monetary Union is another case. The whole issue is wide open for research and I sketch what I see on the agenda.

3.1   One or several central banks? The issue is not really one of provision of liquidity for interventions: this problem can be easily solved by reserves pooling or borrowing agreements. The difficulty lies in reconciling policy divergences in the face of country-specific shocks or asymmetric effects of external disturbances. A closely related issue is the weights of national representations in the Board of the possible Federal Central Bank. Picking a German Governor does not solve the inherent difficulty. Given the European situation, we need to develop models with more than two countries, and which recognize asymmetries in terms of size, initial conditions and market (including the labour market) structures. (The paper by Casella and Feinstein in this volume represents a first step in the right direction.)

3.2   Central bank independence Should there be a unique European central bank, how much independence should it enjoy? The general presumption is that the more independence, the better. The convergence of opinions results from both the recent literature on credibility and (casual) inference from actual experiences. The argument usually boils down to the risks inherent in having a lender (the central bank) subservient to a borrower (the Treasury), and letting the public do the credit rating (credibility and expected inflation). That is a powerful argument, but not the only criterion that must be considered. There also exist inefficiencies in having uncoordinated monetary and fiscal policies. In addition, within the EMU, independent national Treasuries are likely to enact imperfectly coordinated fiscal policies: what is the optimum degree of central bank independence in this (at best) second-best world has not been worked out yet.

3.3 Distribution of seigniorage While revenues of seigniorage are typically limited, this is not as easy an issue as Daniel Cohen wishes it to be: adopting a simple rule is appealing, but does not necessarily yield Pareto superior outcomes. In the presence of country-specific disturbances, some element of contingency may be desirable. Certainly, the difficulties of operating the Common Agricultural Policy are suggestive of the dangers inherent in contingent income redistribution within Europe.

The most serious issue, however, is not one of income distribution. It is more than clear that fiscal policies will assume an increasing role within an EMU. But how is fiscal policy run without a monetary authority? In principle, with the monetization of the debt ruled out, fiscal policy will have to abide by stricter return-on-investment rules. Yet, the return must be properly understood as the social return, which may well include non-pecuniary returns (such as national defence or poverty alleviation). We have therefore to investigate the possibility that programmes which yield returns which are not economically justifiable may become undersupplied.

A related issue concerns the sustainability of temporary fiscal expansions. The Sargent-Wallace logic indicates that the possibility of eventual debt monetization may have inflationary consequences. The same logic applied to the non-monetization case raises issues of insolvency and of illiquidity. Viewed this way, the responsibility of the single central bank becomes prominent and requires more analysis than is currently available. The US experience with fiscal federalism is interesting but of limited applicability when local budgets dwarf the federal budget.

NOTE

1 At this point, it is worth recalling that the EMS zone does not cover the whole of the EC, and that the EEC falls short of being the whole of Western Europe. The self-exclusion of the UK from the EMS, and the half inclusion of the Nordic countries in the EEC weaken this observation.

REFERENCE

De Macedo, Jorge (1983). 'Small Countries in Monetary Unions: the Case of Senegal', unpublished.

8   The monetary unification process in 19th-century Germany: relevance and lessons for Europe today

CARL-LUDWIG HOLTFRERICH

There are few similarities in the discussion and development of the central bank question in the European Community, on the one hand, and in Germany during her unification process in the 19th century, on the other. With economic unification coming before political unification in both cases – the creation of the *Zollverein* in 1834 and of the European Economic Community in 1957 – one similarity is that the reduction of exchange rate risks and of transaction costs by means of agreements on common monetary standards was aimed at in both cases as part of the creation of an internal market without customs barriers. The statutes of the *Zollverein* already demanded a standardization of the coinage systems.[1] The Common Market Treaty already obliged every member state to regard its exchange rate policy as a matter of common concern (Art. 107) and created an advisory currency committee (Art. 105). As in the European Community the central bank question surfaced early in debates about the *Zollverein*'s development. Friedrich List promoted the idea of a central note-issuing bank for the Zollverein with headquarters in Berlin in his journal *Zollvereinsblatt* in 1845.[2] The Prussian government reacted to strong pressure from business circles and from out-of-state competition in note-bank creation and opted for the particularistic state-oriented solution instead of for a centralized *Zollverein* solution. It established the Prussian Bank as a note-issuing bank under government supervision in 1847. This dominant note-issuing bank for Prussia, with its peculiar organizational structure between private ownership and government management, became the *Reichsbank* in 1876; this was after the political unification of Germany was reached at the end of the Franco-German war in early 1871.

But it is important to keep in mind that the circulation of paper money in Germany up to that time was relatively minor compared to the circulation of specie money and that bank notes did not have legal-tender status. They were generally considered as a credit instrument for the purpose of

216

facilitating payments among businessmen, like cheques or remittances in later stages of monetary developments. Consequently, the efforts at monetary unification within the Zollverein were primarily concentrated on the standardization of the coinage systems of the different German states. This process is much more relevant than the creation of the *Reichsbank* for drawing lessons for the present issue of monetary unification in Europe.

In the first section of my paper I will sketch the monetary conditions in Germany before the creation of the *Zollverein*. I will then describe the process of standardization of the coinage systems in the *Zollverein* era. In the following section I turn to the paper money issue which remained unregulated on the interstate level until the foundation of the German Reich. I will then summarize the history of Germany's final monetary unification in terms of specie and paper money in several steps leading up to the foundation of the *Reichsbank* in 1876. My final section will discuss the relevance of and some possible lessons from 19th century German experience for the present issue of monetary unification in Europe.

1 The development of monetary conditions in Germany from 1815 to 1970

1.1 Monetary conditions before the creation of the Zollverein (1834)

As a result of the Vienna Congress of 1815 the 35 principalities and 4 free cities on German territory were left with full sovereignty to regulate their own customs, weights and measures and also their own coinage and money systems.[3] As each prince or city government tended to defend its sovereignty jealously in such matters, the disarray of monetary and trading conditions in Germany was, viewed today, of almost unbelievable proportions. At a time when Germany was in the preparatory stage for industrial take-off, the political organization of Germany ran counter to what was needed for the expansion of commercial and industrial capitalism. This explains why the movement that furthered the cause of German national unification in the following decades was led primarily by members of the liberal bourgeoisie with vested interested in domestic and international trade, industrial production and private finance. The feudal – albeit often enlightened – elites governing the principalities were interested in the preservation of local traditions not only because they hoped to advance the economic cause of their own state at the expense of others from a sort of mercantilistic viewpoint, but also because they had a vested interest in defending independent fiscal revenue sources for the prince and his court in a period when bourgeois strata of society had already succeeded in curtailing the princes' free hand in taxation matters. Customs, therefore, were an important source of revenue for the petty princes.[4] Fees for, i.e. seigniorage from the coinage of money in each state were also of fiscal importance for the feudal elites and a source of revenue not dependent on the consent of quasi-parliamentary institutions which the monarchs had often conceded vis-à-vis the bourgeois demand for power in the constitutional movement of the early 19th century.

In the first decades of the 19th century Germany was replete with coins issued by the many different German states. In addition, foreign coins, such as French, British, Russian and Danish, were circulating and accepted, not only because they were widely used in international transactions, but also because their gold or silver value was roughly equivalent to their face value.[5] But even among German coins the diversity was immense, in sharp contrast to the unified monetary conditions in the economically leading states of the time, Great Britain and France.[6] Not only were the coins of different weights and denominations, but they were part of totally different monetary standards, like the *Thaler* standard in Northern states including Prussia and the *Gulden* standard in Southern states including Austria. These and some other such standards were linked to silver by the currency unit expressed as equivalent to a certain quantity of silver weighted in *Cologne Mark*, i.e. 'mark fine' of Cologne definition,[7] like the US dollar in the 20th century was linked to gold measured in 'ounces fine'.

Except for Bremen, whose overseas connections induced her to adopt the gold standard,[8] the silver standard prevailed in Germany. Gold coins, like *Pistolen*, *Dukaten*, *Friedrichsd'or* and *Louisd'or* were, however, also used, but mainly in wholesale commercial transactions and as a store of value.

What made the comparability of different coins of even the same denomination, like *Thaler*, so difficult, was their different metal value due to the wide range of coinage fees at the mints of the different states. Whoever wanted to have silver coined to a *Thaler* would have to present a certain fixed quantity of silver, the equivalent of the official parity between silver bullion and the respective currency. The coinage fee would be the difference between the quantity of silver demanded by the mints in exchange for a *Thaler* coin and the silver content of the *Thaler* coin. If the difference was 3 to 6%, the coinage fee was relatively low. But one source reports that between 1820 and 1830 it amounted to between 21 and 87% in the states of Nassau, Coburg and Hildburghausen.[9] These states even went so far as to melt down high-silver-content coins of other states, like Bavaria, and to produce their own low-silver-content coins, which as a result of the mechanism described by Gresham's Law tended to penetrate the circulation of money in the surrounding states. The dividing line between full-value specie money, on the one hand, and debased coins, on the other, was therefore very fluid. Whether relatively low or high, the coinage fees were an important source of fiscal revenue for the different states, which at the same time explains their reluctance to sacrifice sovereignty in currency matters and to allow the issue of notes by private banks.

Nevertheless, there was paper money circulating in Germany in the first decades of the 19th century, mainly as a result of fiscal needs of the various governments during the Napoleonic Wars and of the French occupation of German territory. It was above all paper money issued by the different German states themselves, sometimes convertible, sometimes inconvertible, partly legal tender for the discharge of private debts and always accepted by the treasuries of the issuing state. The most notable example were the Prussian treasury notes issued during the Napoleonic Wars to help finance the Prussian war effort.[10] In 1827 as well as in 1835 the Prussian government's total paper money emission amounted to 17 million *Thaler* as compared to 105 million of specie money in circulation in Prussia in 1835.[11] A Prussian state bank, the Royal Bank founded in 1765 by Frederick the Great, was also permitted to issue paper money. But with its concentration on real estate credit, it did so only on a limited scale, until this privilege was terminated by the Prussian government in 1836 as an expression of a preference for government paper money rather than bank-note issue, mainly for fiscal reasons.[12] By then the circulation of the Bank's paper money had risen to 4.5 million *Thaler*.[13]

There were, in addition, two minor experiments with a sort of private note bank: both the Cash Associatoin (*Kassenverein*) in Berlin and the Knighthood Private Bank (*Ritterschaftliche Privatbank*) in Stettin were granted a limited note issue privilege in 1824 by the Prussian government.[14] But as in the case of the Royal Bank, their privileges were withdrawn in the 1830s.

Government paper money had also been issued by other states. Fiscal needs and seigniorage gains were always the driving motive behind it, the same as in the case of the issue of debased coins and of coinage fees charged by the mints of the various governments.

The extensive variety of different moneys in Germany implied high transaction costs on product and factor markets, especially in interstate business. While money-changers and banks were able to realize a comfortable profit from the necessity of frequent exchanges of money, the situation was extremely disadvantageous not only for travellers across Germany, but, more importantly, for the needs of commerce and industry in large-scale operations. The German Federation (*Deutscher Bund*) in 1815 had removed all restrictions on the migration of the citizens of its member states. From that time on labour was as mobile as capital, within Germany at anyrate. The internal customs barriers were finally removed in 1834 according to the *Zollverein* Treaty in which Prussia played the leading role and Southern German states were included, but Austria excluded. It was clear to those who shaped the Treaty that the diversity of monetary conditions was an impediment to the free exchange of goods in Germany, an impediment which ought rapidly to be removed. One of the articles of the Treaty, therefore, stipulated that the governments of the *Zollverein* states should take action in order to bring their coinage systems on to a common standard.

1.2   Towards a unification of the coinage systems, 1837–1867

The Southern *Gulden* states of Germany needed a standardization of their coinage systems most of all. Before it came to a *Zollverein*-wide agreement in 1838, the Munich Coinage Treaty of 1837 was signed by states South of the Main.[15] In preparation of the later agreement among all the states of the *Zollverein*, its articles stipulated coinage standards for the *Gulden* states that a year later became part of the more general agreement. The silver content of a *Gulden*, no matter which state minted it, was prescribed (nine-tenths of the face value) and the *Gulden* coins were to have legal-tender status in all signatory states.[16] Rules for the circulation of small-change coins were introduced, but still left a wide margin for different solutions in different states.[17] Nevertheless, the agreement was a big step forward, as the states had renounced their traditional right of monetary sovereignty, specifically the debasement of their standard coin, and even agreed on routine checks of their coins by representatives by other states.[18]

In 1838 the coinage issue was negotiated for the *Zollverein* as a whole in Dresden and resulted in an agreement called the Dresden Coinage Convention. The government of Saxony – representing the industrially most advanced state within the *Zollverein* – aimed at a radical solution similar to the one later unified the German coinage system in 1871. It proposed one-third of a Prussian *Thaler* as the standard coin in all member states. It suggested several names, among them 'Deutsche Mark' and a decimal subdivision into new *Pfennige* or *Cents*.[19] In contrast to the actual solution of 1871, however, the whole plan was based on silver, not on gold. At the time, it was rejected by the other states. They argued that the changes were too radical to be acceptable to the population. The final agreement of 1838 did not unify the *Zollverein*'s coinage system, but nevertheless brought about a substantial simplification. Each member state had to opt either for the *Thaler* (subdivided in *Groschen*) or for the *Gulden* (subdivided in

Kreuzer) as a basic monetary unit. The link to silver was still expressed in the traditional *Cologne Mark*, which was defined as the equivalent of 233·855 grams. It was agreed that this should be equal to 14 *Thaler* or to 24.5 *Gulden*. Thus one *Thaler* was valued at 1 ¾ *Gulden* and one *Gulden* at $\frac{4}{7}$ *Thaler*. Each state was obliged to mint *Thaler* or *Gulden* according to common metal-content specifications (= the equivalent of the full silver value less the percentage allowed for coinage fees), to withdraw from circulation the many coins that were depreciated from wear and tear and to substitute them by full-value coins at the expense of the state. They were further obliged to restrict the circulation of small-change coins, the intrinsic metal value of which was allowed to be substantially less than the face value, and to reduce their legal-tender status to payment obligations of only small amounts. The member states were not obliged to accept the coins of the other states as legal tender with the exception of a new *Zollverein* coin that was minted by the various states from then on.

In order to advance the idea of a unified monetary system, and to facilitate the exchange between the *Thaler* and *Gulden* areas, the states agreed on the minting of a common coin worth 2 *Thaler* or 3½ *Gulden* with the word *Vereinsmünze* (= union coin) minted on it. The issue of two million such coins by 1842 was aimed at. This coin never played the role for which it was introduced. Its denomination of two *Thaler* or its equivalent in *Gulden* was too big to be of practical value in everyday small-scale business. As it approximated the price of a bottle of champagne, which represented a big luxury to the ordinary citizen, it was nicknamed *Champagne Thaler*.[20] This might have implied that the *Zollverein* coin and with it the *Zollverein* in general was viewed by the public as a rich man's affair without benefit to the ordinary citizen. But even for bigger-scale commerce the new coin, although minted up to the planned quantity, was hardly used, as businessmen found payment in paper money more practical than in these large heavy coins. Instead, the Prussian one-*Thaler* piece penetrated the coin circulation all over Germany and even gained acceptance in the *Gulden* states in Southern Germany. The Prussian *Thaler* became the common coin for all practical purposes: the *Zollverein* coin functioned mainly as the symbol for efforts at interstate monetary unification.[21]

While a common monetary standard on the *Thaler* and *Gulden* level had been fairly well established by the Dresden Convention of 1838, the diversity of small-change coins remained a big problem. It is true that common standards for such coins for each of the two currency areas were agreed on and that the coinage of additional fractional currency beyond the needs of circulation was discouraged by the obligation of the mints to exchange their new small change coins in any amount beyond 100 *Gulden* or *Thaler* against the full-value standard coins. Seigniorage gains from the future minting of small-change coins with their wide difference between face and metal values were thus limited. But the diversity of coins minted before the Dresden convention was left untouched by the agreement. In particular, no obligations were incurred to withdraw them from circulation.[22]

The Dresden Convention in effect established permanently fixed exchange rates between the two currency areas of the *Zollverein* and specified rules for the money supply in subjecting each participating state to the mechanism of the silver standard. As each state accepted the common *Zollverein* coin along with its own coins as legal tender, a double currency system had been adopted with fixed exchange rates between the *Zollverein* currency and each state's currency, as well.

These were achievements, but in the middle of the 19th century monetary unity in Germany was still far off. Not only did the two currency areas exist within the *Zollverein*, in which one *Zollverein* state, namely Luxemburg, did not participate. But there were also a number of city and territorial states within the German Federation (*Deutscher Bund* of 1815), but outside the *Zollverein*, like Hamburg, Bremen, Lübeck and Schleswig-Holstein in the Northern part of Germany and Austria and Liechtenstein in the Southern part. Whereas Bremen was on the gold standard, four other silver coin systems existed in Germany around 1850 besides the two that were regulated by the Dresden Convention. This diversity was multiplied by the fact that each coinage system was subdivided into small-change coins in up to five different ways.[23]

After the 1848 political movement for the unification of German states had failed, Austria's envy of the leadership role Prussia was playing within the *Zollverein* resulted in Austria's application for full membership in the German customs union. Prussia resisted this endeavour with all means at her disposal. It succeeded in keeping Austria outside, but conceded a trade treaty with Austria as a compromise. This was signed in February 1854. It postponed new negotiations concerning full Austrian membership in the *Zollverein* until 1860 and – which is of even more interest in our context here – it provided for a quick start of negotiations of a new coinage convention for both the *Zollverein* and Austria.

The problem was that Austria had been on a paper standard since 1848. It was generally expected that Austria would reestablish the convertibility of the notes of her National Bank before negotiations started in the course of 1854. The Austrian government actually sold its railroads and took a huge loan on the capital market in order to repay the short-term advances from the National Bank and thus to enable the Bank to resume specie payments. But Austria's military mobilization in connection with the outbreak of the Crimean War thwarted the government's plans. The inconvertibility of paper money had to be extended. Negotiations with the *Zollverein* were finally launched in 1854 with the unfavourable starting position that the currencies of the *Zollverein* states were fully convertible, while Austria's was still inconvertible.[24]

Another historical detail needs to be mentioned in order to set the stage for the discussion of the course and results of negotiations that followed. At the end of the 1840s huge amounts of gold had been discovered in California and in Australia. They appeared on the world markets in such quantities that expectations of a relative depreciation of gold vis-à-vis silver were not unfounded. Austria could assume that it might be easier to resume specie payments in gold rather than in silver. Helfferich states that this reasoning probably was behind the Austrian demand in the 1854 negotiations to establish the gold standard in Germany, while the necessity of linking German commerce to the gold-standard world commerce was the official argument presented by the Austrian negotiators. This raising of the currency-standard question was a new element in the negotiations as compared to those on the *Zollverein* level in the 1830s.[25] It was to remain an important issue in the next few decades. In the 1854 negotiations the *Zollverein* states categorically rejected Austria's demand for the introduction of the gold standard, precisely for fear of a weakening of their currency standard. Prussia, in addition, had a specific interest in keeping her silver *Thaler* standard in a dominant position within the *Zollverein*.[26] Negotiations broke down over the gold-standard demand and were resumed in 1856, when Austria had dropped it. The result was the Vienna Coinage Treaty of January 1857.[27]

Although Austria in the end did not become part of the German *Reich* or of the Mark currency area, the agreement that it reached with the *Zollverein* states on the coinage question is discussed here, because it also changed monetary conditions within the *Zollverein* and regulated the circulation of specie money in Germany up to the main reform after the foundation of the *Reich* in the early 1870s. The Vienna Coinage Treaty not only linked Austria to the coinage systems of the *Zollverein*, but modernized and advanced the coinage systems of the Dresden Convention. From now on the basic weight in which the silver metal to number-of-coin relationship was expressed was half a kilo (= one *Zollpfund* = 500 grams). Instead of 14 *Thaler* or 24½ *Gulden* to one *Cologne Mark* (= 233.855 grams) of silver, the new relationship was 30 *Thaler* or 52½ *Gulden* to one *Zollpfund*. This implied a slight depreciation (0.22%) of the two basic monetary units within the *Zollverein*, but left their exchange rate unchanged. The Austrians accepted a more important depreciation (5.22%) of their *Gulden* in adopting a relationship of 45 Austrian *Gulden* to one *Zollpfund*.[28] Thus the parity relations between the three coinage systems were:

1 Thaler = 1½ Austrian Gulden =
1¾ Gulden of the Southern German states.

By choosing a simpler relationship to the Prussian *Thaler* than to the Southern German *Gulden*, the Austrians acknowledged the more important role of the *Thaler* throughout the *Zollverein*.

The Vienna Coinage Treaty went further than the Dresden Convention in regulating the circulation of small-change coins. For the *Thaler* and Austrian *Gulden* currency areas maximum amounts for the circulation of such coins were agreed on. The Southern German *Gulden* states came to an agreement in the following year and called in the old and depreciated small-change coins that had been issued at the beginning of the 19th century and were still inflating the Southern German minor coin circulation.[29] As before, the coins of the now three different currency areas did not receive legal-tender status outside of the currency area the issuing state belonged to. Not even the public treasuries were obliged to accept coins of the other two currency areas.[30]

This had been and continued to be different for the *Vereinsmünze* of 2 Thaler or 3½ Gulden, which enjoyed legal-tender status in all participating states, but, as mentioned earlier, never gained much importance in circulation because of its size and denomination. Therefore, the *Vienna Treaty* provided for a one-*Thaler Vereinsmünze*, in addition, and even granted legal-tender status in all participating states to all one-*Thaler* coins minted before on the 14 Thaler to one *Cologne Mark* (= 233.855 grams) relationship.[31] This was the expression of a total victory for Prussia: her basic monetary unit, the *Thaler*, had been made the common currency all over Germany and even in Austria.[32] While the *Vereinsmünze* according to the Dresden Convention had been put on an equal footing with the respective state coin in each state, the Vienna Treaty accorded a privileged legal-tender status to them: debts that were expressed in state coin could be settled in *Vereinsmünze*, but not vice versa.[33] In practice, the Southern German *Gulden* states thereafter minted more than 90% of their full-value silver coins in *Thaler Vereinsmünze* and less than 10% in *Gulden* state coins.[34] Before 1857 this relationship had been just the opposite. Even Austria coined considerable amounts of *Thaler Vereinsmünze* alongside its own *Gulden*.[35]

Austria's original demand to adopt the gold standard had been blocked by Prussia and the other *Zollverein* states. They even insisted that the 'preservation of the pure silver standard' be expressly written into the

Vienna Coinage Treaty. At the same time, however, the Treaty met Austria's demand for a common 'commercial gold coin' (*Vereins-Handelsgoldmünze*) for use in foreign commerce. It authorized the minting of 10-gram gold coins (*Krone* = crown) and 5-gram gold coins (*halbe Krone* = half crown). From then on the minting of any other gold coins was forbidden. Before 1857 each state was free to issue and treat gold coins as it pleased. The Dresden Convention had not mentioned them. They had no legal-tender status. But in some states gold coins had been accepted by public treasuries at a fixed parity in relation to silver coins; in others its exchange value was completely left to market forces. The Vienna Treaty practically forbade fixed parities for the new common gold coins in all signatory states. As the old state gold coins could no longer be minted, they posed no danger for the silver standard in the future. Therefore, the Vienna Treaty allowed states that had accepted state gold coins on fixed parities with silver coins at their treasuries to continue their practice.[36]

The Treaty ensured that gold could not infiltrate the monetary system as a second currency standard. Its value was decoupled from silver and the standard legal-tender silver coins in all states of the three currency areas. Little demand developed for the new gold coins, and those that were minted mostly disappeared from circulation and probably ended up in the mints abroad.[37]

The Vienna Treaty was the only international monetary agreement of the 19th century that touched on the question of paper money.[38] This was certainly induced by the inconvertibility of the Austrian bank notes. The Treaty forbade a legal-tender status for inconvertible paper money and demanded that Austria restore full convertibility by January 1, 1859. Austria, in fact, made a big effort to meet this Treaty obligation. It actually restored silver convertibility in September 1858, but seven months later involvement in the Italian war of independence, particularly in the battles of Magenta and Solferino, forced Austria back to the paper standard. When Austria was again close to the resumption of specie payments in 1866, the war with Prussia and other German states inter- vened. As a result of defeat and the peace treaty Austria was forced to agree to her withdrawal from the Vienna Treaty in June 1867. The *Thaler Vereinsmünze* which Austria was allowed to mint until the end of 1867 retained its legal-tender status in Germany even beyond 1893, the year when it lost this status in Austria.[39] Austrian silver *Gulden* were allowed to continue to circulate in Germany until 1874 and they did so plentifully, as Gresham's Law drove and kept them out of Austria, which continued to be on the paper standard.[40] The acceptance of Austrian coins in circulation in Germany posed quite a problem when Germany started to turn to the gold standard from 1871 on. The problem, however, is beyond the scope of this paper. It has been expertly dealt with by Helfferich (1894).

1.3   Paper money disarray up to the 1870s

I have discussed the coinage question in the process of German monetary cooperation and unification in such detail, because paper money was not equipped with legal-tender status in Germany at the time and because coins, especially silver coins, constituted by far the largest share in the total circulation of cash on the territory of the German *Reich*. At the start of the main monetary reform, shortly after the founding of the *Reich* in 1871, the circulation of cash in Germany was estimated at 2.6 billion marks, of which 76% were coins (63% silver coins). The rest consisted of state paper money (10%) and of bank notes (14%) not backed by silver and gold coins or bullion.[41] More than 140 different sorts and denominations of paper money circulated in the territory of the German *Reich* in 1873.[42] For 1866 59 note-issuing institutions (banks and state treasuries) in Germany (excluding Austria) have been counted.[43]

State paper money had been issued time and again, mainly in order to satisfy exceptional fiscal needs of the states. The most notable case was the issue of Prussian *Tresorscheine* (treasury notes) during the war with Napoleon (1806), which served until 1813 as legal tender to settle private debts and not only payments due to public treasuries.[44] But in later decades, too, Prussia and other states in Germany issued state paper money. Bavaria did so for the first time in 1866, when the Prussian-Austrian antagonism culminated in war and created urgent fiscal needs. The Kingdom of Saxony with her early start of industrialization had issued state paper money to meet the demand of commercial circles for means of payments more convenient than coin. In contrast, mainly seigniorage motives drove especially the smaller states to issue such paper money beyond the needs of circulation within their own borders in the hope that their paper money would penetrate into the money circulation of the larger states in Germany. After these states were obliged to terminate the minting of debased coins through the coinage treaties of the 1830s, they turned to paper money issues instead.[45] The treasuries mainly issued notes of relatively small denominations (especially one *Thaler* and five *Thaler*). They did so, because the likelihood that they would be presented for redemption in legal-tender coin was much less for small denominations than for the larger ones and according to the Vienna Coinage Treaty of 1857 the states were obliged to guarantee the convertibility of their state paper money into specie.[46] The states therefore preferred the issue of small denominations for seigniorage reasons.

As to the issue of bank notes, their rise to importance began with the foundation of the Prussian Bank, on account of its relative size a sort of central bank for Prussia, in Berlin in 1846. It was an amalgamation of private capital and government management. After the Prussian government – in order to protect the value of its state paper money – had practically ended some early experiments with note-issuing privileges for three banks in the 1830s, it was all the more surprising that it came forth with this relatively big project of ten million *Thaler* in share capital. The reason why it gave up its resistance to note-issuing banks at this point was that a small neighbouring state (Anhalt-Dessau) had announced that it would found a note-issuing bank obviously designed to serve mainly Prussian customers.[47] Without a Prussian institution serving the same needs, the Prussian government would, in fact, have left the control of bank-note emissions on its own territory and the seigniorage gains connected with it to a foreign government. In the crucial take-off phase of industrialization in Germany in the 1840s, the Prussian government finally acknowledged the future potential of bank-note demand and followed the example of Bavaria (1834) and the Kingdom of Saxony (1838), each with a note-issuing bank on the basis of private share capital and government management and supervision.

After the bourgeois revolution of 1848 had failed politically, the Prussian and other German governments at least met some of the demand of industrial and financial circles for removing restrictions on private economic activity. A movement for 'free banking' including the note-issue business developed in Germany.[48] Prussia and other larger states remained reluctant to grant concessions, but the smaller states adopted a more liberal attitude towards the foundation of note-issuing banks, especially with a view towards fiscal or seigniorage gains from serving customers in Prussia and other large states, as long as these were pursuing a restrictive policy towards such private note-issuing institutions. During Germany's first big industrial boom from 1853 to the outbreak of the 1857 world economic crisis the number of note-issuing banks in Germany climbed to thirty, operating in twenty different states. Some ran into difficulties and had to curtail their business as a result of the depression, a fact that somewhat discredited the movement for 'free banking' and strengthened the idea of a privileged central note-issuing bank, especially as the Prussian Bank withstood the crisis unharmed. By 1857 the Prussian government had finally chartered a few smaller private note-issuing banks according to its rather restrictive rules established in 1848 for such ventures. In 1856, on the other hand, it authorized its favourite and by far biggest note-issuing institution, the Prussian Bank, to raise its share capital and to remove the previous ceiling on the amount of note issues.[49]

A few of the 33 note-issuing banks that were in existence just prior to the creation of the *Reichsbank*, were founded in the 1860s. And one each was founded in the states of *Baden* and *Württemberg* as late as 1870 and 1871.[50] The circulation of notes of all these banks increased from about 6 million *Thaler* in 1846 to 100 million in 1857 to 236 million in 1869 and further to 456 million in the 1872 boom.[51] Although still dwarfed by the circulation of coins, it was clear at the time of the foundation of the *Reich* that the regulation of the bank-note issue would become a question of prime importance.

Although Friedrich List had agitated for the idea of a central note-issuing bank for the Zollverein as a whole in the mid-1840s[52] and although in 1848 the National Assembly at Frankfurt discussed the note bank question,[53] there was no agreement among the German states on this issue. This changed when article 4 of the constitution of the North German Federation (*Norddeutscher Bund*) that came into being in 1867 as a forerunner of the German *Reich* empowered its legislature to unify the coinage, the state paper money and the bank-note systems for its territory as a whole.[54] As the Southern German states, with whom monetary cooperation was considered essential, were not yet part of the union of German states, the question was not tackled until after the foundation of the *Reich*. The earlier coinage treaties had not even broached the subject, with the exception of the Vienna Coinage Treaty which only obliged the signatory states not to issue legal-tender paper money unless it was convertible into silver.[55]

Small and big business circles had expressed the most interest in a unified regulation of bank-note emissions. They had been adversely affected by the sort of bank-note war that had broken out between the German states in the 1850s, when bank notes started to rise to prominence all over Germany. The larger states, Prussia, Saxony, Bavaria, Baden and Württemberg, outlawed payments in bank notes issued in out-of-state banks,[56] because they did not want the smaller states to receive an overproportionate share of the seigniorage gains. This prompted businessmen and liberal intellectuals organized in the *Volkswirtschaftlicher Kongress* (= National Economic Congress) to discuss the note bank question extensively in the first half of the 1860s. On the whole, the *Kongress* spokesmen advocated 'free banking' and competition among note-issuing banks as well. They criticized government policies in favour of big central note banks with monopolistic privileges at the expense of private competitive note banks.[57] But their main interest was unification in monetary matters, too, and the debate about competitive private note-issuing banks versus state monopoly note-issuing banks became a matter of secondary importance a few years later. The *Deutscher Handelstag* (= German

Chamber of Commerce), also representing business interests, put the issue on the agenda of its 1870 meetings and finally came out in favour of a big central note bank as well as the smaller private note banks.[58]

2 From Reich to Reichsbank: the final monetary unification of Germany, 1871–76

When the German *Reich* was founded in early 1871, there were still different coinage systems in Germany, but the various efforts at harmonization had brought about a set of rules for the coinage of money in the different states which made the system come close to a common currency already. The situation was, however, totally different for paper money. Except for the Vienna-Coinage-Treaty rule that legal-tender paper money had to be convertible, each state acted on its own terms as far as the emission of state paper money or the regulation of the bank-note issue was concerned. And it was in this area that the final monetary unification process that ended in the establishment of the *Reichsbank* on 1 January 1876, began.

For the following account of the final monetary unification of Germany it is very important to keep in mind that it followed political unification and did not precede it. This is the crucial difference from current plans for a central bank for the European Community. The member states of the North German Federation had given up their sovereignty in currency and banking matters in 1867. The Federation's legislature acted in 1870. On 27 March 1870 it outlawed the creation of new note banks by the states and reserved the right to establish such new institutions to the federal legislature (= *Banknotensperrgesetz*). In addition, the same law forbade the increase of existing note-issue limitations by the states and permitted the extension of lapsing charters of existing note banks only under the condition that a one-year cancellation term was provided for.[59] For the South German states that joined with the states of the North German Federation in the *Reich* in 1871, the *Banknotensperrgesetz* was not to be in force until January 1, 1872, which left Baden, Württemberg and Hessen a free hand to organize their note banking systems according to their own particular wishes.[60] In fact, a central note bank of Baden was established as late as January 1, 1871 and that of Württemberg in 1871 even after the foundation of the Reich.

On June 16, 1870 the North German Federation enacted a law which prohibited the additional issue of state paper money. The immediate effect of this legislation was that the future growth of paper money was reserved to note-issuing banks with unlimited rights for bank-note emissions. This was mainly the Prussian Bank.[61] But as its charter could be cancelled from year to year the control of future paper money developments was actually reserved for the Reich as long as the Prussian government, which represented two-thirds of the *Reich*'s territory and population, went along.

The first definite results of monetary reform and unification of the *Reich*, however, were not achieved in the field of paper money, but on the coinage question. In the 1860s commercial and industrial circles in Germany had not only demanded a unified coinage system, but had proposed to introduce the *Mark* (= one third of a *Thaler*) as the basic monetary unit, itself in turn subdivided into *Pfennig* according to the decimal system.[62] In addition, they had pleaded for the introduction of the gold standard, mainly in order to link the German currency area to the British Pound, the number-one transaction currency in international trade and finance. Ludwig Bamberger and Adolf Soetbeer became the main promoters of the idea of the gold standard in politics and in the public media.[63] The outcome of the Franco-German War with French reparation payments amounting to five billion gold francs in favour of the German *Reich* equipped Germany with the necessary precious metal to be able to substitute gold for silver in her monetary system. The gold standard advocates won a quick victory when the first Coinage Act of the *Reich* of December 4, 1871 allowed for the minting of ten-mark and twenty-mark *Reich* gold coins of specified weight and prohibited the further minting of silver coins by the states. The decimal subdivision for the *Mark* in *Pfennig* was introduced. Silver coins previously minted by the states remained legal tender in addition to gold coins (with a relation of 15.5:1 silver to gold). Only the *Reich*, not private individuals, was permitted to use the mints (those still belonging to the states) for the production of gold coins. This shows that the gold standard had not been fully established yet, but it was designed gradually to take over all the functions that silver had so prominently played before then in Germany.

The second Coinage Act of July 9, 1873, took the issue to its preliminary logical conclusion. The minting of gold coins for private account was permitted. A five-mark gold coin was introduced in addition to the other two denominations. The act provided for the abolition of the legal-tender status for coins minted by the states except for the silver *Thaler*. *Reich* silver coins with 10% less metal than face value were to be minted in five-, two- and one-mark pieces, as well as in fifty- and twenty-*Pfennig* pieces. For ten- and five-pfennig coins nickel was to be used, for two- and one-pfennig coins copper. An upper limit for the coinage of smalll-change money was introduced.[64] Some of these stipulations remained suspended until put in force by an executive order of the *Kaiser*. This occurred in connection with the creation of the *Reichsbank* in 1875/76.[65] With the Coinage Act of 1873, especially with its provision that allowed for the minting of gold coin on private account, Germany had adopted the gold standard for all practical purposes, although the existing silver *Thalers* remained in use as legal tender until 1907.[66]

The Coinage Act of 1873 also touched upon the question of paper money in setting rules for its future issue. It contained the provision that by January 1, 1876 all bank-notes not denominated in *Marks* should be withdrawn and that the lowest denomination for the future emission of bank-notes should be 100 *Marks*. This measure was targeted at and strongly interfered with the business of private note issuing banks, especially in the smaller states. These banks had aimed at filling the money circulation of neighbouring states with small-denomination bank notes for which redemption in specie was rarely demanded for cost reasons. This provision helped to pave the way for the central role to be assigned to the *Reichsbank*.

Article 18 of the Coinage Act of 1873 also contained a provision that required the withdrawal of paper money issued by the individual states by January 1, 1876 at the latest.[67] Since June 1870 the additional emission of state paper money had been forbidden for the territory of the North German Federation and shortly thereafter for the *Reich* as a whole. The withdrawal, however, required considerable funds for which the states expected and received the assistance of the *Reich*. The law that the *Reich* enacted on July 13, 1874 reiterated that by January 1, 1876 the states must have withdrawn their own paper money which altogether amounted to 184 million *Marks*. It was to be substituted by 120 million *Marks* in non-interest-bearing *Reich* treasury notes apportioned to the states according to their population. This amount – in notes of 5, 20 and 50 *Marks*, i.e. in denominations below those stipulated for bank notes – was considered sufficient for the needs of circulation. The difference between 184 and 120 million *Marks* had to be covered by the states themselves, especially by the smaller ones that had issued such paper money overproportionately. The *Reich* treasury notes were not legal tender, but were accepted by all public treasuries and were convertible into gold.

The final act of monetary unification in Germany was the Banking Act of March 14, 1875 that provided for the creation of the *Reichsbank* on January 1, 1876. Bamberger, Soetbeer and others had argued that for the preservation and defence of the gold standard Germany would need a strong central bank like the Bank of England, which managed the gold standard for Britain. This argument and the appeal to the sentiment for national unity helped to weaken the resistance of former advocates of 'free banking' to a note-issuing institution with practically monopolistic powers.[68]

Besides the creation of the *Reichsbank*, the purpose of the Banking Act was to unify the regulations for the running of all note-issuing institutions, as there was no central bank in the modern sense, that is with an absolute monopoly of the note-issue. 33 note-issuing banks were in existence when the Act was passed to standardize their operation. The Act differentiated three categories of rules: first, those that were binding for all note-issuing banks; second, special rules and regulations for the newly created *Reichsbank*; and third, norms and regulations which the private note-issuing banks were expected to accept 'voluntarily', i.e. under soft pressure.[69]

The common rules for all note-issuing banks prescribed among others: notes of under 100 *Marks* were no longer permitted. The banks were obliged to redeem their notes at face value at the banks' headquarters and to accept them in settlement of debts at face value even at their branches. Rules for the balance sheet were set and each bank was obliged to publish certain statistics on its status weekly. Note-issue quotas for emissions beyond the amount of specie reserves were assigned to each bank as a brake against an overextended bank-note emission, in addition to the convertibility requirement that was also prescribed. This double check on the inflationary danger of bank-note emissions reflected fears that had been nourished in the speculative boom of 1871–73, the inflationary pace of which was wrongly, but strongly attributed by many observers to the concomitant expansion of the bank-note circulation.[70]

The *Reichsbank* was assigned 250 out of the original total 'uncovered' bank-note quota of 385 million *Marks*.[71] In addition it was to receive any quotas given up by other note banks. Banks were permitted to exceed their quotas only under the condition that they paid a 5% tax on the excess amount to the *Reich*'s government, which made it unprofitable to do so in view of the interest rates prevailing in Germany at the time.

Especially the prohibition of bank-note emission under 100 *Marks* contributed to the smaller note-issuing banks giving up their privileges. Thirteen did so immediately after the passing of the Banking Act. Most of the others gave up in the following three decades, so that in 1906 only four were left besides the *Reichsbank*, namely those of the larger non-Prussian states: Bavaria, Saxony, Württemberg and Baden.

The second category of rules in the Banking Act concerned the *Reichsbank* itself which was to be founded. The set of rules prescribed in detail the range of its bank business, the one-third specie cover requirement (gold bullion and coin, silver *Thaler* plus the 120 million *Marks* in Reich treasury notes) along with the two-thirds commercial-bill cover requirement for the *Reichsbank* notes and its obligation to redeem its notes in German legal-tender coins (including silver *Thaler* officially, but not in practice, as it turned out) at the *Reichsbank*'s headquarters in Berlin without restriction and at the many subsidiaries all over Germany, as long as the liquidity status permitted. The Banking Act defined the organs and the organizational structure of the *Reichsbank* almost exactly according to the model of the Prussian Bank.[72]

In view of the present issues under discussion in Europe it is noteworthy that the *Reichsbank* was subordinated to the government. The Banking Act made the *Reich*'s Chancellor the head of the *Reichsbank*. In practice, however, the *Reichsbank* enjoyed a considerable degree of autonomy and – with minor exceptions – remained free from government interference. This was due to the fact that the Banking Act prohibited the government from using the *Reichsbank* to serve its own fiscal needs. it is true that the government shared the profits of the *Reichsbank* with the private share-holders, but in contrast to note-issuing through the National Banks and later the Federal Reserve System in the United States, the emission of bank notes in Germany was based mainly not on government paper, but – aside from a small quota for treasury notes – exclusively on gold and silver and on private commercial paper. Thus the formal subordination to the *Reich*'s Chancellor meant that the government could exercise a super-visory role, but nothing more. In contrast to the function of state paper money, the printing presses of the *Reichsbank* were designed to serve exclusively private needs, and the government participated in seigniorage gains from the *Reichsbank* note-issue only in as much as it shared the profits of the Bank.

After having played the role of a leading, and in this sense a central bank for most of Germany in practice, the Prussian Bank was transformed into the *Reichsbank* on January 1, 1876. Ludwig Bamberger, the main spokes-man in parliament for the creation of the *Reichsbank*, and other support-ers considered the central bank creation absolutely essential in times of crisis for the regulation and defence of the gold standard in Germany.[73] Others also maintained that a *Reichsbank* would not be achievable politically, as long as the Prussian Bank remained operative as an independent institution.[74] Resistance to the creation of the *Reichsbank* mainly stemmed from traditionally liberal political circles who had fought privileged central note-issuing banks under government supervision all along and had favoured 'free banking'.[75] In addition, particularistic interests of individual states resisted the idea. It is characteristic that the federal chamber of parliament in the German *Reich*, the *Bundesrat*, started the bank reform legislation with a bill that provided for the regulation of the existing note-issuing banks, but did not contain provision for the creation of the *Reichsbank*. It was the *Reichstag*, the national chamber of parliament, that insisted on the central bank idea.

Even the Prussian government had hesitated to push the *Reichsbank* issues. Especially in the boom years from 1871 to 1873, the Prussian Bank had been a source of considerable revenue for the government that the Prussian finance minister von Camphausen was reluctant to give up. Finally the Prussian government agreed to sell the Prussian Bank to the *Reich* at a considerable price on the basis of a treaty of May 17/18, 1875.[76]

The Banking Act's third category of rules concerned the private note-issuing banks in the different states. A radical elimination of these institutions would have met with too much opposition from the governments of the respective states and from those political circles that had favoured their expansion as an expression of the free-banking principle earlier on. But the rules were set in such a way that the *Reichsbank*'s central role was assured for the future. The Banking Act opened the following option. The private note-issuing banks could either continue to operate with the full range of their mixed business that the individual states' charters allowed, but restricted to business exclusively within the borders of their own state, or they could restrict their operations to types of business that were similarly allowed for the *Reichsbank* and they would thus receive permission to operate with subsidiaries all over Germany.[77] In the latter case the investment of funds in private securities (apart from lombard credit) and in mortgages was not allowed, and bank notes had to be covered according to the rules that also applied for the *Reichsbank*.

The theoretical option hardly left a choice in practice. Especially in the small states the note-issuing banks had been founded with a view to business in the large neighbouring states and even the note-issuing banks in Bavaria, Baden and Württemberg saw no point in assuming a provincial role voluntarily by operating only on their own territory. Of the thirty-three note-issuing banks in existence, thirteen renounced their right to note-issuing immediately and became regular commercial banks. Of the remaining twenty the Prussian Bank became the *Reichsbank*, seventeen others accepted the restrictions on their business operations in exchange for permission to carry out nation-wide activities, and only two banks opted for their traditional business range and thus for the restriction of their business to activities within their state. One of them, the Rostock Bank in Mecklenburg, gave up its note-issue privilege in 1877, the other, the Braunschweig Bank, in 1906.[78]

A change of the Banking Act in 1899 finally restricted the operational freedom of the private note-issuing banks even further. Until then they had been free to set their discount rates and had usually done so considerably below the *Reichsbank* rate in order to attract business. The change in the law limited their power to charge lower rates than the *Reichsbank* to a very small margin and thus secured *Reichsbank* leadership for all discount operations.[79]

3   The relevance of and lessons from the 19th century German experience for the present issue of monetary unification in Europe

A superficial comparison of conditions that led to the creation of the *Reichsbank* as a central bank for Germany, on the one hand, and of present plans and chances for a European central bank, on the other, could easily lead to the following conclusions. The *Reichsbank* was established after political unification had transferred the legislative authority in such matters from the member states to the central government. To reverse the order in the present European case, i.e. to establish a central bank before political unification, would seem to be too ambitious in the light of the German experience. Furthermore, in the German case, the leading note-issuing bank, the Prussian Bank, was simply transformed into the *Reichsbank* and thus assumed central bank functions for Germany as a whole *de jure* that it had previously already performed *de facto*. The comparable case in Europe today would be the transformation of the *Bundesbank* into a European central bank with the money-creation privileges of the other European central banks being phased out gradually, at least in relative terms. This would certainly be unacceptable politically outside Germany. Thus on both counts the German example would not serve to encourage optimism about the chances of current plans for a European central bank.

But are the functions of a central bank today comparable to those of the *Reichsbank* or other note-issuing institutions in 19th century Germany? In many respects, they are not comparable. First of all, bank notes in Germany were *not* legal tender. They were in demand, because they reduced transaction costs whenever business debts could be discharged with bank notes instead of a bag of coins. In this sense bank notes in the 19th century case played the same role as deposit money of commercial banks today. This makes it better understandable that the free-banking movement advocated competition among private note-issuing banks and opposed central banks with monopolistic positions granted by the governments of the various states.

When state authorities in the 19th century granted such note-issue privileges, they did so not only to prevent corrupt firms from taking over the business, but also to control the amount of seigniorage gains from note-issuing and to make sure that the government would participate in it adequately. In the 19th century fiscal needs played a prominent role in shaping the attitudes of the various governments towards money and banking issues. For most of the 20th century up to the present, in contrast, economic policy goals, such as price stability, full employment and high economic growth, dominate in shaping government behaviour in matters of money supply and central banking. The main function of the central banks has been to stabilize economic activity and monetary fluctuations, in short the business cycle, while in the 19th century their main function beyond serving as the government's fiscal agent and contributing to government revenue was their role as a leader of last resort in times of crisis.

Bank notes today are legal tender. The function of a European central bank would not only have to be to exercise central control over money and credit policies for Europe as a whole, but to issue bank notes with legal-tender status in all member states. From this perspective the unification of the coinage systems in 19th century Germany seems to be much more relevant as a historical parallel to the present discussions about a European central bank than the creation of the *Reichsbank*. And common standards for the coinage of money had been agreed on very early in the *Zollverein*, long before political unification made majority decisions on such matters possible. The Munich Coinage Treaty of 1837 for the Southern German states not only standardized the minting of *Gulden*, but also gave them legal-tender status in all the signatory states, no matter where they were minted. The Dresden Coinage Convention of 1838 standardized the coinage of money throughout the *Zollverein* and introduced a common coin (*Vereinsmünze* worth 2 *Thaler*) that no matter where it was minted possessed legal-tender status throughout Germany. It is true that the circulation of small-change coins remained somewhat disorderly, but rules for their future emission were also set.

The gist of these early monetary agreements is that permanently fixed exchange rates were established among the *Zollverein* states which implied their renouncing the debasement of coins as a means of satisfying their fiscal needs. Their willingness to do so was certainly enhanced by the increase in net customs revenues that resulted from the formation of the *Zollverein* and from the revenue sharing scheme which had intentionally been biased by Prussia in favour of the non-Prussian member states.[80] The Vienna Coinage Treaty of 1857 remained rather unimportant, as far as linking the Austrian currency area to the *Zollverein* was concerned. Austria failed to restore the convertibility of its paper money on a permanent basis. But the Treaty of 1857 provided for the legal-tender status for all one-*Thaler* coins in all signatory states, no matter in which state they were minted and whether they had been minted before or after 1857. In this way Prussia's basic monetary unit was in fact transformed into the common currency of the *Zollverein*. Its acceptance by the public was greatly enhanced by the provision that debts expressed in state currencies could be settled in the legal-tender common coins. As the reverse was not provided for, the common currency was equipped with a clear advantage and dominated the Germany monetary scene from then on.

The silver standard agreed on ensured that the value of the currency could not be subjected to government manipulation. In that sense, even though coin money was supplied by the various governments' own mints the coinage rules created a situation as if the money supply was determined by an institution independent of the government. The coinage was 'depoliticized' money. In today's world of fiat money, depoliticizing of the money supply in Europe will be likewise of crucial importance and will have to be secured by appropriate legislation.

In conclusion, let me summarize the lessons I would draw for the European central bank issue from 19th century German experience:

- Far reaching monetary unification is possible prior to political unification.[81]
- The willingness of member states to renounce the right to manipulate their national currencies is a prerequisite for the establishment of a common monetary standard.
- Even a decentralized supply of money with legal-tender status in all member states is an important step towards monetary unification. Rules and quotas for its emission by the existing central banks in Europe could be agreed on as a first step towards a common money.
- It seems to be less important to supply a common money through one central bank than to establish rules for the administration of a common monetary standard that might be administered by a number of central banks, just as *Zollverein* coins were minted in many different states. The crucial point is that the supply of money must be depoliticized.
- Just as government ownership of the mints did not endanger the stability of money values in the 19th-century German experience, the question of autonomy or political subordination of a European central bank becomes all the less important the more firmly rules for the conduct of money and credit policies are fixed, e.g. that governments are definitely refused access to central bank credit. Such rules limit the discretionary decision-making power of central bankers and politicians alike.
- Political drives for an agreement on a common currency in Europe will have to take into account that those national governments that lose seigniorage revenues as a consequence of monetary unification will probably not cooperate unless there is some form of compensation.

NOTES

In revising the earlier draft of this paper I have benefited from comments and suggestions from the following colleagues: John Black, Knut Borchardt, William

Branson, Alessandra Casella, Rudiger Dornbusch, Charles Goodhart, Dieter Lindenlaub, Stefano Micossi, Richard Portes, Wolfgang Rieke, Niels Thygesen, and Gianni Toniolo.

1 Sartorius von Waltershausen (1920), p. 176.
2 *Zollvereinsblatt* (1845), pp. 96, 370, 779 and 818–19. Cited in Lotz (1888), p. 26.
3 Schultz (1976), p. 11.
4 Dumke (1976), pp. 24–42.
5 Schultz (1976), p. 12.
6 Janssen (1911), p. 4.
7 Veit (1969), p. 448.
8 Rittmann (1976), p. 403.
9 Sartorius von Waltershausen (1920), p. 29.
10 Schultz (1976), pp. 26–27.
11 Tilly (1966), p. 78, Lotz (1888), p. 17.
12 Lotz (1888), p. 17.
13 Deutsche Reichsbank (1940), p. 17.
14 Lotz (1888), pp. 15–16.
15 For the text of this and the later treaties, see Grasser (1971), pp. 389–415.
16 Rittmann (1975), p. 536.
17 Schultz (1976), pp. 16–17.
18 Veit (1969), p. 458.
19 Rittmann (1975), p. 538.
20 Rittmann (1975), p. 542.
21 Rittmann (1975), p. 542.
22 Helfferich (1898a), p. 12.
23 Details in Helferich (1850), pp. 389–406, also cited in Janssen (1911), p. 35 and in Veit (1969), p. 460; see also Kahl (1972), pp. 12–21.
24 Helfferich (1898a), pp. 14–15.
25 Helfferich (1898a), p. 20, Helfferich (1894), p. 9.
26 Helfferich (1898a), p. 21.
27 For a short summary see Henderson (1984), pp. 249–52.
28 Veit (1969), pp. 461–62.
29 Helfferich (1898a), pp. 25–26.
30 Veit (1969a), p. 462.
31 Helfferich (1898a), p. 27.
32 Helfferich (1894), p. 10.
33 Helfferich (1894), p. 18.
34 Helfferich (1898b), p. 89.
35 Veit (1969), p. 463.
36 Helfferich (1898a), pp. 23–24.
37 Veit (1969), p. 463.
38 Janssen (1911), p. 65, Veit (1969), p. 464.
39 Cp. Helfferich (1894), p. 1.
40 Details in Helfferich (1898a), pp. 29–30, Veit (1969), p. 466.
41 Helfferich (1898b), p. 136. Detailed quantitative estimates of time series for the development and composition of money supply (coin, paper, and deposit money) in Germany from 1835 to 1913 are compiled by Sprenger (1982).
42 Ströll (1909), p. 386.
43 Deutsche Bundesbank (1963), p. IX.
44 Veit (1969), p. 471.

45 Helferrich (1898a), pp. 40–41, 53.
46 Helffericht (1898a), p. 55.
47 Lotz (1888), pp. 26–27.
48 Lotz (1888), pp. 65–66, Sprenger (1981), pp. 67–69.
49 Lotz (1888), pp. 76–79.
50 Ströll (1909, p. 387) presents a table with key information on all 33 note-issuing banks in 1873.
51 Wagner (1873), p. 202, Helfferich (1898a), p. 57.
52 *Zollvereinsblatt* (1845), pp. 96, 370, 779 and 818–19 as cited in Lotz (1888), p. 26.
53 Lotz (1888), p. 50.
54 Lotz (1888), p. 123.
55 Schultz (1976), p. 32.
56 Lotz (1888), pp. 74, 81, Veit (1969), p. 479, Sprenger (1981), p. 70.
57 Lotz (1888), pp. 94–102, Hentschel (1975), pp. 81–88.
58 Sommer (1931), pp. 47–48.
59 Lotz (1888), p. 127, Schultz (1976), p. 32.
60 Ströll (1909), p. 385.
61 See comparative table in Ströll (1909), p. 387.
62 Schultz (1976), pp. 34–36.
63 Cf. Helfferich (1900).
64 Schultz (1976), pp. 41–42, Rittmann (1975), pp. 771–77, Veit (1969), p. 486.
65 Veit (1969), p. 486.
66 Veit (1969), p. 487.
67 Soetbeer (1874), p. 115.
68 Cf. Helfferich (1898a), pp. 290–92.
69 Lotz (1888), p. 200.
70 Ströll (1909), p. 386.
71 Veit (1969), p. 494.
72 For details see Holtfrerich (1988).
73 Lotz (1888), p. 183.
74 Schultz (1976), p. 47.
75 Lotz (1888), pp. 187–92.
76 Lotz (1888), pp. 143, 196; for the price, see Deutsche Reichsbank (1900), p. 7; for the text of the treaty, cf. Koch (1910), pp. 260–68.
77 Veit (1969), p. 497, Ströll (1909), pp. 391–93.
78 Veit (1969), p. 497.
79 For details Ströll (1909), p. 397, Koch (1910), p. 272.
80 Dumke (1976), pp. 24–49, Hahn (1982), pp. 217–25.
81 In a number of historical settings monetary unification has been agreed on even without aiming at political unification altogether. A prominent example is the Latin Monetary Union of 1865 of France, Belgium, Switzerland, and Italy. Details in Russell (1898), pp. 26–30 and Janssen (1911), pp. 149–408.

REFERENCES

Borchardt, Knut (1976). 'Währung und Wirtschaft', in Deutsche Bundesbank, ed., *Währung und Wirtschaft in Deutschland 1876–1975*. Frankfurt/M.: Knapp, pp. 3–55.

240   **Carl-Ludwig Holtfrerich**

Deutsche Bundesbank (1963). *Deutsches Papiergeld 1772–1870*. Frankfurt/M.: Bundesbank.

Deutsche Bundesbank (1966). *Das Papiergeld im Deutschen Reich 1871–1948*. Frankfurt/M.: Bundesbank.

Deutsche Reichsbank (1900). *Die Reichsbank 1876–1900*. Berlin. Reichdruckerei.

Deutsche Reichsbank (1940). *Von der Königlichen Bank zur Deutschen Reichsbank. 175 Jahre deutscher Notenbankgeschichte*. Berlin: Reichsbank.

Dumke, Rolf H. (1976). 'The Political Economy of German Economic Unification: Tariffs, Trade and Politics of the Zollverein Era', Ph.D. Diss. Univ. of Wisconsin-Madison.

Grasser, Walter (1971). *Deutsche Münzgesetze 1871–1971*. München: Battenberg.

Hahn, Hans-Werner (1982). *Wirtschaftliche Integration im 19. Jahrhundert. Die hessischen Staaten und der Deutsche Zollverein*. Göttingen: Vandenhoeck & Rupprecht.

Helferich, Johann A.R. (1850). 'Die Einheit im deutschen Münzwesen', in *Zeitschrift für die gesamte Staatswissenschaft* 6, pp. 385–437.

Helfferich, Karl (1894). *Die Folgen des deutsch-österreichischen Münz-Vereins von 1857*. Strassburg: Trübner.

Helfferich, Karl (1898a). *Geschichte der deutschen Geldreform*. Leipzig: Duncker & Humblot.

Helfferich, Karl (1898b). *Beiträge zur Geschichte der deutschen Geldreform*. Leipzig: Duncker & Humblot.

Helfferich, Karl (1899). *Der Abschluss der deutschen Münzreform*. Berlin: Leonhard Simion.

Helfferich, Karl, ed., (1900). *Ausgewählte Reden und Aufsätze über Geld- und Bankwesen von Ludwig Bamberger*. Berlin: Guttentag.

Henderson, William O. (1984). *The Zollverein*. 3rd. ed. London: Cass.

Hentschel, Volker (1975). *Die deutschen Freihändler und der volkswirtschaftliche Kongress 1858 bis 1885*. Stuttgart: Klett.

Holtfrerich, Carl-L. (1988). 'Relations between Monetary Authorities and Governmental Institutions. The Case of Germany from the 19th Century to the Present', in Gianni Toniolo, ed., *Central Banks' Independence in Historical Perspective*. Berlin/ New York: de Gruyter, pp. 105–59.

Jaeger, Kurt (1966–1972). *Die Münzprägungen der deutschen Staaten vor Einführung der Reichswährung (1806–1873)*. 12 vols. Basel: Münzen und Medaillen.

Janssen, Albert E. (1911). *Les Conventions Monétaires*. Paris: Alcan & Lisbonne.

Kahl, Hans-Dietrich (1972). *Hauptlinien der deutschen Münzgeschichte vom Ende des 18. Jahrhunderts bis 1878*. Frankfurt/M.: Dr. Busso Peus Nachf.

Koch, Richard (1910). *Die Reichsgesetzgebung über Münz- und Notenbankwesen, Papiergeld, Prämienpapiere und Reichsschulden*. 6th ed. Berlin: Guttentag.

Lotz, Walter (1888). *Geschichte und Kritik des deutschen Bankgesetzes vom 14. März 1875*. Leipzig: Duncker & Humblot.

Rittmann, Herbert (1975). *Deutsche Geldgeschichte 1484–1914*. München: Battenberg.

Russell, Henry B. (1898). *International Monetary Conferences. Their Purposes, Character, and Results*. New York/London: Harper.

Sartorius von Waltershausen, August (1920). *Deutsche Wirtschaftsgeschichte 1815–1914*. Jena: Fischer.

Schachtschabel, Hans G. (1941). 'Die Entwicklung der deutschen Währungsgesetzgebung seit der Reichsgründung' in *Deutsche Geldpolitik* (= Schriften der Akademie für Deutsches Recht. Gruppe Wirtschaftswissenschaften, Nr. 4). Berlin: Duncker & Humblot, pp. 51–85.

Schultz, Bruno (1976). *Kleine deutsche Geldgeschichte des 19. und 20. Jahrhunderts.* Berlin: Duncker & Humblot.
Soetbeer, Adolf (1874). *Deutsche Münzverfassung.* Erlangen: Palm & Enke.
Sommer, Albrecht (1931). *Die Reichsbank unter Hermann von Dechend (1865 bis 1890).* Berlin: Heymanns.
Sprenger, Bernd (1981). *Währungswesen und Währungspolitik in Deutschland von 1834 bis 1875* (= Kölner Vorträge und Abhandlungen zur Sozial- und Wirtschaftsgeschichte, Heft 33). Köln: Forschungsinstitut für Sozial- und Wirtschaftsgeschichte an der Universität zu Köln.
Sprenger, Bernd (1983). *Geldmengenänderungen in Deutschland im Zeitalter der Industrialisierung (1835 bis 1913)* (= Kölner Vorträge und Abhandlungen zur Sozial- und Wirtschaftsgeschichte, Heft 36). Köln: Forschungsinstitut für Sozial- und Wirtschaftsgeschichte an der Universität zu Köln.
Ströll, Moritz (1909). 'Die deutschen Banken im 19. Jahrhundert bis zur Gegenwart', in *Handwörterbuch der Staatswissenschaften.* 3rd ed., vol. 2. Jena: Fischer, pp. 384–99.
Tilly, Richard H. (1966). *Financial Institutions and Industrialization in the Rhineland 1815–1870.* Madison: Univ. of Wisconsin Pr.
Veit, Otto (1969). *Grundriss der Währungspolitik.* 3rd ed. Frankfurt/M.: Knapp.
Wagner, Adolph (1873). *System der Zettelbankpolitik mit besonderer Rücksicht auf das geltende Recht und auf deutsche Verhältnisse.* 2nd ed. Freiburg i.Br.: Wagner'sche Buchhandlung.

Discussion

RICHARD PORTES

I have learned a great deal from Professor Holtfrerich's paper, indeed virtually everything I know about this extremely interesting and relevant topic. My remarks are therefore more in the nature of comments and questions rather than criticisms or points of disagreement.

There are four stories told in the paper. The first and perhaps most important for current concerns is that of the standardization of coinages. Within only four years after the establishment of a customs union, the many and fragmented South German states, jealous of their sovereign powers, had agreed on the harmonization and reduction of coinage fees, the establishment of fixed exchange rates, the common use of a silver standard, with an associated money supply rule, and a common parallel currency.

The second is a quite different story of the slow and difficult imposition of constraints on note issue, against opposition from liberal 'free banking' circles. The third is that of the delayed victory of Prussia, whose one-*Thaler* coin finally became a dominant parallel currency issued by the other states, with a specified silver content. Finally, we learn of the process leading to the adoption of a gold standard, followed closely by the establishment of the *Reichsbank*. The entire period required was only forty-two years, less than Europe has now passed since the end of World War II.

What lessons can we draw from this historical experience? It gives us a clear example of monetary unification preceding political unification. It is indecent haste from today's perspective that a customs union could so quickly give rise to fixed exchange rates with a common monetary standard and even a parallel currency. The parallel currency did not take off – rather, bearing out its appellation as a 'heavy *Thaler*', it sank without trace (in a pool of champagne?). But that too is instructive.

Restrictions on note issue did not become effective until the end of the period, in the transition to the *Reichsbank*. Professor Holtfrerich tells us, however, that this was comparatively unimportant. Note issue was small relative to the value of coins. And whereas coinages could be unified by standardizing their specie content, notes had no natural common denominator. Moreover, the author reminds us, these notes were in any case not legal tender, but rather like deposit money today. Nevertheless, governments today do still try to control the volume of privately extended credit, and one suspects that the lack of perceived urgency in controlling note issue in Germany was due simply to its quantitative unimportance – only 24% of the total stock of money outstanding as late as 1871. There is no attempt to explain this in the paper.

We discover also that a parallel currency can work under proper conditions, even though a previous attempt failed. Here the success clearly came because this was the equivalent of the currency unit of the dominant state, which others could issue according to fixed rules.

Finally, Professor Holtfrerich finds a major lesson in the circumstances surrounding the founding of the *Reichsbank*: that the formal autonomy or political subordination of the central bank is unimportant if the rules for the conduct of monetary policy are firmly fixed and leave no room for policy. In the case of the *Reichsbank*, note issuing was not based on government debt, but rather on its holdings of specie and private commercial paper. In one sense, the conclusion is surely sound – if the central bank has no real independent powers, it matters little who does not exercise them. The author goes further to recommend a specific self-denying ordinance: 'The money supply must be depoliticized' – by which he means that government should not be able to finance any part of its operations through the central bank. That strong medicine is certainly suboptimal as an economic prescription – perhaps paradoxically, 'depoliticization' can only be justified on political grounds.

Further research might deepen our understanding of the relation of these stories to the economic processes operating during the period, the objectives of policy-makers, and their performance. For this assessment, it would be helpful to have in the first instance more data on economic performance, in particular inflation, the money supply, and macro-economic stability. Some measures of the distribution and redistribution of seigniorage would also be useful. And are there any data telling us the quantitative role of factor mobility?

Early in the *Zollverein*, the move to a common monetary standard and fixed exchange rates was, we are told, aimed at reducing exchange risk and transactions costs. We must assume this was expected to stimulate specialization, trade, and output. It would be nice to have some evidence on whether it did.

What about the dynamics? The big gains that might come from the common internal market in Europe are wholly dependent on the response of the private sector. Dismantling barriers and harmonizing will in many cases have only small effects unless firms treat the Community as a truly 'single' market in their pricing and investment policies. I suspect that a common currency is a necessary and perhaps a sufficient condition for this. One would like to have evidence on whether a common monetary standard in the *Zollverein* affected private behaviour in this way.

Finally, what we are told about the objectives in founding the *Reichsbank* seems some distance from the underlying motivations. Preservation and defence of the gold standard and the suppression of private note issuance seem relatively weak as rallying cries, and one doubts that this was what List had been on about thirty years previously. I myself do not know enough to say, nor to judge how successful the *Reichsbank* actually was, *ex post*. I hope Professor Holtfrerich's next paper will tell us.

9 The establishment of a central bank: Italy in the 19th century

VALERIA SANNUCCI

1 Formulating and implementing a common monetary policy: technical problems and political will

Two issues present themselves when discussing the creation of monetary union: firstly, the impact of a common monetary policy on the various economic systems and how far differences in the economic systems should be taken into account when designing a common policy; and secondly, how to solve the institutional problems connected with the implementation of a common monetary policy and what kind of relationship can be established with existing institutions, namely, in the case of European monetary union, the national central banks. In both respects Italian economic history is an interesting case, firstly because at the time of national unity there were marked differences in the political, administrative and economic systems of the States involved – some scholars talked of a sort of 'mutual extraneousness' (Cafagna, 1965); secondly, because no State had yet completed its process of industrialization, thus offering an excellent opportunity to study the interrelationships between political unification, market integration and economic growth.[1]

With specific reference to the *institutional* problems of monetary integration, there are some analogies between Italy at the time of unification and Europe today, since the choice faced by Italian policy makers was not between a note-issuing monopoly and free banking – the term Vera Smith used to describe 'a regime where note-issuing banks are allowed to set up in the same way as any other type of business enterprise, so long as they comply with the general company law' (Smith, 1936, pp. 148–49). Then, as now, the choice was rather between a single bank of issue and the maintenance of a limited number of regulated banks that had previously acted as monopolists in the States that had joined the monetary union.

Nonetheless, the task of identifying aspects of Italy's banking history that are relevant to the present situation in Europe is an arduous one, and

244

for quite obvious reasons. The first is that the function performed by the 19th century banks of issue was quite different from that fulfilled by modern central banks. In the last century most banks of issue were profit-oriented joint stock companies whose credit activities were not different from those of ordinary commercial banks. The second reason is that at the time when the reform of the issuing system was being debated, Italy was already a politically united, albeit economically disparate, nation. It had a single currency, uniform taxes and customs duties and, most importantly, the debts of the former States had been recognized by the new kingdom as its own.[2] Monetary policy was part of a more general economic policy aimed at accelerating the process of industrialization and at reducing the gap between Italy and the major European countries. The banks of issue were entrusted with the task of encouraging the use of credit, fostering the development of the system of payments, and financing long-term investment projects. Within this framework, the creation of a single bank of issue was probably not perceived as a high priority objective, even though the Government pursued it for a while. A single issuing bank could have implied, if not necessarily more or less independence from the Government, better defined relationships between the two, more effective monitoring of compliance with existing laws and, perhaps, more inclination on the part of the bank to pursue objectives of national interest. Instead, the existence of several banks of issue contributed to the maintenance of uncertainties and ambiguities, with the banks being either too preoccupied with pleasing the Government in the expectation of gaining some advantages from it or involved in pursuing exclusively their own private goals. On the whole, however, the existence of more than one bank of issue appears to have exerted some effects on the *way* in which Government policy was implemented rather than on the *general guidelines* on which such policy was based: more specifically, though the inflationary bias of Italian economic policy for most of the period examined in this paper might have been accentuated by the existence of more than one issuing bank, this was not the ultimate cause of that bias.

In trying to look at the events surrounding the Italian banks of issue in the 19th century with today's European problems in mind, it is important to remember that the institutional aspects of monetary union – which are mainly concerned with policy *implementation* – should be viewed as being subordinate to the economic problems that can make the *formulation* of a common policy a difficult exercise. Therefore, when discussing the institutional aspects, one has the uneasy feeling that what is being debated is either a somewhat irrelevant technical issue – which was possibly the case in 19th century Italy – or a political issue that has no long-lasting solution unless all the sovereign States entering the union agree on the final goals to be pursued and on the role to be assigned to monetary policy within a broader programme of economic policy.

Having recalled factors for reasons of caution, let us proceed to examine Italian historical experience. The political unification of Italy did not lead to the creation of a single bank of issue, despite the many attempts made both by the Government and by some of the existing banks of issue. Nearly seventy years were to pass before a monopoly of note printing was actually established. This paper, however, concentrates on developments before the creation of the Banca d'Italia in 1893, after which date coordination between issuing banks was enhanced and the problems that had arisen as a result of the plurality of issuing banks abated. Section 2 contains a discussion of the possible reasons for the maintenance of more than one bank of issue after the unification of Italy. In Section 3 the problems that the existence of several banks of issue created for monetary control in the first thirty years of the Kingdom of Italy are discussed. Section 4 contains a short summary and seeks to highlight the aspects of nineteenth century Italian banking that are still of interest.

2   The maintenance of several issuing banks after the unification of Italy

2.1   Government intentions on unification

At the time of Italian political unification, in 1861, there was no general agreement among either economists or policy makers on the relative merits of a monopoly in paper money creation; indeed, many countries had a pluralistic system.[3] Nonetheless, the Government of the new Kingdom of Italy, following the position held by Cavour,[4] pursued the goal of unifying the issue of paper currency; the fact that France was then in the process of consolidating its centralized system might also have exercised some influence on the unification government.

The government plan to unify paper currency issue did not call for the creation of an entirely new institution. Rather, it relied on one of the existing banks of issue, namely the Sardinian National Bank, based in Liguria and Piedmont – later the National Bank in the Kingdom of Italy (Banca Nazionale nel Regno d'Italia, BNR) – which was to be merged with the Tuscan National Bank (BNT) to form the core of the planned 'Banca d'Italia'.[5] As in such other fields as monetary standard, customs duties, and public finance,[6] the tendency was to extend to all of Italy the systems and regimes that had been established in the Kingdom of Sardinia. There were solid grounds for such an approach in this matter, more so than in many others, perhaps, yet the plan encountered an unreceptive when not overtly hostile attitude to Parliament, and the government plans were not put into practice.

The Government decision to privilege the BNR does not appear to have been biased: indeed, of the private banknote issuing banks in the Italian states prior to unity (the Sardinian and Tuscan banks, Banca Parmense, and Banca per le Quattro Legazioni), the BNR appeared to be the best fitted for a leading role. Not only was it the largest, but it had also twice had the experience of issuing inconvertible currency, in 1848–51 and in 1859. During periods of convertibility, moreover, it had been more heavily engaged than the others in the task of reconciling the government's financial needs with those of the private sector, seeking to maintain a relatively stable supply of credit without drawing so heavily on its precious metal reserves as to undermine confidence in its banknotes.

The Southern banks – Banco di Napoli (BN) and Banco di Sicilia (BS) –, while larger than the BNR if taken together, were vastly different as institutions. Originally entrusted with the task of collecting taxes and making disbursements on behalf of the Treasury, upon unification they were run by the Ministry of Finance and instead of having capital of their own had a fund consisting of retained profits. Any expansion of the territorial scope of their operations would have required an increase in their endowment funds and thus appeared difficult to achieve in a relatively short time. The idea of merging the BN with the BNR, broached in 1861, was dropped by the government at the first signs of opposition from the former. Moreover, since they could not issue notes payable to the bearer on demand, the BN and the BS were not really viewed as issue institutions strictly speaking, though *de facto* the registered certificates of deposit that they did issue performed the function of banknotes. The reorganization of the Southern banks in 1863 did not lead to their privatization: they were recognized as foundations to be administered by the municipality, the province, and the chamber of commerce.

The manifestations of the Government's intention, on the morrow of unification, to create a monopoly of banknote issue by strengthening the position of the BNR are countless. As early as 1861 the BNR was authorized by decree to open new branches in the Centre and South of Italy. The problems of establishment in the Southern provinces, where the silver standard prevailed, were dealt with first by allowing the BNR to meet requests for conversion of its banknotes into gold as an alternative to silver, then by extending legal tender status to decimal gold coins in all regions of the Kingdom of Italy. An attempt was made to give the BNR exclusive control of Treasury payments and receipts. Two bills were introduced, in 1863 and 1865, for its merger with the BNT.

The BNR, for its part, seemed at least initially to be quite prepared to take on the central function the Government repeatedly sought to assign it: it proved willing to revise its corporate strategy so as to meet the needs of the Southern market and it incurred considerable costs in the effort to make sure its notes circulated throughout the country. In December 1860, even before the proclamation of the Kingdom of Italy, its board of directors had discussed the need to open an office in Naples to hasten the formation of a single bank.[7] In order to expand its operations in the Southern regions the Bank started paying interest on the deposits it gathered there. The Board of Directors also amended its statutes in April 1861 to permit advances on goods and on six-month bills and different discount rates in different cities. However, these changes did not obtain the necessary Government approval. The opening of branches in the South implied the need for a capital increase which threatened to upset the established balance among shareholders. The proliferation of branches also engendered the requirement for bullion reserves in a number of different cities and, as Director Bombrini observed, required a higher degree of coverage of circulating notes than would otherwise have been the case, especially on account of the public's great reluctance to accept the BNR's notes, which were not legal tender, in areas where they were unfamiliar or in which bearer notes had never been used. Nevertheless, spurred among other things by the prospect of being chosen to perform Treasury operations, the BNR embarked decisively on expansion, increasing the number of branches from 7 in 1860 to 44 in 1865.

The privileged role assigned to the BNR, however, was not officially sanctioned: its expansion relied exclusively on its ability to meet the demands for banknote conversion. Neither the monopoly of Treasury operations[8] nor the proposed merger with the BNT came about; the strategic importance of such a merger, in any case, was diminished by the shelving of all plans to take over the BN and the BS and by the opening of a second issuing bank in Tuscany in 1863 (Banca Toscana di Credito, BTC, whose establishment had been approved in 1860).

The failure of these early post-unification efforts to centralize currency issue in a single bank was followed by a series of unforeseeable circumstances that ultimately postponed the unification of currency issue until the 1920s. In 1865 the Parliamentary strength of the Southern regions and of the Left increased, reducing the chances of introducing a monopoly of banknote issue. They were reduced still further in 1866 with the introduction of an inconvertible paper money regime, which was viewed by the Parliamentary Committee of Enquiry into Currency Inconvertibility appointed in 1868 as the BNR's deplorable expedient to impose, *de facto* if not *de jure*, its own monopoly on banknote issue. In 1874 Parliament passed a Banking Act formally recognizing the six currency-issuing banks (with the annexation of Rome the Banca Romana, BR, took its place alongside the BNR, the two Tuscan banks and the two Southern banks) and making their notes legal tender. The concern to avoid reopening old controversies and to show a united front to foreign observers as Italy turned to the international market to obtain the resources required for the return to a metal standard prevented any re-examination of the question even during the discussion of Magliani's bill for the resumption of convertibility in 1881 (Atti Parlamentari, 1880a). Even the creation of the Bank of Italy in 1893, which was a milestone on the road to a monopoly of currency issue, was not a definitive solution, enacted as it was in the emergency conditions generated by a wave of bank failures.

With the unification Government being in favour of granting to a single bank the power to issue banknotes, and with a bank prepared to shoulder the costs as well, of course, as enjoying the benefits of the new status, one naturally wonders why the post-unity attempts at centralizing the issue of paper currency failed. The question has been raised by a number of scholars. The most common answer, to put it very summarily, has been that the laissez-faire principles of the day, which opposed any and all forms of monopoly, admitted of no exception for the issue of paper currency. This ideological factor, it is held, was flanked by regional particularism and local interests, sometimes not better defined. In trying to explain the maintenance of several issuing institutions after national unity, I have chosen not to dwell on the importance of a laissez-faire attitude in creating a climate of opinion hostile to a monopoly of currency issue or on the influence that private interests may have had on the course of the Parliamentary debates. Rather I have concentrated on more structural reasons, essentially the differing features of the banks of issue and the difficulty of reconciling banknote issue with the credit function that they had to perform. The reasons for this approach are set forth below.

2.2 Laissez-faire, local interests, and multiplicity of banks of issue

Two arguments, one of expediency and one of substance, can be made in support of the decision to ignore the ideological impediments to the unification of currency issue based on laissez-faire.

The argument of expediency is that this does not appear to be the proper forum to review the doctrinal positions adopted by Italian scholars and politicians of the day. Such a review might perhaps be of interest to or illuminate historians of economic thought, but it does not fit the aims of our seminar.[9]

The argument of substance is that, regardless of the reasoning and tone of discourse employed in the debate on the problem of currency issue, the real choice facing Parliament and Government does not appear to have been between freedom and monopoly of currency issue. If we accept the proposition that 'for private currency competition to be free it is necessary that decisions about the quantity and the price of output, i.e. the supply and the purchasing power of the product money, are left to the private owner or his managers' (Vaubel, 1984, p. 60), an examination of Italy's nineteenth-century history leaves the impression that the practical choice facing policy-makers was simply between one and more than one bank of issue.

First of all, it is worth recalling that none of the Italian states that were brought together to form the Kingdom of Italy had had complete freedom of currency issue prior to unification. Where bearer banknotes circulated, these were issued by a single institution.[10] Second, while the introduction of inconvertibility in 1866 provoked a vehement reaction by the proponents of laissez-faire, as is suggested by the contentious tones of the Parliamentary Committee of Enquiry into Currency Inconvertibility in 1868, the ultimate effect seems to have been more to fuel hostility to the BNR in the defence of other banks than to spur the complete liberalization of currency issue.

In March 1870 a bill was indeed tabled to authorize the issue of currency by all commercial companies meeting a series of requirements, but not even this appears to have been inspired by a genuine intention to achieve full liberalization. Rather, it was an effort to restore orderly conditions, given the prevalent illicit circulation of paper money and the fragmentary, self-contradictory state of legislation. After the introduction of inconvertible currency, the authorization to issue notes was extended to rural banks approved by royal decree, in violation of the previous rules, under which only banks authorized by special law could issue banknotes. Despite this measure, the shortage of money for small transactions (metallic circulation had sharply declined as a result of inconvertibility, while the notes put out by the issue banks were of large denominations) led many unauthorized banks to issue banknotes of their own illegally. The 1870 bill to extend issue authorizations – which was not passed, incidentally – was presumably intended to remedy this *de facto* situation. It also proposed such a restrictive set of rules for firms proposing to issue notes (limits to the volume to be put into circulation, reserve requirements, limits on loan maturities, etc.) that it can hardly be considered as expressing any clear desire to install free competition in the issue of banknotes.

The Banking Act of April 1874 sanctioned the multiplicity of currency issue institutions, but definitively precluded freedom of issue. On the one hand it accorded legal-tender status, in all cities where branches at which

they could be changed existed or were established, to the banknotes of all
the existing issue banks. On the other hand, however, it limited the right to
issue money to those banks alone, and set ceilings on the amount of currency in circulation that largely reflected existing market shares while also
making it quite difficult to modify those shares, which had been sharply
shifted in favour of the BNR by the introduction of inconvertible paper
currency. The law not only moved in a direction diametrically opposed to
liberalization, it also condemned the smaller institutions to remain small,
albeit while ensuring their survival.

We can conclude, then, with De Mattia (1959, p. 19), that the multiplicity
of currency-issuing institutions in Italy 'was not the outcome of an anti-
unity process . . . but stemmed instead from the coincidental confluence of
a series of particular arrangements within a single political system.'

The explanation of the plurality of institutions in terms of regional interests seems to fit the facts better. We still need to know, however, what
economic fundamentals underlay those regional interests, and we still
have to explain why the creation of a single issuing bank met stronger
resistance than did so many other administrative and economic reforms
enacted on the morrow of Italian unification. For this purpose a careful
study of the makeup of the Italian Parliament would be required, in order
to assess the political weight of the representatives of banking interests.
Ignoring political factors – which, while probably crucial to an understanding of the Italian case, appear to offer little light on the themes of this
gathering – I have chosen to concentrate on the possible economic motivations underlying the regional interests that impeded the creation of a
single issue institution.

The analysis that follows starts from the fact that in that era banknote
issue neither was nor was considered an actively distinct from the exercise
of credit in general. An issuing bank was one that, in addition to ordinary
banking business, also created paper money. Having several different
banks of issue could mean having credit at lower cost, credit that could
reach larger portions of the nation, credit, perhaps, better suited to the
various needs of the real economy and better able to transcend the limits
of local financial structures. Later in this section, the essential features of
the banking systems of the various regions will be outlined, to see what
credit function banks of issue might have been called upon to perform
there; the type of credit business carried out by each of the issuing banks
will then be briefly described; finally, I shall examine whether the existence
of several different banks of issue was not at least in part due to the need to
carry on different activities and, if so, whether this need could not have
been met by a single bank of issue taking regional features into account in
its actions.

(Number of banks)

	1860		1873			1880			1890		
	sb	boc	sb	boc (*)	cb	sb	boc	cb	sb	boc	cb
Former Kingdom of Sardinia (1)	18	2	21	56	15	19	39	16	20	12	35
Lombardy, Veneto	7	—	8	16	37	12	18	54	13	27	158
Emilia, Marches, Umbria	50	1	69	9	18	96	10	30	115	10	108
Tuscany	12	1	13	19	10	13	21	10	13	7	35
Latium	4	—	7	11	2	11	5	3	13	3	10
Southern Regions (2)	—	—	18	13	6	32	20	27	44	61	283
Total	91	4	136	124	88	183	113	140	218	120	629

Table 9.1 *Regional distribution of Italian commercial banks (excluding banking houses)*

(*) Figures refer to December 1870.
(1) Includes Piedmont, Liguria and Sardinia.
(2) Includes Campania, Abruzzi, Molise, Puglie, Basilicata, Calabria, and Sicilia.
Legend: sb = savings banks; boc = banks of ordinary credit; cb = cooperative banks.
Sources: Ministry of Agriculture, Industry and Commerce (M.A.I.C.), *Le casse di risparmio ordinarie in Italia dal 1822 al 1904*, Roma, Bertero, 1906; T. Martello and A. Montanari (1875); M.A.I.C., *Statistica delle Banche Popolari*, Roma, Tipografia Bodoniana, 1882; M.A.I.C., *Statistica delle casse di risparmio*, Roma, Bertero, 1896.

2.3   Banking in the various regions and the banks of issue as credit institutions

In 1860 the banking system in Italy was very rudimentary; in the South it was especially backward. There were 91 savings banks and 4 banks of ordinary credit (Table 9.1). None of the foregoing was located in the South, which accounted, instead, for the majority of corn banks (1,145 out of a total of 1,678 in 1861) and pledge banks (226 out of 547 in the same year). Numerous Italian and foreign banking houses existed in various parts of Italy about which we unfortunately have no information.

After 1863 there was an increase in the number of banks of ordinary credit and a few years later the first cooperative banks were set up. In 1873 there were 124 banks of ordinary credit and 88 cooperative banks. Most of

(A: in millions of lire; B: lire per capita)

| | 1860 | | 1880 | |
	A	B	A	B
Former Kingdom of Sardinia	7	1.7	259	55.8
Lombardy and Veneto	89	15.9	519	79.9
Emilia, Marches and Umbria	22	6.5	160	43.3
Tuscany	26	13.2	212	96.2
Latium	14	18.8	75	83.1
Southern Regions	—	—	68	6.5
Total	158	6.3	1,293	45.4

Table 9.2 *Current and savings account deposits at savings banks, banks of ordinary credit and cooperative banks in 1860 and 1880*

Sources: see Table 9.1.

Notes: The 1860 figures refer to savings banks only. The 1880 figures for cooperative banks refer to 124 institutions; those for banks of ordinary credit refer to 31 October 1881 and are calculated from data published in M.A.C.I., *Bollettino semestrale del credito cooperativo, ordinario, agrario e fondiario, Appendice al bollettino del secondo semestre 1886*, Roma, Tipografia Botta, 1888.

the former were located in the former Kingdom of Sardinia (consisting of Piedmont, Liguria and Sardinia), while the latter expanded rapidly in Lombardy and Veneto. In a summary assessment of credit conditions around 1874, Martello and Montanari wrote of the persisting 'disadvantaged state of the Southern regions, with the provinces of L'Aquila, Benevento, Caltanissetta, Girgenti and Trapani totally lacking the benefit deriving from purely local initiatives, since they only have access to the credit supplied by the branches of some banks of issue. At Siracusa, Chieti, Cosenza, Teramo, Avellino and Campobasso the only types of institution to be found, apart from the aforementioned branches, were a cooperative bank at Siracusa and savings banks in the other provinces' (Martello and Montanari, 1874, pp. 183–84).

Twenty years after the unification of Italy, the total number of savings banks, banks of ordinary credit and cooperative banks had risen to 436. The same period also saw the birth of agricultural and real estate credit institutions and an expansion of the activity of the Savings and Loans Fund. However, even though 37% of the population lived in the South, in 1880 no more than 18% of Italian banks were located there (with banks of ordinary credit accounting for only 25% of this total) and deposits in the South were hardly more than 5% of the total (Table 9.2). An indication of the different degree of development of the banking system in the various

| | 1860 | | | | 1880 | | | |
	A	B	C	D	A	B	C	D
Piedmont	2.0	15.7	53.0	17.6	6.9	15.1	45.3	27.4
Liguria	—	4.5	4.5	—	3.2	8.7	5.1	2.0
Lombardy	5.3	75.1	6.9	1.0	1.2	13.4	54.6	12.1
Veneto	11.8	2.9	5.9	79.4	7.3	33.0	33.4	16.6
Emilia	50.5	24.1	5.3	13.6	31.9	16.9	26.5	6.2
Marches	55.9	11.8	—	11.8	63.0	9.4	2.6	6.2
Umbria	50.0	8.3	—	41.7	69.2	11.0	—	5.5
Tuscany	—	6.9	5.4	76.2	0.1	22.1	42.4	22.5
Latium	0.7	43.7	14.8	16.9	2.1	47.5	29.7	1.3
Abruzzo	—	—	—	—	84.6	—	7.7	—
Continental South	—	—	—	—	26.5	7.4	13.2	25.0
Sicily	—	—	—	—	37.0	7.3	49.7	1.2
Total	11.0	49.1	8.2	18.7	10.9	17.9	40.5	12.3

Table 9.3 *Lending operations of savings banks (as a percentage of inter-mediated funds)*

Legend: A = discounts; B = mortgage loans; C = securities; D = unsecured loans (mostly to communes, provinces and public entities).
Source: G.B. Morsiani, *Notizie storiche sulle casse di risparmio dell'Emilia*, Tipografia Compositori, Bologna, 1941.

areas between 1860 and 1880 may be derived also from the composition of the assets of the savings banks (the only category for which an inter-temporal comparison can be made): while in Emilia, Lombardy and Veneto there was a significant decline in discounted bills as a ratio to total assets held by these intermediaries and a rise in securities holdings – suggesting that the entry of other categories of banks enabled savings banks to acquire an asset composition closer in line with that typical of basically philanthropic institutions, such as those in Piedmont had had from the beginning of the 1860s – in the South, by contrast, the proportion of discount business in savings banks' total assets was, in 1880, well above the national average as a result of the relative lack of banks of ordinary credit and the small amount of funds raised by the cooperative banks (Table 9.3).

Due to the growth in the size and services of commercial banks in the first twenty years of the new Kingdom, the vital role that the banks of issue were called on to perform at the turn of the 1860s was gradually reduced over time: issue banks' total assets fell from 68 to 30% of those of the banking system as a whole between 1870 and 1880 (Biscaini Cotula and Ciocca, 1979). However, these aggregate data conceal wide regional

(Number of banks)

	BNR	BNT	BTC	BR	BN	BS	Total	SB + BOC + CB
Former Kingdom of Sardinia	10	—	—	—	1	—	11	74
Lombardy, Veneto	18	—	—	—	2	—	20	84
Emilia, Marches and Umbria	13	1	—	—	—	—	14	136
Tuscany	4	8	1	—	1	—	14	44
Latium	1	—	—	1	1	1	4	19
Southern regions	24	—	—	—	12	7	43	79
Total	70	9	1	1	17	8	106	436

Table 9.4 *Regional distribution of commercial banks and of banks of issue in 1880*

Source: See Table 9.1 for sb, boc and cb. For the banks of issue, see Banca Nazionale nel Regno d'Italia, *Adunanza ordinaria degli azionisti*, 1881, and I. Sachs, *L'Italie, ses finances et son développement économique depuis l'unification du royaume 1859–1884*, Librairie Guillaumin, Paris, 1885.

disparities, the credit function pertaining to the banks of issue in the South decreasing at a much slower pace.

When the regional distribution of the branches of the banks of issue is compared with that of that of the other credit institutions it can be seen that in 1880 the regions of the former Kingdom of Sardinia had roughly the same number of banks as the Southern regions, but the latter had four times as many branches of banks of issue (Table 9.4). Comparison of the volume of discounts and advances granted in 1883 by cooperative banks, banks of ordinary credit and agricultural credit institutions with that of the banks of issue suggests that the latter's expansion permitted more extensive recourse to credit in the areas where the other kinds of intermediary were slow to develop. Even though the figures for the banks of issue include their discount business with other intermediaries, it can safely be claimed that their customer business in the provinces of the former Kingdom of Sardinia was small, while in the South it was preponderant. In the former, the banks of issue disbursed 553 million lire, compared with 989 million by the other kinds of bank (Table 9.5), and the inclusion of interbank discount business results in the importance of the direct financing of the economy effected by the banks of issue being overstated. In the Southern regions, the corresponding figures were 634 million and 367 million. Even if all the other banks' discounted bills had been rediscounted by the banks of issue, the figures indicate that the latter's direct financing of the economy was on a very substantial scale; the

	BNR	BNT	BTC	BR	BN	BS	Total	Others (*)
Former Kingdom of Sardinia	476.7 —	—	—		76.4	—	553.1	989
Lombardy and Veneto	516.5 —	—	—		10.1	—	526.6	677
Emilia, Marches and Umbria	193.6 —	—	—		—	—	193.6	215
Tuscany	136.9	155.2	47.6	—	47.9	3.6	391.2	236
Latium	42.9 —	—	127		34.6	40.5	245.0	301
Southern regions	259.8 —	—	—		297.5	76.2	633.5	367
Total	1,626.5	155.2	47.6	127	466.6	120.3	2,543.0	2,785

Table 9.5 *Discount operations and advances of credit institutions and banks of issue in 1881 (in millions of lire)*

(*) Cooperative banks, banks of ordinary credit and agricultural credit institutions.
Sources: M.A.I.C., *Bollettino mensile delle situazioni dei conti degli instituti de emissione, anno XII*, n. 12, Tipografia Eredi Botta, Roma, 1882; M.A.I.C., *Bollettino semestrale del credito*, cit.

backwardness of the Southern banking system still required the banks of issue to perform a far from negligible role in directly financing the economy.

The picture drawn above indicates that the credit activity that the banks of issue were asked to perform varied from one part of the country to another as a result of the need to fill the gaps left by the non-issuing credit institutions. The force of tradition nonetheless resulted in some banks of issue adjusting to the needs of the local economies of the new state more slowly than others.

The range of operations permitted by the Statutes of the banks of issue was fairly similar – all of them were authorized to discount bills and to grant advances – but some difference did exist. The Statutes of the Tuscan banks (the BNT and the BNC) provided for the discount of bills signed by two persons, while three signatures were required by the other banks of issue. The question of the number of signatures is significant because bills were more likely to be presented for discount by a banker when three operators were involved. The maximum maturity of discountable bills was three months for the BNR, five for the BTC and six for the BS. The BNT used to renew maturing bills almost automatically and at the BN – which allowed a maximum maturity of three months, extended to four in 1863 – there was the longstanding tradition of allowing landowners and

	1861	1865	1866	1874	1884
BNR	61.9	58.5	34.1	46.8	38.6
BNT	57.7	71.8	67.5	49.4	44.9
BTC	72.7*	65.4	52.5	57.6	70.4
BN	39.2	48.8	36.8	45.6	40.9
BS	4.2	7.5	6.1	49.9	46.0
BR	—	—	—	55.6	52.1

Table 9.6 *Credit to the private sector (including banks) granted by banks of issue (as a percentage of total assets)*

(*) The figure refers to 31 December 1864.
Source: Banca d'Italia (1967), Tomo I, tav. 2.

especially small tradesmen to pay a tenth part of the discounted bill at maturity and to issue a new one for the residual amount, a practice that was only abandoned in 1866. Both the BNR and the BNT were allowed to grant advances backed by government and industrial securities, silk, foreign bills, ingots and coins. However, the interest rates charged by the BNT penalized advances against silk, a form of finance considered of importance in the provinces of the former Kingdom of Sardinia, which had a substantial silk industry. Neither the BNR nor the BNT accepted valuables as collateral for advances, as did the BN, which continued to provide pledge credit for a long time.

To some extent the Statutes appear to reflect the features of the regional economy in which each bank of issue was founded and did not always make exceptions for the branches operating in other areas. For instance, even though the BNR had contemplated modifying its Statutes in order better to meet the needs of the Southern market, it generally required bills to carry three signatures. By contrast, the BN, which had decided after much discussion to keep the three-signature requirement when it revised its Statutes in 1863, allowed its Florence branch to discount bills with two signatures, in line with the practice of the Tuscan banks of issue.

Comparison of the issuing banks' balance sheets immediately after the unification of Italy shows that the Tuscan banks (the BNT and the BTC) and the BNR granted a much greater proportion of credit in the form of discounts and advances than their Southern counterparts (the BN and the BS) (Table 9.6). In particular, the credit activity of the BS was reduced almost to zero in the early 1860s as a result of its endowment fund being plundered by the Bourbon Government in 1860 and subsequently by the dictatorship and the national Government. Among the private banks of issue, the Tuscan ones engaged more heavily in credit business than the BNR. Furthermore, the average maturity of the latter's discounts was around 50 days in the period 1861–65, with a peak of 58 days in 1863, while that of the BNT was over 100 days. The average maturity for the BTC in the two years 1863–64 was 144 days, and though it shortened considerably in the two following years, the average remained above 80 days. As regards advances, the proportion backed by industrial securities in the period 1860–67 was much greater for the BNT (21.6%) than for the BNR (3.4%); while advances backed by silk accounted for 3.5% of the BNR's total, the figure for the BNT was only 0.6%.

The distribution of discount credit according to the type of operator presenting the bills reveals the most significant qualitative differences and, as mentioned earlier, reflects the different rules banks adopted for the number of signatures they required. The valuable information published by the Parliamentary Committee of Enquiry into Currency Inconvertibility shows that the BNR had a much higher proportion of rediscount business than the two Tuscan banks. Unfortunately, there is no comparable information on the Southern banks, but it is reasonable to assume, in view of the undeveloped state of the banking system in the South in the 1860s, that there was only a small proportion of rediscount business. The discounts granted by the BNR to bankers, savings banks and other credit institutions accounted for around 58 per cent of the total in 1861–62 and, notwithstanding a downward trend, this proportion never fell below 47% in the following five years. By contrast, rediscounts accounted for only 12.2% of the discount business of the BNT's office in Florence in 1865–67 and the corresponding figure for the BTC was 11%. The gradual reduction in the importance of rediscounts for the BNR, matched by an increase in that of its discounting of bills presented by tradesmen and industrialists (which rose from 36 to 48% of the total between 1861 and 1864), was probably related to that bank's geographical expansion, which led to its operating in regions in which the calls on banks of issue to fill the gaps left by the absence of commercial banks were greater.

The proportion of the BNR's discounts and advances going to Southern provinces rose from 0.5% in 1861 to 7% in the two following years, to 9% in 1864 and to 23% in 1865. It would appear that the BNR's expansion in the South was well received,[11] partly in view of the initial comparative apathy of the Southern banks. As time passed, however, the latter became less and less bankers to the state and began to build up their lending to private customers: between 1861 and 1865 the ratio of discounts and advances to total assets of the BN rose from 39 to 49 per cent, though this was still well below the levels of the other banks of issue. The inexperience of the BN in the field of bill discounting for customers led, however, to

| | 1861 | | 1865 | | 1866 | | 1874 | | 1884 | |
	cred	totat	cred	totat	cred	totat	cred	totat	cred	totat
BNR	55.8	42.6	60.1	55.5	71.1	73.8	55.6	56.1	58.3	61.1
BNT	13.6	11.2	13.4	10.0	10.5	5.5	9.8	9.4	7.5	6.8
BTC	—	—	1.2	1.1	2.0	1.3	2.9	2.5	2.5	1.4
BN	29.7	35.8	24.2	27.1	15.7	15.2	23.6	24.4	24.5	24.2
BS	0.9	10.4	0.9	6.3	0.7	4.2	8.1	7.6	7.3	6.4
BR	—	—	—	—	—	—	7.9	6.7	7.5	5.8
Total	100	100	100	100	100	100	107.9	106.7	107.5	105.8

Table 9.7 *Credit to the private sector and total assets of the banks of issue (percentage values)*

cred = credit to the private sector; totat = total assets.
Source: see Table 9.6

serious operating problems. The committees appointed to manage the discount business had a large and varying membership, which prevented the application of uniform criteria and led to signatures being judged unacceptable on one occasion and creditworthy a short time later. Furthermore, the failure of BN to follow the standard procedure of recording individual credit limits meant that it was unable to avoid excessive risk concentration. In turn, this led to an increase in bad debts and renewals of bills at maturity, a situation that only returned to normal after some years.

When paper currency was declared inconvertible in 1866, the BNR's growing business with the state resulted in its importance among the banks of issue increasing; meanwhile, the rate of increase in its lending to private customers slowed down. In 1874, when the Banking Act which standardized the regulations governing the banks of issue came into force, the proportions of these banks' assets that consisted of private sector loans was very similar – between 46% and 50%, except for the BTC and the BR, which had shares of over 50%.

A comparison between the two years immediately before and after the long period of inconvertible currency (1865 and 1884), reveals a marked change in the classification of issuing banks based on this criterion. In 1865 the portion of total assets destined for loans to private customers, which was highest for the two Tuscan banks, was much higher for the BNR than for the Southern banks; in 1884 the BNR was in bottom place, reserving only 39% of its assets for private customer credit. While the BNR's overall position gained considerable strength following political unification (its share of total assets rose from 43% to over 60% of the total for the issuing banks, excluding the BR), its relative importance as a granter of credit did not change very much (Table 9.7).

While the portion of assets allocated by each issuing bank to financing private customers had gradually become more similar, a number of qualitative differences remained in the type of credit granted. A government inspection of the issuing banks undertaken in 1880 showed that the BNT's discounting transactions concealed long-term credit; it confirmed the preference given by the BNR to paper presented by bankers and by other credit institutions; it emphasized the dynamic management and substantial solidity of the BS and revealed the non-commercial nature of bills of exchange allowed for discount by the BN, as well as the latter's excessive involvement in pledge operations (Atti Parlamentari, 1880b). The market continued to be somewhat fragmented, as is confirmed by the different rates applied by the issuing banks in a single location. For much of the period 1878–79, for instance, all the issuing banks, with the exception of the BS, were able to keep their discount rates above that of the BNR by accepting bills that the latter refused, sticking to more rigorous criteria for the assessment of credit worthiness.[12]

It would seem, in conclusion, that by widening their fields of operation the issuing banks helped to spread the benefits of credit in some areas of the country where they were completely lacking. Their different *modi operandi* nevertheless survived at least partially, in spite of the fact that territorial expansion led to the simultaneous presence of more than one bank of issue in certain locations. Thus the coexistence of several banks of issue would have had a limited impact on increasing competition in the credit market, with the effect of moderating the price of loans. A single bank of issue would perhaps have been equally effective in spreading credit. However, the differences in operations and in customers between the various banks of issue and the dominance of a concept that linked the function of issuing banknotes with that of granting credit to the economy, may have represented a considerable obstacle to the implementation of the government's plans for unification, on account of the difficulties of bringing about a swift change in payment customs.

2.4 *Payment customs and the difficulties of reconciling the granting of credit with the issuing of bank notes.*

At the time of political unification there was more than four times as much currency circulating in the form of metal coins as paper money: in 1859 approximately 90 types of metal coin were legal tender. Consequently, the unification of metal coinage, while probably more urgent, was also

| | | | Percentage shares | | | Lire per capita in the designated area of operation | |
	1861	1865	1866	1874	1884	1860 ca. (*)	1882
BNR	28.1	43.8	72.7	57.3	65.1	13.1	16.2
BNT	11.3	8.9	4.7	9.9	7.8	10.5	25.5
BTC	—	2.0	9.0	2.4	1.7		
BN	47.6	38.4	16.7	24.8	21.0	14.0	11.5
BS	13.0	8.7	5.0	5.6	4.5		9.2
BR	—	—	—	7.9	5.7	18.0	50.7
Total	100.0	100.0	100.0	107.9	105.7		
in millions of lire:							
	233.5	283.2	637.1	648.8	899.1		

Table 9.8 *Paper currency in circulation (including certificates of deposit issued by the Southern banks)*

(*) The notes of the Austrian National Bank circulating in Lombardy and those of the Banca per le Quattro Legazioni circulating in Emilia were approximately equal to three lire per inhabitant.
Sources: Banca d'Italia (1967), Tomo I; De Mattia (1959); Seconda Relazione della Commissione Permanente per l'abolizione del corso forzoso, *Atti Parlamentari, Camera dei Deputati, Legislatura XV, Prima sessione 1882–3*, Doc. XX.

perhaps less traumatic than the unification of banknotes: a public accustomed to handling a large variety of coins would probably be more ready to accept a new coin that would considerably simplify even minor transactions by increasing the uniformity of metal currency in different areas. The fact that, as already noted, the public was almost everywhere accustomed to using paper money issued by only one bank could, on the other hand, have led to less elasticity where paper instruments of payment were concerned.

Around 1860 the use of paper instruments of payment was more widespread in the South than elsewhere (Table 9.8). One of the reasons for this was that the certificates of deposit issued by the BN enjoyed special privileges: they were accepted as cash by public administrations (which was true of BNT, though not BNR notes); they were exchanged for metal by the State cashiers and any contract could be sealed with them, including the purchase and sale of real estate, without paying either stamp duties or registration fees. Finally, as Minister Manna wrote in 1863, 'the confusion generated by the government with regard to private and public deposits had *de facto* extended the latter's guarantee to the former' (Atti Parlamentari, 1868, vol. 1, p. 38), thus strengthening operators' confidence in BN means of payment: the latter also offered depositors, free of charge, the faculty to issue orders payable to third parties on their deposits.

The Southern banks were thus quite active in promoting the development of the system of payments by offering several services to their customers, while, as we have seen, their expertise in supplying credit was less developed. It is therefore hardly surprising that at the beginning of the sixties the territorial expansion of the BNR, which had been given a fairly good reception in its role as a credit institution, should have been met in the South by a marked reluctance on the part of operators to accept its notes.[13] While in areas such as Lombardy and Emilia the BNR's arrival could play a decisive role in encouraging the spread of previously almost non-existent paper means of payment, this was not the case in the South, where the Bank faced the problems of at least partially substituting a well tried and fairly widespread instrument with a new one.

Expansion in the South was thus a very expensive exercise: to the costs of transporting metal from one part of the country to another – an operation further complicated by the lack of communications and by the dangers from banditry – there had to be added those arising from the need to hold much larger reserves than the statute required, in order to meet more frequent and less predictable demands for conversion. In the six years prior to the suspension of convertibility the BNR's level of note cover rose gradually, averaging 52.5% (the minimum fixed by the bank's statute was 33%). The bank probably came to realize that it would be much more expensive to attempt to impose new payment customs than to give in to old ones, at least so long as redemption was compulsory: the former course would have implied a less efficient use of the country's metal stocks than would have been possible by reaching agreements for the reciprocal acceptance of means of payment issued by different banks. This was therefore the approach adopted in dealing with the Southern banks – an approach not without considerable difficulties, since the BN sometimes exchanged certificates with pre-unification coins already withdrawn from circulation. The BNR temporarily suspended acceptance of these certificates by its branches, but it is interesting to note that in justifying this step the Manager, Bombrini, deemed it expedient to point out that the measure did not result from fears of competition from the Southern banks, since the BNR was '. . . convinced that Italy in general and the Southern Provinces in particular (offered) a vast field of operations, in which both the (Southern) banks and the Bank (could) find adequate business.' (Report of the meeting of the Board of Directors of 28 June 1864).

The difficulties encountered in the South were thus presumably responsible for eroding the BNR's confidence in its ability to beat the BN's
competition without the aid of legislation that would remove the Southern
banks' faculty to issue payment instruments having *de facto* the same
functions as banknotes. There being no chance of any such intervention,
the BNR's resolution to conquer new market shares may have weakened,
and the importance it attributed to the possibility of merging with the
BNT also faded. Relations between the two banks had in any case cooled
in the meantime as a result of widely differing views of the role they were
called upon to fulfill.

This controversy, which had arisen during discussion of the stature to be
given to the projected 'Banca d'Italia', centred on three issues: (1) whether
a bank of issue should restrict its discounting activities to bills with three
signatures, leaving bills with only two signatures to smaller banks, as
maintained by the BNR, to which the BNT objected that this would
penalize small traders; (2) whether to entrust the executive with the task of
nominating the Governor of the single bank of issue, as proposed by the
BNT, in contrast with the BNR, which maintained that 'the controller
cannot be the administrator'; (3) whether to decentralize the new bank's
administration, giving it regional head offices with responsibility over
branches, as advocated by the BNT, whose own internal organization
allowed broad local autonomy. The BNR reserved its fiercest criticism for
the last of these issues, pointing out that to allow the branch offices to
decide the allocation of funds assigned to them by the central headquarters for discounting and advances would be sufficient to ensure due
consideration of local needs. The Bank further objected that excessive
decentralization would slow down the administrative machinery '. . . since
there would be no strong hand with the authority to steer it along the path
that (. . .) should be trodden at the speed of light'; finally, that 'the general
interests of the country . . . in matters of credit can never be separated
from the specific interests of each region' (Report of the extraordinary
meeting of shareholders held on 7 October 1863, p. 21).

This dispute between the two major private banks of issue whose merger
was intended to create the Bank of Italy reveals the BNR's concept of the
nature of a bank of issue and suggests that it was not fully prepared to take
on the role of leader on the terms outlined in the government's projects for
unification. The controversy with the BNT seems to suggest that the BNR
was reluctant to expand its role as dispenser of credit to the economy,
tending instead towards a pyramid-shaped banking system within which
to concentrate chiefly on refinancing operations. One also has the feeling
that, while acknowledging the need for public control over issuing
activities, the Bank wished to defend its independence of the government

(albeit probably not in order to guarantee its own margin of independence on issues of 'monetary control', but rather to safeguard the interests of its shareholders); lastly, the Bank seems to have been aware of the national dimension of monetary matters, which were not always compatible with the varying calls made on the banks of issue in their capacity as credit institutions in the regions.

We can thus not exclude the possibility that the government's strategy may have lost some of its credibility: if the Southern banks were maintained and allowed to continue to procure their livelihood by issuing instruments of payment effectively identical to banknotes, the new Bank of Italy's monopoly of issue would be a mere formality. To prevent the Southern banks from issuing certificates of deposit, limiting their activities to those of credit institutions while exonerating the new – single – bank of issue from credit functions would perhaps have encouraged the spread of the latter's notes, at the same time enabling it to reinforce its function as lender of last resort. The Southern banks would, however, have had to create new means of raising funds: they would necessarily have had to seek credit from the bank of issue and would have had to develop their lending activities very rapidly. This solution thus involved overturning the 'comparative advantages' that the banks in question had initially enjoyed: the Southern banks, after years of experience as State banks, would have become bankers to commerce and had to forgo their faculty to issue the liabilities favoured by local operators; at the same time the market would suddenly have been deprived of the credit offered by the two private banks, whose notes still in 1863 represented 40 per cent of the total paper money in circulation. This kind of solution, moreover, while it would probably have been welcomed by the BNR, would have been opposed by the BNT, which was deeply convinced of its mission as a credit-granting institution; lastly, it would have gone against the very banking philosophy of the time, which was based on the premise that banks of issue are created for the purpose of facilitating commerce, that their assets should consist to a large extent of 'real' commercial bills and that any investment of their funds in foreign assets or government securities should be strictly limited.

Having discarded the possibility of preserving the Southern banks while depriving them of certificates of deposit as a form of raising funds, there remained the possibility of incorporating the BN and the BS into the new bank of issue. This option was initially considered by the government, which rejected it in view of the Southern banks' opposition. This solution would have involved solving the question of the legal status to be attributed to the resulting bank, formed by merging two private joint stock companies and two institutions funded originally by government endowments. It would also have made it even more unthinkable to separate the credit and issuing functions, given the almost total absence – at least in the first years of the new Kingdom's existence – of other types of intermediary in the vast area of the Southern provinces. To enable a single Bank to perform such widely varying credit functions as those actually performed by the different banks, it would have been necessary to allow wider decision-making powers at the local level than the BNR was probably prepared to concede. Given the diversity of criteria adopted by the different banks in assessing the merits of loans, it is probable that even if the BNR had been authorized to apply different discount rates in different regions, it would have chosen to ration loans to some Southern bank customers.

   There was thus no easy way out for the government. With the rejection of the compromise outlined in the first half of the sixties and the adoption of inconvertibility, the position of the Southern banks as banks of issue, while gaining legitimacy, declined, to the advantage of the BNR (Table 9.8). On the other hand, as we have seen, the share of total assets granted by the latter as credit to private customers had in the meantime contracted. At this point the possibility of separating the issuing and credit functions gained in feasibility. Nonetheless, there still remained the cultural barrier represented by the inviolable coupling of the two functions, a barrier that became increasingly decisive.

3   A plurality of issuing banks and monetary stability

When he recounted the story of Italian banks of issue to the National Monetary Commission of the US Congress, Canovai noted that it was a particularly instructive one since it clearly illustrated the ruinous effects that are inevitably produced by bad banking systems and went on to assert that a great many of the difficulties encountered at times of political and economic crisis would have been avoided if there had been only one bank of issue (Canovai, 1911).

   In reality, the effects of the plurality of issuing banks on monetary stability in the 19th century are hard to disentangle from those of other factors. In the first half of the 1860s, the country's financial difficulties were primarily due to the growing budget deficit and vulnerability to events on foreign money markets resulting from the size of the foreign debt. It was these factors, together with the need to support some commercial banks, that principally underlay the suspension of convertibility in 1866. The key factors in the persistence with inconvertibility and the heavy depreciation of the lira were the gradual approach adopted to the adjustment of the public finances and the decision to increase the share of monetary financing of the deficit in the initial phase. Competition between the various banks of issue, which had generally been modest in the two previous decades, became fiercer during the eighties. Again, however, the effects of the existence of several banks of issue were intertwined with those of other factors (faulty legislation, ineffective government supervision and the fraudulent behaviour of one of the banks, the BR).[14] These factors, aggravated by a new deterioration in the public finances and periodic crises on foreign stock exchanges, contributed to episodes of excessive money creation and dangerous waves of speculation. The result was a worsening of the quality of the issuing banks' assets, the failure of numerous commercial banks, the depreciation of the lira and, towards the end of the decade, the *de facto* restriction on payments in gold and silver and the return to inconvertibility in February 1894.[15]

Setting the problems that the increase in the public sector borrowing requirement and the high level of foreign debt created for monetary control against the generally positive results obtained in the first decade of the twentieth century in ensuring exchange rate stability[16] and damping the impact of the 1907 international crisis on the domestic market, suggests that the plurality of issuing banks was probably neither a necessary nor a sufficient condition for the monetary instability recorded in Italy during the 19th century. However, even if the inadequate coordination, and sometimes competition, between the banks of issue were not the only causes of the excessive money creation, they certainly contributed to make the money supply less flexible and to the virtual abandonment, even in the periods of convertibility, of the discount rate as an instrument for the control of credit and money.

From the very first years of the new Kingdom, less use was made of the discount rate, which was controlled exclusively by the banks of issue until 1866, than in the other main European countries which were on a metal standard.[17] In a period of full convertibility, with complete freedom of capital movements and a high degree of dependence on foreign markets for the financing of the government, the relative stickiness of the discount rate in Italy can be related to the oligopolistic structure of the note-issuing function, though, as shown above, there was still a degree of market segmentation. Most of the time the signal for the BNR to modify its discount rate was a change in the interest rates on foreign markets, so that its action can be seen as having been purely defensive. When the outflow of reserves from the BNR was thought to have a domestic destination, it preferred not to raise its discount rate, possibly because it feared that the other banks of issue, in whose territories it was expanding its operations, would not follow suit. In these circumstances the BNR countered the reduction in the cover of its note issue by importing gold and silver through the sale of securities on foreign markets or by borrowing from its foreign correspondents, a policy that was frowned on, however, by its own shareholders. It thus cannot be excluded that the plurality of issuing banks may have influenced not only the level of interest rates but also their variability, but the exchange rate was kept basically stable. The crisis of Spring 1866 was due to events that were mostly beyond the control of the banks of issue. The decision to tackle the crisis by suspending convertibility was judged to be inevitable even by the economist Ferrara, one of the fiercest critics of the Italian note-issuing arrangements.

After the suspension of convertibility, the discount rate no longer served to regulate the issuing banks' gold and silver reserves and was almost completely ignored: during the seventeen years of inconvertibility, the BNR's rate was changed only five times. In this period changes in the discount rate had to be resulting from increases. However, the Government failed to replace foreign central banks in providing signals for discount rate changes and, while it opposed some applications for the discount rate to be lowered, it never imposed any increases.[18] The introduction in 1874 of limits on the currency in circulation was a sort of recognition of the Government's difficulties in effectively regulating the discount rate policy of the banks of issue.

With the return to convertibility in 1883, there was a revival of inflows of capital from abroad and market interest rates were pushed down below those of the banks of issue. As already mentioned, the latter's importance within the banking system had declined during the 1870s. They thus found themselves fighting for smaller market shares, which also contained fewer prime customers. In the first two years of convertibility the most active user of the discount rate, which had been returned to the discretion of the banks of issue, was the BN, which sought to expand business by lowering the rate, followed somewhat reluctantly by the BNR. The BNR also criticized the Southern issuing banks' habit of applying a rate below the official one on its discount business with cooperative banks.[19]

The exchange rate, which had remained below the official parity until the Summer of 1884, subsequently began to weaken. This was a cause of concern for the Treasury Minister, who held a meeting with a managing directors of the banks of issue and invited them to suspend their discount business at rates below the official one. The agreement, which made an exception for the BN, was not respected and it was left to the BNR on its own to grapple with the exchange rate problem. With the support of one of the major commercial banks (Società Generale di Credito Mobilaire) and helped by a loan from the Treasury, the BNR intervened on the Paris stock exchange to reduce the gap between the yield on Italian government securities listed there and that available in Italy with the aim of eliminating one of the causes of the depreciation of the lira.[20] Another agreement on preferential discount rates was reached in February 1885, with an exception being made this time for the BS. This agreement was also not respected and another exchange rate crisis developed.

In June 1885 a law was approved that again subjected discount rate policy to Government authorization. The same law provided for preferential rates for the discounting of bills presented by cooperative banks and other intermediaries, though the difference compared with the official rate was restricted to one percentage point. In the ten-year period 1883–93 the latter was even more rigid than during the years of inconvertibility.[21] In the meantime, the banks of issue had been allowed to increase their issues to over three times the value of their capital, provided there was 100% backing for the amount in excess. The measure led the issuing banks to borrow abroad, where credit conditions were easy at the time, to increase their reserves and expand their note circulation and domestic lending. This increased the Italian market's vulnerability to events abroad and when foreign bankers' attitude towards Italy changed, the banks of issue were unable to comply with the reserve requirement. After 1885 it became common for the currency in circulation to exceed the limits laid down by law, and this situation persisted even after the Government had summoned the managing directors of the issuing banks to a meeting during the Autumn 1887 exchange rate crisis and invited them to bring the note circulation back within the prescribed limits. Between 1883 and 1893 the circulation of the BNR expanded by 49%, that of the BS and the BN by 73 and 83% respectively, and that of the BNT and the BR by 110 and 130%. In relation to GDP, the total money supply (including state notes and bank deposits) was nearly always above the long-term rising trend. In 1894 the lira had depreciated by 12% against the French franc and the pound sterling compared with eleven years earlier. In February of that year the convertibility of the lira was suspended once more and was not to return until the 1920s.

It can thus be seen that not even the introduction of ceilings on circulation or reserve requirements were effective. There are at least two reasons for this: on some occasions towards the end of the eighties the Government itself considered it desirable for the BNR to expand the note circulation beyond the legal limit with the aim of supporting commercial banks that ran into difficulties, thereby eroding the credibility of the limits and giving the other banks of issue the impression, confirmed at the beginning of the following decade, that the authorities would ratify overshoots. Furthermore, the mechanisms for the exchange of notes between the various banks of issue were not left to operate freely, often on the grounds that it was necessary to prevent sudden large reductions in the credit available in some regions.

	BNR	BN	BNT	BR	BS	BTC
1885	43.3	40.3	362.1	22.2	102.3	64.3
1886	39.3	46.9	480.9	2.3	—	—
1887	33.8	62.4	480.2	3.8	—	—
1888	32.2	60.4	375.9	3.1	—	—
1889	31.6	57.8	10.5	4.4	—	0.5
1890	28.2	52.9	101.1	2.8	—	78.6
1891	28.7	15.3	116.7	—	14.8	13.3
1892	17.5	—	21.4	—	—	—

Table 9.9 *Note conversion: inter-issuing banks' balances as a percentage of each bank's average circulation*

Source: M.A.I.C., *Bollettino mensile delle situazioni dei conti degli istituti di emissione.*

   While the regime of inconvertibility was in force the only factor able to curb possible excesses of circulation by one institution or another was the note clearing system between issuing banks. The quantitative and temporal limitations imposed on this mechanism – clearing was carried out every seven days and another seven were allowed for the settlement of balances – narrowed the scope for any bank wishing to create the basis for a favourable redistribution of reserves to its own advantage by adopting a more cautious policy. There was thus no incentive to keep circulation below the maximum limit allowed by law.[22] Moreover, in order to fan demand for their own notes and discourage requests for conversion, and since any manoeuvring of discount rates was subject to government authorization, the banks concentrated on non-price competition.[23]

   In preparation for the return to convertibility, further limits to the exchange of notes between issuing banks were introduced in order to safeguard the banks whose geographical areas of operation were limited.[24] In 1883 the interval between clearing operations was lengthened from 7 to 10 days. Towards the end of the 1880s the system was essentially dismantled;[25] as a consequence, the banks most responsible for swelling the creation of money, which for the most part were those whose notes circulated on a more local basis, were obliged only to a very limited degree to reduce their reserves (Table 9.9).

   In concluding this brief reference to the problems raised by the coexistence of more than one bank of issue from the point of view of monetary control, it would seem that while the existence of several banks of issue began to produce effects on monetary growth only some years after the

unification of Italy, it is likely to have had from the start a certain
restrictive effect on the room for manoeuvring instruments of monetary
control. The absence of any spontaneous forms of cooperation and, at
times, rivalries between the banks of issue – which resulted to a large
extent from their commercial nature and from differences in their legal
status, only some of them being private joint-stock companies – was
matched by legislation and government interventions equally unable to
enforce any effective form of stabilization. The government was unable to
encourage coordination either through interest rate agreements or
through quantitative controls; the latter were far too rigid when crises in
the banking system required extraordinary, albeit temporary, supporting
measures by the banks of issue; their effectiveness in any case depended on
the government's determination to compel the banks to respect the 'rules
of the game' on an inter-regional basis, but, as we have seen, this
determination was completely lacking. The problems of monetary control
that arose would thus not seem wholly attributable to the existence of
more than one bank of issue; they would obviously have been less serious
had there been a monopoly of issue, but also if the government had shown
more incisive coordinating abilities and if the albeit imperfect corrective
mechanisms created by the process of reciprocal clearing had been better
implemented. While it is true that these mechanisms cannot necessarily
prevent the excesive expansion of money in circulation when expansion is
uniformly distributed among the banks, it is also obvious that the way in
which they were enforced in Italy during the last century worked to the
advantage of the more unscrupulous of the issuing banks.

4   Summary and conclusions

In 19th century Italy, the failure to unify paper currency issues, in spite of
political unity, resulted jointly from three kinds of weakness that fueled one
another. First of all there was the lack of a sufficiently strong political will
on the part of the *Government* which gave rise to some inconsistencies: the
Government established a privileged relationship with one of the banks,
but it was unable to guarantee official recognition of the role that bank
was called upon to perform; it sometimes defended the position of the
smaller banks, though such defence did not get to the point of seriously
threatening the dominant position of the major bank. The lack of
sufficiently strong Government incentives to reform the system of note
issue was due, in turn, to the economic theories of the time – which
generally speaking did not view banks of issue as performing an activity
inherently different from that of credit institutions – and to the specific
role assigned to monetary policy within economic policy – priority being

attached to promoting economic growth and the development of the credit system.

Secondly, there was the inability of each of the *issuing banks* to 'export' its style of operating: their models of behaviour, which were partly due to their different legal status, contained too many distinctive features reflecting specific structures of the financial and credit markets in which they traditionally operated for any of them to be adopted on a national scale. Furthermore, the differences in working styles sometimes concealed different views concerning the functions an issuing bank was called upon to perform. The bank with enough resources and skills to expand – the BNR – followed a strategy which was the least exportable, precisely because it was the most advanced with respect to the financial structure of large areas of the country and with respect to the theories of the time, which coupled credit and issue activity together. Indeed, in the early 1860s the BNR had proved willing to revise its *modus operandi* so as to meet the needs of the Southern market; subsequently, however, as it became gradually aware of the difficulties imposed by its expansion, and grew less and less confident of its ability to conquer a position of officially recognized supremacy, the BNR may have to some extent lost interest in performing a truly national role and seems to have decided to adhere more strictly to its traditional operating style, which was tailored to a somewhat more mature and articulated financial system than that of the Southern regions.

Thirdly, there was the impossibility of *market forces* bringing about the supremacy of some of the banks over the others. Contrary to the claims by advocates of currency competition, who suggest that the working of Gresham's Law is reversed in the case of convertible bank money, in the Italian experience the existence of more than one bank did not result in those whose assets were qualitatively superior prevailing over the others. The reason is that the first period of competition under a regime of convertibility, which ended in May 1866, was too short to allow for a profound transformation of long-established payment habits, while during the second period of *de jure* and *de facto* convertibility (1883-late 1880s) the working of market mechanisms, such as the note exchange system, was deliberately hampered.

After re-examining the Italian events of the last century it would seem appropriate to conclude that the reasons for the continued existence of more than one bank of issue were due less to ideological hostility towards monopoly in note-issuing than to the defence of local interests, and that it would be small-minded to interpret the latter either as purely private interests or those of restricted lobbies, or to depict them as the typically chauvinistic attitudes common among large sectors of the population. The experience of those years would furthermore suggest that instability was the consequence of the lack of effective mechanisms for cooperaton rather than the inevitable result of there being more than one bank of issue.

The Italian events of the last century seem to hold few lessons for today. In any attempt to draw some conclusions from that experience, due attention should be paid to the enormous changes that central banking has gone through since then; in many respects considerations based on the differences between the problems of today and those of the last century will prove more appropriate than considerations based on similarities.

The diversities of the issuing banks' working methods and of the concepts of their functions, which in the 19th century were enhanced by the banks' commercial nature and by the need for a selective allocation of resources arising from their close relationships with private economic operators, have been slowly diminishing over the years. As a result of the development of the financial structures in which they operate, central banks' activities are now completely distinct from those of commercial banks and the role they play has become more and more similar from one country to another. Coordinating or even unifying institutions that perform similar functions presents fewer difficulties than those met in the Italian historical example. However, if on the one hand the distribution of profits to shareholders is no longer one of the objectives of a modern central bank, nor is the allocation of resources one of its functions, on the other hand this same evolutionary process has strengthened the role of the central banks as institutions specifically established to pursue objectives of general interest; the differences in 'corporate style' have disappeared, but there are still traces of the specific function to which each of them was assigned in the model of economic development adopted by the countries to which they belong.[26] In discussing the creation of a central bank for Europe it thus becomes crucial to take into account the special relationship between national banks and national Treasuries – the intensity of such relationships varying from country to country.

If the issue we are discussing today is not set against a process of political unification, then the problems that may arise in providing European monetary union with an appropriate institutional framework will be faced by the central banks alone, under the pressures exerted by the workings of market forces. In this case the goal of centrally implementing a common monetary policy may still be achieved, but the costs may become so high[27] that market forces would not be left free to operate indefinitely; furthermore, it is possible that different views concerning the final goals to be achieved may give rise to frictions apparently related to differences in the operating techniques of the national central banks. If a 'rule' at least as stringent as that underlying the working of the gold standard were envisaged, it might be easier – but also less relevant – to entrust one of the existing banks, or a newly created institution, with the task of implementing monetary policy for the union as a whole, even if a common economic policy were lacking. In 19th century Italy, for instance, hostility towards any project to unify the issuing banks grew stronger once convertibility was abandoned, indicating that the risks of entrusting a single bank with the privilege of issuing notes were perceived as much greater in the absence of some form of objective control to avoid over-issue. Such a rule does not exist today. In order to define policy guidelines and ensure their credibility, either coordination at a world-wide level must be ensured, or frequent reassessment of the adequacy of the adopted stance would be necessary within the area.

Renunciation of the pursuit of national monetary policies is certainly the logical consequence of increased international economic and financial integration: it is thus no longer one of the possible options, but rather a compulsory stage in the development of options already decided. The means whereby one might think of going ahead towards monetary unification are nonetheless not so pre-ordained and a gradual approach may be desirable.

The European central banks have now accumulated many years of experience in countries that until a few decades ago presented very pronounced differences. The instruments they use have in the process been enriched and become more homogeneous, but traces of the peculiarities of the financial structures within which they operated were still visible in recent times. In setting off down the road that may lead to the establishment of a European central bank, it would be extremely helpful to take a very close look at the reasons for the survival of differences in their working methods, without either immediately writing them off as mere technicalities or considering them as unwarranted deviations from abstract models. In creating new institutional arrangements, any comparative advantages of national banks should be borne in mind and the best possible use made of them. In countries such as Italy, for example, where inflation has in the past been more pronounced than elsewhere and where the share of savings intermediated by the banks has been relatively high – bringing considerable difficulties in reducing that part of the public deficit financed by the creation of money – the monetary authorities have had to expend a lot of energy in interventions to modify the structure of the monetary and financial markets and have amassed considerable experience in stimulating and controlling the banking system. It is important that the abilities developed over the years should not be thrown away.

The process of harmonizing operational methods and pooling the knowledge and abilities evolved by the different national banks may take time. In the meantime, it seems extremely unlikely that the continued coexistence of these banks could ever lead, in Europe, to the kind of instability briefly recalled in this study. There is no parallel today for the almost total lack of cooperation and, later, the bitter competition between the Italian issuing banks of the last century. That experience suggests, however, that problems may arise if one of the existing banks is given *de facto* a leading function without this being formally recognized, since this may reduce its willingness to take upon itself higher responsibilities, while possibly inducing non-cooperative behaviour on the part of others.

One last, specific, comment suggested by last century's events in the Italian banking system concerns the difficulty of enforcing from the centre the continued respect for the intermediate quantitative targets set for each bank over relatively long periods of time. In the face of exceptional circumstances, the rigidity implicit in these targets more than once led the government itself to encourage the largest bank of issue to waive the limits set for money creation. The means should be ensured whereby national banks could tackle unforeseen circumstances without internationally agreed guidelines losing their credibility.

Appendix

(a) Banks of Issue operating in Italy

In 1860 the following banks of issue operated in the states that a year later became part of the Kingdom of Italy:

1 Sardinian National Bank (BNR), established in 1849 through the merger of the Banca di Genova (est. 1844) and the Banca di Torino (est. 1847);
2 Banca Parmense, established in 1858;
3 Banca per le Quattro Legazioni, established in 1855;
4 Tuscan National Bank (BNT), established in 1857 through the merger of six banks of issue operating in Tuscany;
5 Banco di Napoli (BN), established in 1816 as Banco delle Due Sicilie;
6 Banco di Sicilia (BS), established in 1850 as Banco dei Reali Domini al di là del Faro.

In 1861, the BNR absorbed the Banca Parmense and the Banca per le Quattro Legazioni.

In 1863, the Banca Toscana di Credito (BTC), established in 1860, began its operations.

In 1866, with the annexation of Veneto, BNR absorbed the issue bank operating in that region (Stabilimento mercantile di Venezia).

In 1870, with the annexation of Rome, the Banca Romana (BR) was added to the other banks of issue.

In 1893, the BR collapsed. The BNR, the BNT and the BTC were merged to form the Banca d'Italia, which acted as liquidator of the BR.

In 1926, the faculty to issue banknotes was restricted to the Banca d'Italia.

(b) Measures concerning paper currency circulation (1860–1894).

In 1860–1865, banknotes were not legal tender and they were redeemable at par. The note cover regulations were established by the banks' statutes.

In May 1866, the Government obtained a loan from the BNR and the Bank was freed from the obligation to redeem its banknotes. That part of the BNR's circulation which was not a counterpart of the loan to the Government, however, could not exceed its metal reserves by more than three times. Banknotes issued by the Tuscan banks (BNT, BTC) and certificates of deposit issued by the Southern Banks (BN, BS) became legal tender in Tuscany and in the Southern regions; they could be converted into BNR's inconvertible notes; the BNR provided the other banks with its banknotes up to ⅔ of their metal reserves, which had to remain in their vaults.

In April 1874, a consortium of the six issuing banks was formed to issue inconvertible notes on behalf of the State. The notes issued by the banks became legal tender wherever a branch was established; their amount could not exceed the banks' capital or endowment fund, nor their reserves by more than three times.

In April 1883, convertibility was resumed and banknotes continued to be legal tender.

In June 1885, it was established that the circulation of the banks of issue could exceed the limits previously set, provided the excess circulation was 100% covered by metal reserves.

In February 1894 it was established that requests for conversion of bank-notes could be met using either metal or inconvertible State notes.

NOTES

Historical Research Office of the Bank of Italy. I am grateful to my colleagues at the Historical Research Office for their comments and, in particular, to Sergio Cardarelli, who provided numerous stimulating insights during an internal seminar held in December 1987. I would also like to thank Leandro Conte and Curzio Giannini for their many helpful suggestions during all the stages of the work. I am especially grateful to Franco Bonelli for the invaluable help he patiently and generously gave during discussions based on the reading of a preliminary draft of the paper. The responsibility for any remaining errors and omissions is naturally mine alone.

1 In the early 1950s, when a huge research project was set up to examine the process of economic integration following Italy's political unification, the possible relevance of that historical experience in evaluating the different strategies for economic integration that were then being debated with reference to Western Europe was clearly perceived and it was explicitly mentioned in the Introduction to the series of volumes that collected the results of the research and formed the Archivio Economico dell'Unificazione italiana.

2 More than 55% of the debts that the new Kingdom inherited from the pre-unity States pertained to the former Kingdom of Sardinia (formed by Piedmont, Liguria and Sardinia) and had partly been incurred by the need to finance the Wars of Independence. The debts of the Kingdom of the Two Sicilies represented only 29% of the total national debt of the new Kingdom of Italy. As a ratio to the population, the debt of the Kingdom of Sardinia was nearly four times that of the Kingdom of the Two Sicilies (Nitti, 1900, p. 349).

3 Smith (1936) provides an account of the earlier literature on alternative regimes in bank-note creation; some useful references can be found in White (1984). For a brief sketch of the institutional framework of issue of bank notes in the 19th century in several countries, see Goodhart (1985) and Vaubel (1984).

4 At the beginning of the 1850s Cavour had come out explicitly in favour of a single bank of issue, with a strong capital base and branches throughout the Kingdom of Sardinia, whose banknotes would be legal tender and which would be responsible for Treasury payments and receipts. Only a few of his proposals were enacted (the increase in capital and the creation of branches of the Sardinian National Bank) but his position certainly affected the unification Government.

5 For a discussion of the origin, distinctive features and functions of Italian banks of issue see Atti Parlamentari (1868) and (1880b), De Mattia (1959) and Di Nardi (1953). For a more specific discussion of the role of the Southern banks, see De Rosa (1964) and Monzilli (1895). A fairly complete bibliography is in Banca d'Italia (1967). More recently, the origin of the BNR and its role before national unification have been discussed by Conte (forthcoming).

6 In the Spring-Summer of 1861 it was decided to apply the Piedmontese customs tariff to all the Italian provinces and to unify the public debt. In August 1862 the bimetallic decimal monetary system in force in the Kingdom of Sardinia was extended to the rest of Italy. In 1863 the tax system was unified. The impact of these measures was significant, especially in the Southern provinces, which had been accustomed to heavy customs tariffs and comparatively low public debt and taxation, and which were on the silver standard.

7 I am indebted for this and other references to the minutes of the meetings of the Board of Directors of the BNR to A. Finocchiaro, who made available to the Bank of Italy's Historical Research Office a highly useful series of notes based on readings of the Reports.

8 In 1865 an agreement was signed assigning to the BNR all Treasury operations throughout the Kingdom, but Parliament opposed it. In 1869 another agreement divided Treasury operations between the BNR and the BN, but this gave rise to disputes regarding the quotas to be assigned to each bank. In 1871 Treasury operations were attributed to the BNR in 39 provinces, excluding those of Tuscany, Naples and Sicily. It was only with the establishment of the

Bank of Italy that Treasury operations throughout Italy were finally brought together in a single institution.

9 The debate over the issue of one or several issuing banks in Italy between 1860 and 1893, with reference both to positions adopted in Parliament and to discussions in economic reviews of the time, is examined in a study by S. Cardarelli, to be published shortly.

10 The only exception was the Kingdom of Sardinia, where until 1859 there existed, alongside BNR notes, which circulated through the nation, the regionally circulating notes of the Banca di Savoia.

11 In many instances the opening of branches was decided by the BNR's Board in response to solicitation by local Chambers of Commerce.

12 As a result, the quality of the BNR's loans was generally higher than that of the other banks of issue: between 1875 and 1881 the BNR's bad debts as a ratio to credit to the private sector were equal to one third of those of the BN.

13 The difficulties encountered by the BNR in the role of issuing institution are confirmed by the frequency and volume of requests to exchange notes that accompanied its territorial expansion: in 1865 its notes remained in circulation for an average of 75 days as against 121 in 1860; during the first five years of unification the average ratio between payments and receipts in metal coins by BNR outlets was 7.8 in the South and 5.8 in the rest of Italy; in 1865 requests to exchange notes received by the Southern branches reached 28% of the total, while receipts in coin accounted for only 21%.

14 Some interesting remarks on monetary instability being caused, in the 1880s, by specific institutional arrangements rather than by plurality in note issue as such are in Giannini (1988).

15 For a discussion of these developments see Alberti and Cornaro (1931), Atti Parlamentari (1893), Canovai (1911), Confalonieri (1979), Di Nardi (1953) and Supino (1929).

16 See Ciocca (1973) and Fratianni and Spinelli (1984 and 1985).

17 Between January 1860 and April 1866 the coefficient of variation in the discount rate of the BNR, measured on monthly averages, was 0.199, compared with 0.269 for the Bank of France and 0.375 for the Bank of England. It is worth noting, moreover, that the BNR was the most active of the Italian banks of issue in this field; between 1861 and 1865 it changed its discount rate 29 times, while the BN made only 11 changes, the BS 20 and the BNT 15.

18 In one instance, in 1872, the BNR chose to reduce lending rather than accept the government's request to raise the cost of credit; its discount rate had for many years been lower than that applied by the BS and the BNR was aware of the danger of losing some of its market share. There are mentions in the minutes of meetings of the BNR Board of Directors during the early seventies of 'unfair' competition by the BS, which was attracting large numbers of bills of exchange previously presented to the BNR for discounting (Minutes of the meetings of the Board of Directors of 1 March 1871 and 3 January 1872).

19 The Director General of the BNR, Grillo, argued in the meeting of the Board of 25 June 1884 that any attempt to compete with the Southern banks by granting discounts at favourable rates would have been in vain, since the Southern banks' room for manoeuvre was much wider than that of the BNR, which was limited in its operations by having to distribute dividends to its shareholders. Grillo further held that expanding the rediscounts offered to cooperative banks at preferential rates was also risky, since these banks' bills were often renewed on maturity.

20 The Bank of Italy's historical archives contain documents illustrating this episode (Fondo Rapporti con l'Estero, file no. 129).

21 The coefficient of variation of the discount rate applied by the BNR was equal to 0.095, compared with just under 0.3 in the United Kingdom.

22 In spite of the limits that had been set for the reciprocal exchange of notes, the banks whose notes circulated in the more geographically restricted areas often encountered difficulties. In these cases, too, no immediate steps were taken to adjust circulation. Instead, either the government intervened, lending metal to the debtor bank, or the creditor bank was asked to rediscount part of the portfolio of its debtor.

23 As an example, in its desire to compete with the BN, which, in its fervour to offer services to its customers issued certificates of deposit that could be cashed free of charge at any branch, at the start of 1880 the BNR reduced commission charges on the issue of promissory notes and allowed its customers to draw from and pay into their current accounts at several BNR branches without paying charges (minutes of the meetings of the Board of Directors of 28 January and 10 March 1880).

24 It was decided that the BNR would rediscount a part of the BR and BNT's portfolios and hold some of the notes issued by these two banks.

25 After 1890 the minor banks, and in particular the BR, found their difficulties increasing and the BNR was repeatedly invited by the government to grant loans to the debtor banks. In 1891 it was decided that reciprocal outstanding balances need not necessarily be settled and that unexchanged notes could be used by the creditor bank for its own operations.

26 Some stimulating remarks on the 'national physiognomies' of central banks can be found in Bonelli (1988).

27 Revisiting Italy's economic history could be rather instructive in this respect, perhaps more than with reference to the process that led to a monopoly in note-issuing. The fact that after Italy's political unification the economic gap between North and South widened rather than narrowed was the object of numerous studies: I shall recall only those of Eckaus (1961), Nitti (1900b), Pantaleoni (1891) and Saraceno (1961). It would be impossible here even to touch upon the 'Southern question': what is especially relevant to this discussion is that the persistence of Italian dualism after political unity does not seem to have resulted from an aggressive and 'colonialistic' attitude on the part of the North, but, rather, from the 'mutual extraneousness' mentioned at the beginning, the lack of complementarity between North and South (Cafagna, 1965). Thus if the neutral attitude adopted by the Government is sufficient to explain the worsening of regional economic disparities after Italy's political unity, it should not be surprising if there is some resistance in Europe when the creation of monetary union is discussed independently of political integration; fears that some countries may be worse off are not necessaarily based on the assumption that some nations may be willing to play an aggressive role within the union.

REFERENCES

Atti Parlamentari (1868). Camera dei Deputati, legislatura X, sessione 1867–68, *Relazione della Commissione Parlamentare d'inchiesta sul corso forzoso dei biglietti di banca* (10 marzo 1868).

(1880a). Camera dei Deputati, legislatura XIV, sessione 1880–82, *Progetto di legge presentato dai Ministri Magliani e Miceli: Provvedimenti per l'abolizione del corso forzoso* (15 novembre 1880), doc. 122.

(1880b). Camera dei Deputati, legislatura XIV, sessione 1880–82, *Relazione degli ispettori sulle sei banche di emissione*, doc. 122–A bis.

(1893). Camera dei Deputati, legislatura XVIII, prima sessione 1892–3, *Disegno di legge sul riordinamento degli istituti di emissione*, doc. 164.

Alberti, M. and V. Cornaro (19310. *Banche di emissione, moneta e politica monetaria in italia dal 1849 al 1929*, G.U.F., Milano.

Banca d'Italia (1967). *I bilanci degli istituti di emissione 1845–1936*, R. De Mattia (ed.), Roma.

Biscaini Cotula, A.M. and P. Ciocca (1979). 'Le strutture finanziarie: aspetti quantitativi di lungo periodo (1870–1970)', in F. Vicarelli (ed.), *Capitale industriale e capitale finanziario: il caso italiano*, Il Mulino, Bologna.

Bonelli, F. (1988). 'Appunti sulla "via italiana" all'autonomia della banca centrale', in D. Masciandaro and S. Ristuccia (eds.), *L'autonomia delle banche centrali*, Edizioni Comunità, Milano.

Cafagna, L. (1965). 'Intorno alle origini del dualismo economico italiano', in *Problemi storici dell'industrializzazione e dello sviluppo*, Argalia, Urbino.

Canovai, T. (1911). 'The Banks of issue in Italy', in *Banking in Italy, Russia, Austro-Hungary and Japan*, U.S. Congress, National Monetary Commission, Washington.

Cardarelli, S. (1989) *Il dibattito sull'unicità e pluralità degli instituti di emissione nell'Ottocento*.

Ciocca, P. (1973). 'Note sulla politica monetaria italiana 1900–1913', in *Lo sviluppo economico italiano 1861–1940*, Laterza, Bari.

Confalonieri, A. (1979). *Banca e industria in Italia (1894–1906)*, vol. 1, Il Mulino, Bologna.

Conte, L. (1989). 'La Banca Nazionale nel sistema del credito degli Stati sardi', Proceedings of the Conference on 'Credito e sviluppo economico' held in June 1987 in Verona.

De Mattia, R. (1959). 'L'unificazione monetaria italiana', in *Archivio Economico dell'unificazione italiana*, serie II, vol. II, ILTE, Torino.

De Rosa, L. (1964). *Il Banco di Napoli nella vita economica nazionale (1863–1883)*, L'arte tipografica, Napoli.

Di Nardi, G. (1953). *Le banche di emissione in Italia nel secolo XIX*, UTET, Torino.

Eckaus, R.S. (1961). 'The North-South Differential in Italian Economic Development', *Journal of Economic History* 3.

Fratianni, M. and F. Spinelli (1984). 'Italy in the Gold Standard Period', in A. Schwartz and M. Bordo (eds.), *A Retrospective on the Classical Gold Standard, 1821–1931*, University of Chicago Press.

(1985). 'Currency Competition, Fiscal Policy and the Money Supply Process in Italy from Unification to World War I', *Journal of European Economic History*, no. 3.

Giannini, C. (1988). 'L'evoluzione del sistema dei pagamenti: una sintesi teorica', in *Moneta e Credito*, giugno.

Goodhart, C. (1985). 'The Evolution of Central Banks, A Natural Development?', Suntory-Toyota International Centre for Economics and Related Disciplines, London.

Martello, T. and A. Montanari (1874). *Stato attuale del credito in Italia e notizie sulle istituzioni di credito straniere*, Salmen, Padova.

Monzilli, A. (1895). *Il Banco di Napoli: passato, presente, avvenire*, Balbi, Roma.

Nitti, F.S. (1900a). *Il bilancio dello. Stato dal 1862 al 1896–7*, Società Anonima Cooperativa Tipografica, Napoli.

(1900b). *Nord e Sud*, Roux e Viarengo, Torino.

Pantaleoni, M. (1891). 'Delle regioni d'Italia in ordine alla loro ricchezza e al loro carico tributario', *Giornale degli Economisti*, gennaio.

Saraceno, P. (1961). 'La mancata unificazione economica italiano a cento anni dall'unificazione politica', in *L'economia italiana dal 1861 al 1961, Studi nel I Centenario dell'Unità d'Italia*, Giuffré, Milano.

Smith, V. (1936). *The Rationale of Central Banking*, P.S. King & Son, London.

Supino, C. (1929). *Storia della circolazione cartacea in Italia dal 1860 al 1928*, Soc. Ed. Libraria, Milano.

Vaubel, R. (1984). 'Private Competitive Note Issue in Monetary History', in P. Salin (ed.), *Currency Competition and Monetary Union*, Martinus Nijhoff Publishers, The Hague.

White, L.H. (1984). 'Free Banking and Currency Competition, a Bibliographical Note', in P. Salin (ed.), *Currency Competition and Monetary Union*, Martinus Nijhoff Publishers, The Hague.

Discussion

CHARLES GOODHART

Currently we tend to discuss the question of having a single common European currency and a single European Central Bank, as if the two necessarily went hand in hand – that is, in order to have a common Euro-currency, it is *necessary* also to have a common single European Central Bank. This is not in fact so.

We shall shortly hear from Jeffrey Miron in the next session, for example, how many, indeed most, measures of economic variability deterioriated in the United States after the establishment of the Federal Reserve System in 1914. Some supporters of a single unified European currency might, therefore, suggest that the system would be better organised on the basis of a single commodity money, say gold, on which basis the banking system would then be left to operate freely, without being restricted by the interposition of a central bank. As it happens, however, I share Valeria Sannucci's viewpoint, that a return to free banking would not be practical politics; there appears to be little public, and only limited academic, support for such a move to free banking. Yet it is an option that deserves, at least, a hearing.

As an advocate myself of the case that a central bank can, and usually indeed does, play a useful and necessary role within a modern banking system, I much enjoyed this paper; one reason for my enjoyment of the paper is that the competitive, commercial banking system in Italy without a single central bank, that existed in the late 19th century, provided a clear example of certain of the instabilities and disturbances to which such freely competitive systems are prone.

Indeed, one minor qualification that I have about the author's sound historical account is that she somewhat skates over, only lightly touches upon, the 1883–1893 episode: after that date, the 1893 banking law – in conjunction with the reaction to the preceding events – really brought to an end the period of competitive banks of issue. Although this is discussed in the author's text, it is not given much emphasis.

It was, in truth, a thoroughly discreditable period in banking history, and consequently fun to report. Let me give you some of the flavour of the goings-on during this period. I am going to quote, from the section in my own account of this historical period, my monograph on *The Evolution of Central Banks*. First, let me quote Canovai, the Chief General Secretary of the Banca d'Italia, who was giving evidence at the time to the National Monetary Commission in 1911.

> It was at this period [1883–85] that a lively competition arose between the Italian banks of issue, which carried them beyond the bounds to which they should have limited their activity, and had serious consequences for all, showing one of the most dangerous sides of the plurality of banks of issue . . . . Between the desire to rival the Bank of Naples, especially in the south of Italy, and that of not seeming to diminish dividends, the business of the Banca Nazionale became more active and apparently more profitable. (p. 120)

There were a couple of economic problems at the time. First, as a result of growing competition from agriculture in the USA, the prosperity of Italian agriculture, especially in the South, suffered. Second, there was an unstable building boom, centred in Rome and Naples, that took place, and then broke.

Moreover, there was a rotten apple among the six banks of the association of note issuing banks, the Banca Romana. Reverting to the account in my own monograph,

> This bank [the Banco Romana] originated in 1850 when a papal decree founded the Banca dello Stato Pontifico.

> From the start the Banca dello Stato Pontifico distinguished itself for the recklessness with which it committed abuses of all kinds. (Canovai)

It was bankrupt by 1870 (with known losses of 9,000,000 lire relative to capital of 3,000,000 lire), but for political reasons, as it was the only bank in the Papal States annexed to Italy in 1870, it was not liquidated or merged, but reorganised as the Banca Romana. It did not change its ways.

> The institution which was economically and morally most corrupt was the Banca Romana, which, ill conducted under the papal administration, had not had a sound existence under the national Government, and was the veritable poison of Italian credit. (Canovai)

It became deeply involved in the building boom in Rome, and effectively became bankrupt again when that collapsed. Although its weakness became increasingly evident, it fought to maintain its position and was supported on political grounds, as the only indigenous bank of Rome, supporting employment in Rome, and threatened by competition from outside banks, etc. Indeed, the authorities conspired to prop up the bank, and to keep silent about its state. Thus the government had ordered an inspection of the banks of issue in 1888 and found a cash deficit of 8,000,000 lire. The audit was suspended; the Governor of the Banca Romana borrowed the money from the Director General of the Banca Nazionale; the audit was reconvened and

> the cash was found to be correct (p. 121)

> The plug was finally pulled by the economist, Maffeo Pantaleoni, who obtained a copy of the report of the inspection of the Banca Romana, completed in 1889 – which had been hushed up – and made it public in 1893. The result was an uproar in Parliament, the collapse and liquidation of the Banca Romana, and a new banking act, of August 1893. (p. 122)

Not many economists can have precipitated such a massive, though long overdue, crisis. Canovai approved of his action and described him as

> the illustrious economist who is an honor to Italy

Canovai generally thought well of economists, describing another, Ferrara, as

> the glory of economic science.

He was not so well inclined towards politicians, describing their reaction to Pantaleoni's revelation, as follows:

> the politicians, who had suddenly scented, in the sad rotteness of the Banca Romana, a most excellent excuse for giving free play to the cannibal instinct that distinguishes them from the rest of the human race (p. 163)

Central bankers may occasionally still feel the same way, but they rarely express themselves so graphically nowadays!

Another, more analytical qualification, that I would make in respect to the author's generally sound and sensible historical analysis, is that she does not distinguish sufficiently in her text, (though she did in her oral discussion), between the role that bank notes played *then* and the role that they play *now* in our fiat currency system. In the earlier stages of the development of commercial banking, the majority of commercial bank liabilities were actually in note form, not in deposit form. This was certainly true in Italy in 1894, for example. On that date, the note liabilities of the three remaining banks of issue amounted to 1,126 million lire, as compared with demand deposits of 325 million lire. The distinction between notes and deposits was regarded at that time in rather the same light as we now view the difference between bearer bonds, and inscribed and registered bonds.

At that time base money was, of course, metallic, and increasingly represented by gold reserves. So if one wanted to write down the equivalent then of the banking multiplier of today it would look something like the following:-

$$M = G_p + (N + D) \tag{1}$$

$$H = G_p + G_B \tag{2}$$

$$M = H \frac{\left(\dfrac{G_p}{N + D} + 1\right)}{\left(\dfrac{G_p}{N + D} + \dfrac{G_B}{N + D}\right)} \tag{3}$$

where M is the money stock, G_p gold in the hands of the public, G_B gold held by the banks, H high powered money, N commercial bank notes, D commercial bank deposits, $(N + D)$ commercial bank liabilities.

Within this context, what were the main reasons why contemporaries felt the need for a central bank?

(i) The main reason was to concentrate, protect and control the gold stock of the country. This was not only important for the objective of maintaining the external and internal value of the currency; but beyond that, the accumulation of gold pandered to the continuing mercantilist prejudices of many, and also represented for most European countries a war chest which they foresaw having to use on some future occasion.

(ii) Clearly the concentration of gold within one central bank would stabilise the $G_B/(N + D)$ ratio, and would therefore tend to control the banking multiplier, so that banking cycles would be dampened.

(iii) Third, in order to achieve the first two objectives, the central bank was expected to vary interest rates in such a way as to protect the gold stock and also to dampen the banking cycles that would otherwise occur, arising from the interactions within a competitive commercial banking system. In order to do this latter the central bank would have to vary interest rates in a non-competitive, non-commercially orientated way in order to protect the monetary base of gold.

But such central bank functions do *not* necessarily require a monopoly of control over all bank note issues. This latter would have involved the disadvantage during this period, as the author notes, that the monopoly of note issue would also have implied a monopolisation of a certain important kind of commercial banking. What central banking at this time *did* require was:–

(a) A degree of centralisation of gold reserves.

(b) The treatment by the other note-issuing banks of the central bank as their main source of metallic reserve, in order to maintain convertibility, either by holding deposits with, or rediscounting from, the central bank.

(c) The willingness of the central bank to operate in a non-competitive and non-commercial manner in order to maintain the gold stock, i.e. by undertaking open market operations and varying interest rates in a contra-cyclical fashion.

Why then did central banks, in practice, increasingly come, in the late 19th and early 20th centuries, to assume a position as sole note issuer? There were several reasons for this:–

(i) It concentrated seigniorage in a single institution where it could be most easily taxed by the political authorities.

(ii) It provided informational and transaction convenience to the general public.

(iii) The growth of deposit banking at the time meant that the commercial banks did not object too strongly, since they had an alternative to hand.

(iv) It provided the central bank with greater control over the bank multiplier.

By the time that the central bank had become the main, or sole, provider of bank notes within the system, these tended to become part of the cash base of the system. We can then write the basic equations of the banking multiplier as follows:–

$$H = (G_p + CB_n) + (G_B + CB_{BD}) \tag{4}$$

$$M = (G_p + CB_n) + (B_N + B_D) \tag{5}$$

$$B_m = B_N + B_D \tag{6}$$

where CB_n represents central bank notes outstanding, so $G_p + CB_n$ is the total of high powered cash (C_p) held by the public; CB_{BD} are commercial bank deposits held with the central bank, so $G_B + CB_{BD}$ constitute commercial bank reserves (R). $B_N + B_D$ are commercial bank note and deposit liabilities respectively, B_m, commercial bank money.

Obviously the degree of substitution between B_n and CB_n could be high enough to disturb the ratio C_p/B_m, the current equivalent of the C/D ratio.

So, there were various strong forces leading towards the centralisation of the note issue. This trend became then generally irreversibly established with the breakdown of the gold standard, and recourse to fiat currency in World War I. Nevertheless, I would reiterate that we have today a rather different mental vision of the role and functions of bank note issue than they had in the 19th century, and this can cause errors in analysis unless that difference is clearly perceived.

GIANNI TONIOLO

My comments are divided into three brief parts. The first deals with Sannucci's contribution to the monetary and banking history of Italy. In the second I shall try to recall briefly how her story ended and how Italy eventually got its embryo Central Bank. Finally I shall venture some steps along the dangerous path of the 'lessons from history'.

Briefly restated, Sannucci's story runs as follows. The Kingdom of Italy, hastily assembled in 1859–60, inherited a number of banks of issue from the previous component states. Prominent among these, both because of its size and of its links with the Treasury and with the national ruling class, was the Banca Nazionale nel Regno (BNR) which was, therefore, the obvious candidate for the monopoly of currency issue. In the early 1860s, the Government was in favour of granting such a monopoly and BNR was ready to pay the costs that went with the privilege. The project, however, was not implemented during the thirty odd years covered by this paper. Wonderering about the reasons of such an outcome, Sannucci dismisses explanations that call upon ideology and petty local interests. In her opinion, there are better economic reasons for the long-lasting plurality of issuing privileges after political unification. In an area such as the Italian Peninsula, characterized by extreme regional differences in resource endowments, the secular segmentation in a number of independent states produced institutions fairly well adapted to local comparative advantages. Financial intermediation, in particular, took shape in each regional state according to the structure of the real economy, government borrowing needs, customs, legislation and the like. Sannucci implies that by the 1860s banking structures, and particularly individual banks of issue, had adapted to provide each region with the most efficient financial services, given the prevailing transaction costs embodied in the supply and demand functions for credit. Such functions were not quickly modified by political unification since the process of creating a single national market was particularly slow. Entry costs into regions already served by a bank of issue remained high for the others. In the last part of the paper Sannucci looks into the consequences of the long-lasting plurality of banks of issue. She maintains, not surprisingly, that competition among such banks resulted *ceteris paribus* in lower interest rates. She sees, in the eighties, an undesirable (*ex-post*) expansion of money supply and a worsening of the banks' assets, but she attributes them at least partially to an implicit encouragement by the government for BNR to extend credit of last resort to commercial banks in difficulty. Faulty legislation and inaccurate supervision are also to blame for the unscrupulous behaviour of some banks of issue.

The reconstruction of the peculiarities of the individual banks of issue and of how they were shaped to meet specific features of the regional economies is the important and novel contribution this paper makes to the history of Italian banking.

One would, of course, as is always the case with historical research, want more. For instance, Table 9.2 shows a regional distribution of *per capita* deposits largely uncorrelated with whatever guesstimates we may make of *per capita* incomes or wealth. One wonders whether the high intermediation ratios found for Tuscany and Latium could be explained by the presence, precisely in those areas, of the most aggressive, and less 'well behaved', banks of issue.

The role played by ideology in shaping the legislation on the banks of issue is assumed to have been negligible. It may be so but, in view of the 19th century French debate on the subject, the matter should be more closely investigated. In France the battle was not fought in terms of *laissez-faire* versus state intervention but in the more relevant ones of 'expansionists' against believers in 'monetary rules' (one could perhaps say Banking School versus Currency School). The latter – which was certainly closer to *laissez-faire* than the former – strongly favoured monopoly of the note issue by the Banque de France. The opposite view was held by Lafitte, the Pereire brothers and other Saint-Simonians. They endorsed free entry because it meant larger means for the operations of their Crédit Mobilier, a powerful financial innovation of the 1850s. In view of the fact that the Pereire banking style was introduced in Italy by Credito Mobiliare and that the Tuscan banks of issue exhibited a high propensity for long-term industrial investment, for financing social overhead capital (notably railways) and for rather speculative ventures, one wonders if the political stance against the monopoly taken by the Tuscan 'left' was not motivated by an 'expansionist' rather than a merely *laissez-faire* ideology. This interpretation would not be inconsistent with that focussing on the regional basis of the banks of issue held by Sannucci. At the same time it would help in understanding the propensity shown by some banks of issue for expansive money supply and, given the opportunity, for overtrading.

This leads us to the main issue left out of Sannucci's picture, that of financial stability. To make this clear I must pick up the story where she left it and recall briefly how Italy got its embryo central bank.

The investment spurt of the eighties and the following crisis were by no means only Italian phenomena. London financed the boom and, by cutting down its capital exports, brought about the depression. Domestic conditions were favourable to investment. Expectations were raised by Government expenditure for the navy and by its subsidies to steelmakers and shipyards. A second railway boom was under way. Public expenditure in construction, particularly in Naples, Rome and Turin, opened the way to huge private investments in the sector, largely speculative in nature. The main commercial banks and the banks of issue provided credit, mostly long-term, for everybody. Sannucci is right in pointing out that the government was not sorry to see BNR expanding its note circulation at the first signs of difficulties generated by overtrading by commercial banks. But the Tuscan and Roman banks of issue themselves did not avoid overtrading. After 1887 foreign capital began to leave Italy. The reason is to be found in the domestic rather than in the international market since the 1888 Goschen conversion provided a further boost to British foreign investment, which declined only in 1889 and precipitated the Baring crisis one year later. The fact is that in 1887 Italian loans were perceived to be too risky.

From 1888 onward, banks found themselves increasingly burdened with locked-in credits. Lending of last resort operations were undertaken in that year by BNR. They were probably too small in size. Moreover they were not coupled with supervision aimed at inducing the banks to shift the composition of their portfolios to more liquid assets. In 1889 the Roman bank of issue (Banca Romana) was virtually bankrupt. To avoid disaster it resorted to fraudulent issue of notes. The two main commercial banks of the country failed in 1893. In August of that year a Banking Act was passed that provided for the merger of the BNR with the two Tuscan banks of issue to form the Banca d'Italia. The latter was entrusted with the liquidation of the Roman bank of issue.

The story of the banking crisis of 1887–93 poses two questions that are relevant both to Sannucci's paper and to the more general issues discussed in this book. The two counterfactuals are the following: would the crisis have been less severe in the presence of one monopolistic bank of issue? Did the creation of the Bank of Italy significantly improve the stability of the financial system? My answer is yes in both cases.

The first question boils down to who is responsible for supervising the banks and for lending of last resort. The fact that a political muddle paralyzed the decision-making process delaying much needed action is seen as the proof that Government and Parliament rather than the lack of a monopolistic bank of issue were responsible for the most serious Italian banking crisis to date. But, in my opinion, when governments and parliamentary majorities come and go, when they see the economy merely as an arena for their power struggles, when consistent policies are not in sight, an authoritative and independent central bank may take correct and timely decisions that will offset some of the dangers deriving from lack of political leadership.

Did the Bank of Italy, after 1894, perform some important functions of a central bank improving the system's financial stability? For all practical purposes the Banking Act of 1893 created the prerequisites for the Bank of Italy to act as a public institution responsible for money supply, exchange rates and short-term Treasury finance, thus making it *de facto* responsible for the implementation of monetary policy. Moreover it took upon itself the task of stabilizing the financial system and of avoiding the failure of major commercial banks. Its handling of the 1907–8 crisis provides a good counterfactual of how the previous 1888–93 crisis could have been managed in the presence of a well-established and competent monopolistic bank of issue. Crisis management in 1921–22 and in 1931–33 confirms this view.

Of the three historical cases examined in this book, that of Germany seems to be the most relevant to the present European situation in view of the fact that the creation of a single national market paved the way to the process of political unification. Italy became a unique political entity almost overnight; the economy adapted very slowly to the new reality. Each country had a banking institution that was the obvious candidate for the role of leading bank of issue and later of central bank. The Bank of Prussia became the Reichsbank within four years of the proclamation of the German Empire while it took the former National Bank of Piedmont 32 years to become the Bank of Italy. We may argue that Prussia's power *vis-à-vis* the other German states was stronger than that enjoyed by Piedmont in Italy and, in fact, we may wonder whether any European country enjoys, at present, the relative strength of 19th century's Prussia within Germany.

Sannucci's paper draws attention to a neglected aspect of European monetary integration. The received wisdom is that national governments have vested interests that will delay the creation of a European Central Bank. But if we think of national central banks as institutions well tailored to serve the specific needs, advantages and shortcomings of their own national markets – as were Italy's banks of issue within their original regions – then governments may not be entirely responsible for slow progress in the creation of a European Central Bank.

History gives us another hint. Financial crises have acted as powerful catalysts for the creation of modern central banks. I have recalled the case of Italy in 1893. The Fed was originated by the crisis of 1907–8. The Depression of the early 1930s produced not only the Canadian National Bank but relevant central banking legislation in almost every country as well as the Bank for International Settlements, a timid attempt to give an international body lender of last resort responsibilities. The present situation is difficult to judge in this respect. The fragility of financial markets calls for experienced action that in ordinary conditions is likely to be better carried out by existing central banks with their fifty-year-old experience in crisis management. A depression coming during the process of power devolution from national monetary authorities to a European Central Bank is likely to be made more severe by the lack of swift and experienced action. On the other hand, we may think of a scenario, similar to that of 1931, in which mechanisms of international transmission make it impossible for national authorities to act effectively and in which coordination is difficult for technical and/or political reasons. In such a case, a supranational monetary authority, even one with limited powers, is likely to be of great help. And probably, such a crisis would precipitate the devolution of much additional power into its hands. Judging from the historian's vantage point, I cannot help seeing dangers both in upsetting the existing arrangements in the field of central banking, supervision and lending of last resort and in leaving things as they are.

10 The founding of the Fed and the destabilization of the post-1914 US economy

JEFFREY A. MIRON

1   Introduction

A standard assumption in the literature on optimal monetary policy is that the proper goal of policy is the reduction of the variation in output around its natural rate level (e.g., Friedman, 1953; Brainard, 1967; Fischer, 1977; Taylor, 1980).[1] Indeed, one of the apparent triumphs of Keynesian economics is the fact that fluctuations in real activity have been smaller since World War II than they were prior to 1930 (e.g. Burns, 1960; Modigliani, 1977; Mayer, 1978). Although recent research by Romer (1986a, 1986b) suggests that the degree of stabilization is smaller than previously believed, there is still widespread agreement that such a stabilization would be desirable if it could be achieved.[2]

The stabilization of output has not always been accepted as the primary goal of policy, however. This paper argues that neither the founders of the Fed nor the central bankers in charge during the first twenty-five years of the Fed's existence viewed the elimination of short-term movements in output as an important objective for policy. Instead, the framers of the Federal Reserve System and the early practitioners of central banking in the United States apparently thought that 'stabilization' of asset markets was the crucial task for the monetary authority (along with maintenance of the gold standard). Of course, the policy makers of that period presumably believed that calming financial markets led, in some longer-term sense, to better performance of the economy. This improved performance, however, did not include the elimination or reduction of the short-term, 'business cycle' swings in output. As a result, the Fed pursued policies that destabilized output in several important instances.

The paper begins in Section 2 by comparing the performance of the United States economy during the twenty-five year periods before and after 1914. I show that after the founding of the Fed the variance of both the rate of growth of output and of the inflation rate increased

290

significantly, while the average rate of growth of output fell, and real stock prices became substantially more volatile. At the same time, nominal interest rates, which had exhibited significant seasonal and other mean-reverting variation prior to 1914, became close to a random walk. All of these conclusions hold even when one excludes the Great Depression from the post-Fed sample period, although they are generally made much stronger by inclusion of these sample points.

The fact that the economy was less stable after the founding of the Fed does not necessarily imply, of course, that the Fed was responsible for the increased volatility. There were a number of other important changes in the United States and world economies, including World War I and the suspension of the international gold standard in the United States and Europe. In order to make plausible the hypothesis that the change in the behaviour of the economy was the result of Federal Reserve policies, rather than the result of other exogenous factors, it is necessary to explain why the Fed might have pursued policies that destabilized the economy and to present direct evidence that the Fed's actions were responsible for the increased volatility of economic variables.

The remainder of this paper shows that the deterioration in the performance of the economy after 1914 can be attributed directly to the actions of the Fed. Section 3 reviews the structure and behaviour of the monetary system in the United States during the period preceding the founding of the Federal Reserve System. The dominant institutional feature of the National Banking System was the absence of a central bank, and the noteworthy characteristic of the performance of the economy was the recurrence of financial panics, involving bank runs and stock market crashes. These economic ills of the pre-1914 period shaped directly the kinds of policies that the Fed pursued during the early years of its existence, particularly the desire to 'provide an elastic currency'.

In Section 4 I examine the monetary policies advocated by the founders of the Fed, discuss possible justifications for these policies, and consider the likely effects of the policies on the economy. The dominant theory of central banking of the early 20th century, the real bills doctrine, suggested that central bank lending should make the money stock elastic with respect to shifts in the level of economic activity, thereby smoothing nominal interest rates.[3] The analysis of Poole (1970), however, shows that smoothing interest rates in the face of IS shocks destabilizes output, so it is hard to rationalize the real bills doctrine from this perspective. Instead, contemporary observers appear to have believed that by maintaining orderly credit markets they would eliminate the tendency for financial panics, thereby preventing truly violent swings in output, even if this caused some increased short-term instability.

An additional concern of contemporary bankers and academics, however, was the high incidence of stock market speculation during the pre-1914 period. Since most stock was purchased on credit, central bankers worried that a policy of increased lending in response to higher interest rates (the 'accommodation of business') might also fuel speculation. This meant that they did not believe in adhering strictly to the real bills doctrine but instead thought it important to restrain the provision of credit if they believed it was being used for speculative purposes. This view of appropriate policy implies that the Fed would restrain credit, drive up interest rates, and moderate or depress output growth on occasions when there was significant evidence of speculative activity in asset markets.

Thus, the founders of the Federal Reserve System believed that the overall objective of monetary policy was the stabilization of asset markets, particularly the elimination of financial panics. At a practical level, this meant that monetary policy was supposed to eliminate the transitory variation in nominal interest rates and reduce the major swings in stock prices. As explained below, these two objectives were not always compatible and may even have been systematically in conflict. The Fed's inability to adequately resolve this conflict provides the key to understanding its policies after 1914.

Section 5 of the paper evaluates quantitatively the Fed's actions during the post-1914 period. The Fed was highly successful in providing an elastic currency and thus in smoothing the process for nominal interest rates. At the same time, on three particular occasions the Fed abandoned its commitment to smoothing rates and deliberately restrained money growth in order to stop speculation in stock or commodity markets. As a result, the Fed appears to have caused output and the price level to become significantly more volatile after 1914 than they were before 1914 and more volatile than they otherwise would have been.

Section 6 concludes by discussing the implications of the findings for the current conduct of monetary policy. The results in the paper do not imply that the founding of the Fed has, on the whole, harmed the economy, nor do they necessarily provide support for a monetary rule as opposed to interest rate stabilization. The results do suggest, however, that sole reliance on interest-rate or other asset-market targets, without explicit attention to the behaviour of output and prices, can have adverse consequences for the performance of the economy.

2   The macroeconomic performance of the post-1914 economy

This section of the paper evaluates quantitatively the performance of the United States economy before and after 1914. A great deal of research

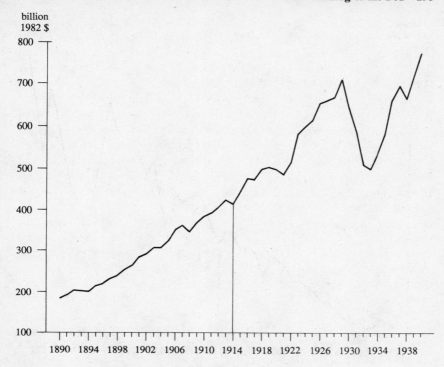

Figure 10.1   US real GNP, 1890–1940 (annual data)

compares the pre-WWII and post-WWII economies, and considerable attention has been directed at the behaviour of monetary and financial market variables before and after the founding of the Fed.[4] There has been considerably less effort, however, devoted to examining the behaviour of real output before and after 1914, or to relating these results to those on other variables. The thrust of the analysis in Sections 4 and 5 below is that the changes in the behaviour of real variables were the result of those in monetary and financial variables, so it is important to consider them jointly.

I begin by considering the behaviour of real output. Figures 10.1 and 10.2 present annual data on real GNP and industrial production for the period 1890–1940; the vertical line in each graph is located at 1914. Tables 10.1 and 10.2 show the mean, standard deviation and first-order autocorrelation of real GNP and industrial production, respectively, for a number of different sample periods.[5]

Both measures of output convey the same message, which is that real activity was much more volatile after 1914 than it was before 1914. This

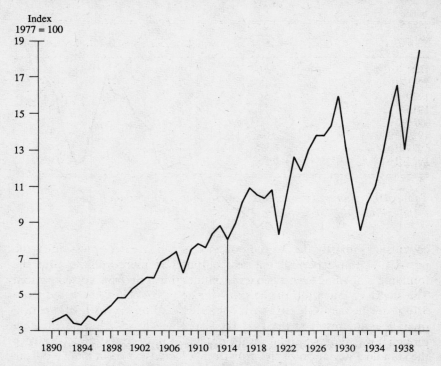

Figure 10.2   US industrial production, 1890–1940 (annual data)

Sample Period	Mean	Standard Deviation	Autocorrelation
1891–1914	3.42	3.19	− 0.177
1915–1940	2.40	6.63	0.416
1919–1940	1.99	7.03	0.440
1915–1928	3.42	4.02	0.109
1919–1928	2.95	4.28	0.217
1929–1940	1.20	8.82	0.463
1929–1933	− 5.89	7.90	− 0.166
1934–1940	6.26	5.40	0.029

Table 10.1 *Summary statistics, US real GNP, 1890–1940 (Annual data, log growth rates)*

Sample Period	Mean	Standard Deviation	Autocorrelation
1891–1914	3.48	8.66	− 0.313
1915–1940	3.18	14.72	0.007
1919–1940	2.54	15.73	− 0.017
1915–1928	4.13	12.06	− 0.238
1919–1928	3.10	13.72	− 0.328
1929–1940	2.08	17.83	0.126
1929–1933	− 6.98	19.23	− 0.190
1934–1940	8.55	14.81	− 0.220

Table 10.2 *Summary statistics, US industrial production, 1890–1940 (Annual data, log growth rates)*

conclusion is partly due to the presence of the Great Depression in the post-1914 sample period, but real output was more volatile after the founding of the Fed even when one excludes the 1930s from consideration. The standard deviation of the growth rate of real GNP increased from 3.19% during the 1891–1914 period to 4.28% during the 1919–1928 period (mainly as the result of the 1921 recession, which was quite severe even though it was short). Similar results obtain for industrial production, with the standard deviation of the growth rate increasing from 8.66% during the 1891–1914 period to 13.72% during the 1919–1928 period. From 1929 to 1940, the variability of output growth was extremely high. The standard deviation of real GNP growth was 7.90% during the 1929–33 sample and 5.40% during the 1934–1940 sample.

These increases in the volatility of output were, in general, accompanied by decreases in the average rate of growth of output. Over the entire 1890–1914 sample the mean rate of growth of output was 3.41% while during the 1919–1940 period it was only 1.99%. This overall average during the post-1914 sample reflects several periods with very different average growth rates. Average output growth was fairly strong during the 1919–1928 period and quite strong during the 1934–1940 period. During the 1929–1933 period, however, the rate of growth fell to − 5.89% for real GNP and − 6.98% for industrial production.

In Figures 10.3 and 10.4 I present annual data on the implicit price deflator for real GNP and on the wholesale price index; Tables 10.3 and 10.4 present summary statistics.[6] The results show that the inflation rate was more variable in every post-1914 sample period than it was during the 1890–1914 period. Between the 1891–1914 and 1919–1928 periods the standard deviation of the inflation rate rose from 2.73% to 7.30% as

Index
1982 = 100

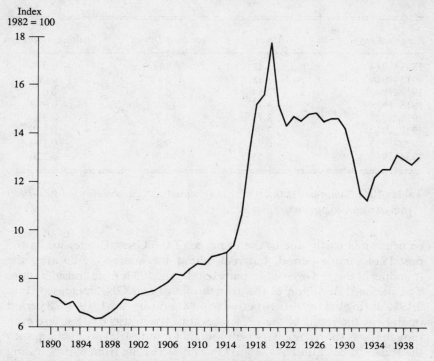

Figure 10.3   US implicit price deflator, 1890–1940 (annual data)

Sample Period	Mean	Standard Deviation	Autocorrelation
1891–1914	0.95	2.73	0.128
1915–1940	1.37	8.03	0.401
1919–1940	− 0.71	6.27	0.037
1915–1928	3.37	9.39	0.329
1919–1928	− 0.41	7.30	− 0.235
1929–1940	− 0.96	5.59	0.409
1929–1933	− 5.29	5.07	0.104
1934–1940	2.13	3.64	− 0.010

Table 10.3 *Summary statistics, US implicit price deflator, 1890–1940 (Annual data, log growth rates)*

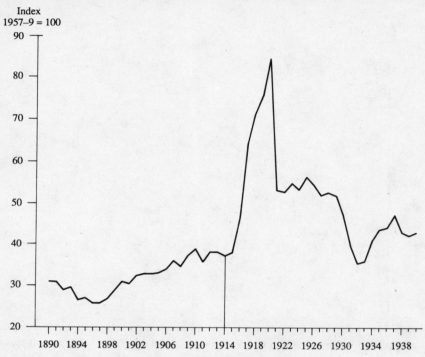

Figure 10.4   US wholesale prices, 1890–1940 (annual data)

Sample Period	Mean	Standard Deviation	Autocorrelation
1891–1914	0.77	5.04	− 0.173
1915–1940	0.55	13.81	0.228
1919–1940	− 2.33	12.13	− 0.050
1915–1928	2.51	17.15	0.152
1919–1928	− 3.03	15.82	− 0.249
1929–1940	− 1.74	8.68	0.468
1929–1933	− 7.68	7.49	0.029
1934–1940	2.50	7.10	0.118

Table 10.4 *Summary statistics, US wholesale prices, 1890–1940 (Annual data, log growth rates)*

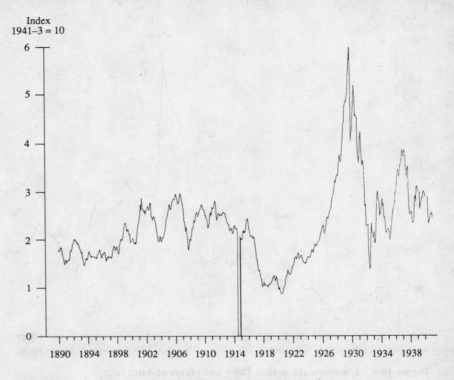

Index
1941–3 = 10

Figure 10.5   US real stock prices, 1890–1940 (monthly data)

measured by the implicit price deflator and from 5.04% to 15.82% as measured by the wholesale price index. The average inflation rate was negative until 1896 but was the moderate and positive during most of the pre-Fed sample period.[7] In the post-1914 period, the mean inflation rate was highly sample dependent. There was rapid inflation starting in 1914 and continuing for two years past the end of the war, followed by rapid deflation from the middle of 1920 to the end of 1921. The middle 1920s witnessed relative price stability, followed by extreme deflation during the 1929–1933 period.

The next variable that I consider is an index of real stock prices, presented in Figure 10.5.[8] There were several significant swings in stock prices during the pre-Fed period, the most dramatic being the decline of 1906–1907, when real stock prices fell by over 40% from September, 1906 to November, 1907. The volatility of the stock market during the post-1914 period was much greater than during the pre-1914 period, however. Between the middle of 1922 and the end of 1929, real stock prices

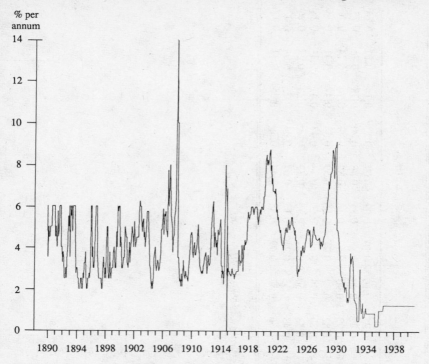

Figure 10.6 US nominal interest rates, 1890–1940 (monthly data)

rose by a factor of five; they then fell to approximately their 1922 level over the next three years. Even excluding this episode, stock prices moved on several occasions by as much as 30% over the space of a year or less.

Figure 10.6 shows monthly data on the short-term nominal interest rate while Table 10.5 reports the autocorrelation function for the nominal rate in each of the sample periods considered above.[9] The stochastic behaviour of the nominal rate became systematically different after 1914, displaying more persistence than previously. The sample autocorrelation function for the pre-1914 sample period dampens fairly quickly, indicating that the nominal rate was stationary. In all of the post-1914 sample periods except 1929–1933, the nominal rate was much more persistent and appears to have been close to a random walk.[10] As the tables suggest, and as Mankiw, Miron and Weil (1987) demonstrate more rigorously, this change took place quite rapidly after November of 1914.[11]

The other major change in the behaviour of the economy after 1914 was the disappearance of seasonality in nominal interest rates. Figure 10.7 plots the estimated seasonal patterns in nominal rates for the periods

Sample Period	Standard Deviation	Autocorrelations											
1890:2–1914:11	1.49	0.75	0.58	0.37	0.25	0.16	0.10	0.09	0.09	0.12	0.14	0.17	0.16
1914:12–1940:12	2.24	0.98	0.96	0.94	0.92	0.90	0.88	0.85	0.83	0.80	0.78	0.75	0.73
1919:1–1940:12	2.37	0.98	0.96	0.94	0.92	0.90	0.87	0.85	0.82	0.79	0.76	0.74	0.71
1914:12–1929:10	1.60	0.95	0.91	0.96	0.82	0.77	0.71	0.65	0.59	0.53	0.47	0.41	0.35
1919:1–1929:10	1.54	0.95	0.90	0.84	0.80	0.74	0.68	0.60	0.54	0.47	0.41	0.34	0.28
1929:11–1940:12	1.02	0.86	0.77	0.67	0.58	0.50	0.41	0.36	0.32	0.29	0.28	0.27	0.26
1929:11–1933:12	1.35	0.81	0.69	0.56	0.43	0.33	0.21	0.13	0.07	0.04	0.05	0.04	0.02
1934:1–1940:12	0.28	0.91	0.83	0.74	0.66	0.57	0.49	0.48	0.44	0.39	0.35	0.31	0.27

Table 10.5 *Summary statistics, US nominal interest rates, 1890–1940 (Monthly data, levels)*

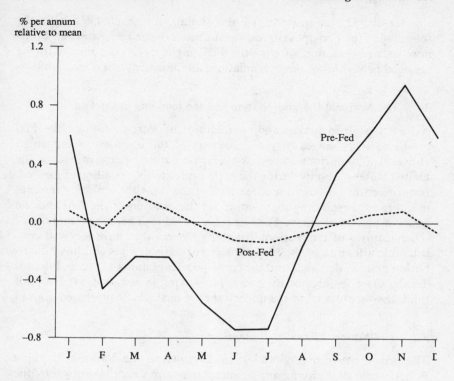

Figure 10.7   The seasonal pattern in US nominal interest rates

1890:2–1914:11 and 1914:12–1940:12.[12] The patterns were calculated by regressing monthly observations of the nominal rate on a set of twelve seasonal dummies and then subtracting the mean value of the coefficients. There was a dramatic decline in the importance of seasonality, with the amplitude of the cycle falling from over 160 basic points to fewer than 40 basic points.[13] Seasonal fluctuations, which were one of the most pronounced sources of transitory variation in nominal rates before 1914, were almost entirely absent after 1914.[14]

The results presented in this section demonstrate that the behaviour of the United States economy changed significantly after 1914. Output growth, the inflation rate, and real stock prices became more variable, and nominal interest rates became close to a random walk. The fact that these changes occurred after 1914 does not, by itself, mean that the Fed caused the changes. There were other significant changes in the United States and world economies during this period, particularly World War I and the departure of the United States and Europe from the international gold standard.[15] The coincidence of the timing of the changes with the founding of the Fed does suggest the influence of the Fed, however. I turn now to an evaluation of why the Fed might have contributed to the changed behaviour of output, inflation, and financial market variables.

3   The National Banking System and the founding of the Fed

As a first step in understanding whether the introduction of the Fed produced the changes in the behaviour of the economy documented above, it is important to review the structure and performance of the United States economy during the period prior to the founding of the Fed. In this section I discuss those features of the pre-1914 economy that are useful in understanding the reasons for the creation of the Fed and the kinds of policies it pursued during its early years. There are a number of other features of the National Banking System that have received considerable attention in the literature, particularly the geographical distribution of asset demands and the correspondent banking system. I do not discuss these features of the pre-1914 banking system because I do not think they are crucial to the understanding of the facts presented above.

3.1   The National Banking System

The period between 1863 and 1913 is known as the National Banking Period, since the banking and financial structure were determined by the provisions of the National Banking Acts of 1863, 1864 and 1865.[16] The National Banking Acts were both a response to problems of the financial system that existed before the Civil War and a measure designed to raise revenue for the North during the War. The Acts were successful in generating revenue and in curing some pre-War financial ills (notably the multiplicity of note issue). The National Banking System was nevertheless regarded as fundamentally flawed by those in academia, the banking community, and government, and the Federal Reserve System was created in response to those problems that remained despite the many attempts to fix them through repeated revisions of the National Banking Acts.[17]

 Before the Civil War the United States banking system consisted of a collection of state banks organized under the laws and chartering systems of the individual states; there were therefore as many different sets of laws governing banks as there were states.[18] A distinctive characteristic of this system was that each bank could issue its own notes. Consequently, there were hundreds of different types of bank notes circulating throughout the country, and the notes of a given bank traded at a premium or discount relative to those of other banks and at a discount relative to gold.[19] The transactions costs involved in determining the quality of a particular note, which were increased by the possibility of unethical note issue, made this system less than satisfactory. There was little regulation of the note issue of state banks, and there were instances in which banks attempted to make a quick profit by using their own notes to acquire other assets and then closing down before the notes could be presented for redemption.[20]

The Civil War was the occasion of a major restructuring of this system, motivated more by the North's need to finance the War than by the desire to reform the banking system. The National Banking Acts imposed a tax of 10% on notes issued by state banks and authorized the Federal government to charter national banks that could issue notes backed by government bonds. It was thought at the time that this would lead to the demise of state chartered banks because of the *de facto* loss of the power of note issue.[21] As it turned out, state banks declined only temporarily and eventually became more prominent than national banks. The explanation is that state banks discovered that deposit creation was a good substitute for note issue. Since capital requirements and reserve/deposit ratios were lower for state banks, and since state banks were allowed to lend against real estate collateral while national banks were not, state banks were able to compete successfully with national banks. The United States banking system thus consisted of two sets of banks, one state chartered, the other federally chartered.[22]

The most distinctive feature of the National Banking System, at least by modern standards, was the absence of a central bank.[23] There had been some kind of central bank in the United States during much of the Ante-Bellum period,[24] and by the last quarter of the nineteenth century most important economic powers other than the United States had established central banks.[25] The absence of a central bank left an important void in the workings of financial markets, and a number of agents or institutions attempted to fill this void. The most important were the Independent Treasury and the New York Clearinghouse Association.

The Independent Treasury was created by Congress in 1846 to fill a deficiency in the day-to-day operation of government created by the demise of the Second Bank of the United States.[26] The original Act required that all payments to and from the Federal government be in the form of specie or Treasury notes and that only government strongboxes, not banks, could be the depositories for these funds.[27] These restrictions were weakened by subsequent legislation, but since government fiscal actions had a direct effect on the money stock, there were inadvertent and capricious disruptions of the money market that would not have occurred had all funds been kept in banks.

Over time the Independent Treasury began to function more as a central bank, making loans and injecting or withdrawing funds with the explicit purpose of stabilizing the money market. The Treasury secretary who pursued these policies most vigorously was Leslie M. Shaw, who served from 1902 to 1907. The most important of Shaw's policies was the deliberate attempt to offset seasonal shifts in asset demands by moving treasury funds into banks, where they could serve as reserves against deposits and loans (Timberlake, 1963). Shaw was successful (or lucky) in preventing any serious financial panics during his tenure, which ended in March, 1907, six months before the October panic.

Shaw was vilified in both the academic and popular press for his attempts to turn the Treasury into a functioning central bank.[28] The opposition to his actions arose both from those who thought that central banking actions were undesirable, whether carried out by the Treasury or by a true central bank, as well as from those who thought Shaw's actions were unconstitutional, even if they were ultimately desirable.[29] The political opposition to Shaw's actions, the constraints placed on his activities by the normal demands of operating the Treasury, and the modest quantity of funds he had available for stabilizing money markets meant that Shaw only partially eliminated seasonal fluctuations in nominal rates.

A second institution of the National Banking System that engaged in central banking activities was clearinghouse associations. These associations were originally devised as a means of reducing the costs of clearing claims between banks within the same city. The first and prototype clearinghouse, the New York Clearinghouse Association (NYCA), was created in 1854. The member banks appointed a manager who kept track of all inter-bank claims and issued coin certificates (which constituted legal reserves) to account for any net differences. The clearinghouses therefore reduced significantly the movement of specie around the city. The NYCA was sufficiently successful that other cities established their own clearinghouses, and by 1913 there were 162 such associations.[30]

The next step in the development of the clearinghouses, and the one that gave them the appearance of possessing central banking powers, was the use of clearinghouse loan certificates. Clearinghouse members had the right to deposit non-reserve assets (such as stocks or treasury bills) with the clearinghouse and receive in exchange loan certificates with face value equal to 75% of the value of the assets deposited and bearing an interest rate of 7%. These loan certificates were accepted by other clearinghouse members in settlement of interbank accounts, although they did not constitute legal reserves.[31] The issuance of these certificates reduced somewhat the need for a central bank to provide liquidity during crises, but there were numerous crises despite the use of the certificates. It should be clear that the loan certificates could, at best, moderate the effects of shifts in asset demands that forced lower reserves ratios on banks. There were costs to the banks of increasing their reserve base by using the loan certificates (the 7% interest), and the loan certificates were not generally accepted for settlement of debts outside of the clearinghouse. Essentially, the arrangements meant that, amongst themselves, the member banks counted non-specie assets as reserves.[32]

3.2 Economic performance under the National Banking System

The National Banking Acts were effective in accomplishing their immediate goal of raising revenue for the North, since the requirement that nationally chartered banks hold government securities as backing for their notes created a ready market for these securities. The Acts were also successful in creating a uniform national currency: during this period the notes of different national banks traded at par since they were, by law, backed more than 100% by government securities and therefore virtually without risk.[33] The creation of a uniform currency, however, did not solve all the problems of the banking system. The most important problems that remained were the frequency and severity of the financial panics, which were blamed on the inelasticity of the money stock.

The inelasticity of the money supply referred to the fact that the National Banking System operated, at least in the short run, with a fixed quantity of high-powered money. There was no central bank to provide funds in times of high demand, and the Independent Treasury and the New York Clearinghouse Association were not sufficiently powerful to have major effects on the quantity of reserves. In theory there should have been significant elasticity in the money stock coming from international sources, since between 1879 and 1914 the United States participated in the international gold standard. In practice, however, this source of liquidity was limited by short-term frictions in the international capital markets (Friedman and Schwartz, 1963, pp. 89–90) and by the fact that the other major countries of the gold standard experienced seasonal shifts in asset demands similar to those in the United States (Clark, 1986).[34]

The inelasticity of the money stock was widely blamed for the frequency and severity of the financial panics that occurred in this period, which were combinations of bank failures, bank runs, and stock market crashes. The immediate cause of the panics varied considerably, with some resulting from the failure of specific banks or investment houses in New York, others resulting from rashes of bank failures in the agricultural regions, and one stemming from an external shock (the Baring Crisis of 1890 in England). When an initial shock caused one or a few banks to fail, other banks anticipated the possibility of bank runs and called in some of their loans. Since many of these were stock market call loans, the cumulative effects of loan recall by many banks depressed the stock market. At the same time, the non-bank public increased its desired currency-deposit ratio, and this caused additional bank failures and runs on many banks. The most serious panics (1873, 1893, and 1907) ended only after suspensions of convertibility by the banks.[35]

The inelasticity of the money supply was particularly a problem with respect to *seasonal* shifts in asset demands. In the Spring and Fall of each year, seasonal increases in loan demand were accompanied by seasonal increases in the demand for currency relative to deposits.[36] With the reserves of the banking system held fixed, these shifts in asset demands meant that interest rates rose sharply and reserve-deposit ratios fell. The likelihood that an event such as a large loan default precipitated a panic therefore increased systematically in the seasons with high loans and currency demand, since the probability that any given size shock caused banks to fail increased with reserve-deposit ratios were low. The seasonal shifts in asset demands did not, by themselves, cause the panics, but they produced the conditions that made panics likely to occur. As Miron (1986) documents, the probability of a panic was much higher in the Fall than it was during the rest of the year, consistent with the high interest rates and low reserve-deposit ratios that prevailed during this season.[37]

The major panics during the National Banking Period occurred in 1873, 1884, 1890, 1893, and 1907 (Sprague, 1910). In addition, there were twenty-four other minor panics during the 1873–1909 period (Kemmerer 1910). The economic costs of these panics are difficult to estimate, but it is plausible that the widespread bank failures and the suspensions of convertibility produced serious disruptions in the provision of financial intermediation services, as Bernanke (1983) emphasizes with respect to the Great Depression. The effects of the panics during the pre-1914 period may not have been as severe as they were during the Depression, since the National Banking System had developed ways of moderating the effects of the crises (suspensions of convertibility and clearinghouse loan certificates).[38] Nevertheless, the considerable attention that the panics received in the popular and academic press, and the amount of energy devoted to preventing them (for example, by setting up a central bank), suggest that the costs were substantial. It is possible, of course, that the important effects of the panics were redistributional rather than allocative; this does not necessarily mean that they were a less compelling problem.

3.3   The creation of the Federal Reserve

The recurrent financial panics during the National Banking Period led to extended discussion of reforms of the system, especially the creation of a central bank. Conflicts between competing interest groups, however, prevented agreement on major reform for many years. The agricultural (western) banks were leery of a central bank, partly because they thought it would be controlled by New York banks, partly because of lingering resentment over the actions of the Second Bank of the United States.[39] Although there were numerous modifications of the National Banking System, none of these represented substantial change. Moreover, between 1893 and 1907 the economy did not experience any significant panics, and output growth was quite strong.

The panic of 1907, which coincided with a significant decline in output and a major stock market crash, spawned renewed interest in the creation of a central bank. The immediate result of the 1907 panic was the Aldrich-Vreeland Act of 1908, which granted emergency powers to groups of ten or more national banks and created the National Monetary Commission, a congressional committee assigned to study the United States and foreign banking systems. The Commission's *Report*, published in 1910, laid the basic blueprint for the Federal Reserve System. The Report suggested that a central bank patterned directly after the European central banks, with their monolithic structure, would not be suitable for the United States, but a more de-centralized system, with some method for coordination of the component parts, would be acceptable to a sufficiently large constituency. In response to the political demands of the time, the Act created a system consisting of twelve Federal Reserve Banks organized under the umbrella of a Board of Governers.

The Federal Reserve Act became law in December of 1913, and the banks opened for business in November of 1914. The proponents of the System promised a host of benefits from its creation. The Fed was intended to be the guardian of the nation's gold reserve and thus maintain the United States' position in the international gold standard.[40] It was assumed that the Fed would clear all checks at par and thereby eliminate the complicated system of charges associated with transporting checks between distant parts of the country. In addition, the founders expected the Fed to reduce interregional interest rate differentials by transferring funds to the parts of the country where demand was greatest. The primary goal of monetary policy, however, as stated in the Fed's charter, was 'to furnish an elastic currency.' According to H. Parker Willis (1915, p. 75), an expert consultant to the House Banking and Currency Committee in 1912–1913 and a future Secretary of the Federal Reserve Board, the potential benefits of the System were that 'there will be no such wide fluctuations of interest rates . . . from season to season as now exist . . . and no necessity of emergency measures to safeguard the country from the possible results of financial panic or stringency.'

4   The real bills doctrine and the lender of last resort

The discussion in Section 3 above suggests that the Fed was created with one dominant goal in mind: the elimination of financial panics through provision of an elastic currency. Although the goal of eliminating financial panics was widely accepted, the exact means of attaining this goal were not. The controversies centred around the interpretation of the real bills doctrine and the role of a lender of last resort.[41] In this section I review the discussions of monetary policy by the founders and early practitioners at the Fed, and I analyze the likely impact of these policies on the behaviour of the economy.

4.1   The real bills doctrine and the lender of last resort

The dominant theory of central banking during the 19th and early 20th century was the real bills doctrine. This doctrine held that lending by a central bank should 'accommodate the needs of commerce and business' and that central banks should confine their discount and open market operations to 'short term, and self-liquidating' paper.[42] In practice, real bills lending meant that the central bank should conduct discount or open market operations only for commercial paper, rather than for stock market call or time loans. Much of the credit extended by commercial banks during this period was to stock market brokers, and stocks were purchased on much thinner margins than they are today (Myers, 1931, p. 313). Changes in interest rates therefore had enormous effects on stock prices. The predominant worry of central banking practitioners was that increased lending in response to higher loan demand would finance stock market loans and therefore fuel speculation.

The archetypical real bills lending was the accommodation of the seasonal variation in asset demands, and essentially all observers agreed that the sterilization of seasonal fluctuations in interest rates was desirable.[43] To begin with, seasonal movements in asset demands were assumed to result from seasonal variations in business activity, particularly but not exclusively agriculture, so these shifts in asset demands 'arose out of business' and 'corresponded to the needs of trade.' In addition, seasonal fluctuations are transitory ('self-liquidating'), so accommodating seasonals does not produce any general increase in the price level or in speculation. There are always off-setting decreases in asset demands that approximately cancel out the increases resulting from the seasonal peak in loan demand. Jevons (1884) argued that the Bank of England should not raise the Bank's discount rate in response to the regular autumnal drains on the Bank's reserves since these replenished themselves in the normal course of business.

The real bills doctrine became controversial when it was applied to non-seasonal variation in the demand for credit.[44] Some proponents did advocate the interest smoothing policies implicit in the doctrine with respect to non-seasonal variation in economic activity. For example, Hardy (1932) wrote that the Fed

> ... should adapt its policy to the change in cyclical situation just as it does to the changing seasonal situation, curtailing credit when business declines and expanding it when business expands ... This line of analysis points to the conclusion that it is not the business of the Reserve system to stimulate business by making money artificially cheap in periods of depression or dear in periods of boom, but merely to adapt itself to conditions as it finds them.

Many were fearful of such a policy, however, because the non-seasonal variation in demand is not necessarily transitory and because there is no effective way to ensure that the increased credit is used for business rather than speculative purposes. Much discussion of monetary policy during the early years of the Fed focused on ways of channeling credit selectively to the ultimate users. There was not widespread appreciation of the fact that as long as different kinds of assets are substitutable in private agents' portfolios, any attempt to differentially affect interest rates will be only partly successful at best.[45]

The second main reason for the establishment of a central bank in the minds of contemporary observers was the need for a lender of last resort. The idea that the role of a central bank is to moderate financial crises by providing liquidity in times of unusually high demand for currency and reserves dates back at least to Bagehot (1873). He wrote in *Lombard Street* that the Bank of England had an 'inescapable duty' to act as lender of last resort, and that the appropriate response by a central bank to a crisis was 'to lend freely, but at a high rate of interest.' This aspect of central banking activity was much more controversial than real bills lending, however. The financial panics of the pre-1914 period were associated with dramatic movements in stock prices, so it was feared that by lending in response to increases in interest rates the central bank would fuel speculation and make the size of the eventual crash larger.

The discussion above suggests the following characterization of the policies that the founders of the Fed expected it to carry out. The Fed would make the money stock elastic with respect to seasonal variations in the needs of business, providing additional credit in high demand seasons and removing it again during the low demand seasons. The Fed would also make the money stock elastic with respect to the non-seasonal variation in business, especially to the extent that these variations appeared transitory, and it would, perhaps, provide additional funds in times of crisis. The Fed was also meant to avoid accommodating the demand for stock market loans, however, and the framers for the most part expected it to exercise restrictive policies in response to any evidence of speculation.

4.2   *Interest smoothing and output stabilization*

I turn next to analyzing the likely effects of the policies advocated by the framers and early practitioners of monetary policy. The analysis is based on the Poole (1970) model, in which standard *IS* and *LM* curves are buffeted by shocks that perturb real output from its natural rate level. The monetary authority's objective is to stabilize output around this level, either by fixing the money stock or by pegging the nominal interest rate. The conclusion of the analysis is that if *LM* shocks are more prevalent than *IS* shocks it is optimal to smooth interest rates, but if *IS* shocks are more prevalent then it is optimal to fix the money stock. A policy of smoothing interest rates in a world dominated by *IS* shocks destabilizes output.

The lending policy implied by the real bills doctrine runs directly counter to this analysis. An increase is the underlying 'needs of business' is plausibly interpreted as an exogenous, outward shift in the *IS* curve, and the proper response to such a shift in the Poole framework is a contractionary policy that raises interest rates. According to the real bills doctrine, however, monetary policy should accommodate the needs of trade, implying that the appropriate response to an outward shift in the *IS* curve is an expansionary policy that keeps interest rates from rising and causes the expansion in output to be larger than it otherwise would have been. Application of the real bills doctrine destabilizes output, so any justification for the real bills doctrine must proceed along lines other than those suggested by Poole.

The contemporary justification for the policies implied by the real bills doctrine was, I believe, essentially the following. The founders and early practitioners of the Fed associated financial panics with high interest rates and a scarcity of reserves. They believed that by accommodating the needs of trade they could eliminate the periods of high nominal rates and low reserve-deposit ratios that constituted the conditions necessary for panics. It is not clear whether they adopted this point of view because they believed monetary policy had no effect on real variables (the classical dichotomy), or because they thought that a modest increase in the short-term variance of output was a fair price to pay to avoid panics, which were associated with serious recessions.

It is important to note that, if the justification for the real bills doctrine given above was the one accepted by contemporary observers, then they were correct in focusing on nominal rather than real interest rates. Just as it is the nominal rate that determines desired money holdings in the standard Baumol-Tobin framework, it is the nominal interest rate that determines a bank's desired reserve-deposit ratio so long as the asset that is used as the ultimate means of payment carries a nominal return that is fixed (usually at zero). By smoothing nominal interest rates, the Fed could have eliminated the periods of low reserve-deposit ratios that led to panics, whether or not this policy affected real rates and output.

The Fed's views concerning stock market speculation are somewhat less at odds with the Poole analysis than is the real bills doctrine. Increases in stock prices raise consumers' wealth, increase consumption, and shift out the *IS* curve, so the proper response in the Poole model is a restrictive policy. This is what the Fed planned to carry out, although its desire to restrain stock prices does not appear to have come from a view that doing so would moderate output fluctuations. Instead, it only desired to restrain stock prices when the increases were thought to be 'speculative'. The rationalization of this view may be that speculative increases in stock prices are likely to end in collapses and panics, producing costly disruptions of financial markets, with the eventual costs of the panic an increasing function of the size of the speculative increase in stock prices. This view is similar to the Fed's justification for the real bills doctrine: by maintaining stable financial markets, the violent swings in output that accompany financial panics are eliminated.

There is, of course, a potential conflict between the Fed's desire to smooth interest rates and its desire to smooth stock prices. In Blanchard's (1981) model of output, interest rates, and the stock market, an interest rate stabilization policy in the face of *IS* shocks can increase the variance of stock prices. A positive *IS* shock raises both output and interest rates; depending on the relevant elasticities, this may produce an increase or decrease in stock prices. An expansionary monetary policy increases output and lowers interest rates, thereby unambiguously raising stock prices. Thus, if the conditions for the positive *IS* shock to raise stock prices hold, an interest rate stabilization policy increases the volatility of stock prices. A commitment by the Fed to smooth both interest rates and stock prices is therefore guaranteed to fail.

The Fed's desire to act as a lender of last resort is the one of its three major goals that fits most consistently into the Poole analysis. Increases in desired currency-deposit ratios and reserve-deposit ratios, the two key features of financial panics, lead to decreases in the money multiplier and backward shifts of the *LM* curve. The appropriate policy response in the Poole model is an expansionary one that keeps interest rates from rising, and this is precisely what the proponents of a lender of last resort expected

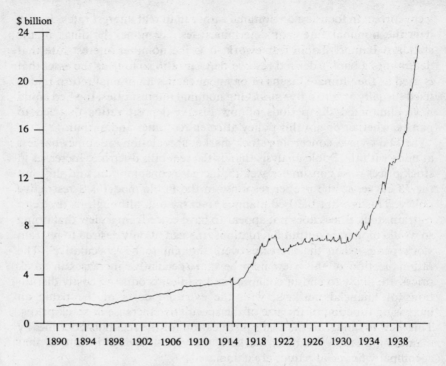

Figure 10.8   US high-powered money, 1890–1940 (monthly data)

the Fed to do. In practice, however, the desire to act as lender of last resort was in conflict with the desire to restrain speculation: the periods of high volatility in stock prices were also the ones when panics forced desired reserve-deposit and currency-deposit ratios upward. The manner in which the Fed resolved this conflict is the key to understanding Fed policy during the early years of its history.

5   Federal Reserve policy, 1914–1940

I turn now to a quantitative evaluation of Fed policy during the 1915–1940 period, with two main goals in mind. The first is to see in what ways the policies pursued reflected the economic problems of the pre-Fed banking system and to what degree they matched the description of desirable monetary policy found in the literature of the time. The second is to assess the extent to which the policies pursued by the Fed caused or contributed to the changed behaviour of both real and financial market variables after 1914. The conclusions of this section are that the Fed's behaviour was

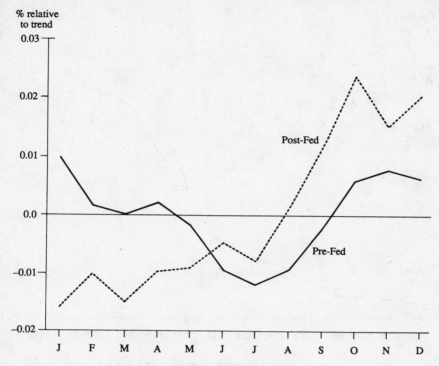

Figure 10.9   The seasonal pattern in US high-powered money

consistent with what the founders desired, but that this behaviour was also largely responsible for the worsened performance of output and inflation after 1914.

Figure 10.8 plots monthly data on the monetary base for the 1890:1–1940:12 sample period.[46] There are three features of the data that deserve comment: the seasonality of the monetary base increased substantially after 1914; the non-seasonal variability of the monetary base also increased significantly; and the rate of growth of the base slowed immediately before the three major downturns in economic activity of the 1915–1940 period (1920–21, 1929–33, and 1937–38). I discuss the importance of each of these features in the data in turn.

The increased seasonality of the monetary base is the most easily understood of the three results just described. Figure 10.9 plots the seasonal in the detrended log level of the base for the 1890–1914 and 1914–1940 sample periods.[47] The base is much more seasonal after 1914, with the standard deviation of the seasonal coefficients increasing from

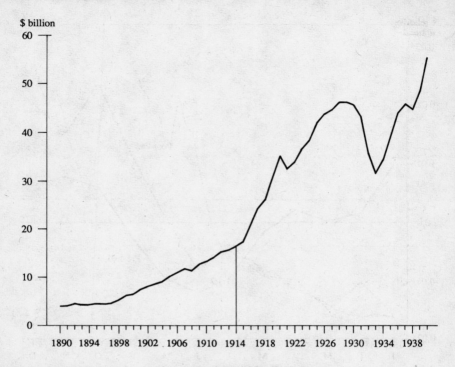

Figure 10.10   US money stock, M2, 1890–1940 (annual data)

0.70% to 1.41% and the amplitude rising from 2% to 4%. In particular, the level of the base is much higher during the fall after 1914, consistent with the Fed's desired to prevent the usual Autumn increases in interest rates. The change in the seeasonal behaviour of the base is thus plausibly the reason for the change in the seasonal behaviour of nominal interest rates documented in Figure 10.7.[48]

The second fact about the behaviour of the monetary base is that the non-seasonal component was more variable after 1914 than before. There are a number of possible explanations for this increased variability. The Fed may have made the base more variable in order to offset shifts in the money multiplier and thereby caused the money stock itself to grow smoothly. Alternatively, the Fed may have made the base more variable in an attempt to offset velocity shifts, thereby making nominal income grow smoothly. To address these issues, Figures 10.10 and 10.11 present data on the nominal money stock (M2) and nominal income for the 1890–1940 sample period. The plots of the money stock are for annual data, since monthly data on the money stock do not begin until 1907. The results in

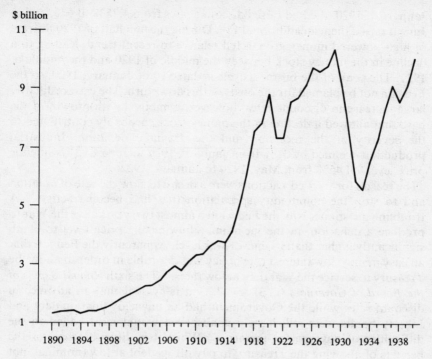

Figure 10.11   US nominal GNP, 1890–1940 (annual data)

the graphs show that neither 'explanation' for the increased volatility of
the base is correct: the money stock is much more volatile after the
founding of the Fed, and the increase in the volatility of nominal income
after 1914 is even more dramatic than that in real income.

The increased volatility of the monetary aggregates does not by itself
mean that monetary policy was responsible for the increased volatility of
output and inflation. If the post-1914 economy was perturbed more by
external shocks than the pre-1914 economy, both money and output
would have become more variable even in the absence of the Fed. Further,
an optimal policy might well be a more variable one if variation in policy
were required to offset shocks to the economy. In order to demonstrate,
therefore, that the increased variability of output was in fact due to the
actions of the Fed, it is necessary to examine the third fact noted above,
namely, that the rate of monetary growth slowed before each of the three
major innovations in output during the 1915–1940 period.

The severity of the 1920–21 recession is widely regarded as the direct
result of Fed policy (Friedman and Schwartz, 1963, pp. 231–9).[49] In

January of 1920, the Fed raised discount rates from 4.75% to 6%, and in June it raised them an additional 1%. During the first half of 1920 the rate of high-powered money growth fell relative to recent trend, leading to a decline in the money stock between the middle of 1920 and the middle of 1921. The peak of the business cycle is dated to be January, 1920, so the Fed can not be blamed for the onset of this downturn. The extraordinarily large increase in discount rates, however, combined with growth of the base that allowed a decline in the money stock, probably contributed to the severity of the recession and the dramatic deflation. Industrial production declined by 31% from January, 1920 to June, 1921, while the price level fell 45% from May, 1920 to January, 1922.

The reason for the Fed's actions were a desire to slow the rate of inflation and to stop the commodity speculation that had become active.[50] A troubling question is why the Fed waited almost two years after the War to produce a deflation, in the meantime allowing the price level to climb significantly higher than its end-of-war level. Apparently the Fed felt that an easy money, low interest rate policy was desirable in order to allow the Treasury to service the War debt at low rates.[51] The sixth *Annual Report of the Board of Governors* (p. 3) says '. . . it is evident that an advance in discount rates while the Government had an unwieldy floating debt and Liberty bonds were still largely unabsorbed would have added to the difficulties of government financing.' While it is difficult to assess the benefits of allowing the Treasury to pay off its debt at low (nominal, not necessarily real) interest rates, it seems likely that by delaying the end of the World War I inflation, and then ending it so abruptly, the Fed made output more volatile than necessary.

The second major downturn in output during the 1915–1940 period is the 1929–1933 episode. There are two distinct questions concerning the Fed's role in the Great Depression, the first being whether it caused the initial downturn and the second being whether, whatever the initial cause, the Fed could have prevented the magnitude of the decline. I discuss each of these issues in turn.

In a recent paper, Hamilton (1987) shows that according to every standard measure of the tightness of monetary policy the Fed began a contraction in early 1928.[52] Figure 10.5 suggests clearly why this might have occurred. During the 1923–1928 period there was an unprecedented increase in stock prices, which many observers of financial markets, including those at the Board, feared represented speculation and should therefore be restrained. There was, of course, strongly dissenting opinion, which argues that any attempt to restrict lending in the stock market would produce a crash. As Friedman and Schwartz (1963) have emphasized, the two points of view corresponded, roughly, to that of the Board of Governors and that of the New York Fed. Benjamin Strong, the president of the New York Bank, was a leading force in the fight to keep policy on an even keel, but Strong suffered from poor health that effectively removed him from power early in 1928 (Chandler, 1958). With Strong absent, the balance of power shifted to the Board and a tighter policy resulted.

There has been much debate over the Fed's role in the severity of the contraction from 1929 to 1933, since, while the nominal money stock declined sharply, the real money stock and both the real and nominal base actually rose.[53] An advocate of the view that monetary policy could have limited the severity of the recession would have to argue that the Fed could have prevented many of the bank failures if it had taken a more aggressive stance, both by pumping in reserves at an even faster rate and by bailing out specific banks that were on the verge of collapse. Friedman and Schwartz (1963) argue that it was crucial for the Fed to take this course of action because the economy's pre-1914 means of moderating the effects of bank runs, suspensions of convertibility, had been outlawed. The resolution of this issue is not crucial to the analysis here, since there is ample evidence of the Fed's role in producing economic instability even when the Depression is excluded from consideration. Suffice it to say that if the Fed bears even partial responsibility for the depth of the Depression, then the case that it destabilized output becomes even stronger.

The circumstances of the 1937–1938 recession were in many ways quite similar to those of 1928. There was an increase in real stock prices during 1936 and 1937 which, although modest in comparison to the increase preceding the Depression, was substantial. As in 1928, the Board became concerned with the possibility of speculation (Friedman and Schwartz, 1963, pp. 511–34), and between the middle of 1936 and the middle of 1937 it doubled reserve requirements, leading to a temporary but sharp decline in the money stock.[54] The recession from 1937 to 1938 was similarly sharp but brief. Industrial production fell 33% between May, 1937 and May, 1938, while wholesale prices fell 11% from July, 1937 to May, 1938.[55]

The general results that emerge from this discussion are as follows. During the period 1915–1940, the Fed usually followed a policy of smoothing interest rates. This had the desired effect of eliminating the seasonal in nominal rates, as well as of removing most of the non-seasonal transitory variation in rates. The Fed deviated significantly from its policy of accommodating shifts in assets demands on three notable occasions. In each case, the Fed was concerned with reducing speculation, and in each case the Fed's policy was sufficiently restrictive that it caused or contributed significantly to major reductions in output and increased variability of prices.

6   Conclusions

The analysis of Fed policy presented above is troubling because it suggests that the Fed, perhaps knowingly, destabilized output and the price level. On the one hand, the Fed deliberately accommodated some shifts in interest rates because the cost of the increased output volatility resulting from this policy was lower than the cost of a true panic. On the other hand, in certain instances the Fed deliberately contracted the economy because it thought this was necessary in order to restrain speculation in stock or commodity markets.[56]

One possible objection to the conclusions offered above arises from the fact that the variance of output increased after 1914 in countries that possessed central banks continuously over the entire 1890–1940 period. This fact might be taken to suggest that an increase in the variance of shocks to the world economy after 1914, rather than the actions of the Fed, led to the deterioration in the performance of the United States and other economies. In fact, it is plausible that the increased variance of output in countries other than the United States resulted from attempts by their central banks to pursue objectives other than output stability. The best example of this phenomenon is Britain, where the desire to return to gold at the pre-war parity required the Bank of England to engineer a major recession and deflation. A proposed reason that these central banks pursued active policies only after 1914 is that the suspension of the gold standard permitted them the freedom to move interest rates without inducing large gold flows (Barsky, Mankiw, Miron and Weil, 1988).

The results in this paper should obviously not be interpreted to suggest that the actions of the Fed have, over its entire history, been bad for the economy. They do suggest that a policy of smoothing interest rates, or of focusing exclusively on asset markets, has the potential to produce undesirable effects on output and prices. The view that maintaining full employment is an important goal for economic policy was acknowledged in 1946 by the Full Employment Act which states that 'it is the continuing policy and responsibility of the Federal Government . . . to promote maximum employment, production, and purchasing power.'[57] Thus, while it is true that the Fed has placed considerable emphasis on the stability of asset markets since 1940, it has apparently learned to give sufficient weight to other objectives (output and the price level) so as to avoid the dramatically undesirable consequences of its actions before 1940.

Data appendix

Real GNP: 1890–1929, Real GNP in billions of 1982 dollars, from Romer (1987), Table 2. 1930–1940, Real GNP in billions of 1982 dollars, U.S. Department of Commerce (1986), Table 1.2. Available annually.

Implicit Price Deflator: 1890–1929, Implicit Price Deflator for GNP, 1982 = 100, from Romer (1987), Table 2. 1930–1940, Implicit Price Deflator for GNP, 1982 = 100, from U.S. Department of Commerce (1986), Table 1.2. Available annually.

Wholesale Price Index: 1890:1–1912:12, Index of wholesale prices for all commodities (1913 = 100), from Bureau of Labor Statistics (1928), Table 1, pp. 2–6. 1913:1–1940:12, Wholesale Price Index for All Commodities (1957–59 = 100), from Bureau of Labor Statistics (1963), mimeo of Table. The pre-1913 numbers have been adjusted to the 1957–59 = 100 scale. Available monthly, not seasonally adjusted.

Industrial Production: 1890:1–1912:12, Index of Physical Volume of Business Activity (Babson), 1923–27 = 100, from Moore (1961), Table 15.1, p. 130. 1919:1–1940:12, Index of Industrial Production, 1977 = 100, from Board of Governors of the Federal Reserve System (1986), Table A.5, p. 171. The Babson numbers have been adjusted so that the average for 1919 equals the average of the Index of Industrial Production in 1919. Available monthly, seasonally adjusted.

Interest Rates: 1890:1–1940:12, Three-month Time Loan Rate, from Mankiw and Miron (1985), Data Appendix. See also footnote 9. Available monthly, not seasonally adjusted.

Money Stock: 1890–1940, M2 for June, in billions of dollars, from Friedman and Schwartz (1970), Table 1, column (9). Available annually, seasonally adjusted.

High-Powered Money: 1890:1–1914:10, Currency in Circulation, end of month figures, in millions of dollars, from NBER files, series # 14,135 (Raw). 1914:11–1940:12, high-powered money is equal to currency in circulation plus member bank deposits at the Fed. The currency in circulation series is from Board of Governors of the Federal Reserve System (1943), Table No. 110, pp. 409–13, end of month figures, in millions of dollars. For 1917:1–1940:2, the member bank deposit series is from the same source, Table No. 102, pp. 373–7, end of month figures, in millions of dollars. From 1914:11–1916:12, the member bank deposit series was provided by Robert Barro, from Anna Schwartz. Available monthly, not seasonally adjusted.

Stock Prices: 1890:1–1940:12, S&P's Index of Stock Prices for 500 Companies, monthly averages of daily figures, 1941–1943 = 10, from *Daily Record of Stock Prices*, Standard and Poor's (1984). Available monthly, not seasonally adjusted.

NOTES

I am grateful to Robert Barsky, Marcello de Cecco, Brad Delong, Rudi Dornbusch, Barry Eichengreen, Rick Mishkin, Christina Romer, Bill Schwert, and David Weil for helpful comments and to Joe Beaulieu for research assistance.

1 Much of this literature also considers the tradeoff between output stabilization and other goals, particularly price stability. See especially Friedman (1968).

2 Two recent papers that adopt this perspective are Basu, Kimball, Mankiw and Weil (1987) and McCallum (1988).

3 Many contemporary observers also felt that the role of a central bank was to act as a lender of last resort. I discuss this issue below.

4 On the first topic see Burns (1960), Moore (1961), Modigliani (1977), Mayer (1978), and Romer (1986a, 1986b). On the second, see especially Friedman and Schwartz (1963, 1982), as well as Shiller and Seigel (1977), Shiller (1980), Miron (1986), Barsky (1987), Clark (1986), Canova (1987), Mankiw, Miron and Weil (1987), Goodfriend (1988), and Barsky, Mankiw, Miron and Weil (1988).

5 The real GNP series is from Romer (1987); it has been constructed in a consistent way for the entire 1890–1940 sample period, so the kinds of issues raised by Romer (1986a, 1986b) probably do not affect the analysis here. The industrial production index is the Babson Index, from Moore (1961), for the period 1890–1918, and the Fed's Index of Industrial Production for the period 1919–40. The Babson Index is available through 1938 and matches the Fed's Index closely during the period of overlap. The Data Appendix describes the sources of the data in detail.

6 The implicit price deflator is from Romer (1987); the wholesale price index is from the Bureau of Labor Statistics. See data appendix for details.

7 Barsky (1987) and Barsky and Delong (1988) discuss the properties of inflation during the pre-1914 period.

8 This is the index for Standard and Poor's 500 companies, deflated by the monthly wholesale price index. The observations for 1914:8–1914:11 are missing because the New York Stock Exchange closed for four months after the outbreak of World War I.

9 The interest rate considered here is the rate on three month time loans, from the first week of each month, as reported in Mankiw and Miron (1985). This series differs from the series on three month time loans reported in Macaulay (1938) for two reasons. First, Macaulay's series is for monthly averages of weekly data while Mankiw and Miron's series is for first week of the month data. Second, there are a few unusual observations that Macaulay treats differently from Mankiw and Miron. In a few weeks, the source of the data (the *Commercial and Financial Chronicle*) reports numbers such as '6 + com', which means that the rate on loans was six percent plus commissions, or '6 nom', which means that a rate of 6 was posted but there was little or no trading at this rate. Macaulay adjusts the reported numbers using information from the text of the *Commercial and Financial Chronicle*, whereas Mankiw and Miron simply report a value of '6'. Macaulay does not provide a precise explanation of how he adjusts these observations. The characteristics of the data series that are important for the conclusions of this paper and other papers using the data series (Mankiw and Miron, 1985; Mankiw, Miron and Weil, 1987; and Barsky, Mankiw, Miron and Weil, 1988) are not sensitive to inclusion of the sample points in question. Indeed, since the actual rates paid during panics were at least as high as the rates reported by

Mankiw and Miron, there was if anything even more transitory variation in short rates during the pre-1914 period than the estimates presented above suggest.

10 Barsky, Mankiw, Miron and Weil (1988) report regressions of the nominal rate on its own lagged value. In the pre-1914 period the coefficient on the lagged rate is about 0.75 and significantly less than one. During the post-1914 period the estimated coefficient is quite close to one and never significantly different from one. The nominal rate changed from being a stationary process to being close to a random walk after the founding of the Fed.

11 Mankiw, Miron and Weil (1987) also demonstrate that the end of 1914, rather than any other date, is the most likely point of the change in the stochastic process for nominal rates.

12 The results described in this paragraph are not substantially affected if alternative post-1914 subsamples are employed.

13 The discussion above does not address the question of whether the Fed affected the seasonal behaviour of real interest rates. Both Shiller (1980) and Barsky, Mankiw, Miron and Weil (1988) find that point estimates of the seasonal pattern in real rates differ after 1914, but there is so much noise in the inflation rate series that one cannot reject any interesting hypothesis.

14 For more detailed analyses of the disappearance of seasonality, see Shiller (1980), Clark (1986), and Miron (1986).

15 The suspension of the gold standard in 1914 was the direct result of the outbreak of World War I in August 1914. Within a few months of the outbreak of war (indeed in some cases even before the formal declaration), most countries had suspended gold payments either *de jure* or *de facto* (Brown, 1940, pp. 7–26). When the war ended, most countries had experienced such rapid inflation during the previous four years that an immediate return to convertibility at anything like the pre-war parities was unthinkable. It was the announced aim of virtually all countries, however, to return to the gold standard quickly, and a great deal of macroeconomic history of the subsequent period can only be understood in this light. See, for example the *First Interim Report* of the Cunliffe Committee (1918) in Britain. Keynes (1923), was an outspoken opponent of the return to gold.

16 The original Act was passed in February, 1863, and amended in June 1864 and February, 1865. The Acts became fully effective on August 1, 1866. See Friedman and Schwartz (1963), pp. 18–19.

17 One of the most important changes in monetary arrangements that occurred during this period was the remonetization of gold in 1879 (Friedman and Schwartz, 1963, pp. 44–59). Other changes included adjustments in reserve requirements against national bank notes, minimum reserve-deposit ratios, minimum capital requirements, and the number of greenbacks in circulation.

18 The legal constraints imposed on banks (such as minimum capital requirements and minimum reserve-deposit ratios) were similar in spirit across states but different in detail. (James, 1978, pp. 39–44).

19 The discount on a particular issue was determined by the distance to the issuing bank, the reputation of the bank, and the length of time since the note had been issued. (Myers, 1970, pp. 70, 80, 94, 121).

20 One of the important causes of the destruction of the Second Bank of the United States (in 1837) was that Nicholas Biddle, its president, made a concerted effort to collect state bank notes and then present them quickly to the bank of issue, thus discouraging overissue. This practice was unpopular with

rural banks, where excessive note issue was more prevalent, and they lobbied hard and successfully against the renewal of the Bank's charter. (Beckhart, 1972, pp. 4–13).

21 Indeed, the collection of data on state banks stopped in 1863 and did not resume until 1867.

22 In 1870 there were 261 state banks and 1,612 national banks. By 1910 there were roughly 15,000 state banks and 7,000 national banks (James, 1978, p. 25).

23 The period after 1879, when the United States resumed specie payments, is also unusual because the world was operating on the international gold standard. As the result of World War I, the international gold standard was suspended in 1914 in most countries, and it returned for only a limited time and in much weakened form. The correct characterization of the system of international monetary arrangements varies considerably over the 1914–33 period. During the War there were sufficient controls on prices, gold movements, and international capital flows that any attempt to describe the system in simple terms is bound to be inaccurate. The period from 1919–25 seems to be a relatively clean case of floating rates. From 1926–31, several countries resumed convertibility, so that the world moved back toward an international gold standard. It appears to be the consensus, however, that the operation of the gold standard during this period did not approximate its smooth operation before 1914 (Hamilton, 1988). Beginning with Britain's devaluation of sterling in the Fall of 1931, a number of countries left the gold standard, this time for good. The final blow to the international gold standard was the departure of the United States in 1933 (Eichengreen, 1985, pp. 19–24).

24 The First Bank of the United States operated from 1791 to 1811; the Second Bank from 1817 to 1836 (Beckhart, 1972, pp. 5–11).

25 These banks included the Bank of England, established in 1694, the Bank of France (1800), the State Bank of Russia (1860), the German Reichsbank (1876), and the Bank of Japan (1882). Bloomfield (1959) counts an additional sixteen countries with central banks or quasi-central banks by 1880 and three more by 1907.

26 The Independent Treasury Act was originally passed in 1840 but repealed in 1841. The Act was then re-adopted in 1846, with the System becoming operational on January 1, 1847 (Beckhart, 1972, p. 14).

27 Taus (1943), pp. 49–50.

28 The *Nation*'s was the most vocal attack in the popular press, Andrew's (1907) and Patton's (1907) the most famous in the academic literature. Timberlake (1963) provides an interesting analysis of Andrew's criticisms.

29 See Timberlake (1978), pp. 175–85.

30 White (1983), pp. 74–5.

31 White (1983), p. 76.

32 Timberlake (1978, 1984) provides a detailed account of the central banking activities of the Clearinghouse Associations.

33 See Myers (1970), p. 163 and James (1978), p. 75.

34 Calomiris and Hubbard (1987) present evidence that the short-term frictions in the international capital markets during the 1879–1914 period were too small to be consistent with the large seasonals in United States interest rates unless there were similar seasonals in interest rates in other countries. Clark (1986) documents that these other seasonals were indeed present.

35 Sprague (1910), pp. 1–225.

36 These seasonal movements in loan and currency demand were attributed to

many causes, the principal one being the need for both currency and credit by the agricultural sector of the economy in the spring planting season and the Fall crop-moving season. Additional currency was indeed because the volume of transactions was higher in these periods. Credit demand was high because farmers borrowed to finance the planting and harvesting of the crops (Laughlin, 1912, pp. 309–42). Kemmerer (1910) also mentions holidays, increased rail and barge activity during warm weather, and quarterly interest and dividend settlements as additional reasons for seasonal activity in the financial markets.

37 It is theoretically possible that the frequency of panics was higher during the fall season because the variance of shocks to the financial system was greater in the fall. Miron (1986) argues that according to this hypothesis there should have been a negative correlation between the seasonal in interest rates and the seasonal in reserve-deposit ratios during the pre-1914 period; in fact, the correlation was strongly positive.

38 This is a point emphasized by Friedman and Schwartz (1963), pp. 328–9.

39 After the charter of the Second Bank expired, in 1836, the bank became the United States Bank of Pennsylvania. The president, Nicholas Biddle, engaged in reckless speculation, including an attempt to corner the cotton market. As a result, the Bank failed in 1841, the private stockholders lost everything (Beckhart, 1972, p. 13).

40 The Fed was conceived and created before the outbreak of World War I and the suspension of the gold standard, and the founders expected that it would operate the gold standard regime that had come to be the accepted system of international monetary arrangements (Friedman and Schwartz, 1963, p. 191). As events turned out the gold standard was suspended just months before the Fed began operations, and it never returned in full form. The maintenance of a gold reserve for international settlements was therefore never a major issue for the Fed.

41 An additional issue that receives considerable attention in the literature is whether the Fed should employ open market operations or discounting as a means of affecting credit conditions in the economy. The amount of attention devoted to this topic appears misplaced. First, both notions were widely understood before the Fed began operations, and explicit provisions in the Federal Reserve Act made it legal for the Fed to conduct open market operations and to discount private debt. Second, contemporary observers clearly understood that a pure discount policy would not allow the Fed to achieve all conceivable monetary policies; in some cases it would need to use open market operations to 'make its discount rate effective.' Third, as a matter of practice, the Fed used both tools, as had the Bank of England in the pre-Fed period (Beckhart, 1972).

42 See especially the 1923 *Annual Report of the Board of Governors*.

43 See, for example, Laughlin (1912), Willis (1915), Glass (1927), and Warburg (1930).

44 The *First Interim Report* of the Cunliffe Committee (1918) suggested that the *Bank Rate* be raised in response to permanent but not temporary disturbances in the money market.

45 The Fed's confusion on the total amount of credit versus the composition of credit is summarized by Warburton, who says, 'Flexibility (elasticity) in currency – *not in total bank credit* – was the aim of the founders of the Federal Reserve System, and this flexibility was desired as a means of producing stability in total bank credit by providing stability in bank reserves' (Warburton , 1950, pp. 154–5). See also Friedman and Schwartz (1962), p. 193.

46 In the 1890: 1–1914: 10 period the base is equal to the stock of currency in circulation. Beginning in 1914: 11, the base is equal to currency in circulation plus member bank deposits at Federal Reserve Banks. The numbers for the period 1914: 11–1915: 5 are not strictly comparable to those for earlier or later periods and should be interpreted with caution; see the data appendix for details.

47 The patterns are calculated by regressing the log level of the base on twelve seasonal dummies, time and time-squared, and plotting the de-meaned values of the twelve coefficients on the dummies.

48 Clark (1986) points out that the increased seasonality of the monetary base does not appear very strongly until the middle of 1917, two and a half years after the founding of the Fed. Clark interprets this result as evidence that the change in the seasonality of interest rates could not have been the result of Fed policy. I do not find this point convincing. As noted above, the statistics on the monetary base are of much worse quality during the 1914: 11–1917: 5 period than during either the earlier or later period; the Clark result may therefore be an artifact of the data collection procedures. The other fact that Clark presents as evidence against the view that the Fed eliminated interest rates seasonals in the United States is that the seasonals disappeared at the same time in Europe. Barsky, Mankiw, Miron and Weil (1988) and Goodfriend (1988) provide explanations of this fact that are consistent with the hypothesis that the Fed eliminated the seasonals in the United States.

49 For a related analysis, see Huizinga and Mishkin (1986).

50 See Friedman and Schwartz (1963), pp. 221–30.

51 There was also some question as to whether the Fed had the legal authority to raise discount rates without the Treasury's consent. See Friedman and Schwartz (1963, p. 228).

52 See also Miron (1986), who emphasizes that the Fed moderated its accommodation of the seasonals in credit markets beginning in 1928.

53 See especially Temin (1976). Cecchetti (1988) disputes Temin's principal conclusion by presenting evidence that the deflation was anticipated. Hamilton (1987) and Dominguez, Fair and Shapiro (1988) conclude, however, that the deflation was probably not anticipated.

54 The Federal Reserve claimed later that the increase in reserve requirements should have been expected merely to absorb reserves, rather than to produce a decline in the money stock, because banks were holding unusually large excess reserves (Friedman and Schwartz, 1963, p. 543). This line of argument obviously ignores the plausible hypothesis that the experiences of 1929–33 led banks to desire much larger levels of precautionary reserves.

55 Brown (1956) discusses the stance of fiscal policy in the 1930s. He finds that fiscal policy was expansionary in 1936, contractionary in 1937, and expansionary in 1938. Given plausible lags in the effects of changes fiscal policy, it is not clear whether these changes contributed significantly to the decline in output from 1937 to 1938.

56 An alternative interpretation is that the Fed meant to move the economy in the directions that it did, but not by anything like the amount that occured. This perspective raises the question of why monetary policy may have been more potent than the Fed expected. One possibility is that the Fed required experience in order to have reasonable estimates of the feedback from its actions to the economy. A second is that the Fed implicitly assumed the conditions of fixed exchange rates, in which case their own policies would have been moderated by international forces. Alternatively, the responsiveness of

the economy to contractionary forces may have changed because the institutions that the privte economy had developed in order to ameliorate panics, such as suspensions of convertibility and clearing house loan certificates, were no longer allowed to operate.

57 The Act also created the Joint Economic Committee of Congress and the Council of Economic Advisors.

REFERENCES

Andrew, A. Piatt (1907). 'The Treasury and the Banks Under Secretary Shaw', *Quarterly Journal of Economics* 21, 3 (Aug.), 529–68.

Bagehot, Walter (1973). *Lombard Street*, London.

Barsky, Robert B. (1987). 'The Fisher Hypothesis and the Forecastability and Persistence of Inflation', *Journal of Monetary Economics* 19, 1 (Jan.), 3–24.

Barsky, Robert B. and J. Bradford DeLong (1988). 'Forecasting Pre-World War I Inflation: The Fisher Effect Revisited', manuscript, University of Michigan.

Barsky, Robert B., N. Gregory Mankiw, Jeffrey A. Miron and David N. Weil (1988). 'The Worldwide Change in the Behavior of Interest Rates and Prices in 1914', *European Economic Review* 32, 5 (June), 1123–47.

Basu, Susanto, Miles S. Kimball, N. Gregory Mankiw and David N. Weil (1987), 'Optimal Advice for Monetary Policy', manuscript, Harvard University.

Beckhart, Benjamin H. (1972). *The Federal Reserve System*, New York: Columbia University Press.

Bernanke, Ben (1983). 'Nonmonetary Effects of the Financial Crises in the Propogation of the Great Depression', *American Economic Review* 73, 3 (June), 257–76.

Blanchard, Olivier (1981). 'Output, the Stock Market, and Interest Rates', *American Economic Review* 71, 1 (Mar.), 132–43.

Bloomfield, Arthur I. (1959). *Monetary Policy Under the International Gold Standard: 1880–1914*, New York: Federal Reserve Bank of New York.

Board of Governors of the Federal Reserve System (1943). *Banking and Monetary Statistics, 1914–1940*, Washington D.C.: National Capital Press.

(1986). *Industrial Production*, Washington, D.C.: Board of Governors.

Brainard, William C. (1967). 'Uncertainty and the Effectiveness of Policy', *American Economic Review*, May.

Brown, E. Cary (1956). 'Fiscal Policy in the 'Thirties: A Reappraisal', *American Economic Review* 46, 5 (Dec.), 857–79.

Brown, William Adams, Jr. (1940). *The International Gold Standard Reinterpreted*, New York: National Bureau of Economic Research.

Bureau of Labor Statistics (1928). *Index Numbers of Wholesale Prices on Pre-War Base, 1890–1927*, Washington, D.C.: Government Printing Office.

(1963). 'All Commodities Wholesale Price Index', mimeo.

Burns, Arthur F. (1960). 'Progress Towards Economic Stability', *American Economic Review* 50, 1 (Mar.), 1–19.

Canova, Fabio (1987). 'Seasonality, the Creation of the Fed and Financial Panics: A Reinterpretation', manuscript, Brown University.

Cecchetti, Stephen G. (1988). 'Deflation and the Great Depression', manuscript, Ohio State University.

Chandler, Lester (1958). *Benjamin Strong, Central Banker*, Washington, D.C.: Brookings Institution.

Clark, Truman (1986). 'Interest Rate Seasonals and the Federal Reserve', *Journal of Political Economy* **94**, 1 (Feb.), 76–125.

Calomiris, Charles W. and R. Glenn Hubbard (1987). 'International Adjustment Under the Classical Gold Standard: Evidence for the United States and Britain, 1879–1914', NBER Working Paper # 2206.

Cunliffe Committee (1918). *First Interim Report*, London.

Dominguez, M. Kathryn, Ray C. Fair and Matthew D. Shapiro (198). 'Forecasting the Great Depression: Harvard Versus Yale', *American Economic Review*, forthcoming.

Eichengreen, Barry J. (1985). 'Editor's Introduction', in *The Gold Standard in Theory and History*, Barry J. Eichengreen, ed., New York: Methuen.

Fischer, Stanley (1977). 'Long-Term Contracts, Rational Expectations, and the Optimal Money Supply Rule', *Journal of Political Economy* **85**, 1 (Feb.), 191–205.

Friedman, Milton (1953). 'The Effects of Full-Employment Policy on Economic Stability: A Formal Analysis', in *Essays in Positive Economics*, Chicago: University of Chicago Press.

　(1968). 'The Role of Monetary Policy', *American Economic Review* **58**, 1 (Mar.), 1–17.

Friedman, Milton and Anna J. Schwartz (1963). *A Monetary History of the United States, 1867–1960*, Princeton: Princeton University Press.

　(1970). *Monetary Statistics for the United States*, New York: National Bureau of Economic Research.

　(1982). *Monetary Trends in the United States and the United Kingdom*, Chicago: University of Chicago Press.

Glass, Carter (1927). *An Adventure in Constructive Finance*, New York: Doubleday, Page and Co.

Goodfriend, Marvin (1988). 'Central Banking Under the Gold Standard', *Carnegie Rochester Conference Series*, forthcoming.

Hamilton, James D. (1987). 'Monetary Factors in the Great Depression', *Journal of Monetary Economics* **19**, 2 (Mar.), 145–70.

　(1988). 'The Role of the International Gold Standard in Propogating the Great Depression', *Contemporary Policy Issues* **VI**, (April), 67–89.

Hardy, Charles O. (1932). *Credit Policies of the Federal Reserve System*, Washington, D.C.: Brookings.

Huizinga, John and Frederic S. Mishkin (1986). 'Monetary Policy Regime Shifts and the Unusual Behavior of Real Interest Rates', *Carnegie Rochester Conference Series* **24**, 231–74.

James, John A. (1978). *Money and Capital in Postbellum America*, Princeton: Princeton University Press.

Jevons, William Stanley (1884). 'On the Frequent Autumnal Pressure in the Money Market, and the Action of the Bank of England', in *Investigations in Currency and Finance*, London: Macmillan.

Kemmerer, Edwin W. (1910). *Seasonal Variations in the Relative Demand for Money and Capital in the United States*, National Monetary Commission, S. Doc. 588, 61st Cong., 2d. session.

Keynes, John M. (1923). *A Tract on Monetary Reform*, London: Macmillan.

Laughlin, J. Laurence (1912). *Banking Reform*, Chicago: National Citizens League for the Promotion of a Sound Banking System.

Macaulay, Frederick R. (1938). *Some Theoretical Problems Suggested by the Movements of Interest Rates, Bond Yields and Stock Prices in the United States since 1856*, New York: National Bureau of Economic Research.

Mankiw, N. Gregory and Jeffrey A. Miron (1985). 'The Changing Behavior of the Term Structure of Interest Rates', NBER Working Paper # 1669.

Mankiw, N. Gregory, Jeffrey A. Miron and David N. Weil (1987). 'The Adjustment of Expectations to a Change in Regime: A Study of the Founding of the Federal Reserve', *American Economic Review* 77, 3 (June), 358–74.

Mayer, Thomas (1978). 'A Comparison of Unemployment Rates and Income Fluctuations Prior to the Great Depression and in the Postwar Period', *Review of Economics and Statistics*, 142–46.

McCallum, Bennet T. (1988). 'The Role of Demand Management in the Maintenance of Full Employment', National Bureau of Economic Research WP # 2520.

Miron, Jeffrey A. (1986). 'Financial Panics, the Seasonality of the Nominal Interest Rate, and the Founding of the Fed', *American Economic Review* 76, 1 (Mar.), 125–40.

Modigliani, Franco (1977). 'The Monetarist Controversy', *American Economic Review* 67, 1 (Mar.), 1–19.

Moore, Geoffrey H. (1960). *Business Cycle Indicators, Vol. I*, Princeton: Princeton University Press.

(1961). *Business Cycle Indicators, Vol. II, Basic Data on Cyclical Indicators*, Princeton: Princeton University Press.

Myers, Margaret (1970). *A Financial History of the United States*, New York: Columbia University Press.

Patton, Eugene (1907). 'Secretary Shaw and Precedents as to Treasury Control over the Money Market', *Journal of Political Economy* 15, 65–87.

Poole, William (1970). 'The Optimal Choice of Monetary Policy in a Simple Stochastic Macro Model', *Quarterly Journal of Economics* 84, 2 (May), 197–216.

Romer, Christina (1986a). 'Spurious Volatility in Historical Unemployment Data', *Journal of Political Economy* 94, 1 (Feb.), 1–37.

(1986b). 'Is the Stabilization of the Postwar Economy a Figment of the Data?', *American Economic Review* 76, 3 (June), 314–34.

(1987). 'The Prewar Business Cycle Reconsidered: New Estimates of Gross National Product, 1869–1908', manuscript, University of California, Berkeley.

Shiller, Robert J. (1980). 'Can the Fed Control Real Interest Rates?', in *Rational Expectations and Economic Policy*, Stanley Fischer, ed., Chicago: University of Chicago Press.

Shiller, Robert J. and Jeremy Seigel (1977). 'The Gibson Paradox and Historical Movements in Real Interest Rates', *Journal of Political Economy* 85, 891–907.

Sprague, O.M.W. (1910). *History of Crises Under the National Banking System*, National Monetary Commission, S. Doc 588, 61st Cong., 2d. session.

Standard and Poor's (1984). *Daily Stock Price Record*, New York: Standard and Poor's.

Taus, Esther Rogoff (1943). *Central Banking Functions of the United States Treasury, 1789–1941*, New York: Columbia University Press.

Taylor, John (1980). 'Aggregate Dynamics and Staggered Contracts', *Journal of Political Economy* 88, 1 (Feb.), 1–23.

Temin, Peter (1976). *Did Monetary Forces Cause the Great Depression?*, New York: Norton.

Timberlake, Richard H. (1963). 'Mr. Shaw and His Critics: Monetary Policy in the Golden Era Review', *Quarterly Journal of Economics* 77, 1 (Feb.), 41–54.

(1978). *The Origins of Central Banking in the United States*, Cambridge: Harvard University Press.

(1984). 'The Central Banking Role of Clearinghouse Associations', *Journal of Money, Credit and Banking* **15**, 1 (Feb.), 1–15.

United States Department of Commerce (1975). *Historical Statistics of the United States, Colonial Time to 1970, Part 1*, Washington, D.C.: Government Printing Office.

(1986). *The National Income and Product Accounts of the United States, 1929–83, Statistical Tables*, Washington, D.C.: Government Printing Office.

Warburg, Paul M. (1930). *The Federal Reserve System: Its Origins and Growth, Vol. II*, New York: Macmillan.

Warburton, Clark (1950). 'Co-ordination of Monetary, Bank Supervisory, and Loan Agencies of the Federal Government', *Journal of Finance*, June, 153–55.

White, Eugene N. (1983). *The Regulation and Reform of the American Banking System, 1900–1929*, Princeton: Princeton University Press.

Willis, H. Parker (1915). *The Federal Reserve: A Study of the Banking System of the United States*, New York: Doubleday, Page and Co.

Discussion

MARCELLO DE CECCO

This is obviously not a paper on monetary unification, and it could not be otherwise, given its subject. It places itself in the well established line of economic research which, in the USA, has been concerned for a very long time with what can be called 'the economic consequences of the Fed'. I will not make even a faint attempt at reviewing the predecessors to this paper, of which there have been many, by many well known economists. Generally speaking, however, their line of argument has hovered around two questions:

(1) Is a central bank good or bad for the economy?
(2) Is a central bank good for the economy only if it follows certain policy lines, and what policy lines should it follow?

Miron's paper is not particularly aimed at discussing the first question. Rather, it wants to address the second, and to try to give an unambiguous answer to it. It is not, however, a theoretical answer. The theoretical framework he uses is the one developed by Poole in 1970. Miron's job in the present paper is to find an empirical answer, based on an anlysis of historical experience.

Quite rightly he begins by enquiring what the founders of the Fed and its inter-war managers wanted its policy to be. He concludes that, without the slightest doubt, as followers of the 'real bills doctrine' they wanted it to stabilize interest rates and to prevent a repetition of the speculative waves which had characterized the period from 1890 to 1914. Thus they wanted the Fed to stabilize the asset market.

There is very little doubt that the real bills doctrine exercised a strong influence on the making of the Federal Reserve System. The story is, however, rather more intricate than Miron reports in his paper. The real bills doctrine is indeed inscribed forever in the articles of the Federal Reserve Act of 1913. But the Act itself was, in reality, a compromise among a variety of economic interest groups which had, up to 1913, fought for sometimes radically opposed causes. It is certainly excessive to call the real bills doctrine, as Miron does, 'the dominant theory of central banking of the early 20th century'. He might have been more correct if the had added to the sentence the qualification 'in the United States'. Even in that country, however, the real bills doctrine had been bitterly opposed by the most authoritative group of academic economists in the US, who had united their forces with the largest industrials and bankers in what was called the 'sound money league'.

This group of economists, whose most illustrious members and spokesmen were Charles Conant of Harvard and Erwin Kemmerer, of Princeton, and whose business members included the best names of corporate America, like Frank Vanderlip and Paul Warburg, fought, since the 1890s, a running battle against all sort of partisans of unit banking, small scale industry, easy money, and the strong and ubiquitous 'silver lobby'. Their aim was to establish in the US a banking and monetary system like the European ones. They were, in years still dominated by the large price depression which had spanned twenty years from the middle seventies to the middle nineties, more than to anything else, opposed to an excessive creation of productive capacity in all sectors of industry, which in their opinion was the inherent tendency of a monetary and banking system like that inaugurated in the US during the Civil War and which continued until 1914.

They were opposed to the real bills doctrine on theoretical grounds. But they also opposed the American banking practice, which had done so much to promote growth in the US, of lending money on the security of one-signature promissory notes, which could not, for all practical purposes, be considered 'real bills', as they did not really relate to one particular commercial transaction, but were a loan to a single person, based on the banker's knowledge of that person's business situation, of his character and of his integrity.

Seen with our eyes, the economists of the 'sound money league' tried to promote a drive towards securitization in the American banking system. If discounting and rediscounting had been restricted to two-signatures bills, these would have had a life of their own, and would have constituted an alternative on which to base an English-type money market, where banks would hold reserves in rediscountable commercial bills and thus would not be induced to put their reserves at the disposal of stock exchange speculators, in the form of call loans.

The sound money economists and business men were also in favour of branch banking and of centralized reserves.

It is not incorrect to see their battle against the partisans of 'real bills' as a continuation of the English fight between defenders of the 'banking school' and partisans of the 'currency school'. In Britain, that dispute was definitively won by the Currency School in the 1840s, and the banking and monetary system which was built by Robert Peel constituted the true measuring rod to gauge other monetary systems for decades to come. It was thus the Currency School, and not the Banking School, which prevailed all over the world at the theoretical and institutional level. Its direct offspring was the theory of the International Gold Standard, which again prevailed in academic and institutional circles, after a long fight against bimetallism, in the late XIX and early XX century.

It is thus perhaps more appropriate to say that the Federal Reserve Act embodied a bit of each of the two schools. It tried to establish a money market like the English one and a centralized reserve. But it also followed the real bills doctrine and did not favour branch banking. Farmers, small scale industralists and unit bankers were just too strong for the sound money league. The latter however were also too strong to be swamped altogether. The Fed thus represented a theoretical and institutional compromise, almost a stalemate.

What monetary policy did the Fed promote, once it was firmly established after the first World War? Miron thinks that the Fed, having been founded to stabilize the asset market and prevent the repetition of the frequent pre-war financial panics, followed a policy of interest rate smoothing, to iron out the seasonal variations in US interest rates, which had so worried central bankers all over Europe, and especially the Bank of England, before the war, and which were known as 'Autumn drains'.

By using Poole's theoretical framework Miron is led to conclude that if the Fed managed to smooth interest rates and change seasonal variations into a random walk, it could do so only by making real output more unstable. He then sets out to discover whether that is true, and finds in the relevant series of output, industrial production and prices, that reality concurs with theory. Real output varies much more in the period 1914–40

Period	US Mean	S.D.	UK Mean	S.D.	Italy Mean	S.D.	Sweden Mean	S.D.
1891–1914	3.41	3.19	2.45	3.20	1.78	3.75	4.51	5.63
1915–1940	2.40	6.63	1.51	6.04	1.49	4.01	2.98	7.85

Table 10A.1 *Real GNP (annual data, log growth rates)*

than it does in the period 1890–1913. Interest rates, on the contrary, lose their seasonal pattern. Prices also vary much more after 1914 than they did before. The proof stands even a break-down of the post-war series into sub-periods, to allow for the elimination of the influence exercised on data by the Great Depression.

Did the Federal Reserve then cause the greater output and price oscillations after the First World War in the US? Miron is convinced that it did, on the strength of his econometric evidence.

The inception of the Fed was a major institutional change which must certainly have had an impact on the American economy and even the world economy. The trouble, however, is that it coincides with the outbreak of the First World War. It is obviously difficult to disentangle the economic consequences of these two major events from one another.

To demonstrate what I just said, I subjected output and industrial production series for three European countries for the same periods examined by Miron to the same econometric tests he used. (In the short time I had to write this comment, I could not find price and interest rate series long enough to fit the job.) The countries, Great Britain, Sweden, and Italy, were chosen only because Mitchell's book on European historical statistics had consistent time series for them. The results are shown in Tables 10A.1 and 2.

It is interesting to see that the three countries I examined, where indeed no new central bank was established or other major changes occurred in

Period	US Mean	S.D.	UK Mean	S.D.	Italy Mean	S.D.	Sweden Mean	S.D.
1891–1914	3.48	8.66	4.66	8.68	8.22	9.89	9.31	11.62
1915–1940	3.18	14.72	5.31	19.59	6.54	20.56	11.28	25.47

Table 10A.2 *Industrial production (annual data, log growth rates)*

the monetary institutions, the same phenomena can be detected as Miron observed in the United States. Real output and industrial production oscillate much more widely after 1914 than they did before, and both mean and standard deviation behave exactly as they do in Miron's analysis of US data.

At this point we have two options:

(1) All series in the US and elsewhere, were affected by the shocks represented by the war and its aftermath.
(2) Federal Reserve policy becomes, after the Great War, the monetary policy of the whole world, and is to be considered responsible not only for trouble in output and prices in the US, but in the main macroeconomic variables in the whole of Europe and perhaps the whole world.

In this case, we ought to move back the official beginning of the dollar standard to 1918, that is to say, by a good 25 years earlier than its traditional starting point, in 1944.

I have always had an inclination to believe that, and so I would favour the second hypothesis. A corroborating element to its validity I found in comparing the seasonal pattern in Bank Rate changes in Britain, as reported in Hawtrey's *A century of Bank Rate*. Before 1914 they reflect extremely well the presence of 'Autumn drains'. After 1914 that pattern is completely lost. The oscillations cut across whole calendar years, tracing considerably longer cycles.

I would be, however, quite cautious about declaring the international dollar standard officially moved back 25 years. Much more is required in the way of econometric testing, especially to establish which variables lead and which follow, timewise.

I would also suggest in closing, that Miron give some thought to the possibility that the US monetary authorities in the interwar years might not yet have realized that they were the nth country of the system and might have been induced to change policy, especially on those three fateful occasions when they restricted the money supply, by a drain of reserves towards foreign financial centres. This has been often advanced as an explanation of their behaviour, and I have a certain disposition to take it seriously.

BARRY EICHENGREEN

The discussant's nightmare is a paper that is constructed so carefully and argued so convincingly as to leave him virtually nothing critical to say. I more or less find myself in this position with Jeffrey Miron's excellent paper on the founding of the Fed and its first quarter century of operation. The author has read carefully through historical sources – both contemporary and modern – on the operation of 19th century American financial markets and the controversies leading up to the foundation of the Fed. He provides an illuminating analysis of the sources of business cycle disturbances through sensible application of the theoretical literature on the assignment problem and through the presentation of some summary statistics. This leads Miron to his provocative and undoubtedly controversial conclusion that monetary policy did much to undermine the stability of the American economy in Fed's first quarter century of operation.

Essentially, Miron presents an argument in two parts. Part 1 reconstructs the rationale for the founding of the Fed. Part 2 analyses the actions of the new central bank to the eve of World War II. An elegant aspect of the argument is how Miron links the two parts together, arguing that the perceived problems in response to which the Fed was founded served to condition the institution's subsequent actions.

I agree almost without reservation with Miron's characterization of the rationale for the founding of the Fed. I agree almost without reservation with his characterization of the Fed's actions over its first quarter century. I disagree only over the extent to which changes in the behaviour of the macroeconomy over the pre- and post-Fed periods are properly attributed to the presence or absence of that institution.

1   The founding of the Fed

The most important problem in response to which the Federal Reserve Act was passed was the 'inelasticity' or 'perverse elasticity' of the currency under the National Banking System. A subsidiary problem was the recurrence of financial crises – that is, periods of contagious bank failures, liquidity crises and macroeconomic difficulties. The main function of the Fed was perceived to be to provide 'an elastic currency' (in the words of the Federal Reserve Act). Its secondary function was to serve as lender of last resort.

The problem of an inelastic currency was that each Spring, with the planting season, and each Autumn, with the harvest and crop moving season, the demand for money in the US rose. With little increase in supply, interest rates were driven upward. Banks were induced to run down their excess reserves, increasing their vulnerability to runs. As Charles Forgan, President of the First National Bank of Chicago, told an audience of bankers in 1903,

> the supply of money periodically oscillates between overabundance and inadequacy, in accordance with the demand for it, which varies with the seasons. The supply being arbitrarily fixed in quantity, bears no relation to the varying demands of commerce, and there is not even an attempt in our monetary system to adjust the supply to the demand. (cited in Eichengreen, 1984, p. 97)

An even stronger view, which I associated with David Kinely (1895, 1910), is that the supply of money actually declined precisely when the demand rose. The mechanism was the unusually high currency/deposit ratio in the South and parts of the West. Blacks, farmers and residents of rural areas where financial markets were relatively underdeveloped relied on checks and bank deposits to a lesser extent than residents of other regions. In the Autumn, the increase in money demand was concentrated in the agricultural regions of the South and West, which imported money through capital inflows in anticipation of the harvest and the subsequent interregional trade surplus. As the demand for money shifted from low currency/deposits ratio regions to high currency/deposit ratio regions, downward pressure was placed on the national currency/deposit ratio and on the national money supply.

This problem provided the primary rationale for the founding of the Fed. Indeed, one can argue that it provided the sole rationale. Miron's subsidiary factor, the need to contain financial crises, was not independent, since crises were concentrated in the Autumn when interest rates peaked. It was widely argued that by providing the accommodation needed to moderate these peaks, the danger of crisis could be headed off. Smoothing interest rate seasonals and acting as lender as last resort could and often were viewed as one and the same.

Given that a central rationale for the founding of the Fed was to moderate interest rate seasonals, I am entirely convinced by Miron's evidence that this is in fact what the Fed did.

2   Effects of the Fed

I begin to have trouble when Miron attributes the increasing instability of the macroeconomy in the period 1919–40, compared to 1890–1914, to the monetary policy of the Federal Reserve. I do not dispute that the macroeconomy was more volatile immediately after 1919 than before

1914. The question is why. The period 1919–40 was marked by three significant recessions separated on average by 8½ years. This is not an unusual frequency by 19th century standards; if anything the opposite is the case. Contemporaries were struck by the unusual length and persistence of the expansion of the 1920s (much like their counterparts have been struck by the persistence of the expansion of the 1980s). The difference between periods lies not in the frequency but in the severity of recessions. The point is obvious in the case of 1929–33. This brings Miron face to face with the large and contentious literature on the causes of the Great Depression. I think he is too quick to follow Hamilton in attributing the 1929 downturn to monetary policy and Friedman and Schwartz in attributing the depth and duration of the slump to monetary forces. He makes little mention of the consumption and investment shocks to which authors in the Alvin Hansen–Aron Gordon–Peter Temin tradition attribute the initial downturn. He minimizes the possible role of fiscal policy, as argued by Cary Brown, and that of the NIRA, as suggested by Michael Weinstein, in the Depression's singular depth and duration. He ignores the international dimension of the slump. In several European and Latin American countries, the downturn preceded that in the United States. International factors limited the scope for the Fed to reflate in the absence of comparable policies abroad, given its preoccupation with the defensibility of the dollar's gold standard parity. An impartial jury of his peers would probably conclude that Miron's case that the Great Depression was due to the Federal Reserve remains to be proven.

Once one puts aside the Depression, the case rests on the comparison of 1890–1914 with 1919–29. Miron's Table 10.1 shows that GNP was 33 per cent more volatile in the later period. This is due, of course, to the severity of the short but sharp 1919–21 boom and slump. Miron attributes this convulsion to the Federal Reserve, which during the expansion failed to raise its discount rate in response to inflation and commodity market speculation, raised that rate dramatically as the economy peaked, and failed to lower it as activity turned down. This is a critical episode for Miron's argument, since it seems a clear instance of interest-rate pegging. He writes, 'A troubling question is why the Fed waited almost two years after the war to produce a deflation, in the mean time allowing the price level to climb significantly higher than its end-of-war level. Apparently the Fed felt that an easy money, low interest rate policy was desirable in order to allow the Treasury to service the War debt at low rates.'

This is correct. So long as the Treasury retained effective control of discount policy, as it did while the US was engaged in World War I and into early 1920, considerations related to debt service remained paramount. Precisely when control was restored to the Fed, discount rates began to rise. If blame for the 1918–20 inflationary boom is to be parceled out, therefore, it should be bestowed mainly on the Treasury, not the Fed. This observation has important implications for Miron's argument, for it is hard to imagine that things would have been any different under pre-1914 institutional arrangements. If anything, the absence of a central bank would have heightened Treasury control and given Treasury officials even greater freedom to pursue parochial objectives incompatible with macroeconomic stability.

But what about the 1920–21 recession, by which time the Fed has regained control of its discount rate? Why was the Fed inactive in the face of a 9 per cent decline in the money supply in the year and a half from September 1920, a decline that outstrips anything experienced during late-19th-century financial crises? I would emphasize two considerations. First, US officials, and not just within the Fed, were concerned to deflate to 1913 levels to enhance the competitiveness of American goods, in anticipation of the fact that America's trading partners were committed to deflating to that level. In retrospect, this presumption that 1913 prices would be restored elsewhere seems curious; it was widespread nonetheless. Second, contemporaries were preoccupied by the spectre of a global shortage of gold. Reducing prices was a way to increase the real value of existing gold stocks and to raise the profitability of gold mining. Again, this preoccupation seems curious in retrospect, but it was limited neither to the Fed nor to the United States.

Thus, while I too view the 1920 and 1929 recessions as consequences of policy mistakes, I do not attribute these policy mistakes solely to the Fed, nor solely to the United States. The lesson I draw is not simply that interest-rate pegging can be destabilizing, but that misguided policy can be destabilizing. Policy is most likely to be destabilizing when inexperienced policymakers and new policymaking institutions are confronted by unfamiliar situations, and when their efforts to stabilize financial markets conflict with their desire to stabilize economic activity. As Jeffrey Miron ably reminds us, both sets of factors played at least a supporting role in the economic catastrophe that began in 1929.

REFERENCES

Eichengreen, Barry (1984). 'Currency and Credit in the Gilded Age', in Gary Saxonhouse and Gavin Wright (eds.), *Technique, Spirit and Form in the Making of the Modern Economies: Essays in Honor of William N. Parker*, New York: JAI Press, pp. 87–114.

Kinley, David (1895). 'Credit Instruments in Retail Trade', *Journal of Political Economy* 3, pp. 203–17.

Kinley, David (1910). *The Use of Credit Instruments in Payments in the United States*, Washington, DC: GPO.

11 Panel discussion: the prospects for a European Central Bank

RAINER S. MASERA

1.1 The Single European Act and monetary integration

The Single European Act of 17 February 1986 aims at the establishment of an area without internal frontiers permitting the free movement of goods, persons, services and capital by 1992 so as to improve the allocation of resources and put a seal, thirty-five years after the signing of the Treaty of Rome, on the integration of Europe. The liberalization of all capital movements – which will take place by 1990 – and the creation of a European financial market are therefore key objectives that will influence not only the conduct of monetary and credit policies in the coming years but also the structure of financial systems.

It should indeed be recognized that *complete* integration of national financial markets entails exchange rates remaining fixed. Otherwise, financial assets held in different currencies will not be perfectly substitutable, an indispensable condition for full integration. Financial integration itself calls for monetary convergence. In principle, sovereignty in monetary matters, which takes the form of autonomy in controlling the money supply and the exchange rate, is not compatible with the objective of creating by 1992 a *single* European financial market.

The benefits associated with currency integration depend in the final analysis on the ability to ensure, after a period of steady convergence, permanently stable exchange rates within the area and, ultimately, a single currency. The advantages depend, in practice, on the scope for exploiting money more completely in terms of its three basic functions: as a unit of account, as a medium of exchange and as a store of value. In principle, a common currency reduces information and transaction costs, narrows the gap between private and social rates of return, leads to a more efficient allocation of resources both through space and over time, and diminishes the impact of destabilizing shocks insofar as it implies the aggregation of diversified macroeconomic risks.

337

It is obvious, however, that these advantages can only be gained to the extent that the currency area is able to ensure conditions of internal monetary stability, in terms of inflation and interest rates, at least equal to those ruling in the countries with more firmly established monetary discipline. It is also necessary for there to be – as indeed the Single European Act envisages – freedom of movement for products and factors of production. Otherwise, there would only be a switch in risks, in the sense that variable barriers to transactions would take the place of variable exchange rates, in all probability at a higher real cost.

Lastly, it is necessary to limit and prevent rigidities – or even perverse movements with respect to productivity – in wage rates in the countries forming the area. The minimization of the costs associated with overcoming balance-of-payments problems cannot be achieved exclusively by exploiting the mobility of factors of production, but must also be able to rely on fiscal measures that are coordinated at the area level and, when necessary, on recourse to corrective instruments such as incomes policy.

There is thus a close link between monetary and currency unification and the integration of financial markets. The final objectives to be achieved must be clearly defined: in the first place, to permit the related costs to be assessed, with special reference to the renunciation of national sovereignty in monetary affairs and the partial loss of sovereignty in the use of deficit financing, as the budget constraint indicates; in the second place, once the choice has been deliberately made, to permit the steps leading to the achievement of the objective to be clearly set out.

In sum, the major change with which the European countries and the European Monetary System will have to come to grips in a period of exchange liberalization, financial integration and the completion of a single market is the gradual loss of national monetary autonomy. It will therefore be necessary to mark out a course that will allow controlled progress to be made while new methods and instruments are developed for the management of the monetary autonomy of the area as a whole.

This basic problem raises, in turn, the issue of the relation between monetary integration and the creation of a European Central Bank. Indeed, irrevocably fixed exchange rates between European countries may well ultimately require a *single* currency and central bank, as the experience of the British pound and the Irish punt in the EMS shows.

On these questions, important new ideas have recently been put forward by President Poehl, with which I find myself broadly in agreement.

If I understood him correctly, he considers it necessary to identify *ex ante* both the model of a European Central Bank, and the preconditions to be met before enacting this institutional change. The European Central Bank must primarily pursue the target of monetary stability. This requires its independence from national Governments and Community institutions – notably the Council and the Commission. Finally, the European Central Bank should have a federal structure.

I will not elaborate these points, which have been so well analyzed by President Poehl. Also in my view, they set out the prerequisites to be satisfied before moving to European monetary unification and the full institutional setup of the European Central Bank. Here I would rather attempt to consider the practical steps which could be followed, in order to advance towards achievement of the final goal. I identify three of them: (i) the inclusion of all the countries participating in the EMS mechanism, in a stricter, but not yet rigid, exchange rate mechanism, that would gradually reduce the freedom to change central rates and promote the stabilization of exchange relations in Europe; (ii) closer monetary policy and interest rate coordination by the Committee of EC central bank governors (to become the European Monetary Board), with the monetary effects of interventions – which should be extended to the forward exchange market – in principle not being sterilized, and joint determination of aggregate monetary base creation in the Community; (iii) the integration of the private and official markets for the ECU, which would come to play the role of a real European currency both inside the area and in international relations under the supervision and control of the European Monetary Board.

2   A path towards a European Central Bank

As long as differences in the performances and policies of the EMS countries persist, and the international environment continues to be a source of destabilizing pressure within the EMS, the liberalization of capital movements might well be accompanied by large speculative flows in anticipation of central rate realignments.

The transition to full monetary and currency unification therefore requires an adaptation of the EMS mechanisms, to enhance the rigour of the exchange rate system, without exposing it to destabilizing speculative attacks. The proposal I make consists of a two-pronged manoeuvre.

In the first place, the strictness of the system should be guaranteed by the commitment of all the countries participating in the exchange rate mechanism – with their currencies included in the ECU basket – to keep the annual changes in their bilateral central rates within a given limit, say 4% in present circumstances. This commitment should be supported by a parallel explicit undertaking to correct domestic factors of cost/price pressure, notably in respect of wages and the budget. I am not therefore in favour of dedramatizing central rate changes. They should instead be as infrequent as possible, and always accompanied by supporting measures of other economic policies.

In the second place, I would suggest that the constraint on central-rate variations could be supplemented by the *immediate* adoption of a bilateral fluctuation range for *all* countries – including notably the United Kingdom, Spain and Italy – of the order of 3%, without in any way loosening the discipline of the exchange rate commitment.

Since this bilateral margin would allow over time a maximum swing of 6% to emerge, it appears suitable in today's circumstances, insofar as it would allow both sizable movements in interest rate differentials, without taking forward exchange rates outside the fluctuation band for spot rates, and less frequent realignments of central rates (*on average less than once a year*), without this implying discontinuities in market rates. Both the constraints – presumptive for central rates and operative for the range of fluctuation – should be *gradually tightened* in line with the objective of monetary and financial unification.

Indeed, I believe that greater fluctuation of exchange rates and interest rates around more stable central rates – together with recourse to interventions in forward market, consistently with the commitment to set a ceiling to maximum variations of parities – would counter destabilizing speculative movements of capital and permit achievement of the objective of monetary unification with a greater convergence of the economic fundamentals in all participating countries.

A similar problem to that of greater strictness in exchange rate relations is that of strengthening monetary cooperation through the adoption of rules of the game consistent with the objective of unification.

A first model of coordination is based on the 'asymmetrical' role of the country whose currency is at the centre of the system. This country keeps the growth in its monetary aggregates consistent with domestic price stability, while the other countries manage their exchange rates vis-à-vis the dominant currency by suitable changes in their interest rates. This model has the advantage of providing the system with a nominal anchor represented by the discipline and the credibility of the leader country. On the other hand, the other EMS countries would have difficulty in accepting this solution, especially if it is not set within the framework of an overall design for economic policy based on cooperation and intended to promote the growth of the European economy as a whole. Moreover, the leader country itself might be unwilling to accept the constraint inherent in a passive exchange rate policy within the area.

A second model could be based on *coordinated management* of individual central banks' expansion of both the *domestic component* of the monetary base and domestic credit. At aggregate level this would clearly imply joint decision of the overall monetary base creation of the area.

In my view, a progressive path to guarantee the attainment of these objectives, without weakening the commitment to monetary stability in the area, would consist of the following steps:

(i) The existing tasks and responsibilities of the Committee of EC central bank governors should be broadened and deepened to encompass *ex ante* joint setting of monetary targets and coordinated management and monitoring of credit and financial developments. To strengthen the management of exchange rates within the fluctuation band, the impulses deriving from changes in the external component of the monetary base would have to be promptly reflected in changes in interest rate differentials. More generally, the processes whereby liquidity and credit are created will have to be carefully monitored and coordinated, in part through the use of 'objective' economic indicators, and analyzed as part of the determination of overall portfolio equilibria.

(ii) A joint policy vis-à-vis third currencies should also be developed within this body, leading to concerted European interventions.

(iii) A crucial element here would be represented, as already indicated, by the participation of *all* European currencies in the exchange rate mechanism on an equal footing and the evolution of the Committee of EC central bank governors towards a European Monetary Board. The institutional creation of the EMB would have to be based on standards set by the Bundesbank model, with binding institutional guarantees of its adopting a non-accommodating monetary stance in its surveillance of the monetary and exchange rate policies pursued by the individual countries and their impact on the EMS as a whole. The European Monetary Board could gradually evolve to become a true European 'federal' central bank, with full 'constitutional' guarantees of independence.

It is worth recalling in this connection that the Federal Reserve System was conceived at the time of the gold standard as a system of twelve federal banks, coordinated but endowed with considerable autonomy in the management of their 'domestic' credit markets.

It would also be desirable to give the ECU a truly central role both as an international reserve asset and as a European currency, in parallel with national ones.

In my view, this requires not only removing the limits to the acceptability of the official ECU but also linking the official and the private ECU markets, so that central banks could transform their official ECU holdings into private ECU balances and vice versa. As I submitted in a recent proposal for linking the two circuits, this could be effected by way of an institution, such as the BIS, acting both as the clearing house for private ECUs and as a recognized holder of official ECUs.

The creation of private ECUs would be subjected to similar controls to those existing for individual currencies and take account of growth in the latter.

The European Monetary Board would be entrusted with the task of supervising the ECU creation process, notably by setting appropriate reserve requirements, preferably in terms of high-powered ECUs. The gradual increase in the circulation of the ECU would also foster the necessary adaptation and harmonization in the fiscal treatment of financial assets in Community countries. Let it be noted here that, in the model I am presenting, the ECU should be – even in its present basket formula – a relatively *strong* asset vis-à-vis the DM. This is so because all potentially depreciating countries – tied by the Exchange Rate Mechanism – would have in the transitional phase to maintain nominal interest rates higher on average than the expected devaluation.

The EMB would thus act as the nucleus of the central bank system. It would also be responsible: (i) for the centralized management of a part of the European foreign currency reserves and the counterpart effective creation of official ECUs, thereby superseding the present three-month revolving swap arrangement – in accordance with the original plan for the EMS – and (ii) for the short-term credit mechanisms for the support of currencies, designed to discourage and repel speculative attacks on the currencies of participating countries. The medium-term credit facilities should instead be the responsibility of governments.

The ECU, if necessary redefined, could eventually become *the* European currency: ECU liabilities of the European Monetary Board would represent the monetary base of Europe.

3   Conclusions

The key to progress in the fields of European integration and monetary stability remains convergence of economic fundamentals and, in particular, the state of public finances and the processes underlying the determination of costs. Without progress in these two areas, it will not be possible to strengthen Europe's monetary cohesion.

The proposal made here for acceptance of a maximum variation over a twelve-month horizon of central exchange rates is advocated on the assumption that it will force greater discipline in nominal wage demands and in budgetary processes.

I conclude, however, by stressing that the move towards greater monetary discipline, gradual abandonment of the exchange rate as a policy instrument, and full capital liberalization will proceed only to the extent that this will actually prove the cornerstone for growth and the gradual reabsorption of unemployment in Europe.

Price stability, *per se*, will help towards attainment of this objective, but the policy adaptations – of a micro (structural) and macro nature – may well be necessary also, in countries which have already ensured domestic monetary stability, but have failed so far to meet their medium-term growth objectives.

WOLFGANG RIEKE

For obvious reasons, the views I shall express will largely reflect the Bundesbank's position on the issue of a European Central Bank. But given the dynamics of the debate that is under way, I would prefer if my remarks were not taken too literally as being those of the institution for which I work.

The debate on a future European Central Bank (and on a future European currency) was opened late last year, at the official level, by the French Minister of Finance, M Balladur. Other Ministers followed, among them the Italian Treasury Minister, S Amato, and the German Federal Minister of Foreign Affairs, Herr Genscher. Even though it was stressed that Herr Genscher did not then speak for the German Federal Government, the issue of a European Central Bank and currency has been on the official German agenda ever since, not least because the Federal Republic currently occupies the Presidency of the European Communities. Indeed, Herr Stoltenberg, the German Federal Minister of Finance and as such competent in the matter, also issued a statement putting the official German position on record.[1]

The Bundesbank is required by law to 'advise the Federal Government on monetary policy matters of major importance'. Consideration of the creation of a European Central Bank and a European currency is, of course, a monetary policy matter of major importance. Accordingly, the statement by the Finance Minister also reflected the Bundesbank's viewpoint on the issue.

Thinking about the matter prior to this conference I was reminded of the situation exactly 10 years ago in 1978, when the European Monetary System was under preparation. Very little information was made available by those working on the project. The maxim was: 'The less involvement of bureaucrats (including central bank bureaucrats), the better!' One had to resort to one's imagination and ask oneself: What on earth can they have in mind?

This time, M Balladur merely asked a few questions without giving answers himself; others provided lengthy answers without necessarily asking all the relevant questions; still others firmly stated what they felt should be done without further delay, leaving one with some doubts as to whether they knew what they were talking about.

If the immediate creation of a European Central Bank and of a European currency is the objective, this could surely not mean the immediate replacement of all national central banks and national currencies by a European Central Bank and a European currency. Hardly anyone has the courage to suggest that the time is ripe for so radical a step. So it could only mean the creation of a 'parallel' European currency, to be issued by the new European Central Bank in the expectation that it would gradually replace the national currencies.

It is not difficult to see why such an approach finds some support. It would be an act of some considerable symbolic value, likely to be applauded as a courageous step forward. It could be achieved without much need to sacrifice national sovereignty and it would allow politically difficult choices to be avoided, at least for the time being. For instance, determining the status of a European Central Bank could be postponed until later. There might be reasons to expect that the European currency would assume a 'key currency' role within the EMS, hopefully (in the view of some critics) replacing the DMark in that role. And perhaps one could rely on the 'march of time' taking one forward to the stage when the European currency would replace the national currencies and the European Central Bank would be 'omnipotent'.

Some of these arguments seem to me to argue against rather than for the 'parallel currency' concept. A merely symbolic act could easily end in disappointment, if it was found to be without real content. What if the many European tourists found out that it was easier to buy Italian Lira against their domestic currency (either at home or in Italy), and pay for hotel and restaurant bills without further trouble rather than buy the European currency and then find it troublesome to use it for such payments? This would give the European currency a bad reputation from which it might not quickly recover. It is indeed likely that the cost of everyday transactions in a European parallel currency would be perceived to be rather high.

As far as industry and business are concerned, they are not likely to be much impressed by merely symbolic action either, unless it is positively reflected in their profit and loss accounts. In a very unstable exchange rate environment the basket-ECU has offered certain advantages, but it is not clear what advantages a parallel European currency would offer. It would not be a ready-made hedging device if it were no longer based on a currency basket. So its attraction would have to depend on other qualities which are difficult to detect.

I see no merit in avoiding difficult political choices and leaving national sovereignty untouched by action that is expressly intended to advance European integration. Those who favour a European currency and a European Central Bank should not be allowed to simply ignore the implications of such an undertaking. After all, the parallel currency approach is supposed to pave the way to a single European currency for the whole Community eventually. It would initially owe its existence to its ability to compete with existing national currencies. The strongest currency would set a tough standard for its behaviour, as the DMark does for its partner currencies in the EMS (and beyond), due to the existing exchange rate constraint. As the European currency gained in importance, the criteria underlying its management by the European Central Bank would become more relevant. Unless these are agreed upon right from the start, difficulties could well arise later in the attempt to find a consensus on such criteria. Undesirable consequences for one or more partners arising in the meantime could not easily be corrected later.

There are also technical reasons that cast doubt on the parallel currency concept; they have never been spelled out in clear terms. Even though decisions on interest rates are all-important for the relative performance of the competing currencies, development of the monetary and credit aggregates provides an important basis for necessary policy actions. How would national central banks take account of parts of their money stock (including possibly unknown cash positions) being held in the European currency, and what would be the criteria for the creation of 'European Central Bank money'?

Furthermore, could the new European currency be given the same status as the national currency in each country, which would be required if the process of currency competition is to function at all? Once all the conditions for currency competition working properly are in place, i.e.

same status as national currencies,
ability to compete with the strongest currency especially as regards interest rates and exchange-rate developments,
low transactions costs,

this would be virtually equivalent to the final stage of monetary union. If this is correct, it would seem reasonable to define the conditions of the final stage at the outset and lay down the path to monetary union rather than rely on a roundabout 'parallel currency' approach. This would meet the concerns of those who feel that there might be an unfortunate inclination to try and avoid difficult choices.

What one should endeavour to define in broad but clear terms at the outset are

1.   the *requirements of the final stage of economic and monetary union,*
2.   the *tasks, status and instruments of a future European Central Bank system* and
3.   the *path of ever closer cooperation* to be followed on the way to the final stage.

Such an approach would leave no doubts about the objective, the necessary commitments and the steps required. As a practical matter, the Committee of central bank governors might be entrusted with the necessary examination of all aspects. They would bring their full knowledge of the relevant problems to the task, including their experience and judgement of the relative merits of the available institutional variants of a European Central Bank. The Committee of central bank governors could also be used as the instrument of progress towards full monetary union, moving from mutual *ex post* information on national monetary policy action to *ex ante* information, and ever closer coordination. Attendance by the chairman (and individual members on a rotating basis) of meetings of national central bank councils could be considered at some stage. Eventually decision-making on a Community basis could be introduced, with proper safeguards in place. This would be an ambitious agenda for central bank governors. It would clearly fall short of more ambitious projects aiming at the immediate establishment of a European Central Bank. But it might best meet the concerns of those who prefer pragmatic approaches to grand designs and are wholly unprepared at this stage to entertain the idea of a European currency and Central Bank requiring a major transfer of sovereignty from national to community level.

In the meantime, efforts at both national and community levels to achieve complete capital liberalization should be rigorously pursued. Capital liberalization is desirable for a variety of reasons. It should be accepted as an additional discipline, supplementing the exchange rate discipline of the EMS, but offering mutually reinforcing benefits for economic welfare over time. Where necessary the commitment to monetary stability should be further strengthened. Questionable notions of asymmetry, hegemony *et al.* should not be allowed to interfere with effective cooperation and the smooth functioning of the EMS. The progress made so far in European monetary integration owes more to the adoption of non-inflationary policies by all partners and the general acceptance of the DMark as a stable currency anchor than to the intervention and settlement rules agreed upon at the outset. It would clearly be undesirable if attempts to alter the balance of obligations within the EMS were to weaken the commitment to monetary stability and deprive the system of its anchor without a reliable alternative standard being firmly in place.

MASSIMO RUSSO

The current debate

The current debate on the strengthening of the EMS takes as a starting point the achievement of greater exchange rate stability and convergence of inflation to a low level and puts the emphasis on three major interrelated issues:

1. Should there be more 'symmetry' in the working of the System?
2. Accepting the importance of a suitable 'anchor' for price stability, should there also be an 'engine for growth'?
3. How will the complete liberalization of capital movements that is planned by the EC under the Single Act affect the working of the System?

1.1 Symmetry and monetary policy coordination The search for symmetry is intimately linked with the issue of monetary policy coordination and the role of Germany as it has evolved. In a recent paper, Mr Tullio and I have tried to address this issue drawing on the lessons from the gold standard and the Bretton Woods regimes and on recent proposals for the coordination of monetary policies presented within the context of the reform of the international monetary system. Our main conclusion was that, in the present state of economic and financial integration and within the existing institutional framework, it is undesirable to devise automatic rules that would ensure a symmetric response in *all circumstances*. A preferred solution would instead be to focus on the achievement of a final target (e.g., inflation) and to adapt the policy response to the nature and origin of the shocks affecting the System. This implies a considerable strengthening of surveillance in appropriate fora, i.e., the Committee of Governors and the Monetary Committee.

Of particular importance in this context is the monetary variable to be used as the intermediate target. If a monetary aggregate is chosen, the only symmetric rule so far proposed (McKinnon) requires the existence of a stable demand for money function for the area as a whole and an operating rule for setting individual domestic credit targets accompanied by a commitment to nonsterilized interventions. It has already been shown, however, that such a rule is not optimal if there is a shift in the demand for money in the currency area as a whole. It is also inappropriate in the case of asymmetric demand or supply shocks, whether originating within or outside the EMS, and in the presence of an asymmetric monetary shock deriving from an autonomous change in money demand (or money supply shock) in one member country only. In these cases an asymmetric policy response (monetary and fiscal) and/or a realignment will be necessary.

To avoid some of these problems, adapting from another proposal, the monetary authorities in concert could instead focus on the 'appropriate' reference interest rate, compatible with an external exchange rate target (e.g., vis-à-vis the US dollar) and a desired level of nominal domestic demand for the area as a whole. Under this rule, fiscal policy would be geared to achieve domestic equilibrium in each member country, while monetary policy would try to ensure the *interest rate differentials* needed to defend the agreed parity grid. The crucial issue would be to find agreement on the 'reference' interest rate (and on the common external exchange rate target), without jeopardizing price stability. However, in the original proposal the exchange rate targets are expressed in terms of real exchange rate zones rather than a nominal exchange rate grid as in the EMS, thereby permitting the accommodation of different inflation preferences; there is therefore no inflation 'anchor.' The need for an inflation anchor has resulted in the German interest rates becoming the 'reference' rate for the other members of the System.

In the absence of a common central bank setting a monetary (or interest rate) target for the area as a whole, there remains the need to leave to a country, of sufficient size and firm past record, the role of inflation anchor. When translated into intermediate monetary targets, this rule could be applied with more flexibility by establishing a medium-term money supply target (say, for a two-year period), temporary deviations from the target being decided during the process of surveillance, with due regard to the nature and origin of the shocks affecting the System. The concerted moves in interest rates that followed the agreement of Basel and Nyborg of September 1987, are an example of such an approach which, however, needs to be further strengthened.

1.2 The 'engine of growth' issue The need for an inflation 'anchor' and the asymmetry which has resulted from it are also at the origin of the call for 'an engine of growth'. That this call is addressed to Germany is not surprising given the special role described above. Analytically, the issue can be summarized in the following question: under what conditions can countries, other than the nth country, realize their (assumed) higher potential growth of output while respecting the exchange rate regime of the EMS? This is possible if, starting from a situation of current account equilibrium, the elasticity of exports with respect to external demand of the country at the periphery is larger, by a sufficient margin, than the elasticity of imports with respect to its own domestic demand. In other words, this condition implies the establishment and maintenance of a strong competitive position vis-à-vis the country at the centre of the System. But is that likely to prove feasible if the latter is also *by definition* the country with the lowest inflation performance?

The answer to this question is a complex one and needs to be more fully analyzed. Suffice it here to say that, over the shorter term, realignments would have to continue to ensure the needed degree of competitiveness at the obvious cost of slower progress in inflation convergence. Over the longer run, however, it would not be reasonable to expect lasting real effects through regular changes in nominal variables. Thus the continuing relative price changes that would be required while the differences in growth rate are present, can only be expected if there are forces in the economy which are fostering such relative price changes. If these forces exist, then, over the medium to longer run, the appropriate relative price changes can emerge even in the absence of exchange rate changes, particularly if the relative price changes are occurring in a favourable environment for real factor returns. This is not to deny that in many circumstances the exchange rate may be an efficient means of facilitating the desired relative price changes, particularly if, given German inflation, the country at the periphery with faster growth potential needs to see its price level decline to allow the relative price changes to take effect.

1.3   The EMS, full capital liberalization and the Single Market

Capital liberalization in the Treaty of Rome was an obligation only to the extent that it was required for the smooth functioning of the common market. It is, therefore, not surprising that no progress was made for a long time in this area following the 1962 directives. Divergences in economic policies and performance indeed precluded any such progress. The convergence achieved within the EMS and the adoption of the Single Act make full capital liberalization not only possible but obligatory for the establishment of a single market in financial services by 1993. Can the

EMS in its present form and way of operation survive it? As could be expected, opinions differ.

On the one hand, it is stressed that the greater discipline that would ensue would reinforce the System. On the other, the emphasis is put on what Padoa Schioppa has called the 'inconsistent quartet', with some considering that the EMS has indeed been able to operate successfully *because* of the existence of capital controls in the weaker countries. To solve the inconsistent quartet, the remedies suggested go from a loosening of the margins to a degree of monetary policy coordination involving practically the establishment of a common monetary policy (and central bank). Since the last point will be discussed later, I will deal here only with the issue of wider margins, the management of realignments, and some medium-term considerations.

The proposal for wider margins, *for all members*, even if for a temporary (but indefinite) period, while giving more flexibility to the System, would in fact be a step backward and might seriously reduce discipline. Moreover, not all members would be prepared to use them and the System would be divided, most likely, into two groups. More in line with the EMS experience and the future objective of monetary union, would be to agree on realignment rules that, given the convergence of inflation, would limit realignments to: (i) infrequent changes in central parities, (ii) within an overlapping band, and (iii) to changes which would not fully accommodate inflation differentials, unless accompanied by supporting changes in other policies. Such rules should help maintain the System, particularly if accompanied by full use of the band and appropriate interventions as well as timely and shared interest rate changes.

While managing realignments in this way (together with improved surveillance) may prove adequate to deal with the existing (and progressively smaller) differentials in inflation rates within the system, it may not be sufficient in the case of a large external exchange rate shock in the presence of still imperfect substitutability of EMS currencies. The appropriate response in this case would be to recognize the special role still played by the Deutsche Mark and, within the framework of a community procedure (as opposed to a unilateral decision), for a temporary period allow wider margins only for the currency whose demand is assumed to increase more than proportionately.

The proposed management of realignments should not produce undue tensions on interest rates in the weaker currencies, unless policy credibility is affected by other, more fundamental imbalances. Apart from current account imbalances, the most important of these is probably the still wide divergence in budgetary performance and deficits among members. As experience so far and economic theory prove, such divergences are not a threat to exchange rate stability in the short to medium run, since appropriate short-term interest rate differentials can always offset their impact on exchange rate expectations; they are, however, a serious threat in the longer run, particularly when full capital liberalization is achieved.

2. The future of European monetary cooperation

Springing from the renewed momentum of European integration created by the Single European Act (which adds monetary integration to the Treaty of Rome which had left that area to the IMF and its par values), good harvests of ideas and proposals for a major reform of the EMS have been reaped recently. Within a comprehensive political union, full monetary union, with integrated capital markets, is the logical solution. The EMS agreement did not attempt to map out the entire route to monetary union but it did envisage the evolution of the System into the European Monetary Fund (EMF) as an essential second phase and major advance for monetary cooperation and convergence.

The need for an evolutionary intermediate scenario remains. Such a scenario should build on the progress made so far within the EMS, create an institutional framework sufficient to address the issues to be faced now, and be able to develop later into the future European central bank. The new institution could well be a European Monetary Fund, with its roots firmly in the history of the EMS. From the start, the EMF would have to have complete operational independence from national governments and other EC bodies.

2.1 The role and institutional character of the EMF

The EMF should not replace the EMS but provide an institutional centre for the System. More practically, the EMF should from the outset be given the task of directing and handling all of the Community's balance of payments lending to member states. With a view to supporting the Community policies of complete capital liberalization and convergence of economic performance, the EMF could marshal substantial contingency credit lines, combining resources from several loan facilities under appropriate conditionality, which, given its independence, could be applied without undue political considerations.

The exchange rate mechanism would be operated as an integral aspect of the proposed EMF, retaining the fixed but adjustable exchange rate grid, with the ECU as the numéraire. In particular, the EMF would become the centre for the surveillance of economic policies and coordination of monetary policies with a view to maintaining exchange rate and monetary stability. Apart from the future role of a 'reformed' ECU in this regard, the Deutsche Mark would *remain* the inflation anchor of the System and therefore the fulcrum for the coordination of monetary policies. Normally, the monetary policies of the other member countries would need to be geared toward maintaining covered interest rate parity vis-à-vis interest rates in the anchor currency. Declining and converting inflation would lead toward Community-wide interest rate equality, facilitating progress toward monetary union. The central banks of member states would uniformly abstain from any involvement in the financing of public sector deficits which therefore would be financed in the increasingly integrated financial markets. In the medium term this would promote a better compatibility of fiscal policy and thereby strengthen monetary and exchange rate stability.

2.2   Reform of the ECU and the European Monetary Fund   At present, the ECU lacks most of the characteristics of a real currency. The official ECU is basically a credit instrument and its use is severely limited while its supply depends on temporary foreign exchange swap operations of member central banks with the EMCF. The private ECU lives a life of its own, with no link with the official ECU, except for its definition. The attractiveness of both suffers from their design as a basket of national currencies of varying quality, not all participating in the ERM.

A common European currency has to be at least as good as, but preferably and by design better than, the strongest member currency. This would be the case if the ECU were defined in terms of a parity grid vis-à-vis the member currencies, with a proviso that it could not depreciate vis-à-vis any member currency, and was given legal tender status in every member state, thus acquiring convertibility. This would provide the basis for its development into a European parallel currency, with the advantage over the strongest national EC currency that it could not depreciate vis-à-vis it and at the same time could be used throughout the Community. An independent European central bank would eventually be responsible for the supply of the new ECU, but initially this task would be undertaken by the proposed EMF.

The first step would be to base the emission of the new ECU on a permanent basis rather than on temporary swaps. To this end, the EMF would be endowed with a certain percentage of each member state's gold and foreign exchange reserves.

The next step would be to introduce a periodic reappraisal of the assets of the EMF, and thus the supply of ECUs. Ultimately the increase in the supply of ECUs would have to be such as to be linked to the potential growth of the whole area with no allowance for inflation (i.e., it would be targeted at zero inflation) consistently with the proviso that it could not depreciate vis à vis any member currency.

Who would demand and hold the new ECU? As it would be issued to member central banks in exchange for their contribution to the EMF, it would become *the* international reserve currency in the EMS, a status which the old ECU has never achieved. But there would also be room for private holders, i.e., there would be no more separation between the 'official' and 'private' ECU circuits. If the ECU were periodically revalued against the strongest currency of the system, it would become an attractive asset also in the stronger currency countries, on this account at least.

What if demand for ECUs by the private sector exceeds the supply? This situation is entirely possible even at the beginning, particularly in a weak currency country when confidence in that country's currency is declining. In this situation, the national central bank may run out of ECUs. It would then have the option of obtaining more ECUs, either through conditional borrowing from the EMF or purchases from other central banks or against an additional transfer of its international reserves to the EMF. It could also attempt to reduce the demand for ECUs by devaluing its currency against the ECU (and the other member currencies), or by supporting its currency by higher interest rates. The option of devaluation would, of course, be a risky one as it might lead to a vicious circle of further attacks and devaluations and, in the extreme, to the complete 'ECU-ization' of the economy. Thus, the incentive to improve economic convergence with the stronger partner countries would be reinforced.

What if the supply of ECUs exceeds the private demand? In this case, member central banks would simply buy back the ECUs sold earlier to the private sector against their own currency and keep or use the ECUs as international reserves until private demand bounces back. Since the supply of ECUs is limited, any intervention to support the ECU can always be sterilized if considered appropriate.

What would be the implications for monetary policy in the EC member states? Under the proposed scheme, member central banks would remain in control of their national money supply, to the same (unequal) degree that is possible at present. If there were non-sterilized intervention of member central banks vis-à-vis the ECU, domestic money supplies would change and so would the supply of ECUs. In the case of sterilized intervention, the supply of ECUs would be affected but not the national money supplies.

How could this provisional system be transformed into a genuine European monetary union? This question arises only after a strong and independent European central bank has been established *which is able to issue ECUs ex nihilo*. But when this has been achieved, the infrastructure needed by the central bank to issue and control the supply of ECUs would be largely in place. ECU interest rates would already have become the 'reference' interest rates of the System and would be the result of a European monetary policy. Commercial banks' minimum reserve requirements on ECU deposits, originally established only for prudential reasons, could then become policy instruments.

3.   Conclusions

The European Monetary System is clearly at a crossroads. As its initial aims of exchange rates and monetary stability are progressively attained and the requirements of the Single Act approach, with full capital liberalization occurring even earlier, the demands on the System are beginning to exceed its capabilities. The fine balance between rule and discretion so far maintained needs to be strengthened. This can only be achieved through some institutional step. Some have suggested the creation of a fully fledged European Central Bank by 1993. Others – and I share these views – believe that such a step is still premature. An intermediate solution – which nevertheless requires institutional changes – seems more feasible. Building on the experience of cooperation so far, it would seem logical to move first toward the establishment of a European Monetary Fund, as was indeed envisaged originally.

Such a Fund would consolidate the current achievements and permit new progress by strengthening surveillance and the financial defences of the System and by developing a more effective exercise of conditionality, without undue political interference. It would also assume some functions of a European Central Bank with regard to a reformed ECU, which would progressively become the true common inflation anchor and parallel currency. But the movement would remain gradual and evolutionary in character.

Article 102A of the Single Act would seem to require approval for such a step by national Parliaments. Would it be worthwhile to embark on such a complex process for an intermediate solution? The answer could be that aiming too high may make progress so slow as to endanger not only what has been achieved but the establishment of the Single Market itself. However, staying put makes the latter virtually impossible and the EMS only a useful experience, but for how long?

NIELS THYGESEN[2]

Two positive achievements in the present EMS and two indications that these achievements may not be fully sustainable as the EC moves towards a stage of deeper integration of its markets for goods and finance have combined to make the idea of a common European currency and a central banking system to manage it look less radical than for the past two decades.

The first achievement is that of macroeconomic convergence. To a degree which could hardly have been envisaged a decade ago, the EMS has achieved its aim of becoming 'a zone of monetary stability' in the double sense which has been given to this term: stabilization of exchange rates within the area and convergence towards a low level of inflation. Exchange rates have become more stable in the sense that short-term variability has been greatly reduced. Major temporary distortions in competitive relationships which marked the 1970s within Europe and which have continued to mark the floating exchange-rate regime between the world's major currencies have been well contained within the EMS. Inflation differentials which had come to be regarded as an insurmountable barrier to stable exchange rates within Europe have narrowed considerably. This has not been the outcome of an averaging process in which the low-inflation countries, Germany and the Netherlands, have had to accept a deterioration of their performance – on the contrary, these two countries have temporarily achieved near-zero inflation over the past couple of years. The EMS has become a framework that operated not only as a disinflationary mechanism for the weaker currencies; it did not prevent the stronger currencies from improving their price performance.

These trends which have become gradually more visible after the period of relatively large and frequent realignments came to an end in March 1983 suggest that the EMS currencies are closer today to meeting the prerequisites for more permanently fixed exchange rates than at any time since the 1960s. Current account imbalances are still evident within the EMS, but the macroeconomic experience of the 1980s suggests that changes in intra-EMS exchange rates will not have to be assigned an important role in the remaining adjustment. Some redistribution of demand through fiscal policies, combined with supply-oriented measures, particularly in relation to the completion of the Internal Market offer sufficient prospects of adjustment to leave only a modest residual role for realignments for a few more years. By the early 1990s fully fixed exchange rates among the present EMS members appear feasible. This is the main achievement of the system, making consideration of the option of having at least some elements of a joint monetary authority increasingly logical.

The second achievement of the EMS that makes new institutional developments appear less radical than in the first, more experimental decade of the system, is that participants have in important respects become accustomed to taking joint decisions. This is particularly the case with respect to realignments. In earlier examples of fixed-but-adjustable exchange rate systems – the Bretton Woods system which operated globally prior to the early 1970s and the joint float of some European currencies in the 1972–78 period – changes of a parity or a central rate were essentially decided unilaterally. Through their domestic political process countries arrived at decisions on devaluations and revaluations which were subsequently communicated to their trading partners through the International Monetary Fund or at meetings of Finance Ministers in the European 'snake'. In the EMS, realignments have resulted from negotiations in which the participating countries could not count on obtaining the adjustment they would have preferred. In particular, devaluations have on occasions been smaller than requested by the initiating country.

Gradually the capacity to take genuinely joint decisions has been extended beyond the crucial area of agreeing on realignments and the exercise of some mutual influence on accompanying domestic measures to tighten fiscal policies and weaken indexation mechanisms, as happened on several occasions in the early 1980s. Monetary management has also become more smoothly coordinated. In particular, short-term interest rates have been geared more and more explicitly to external considerations. With the so-called Nyborg Agreements of September 1987 – negotiated by the EMS central banks and confirmed by the Council of Ministers – the participants have developed a flexible set of instruments for containing incipient exchange-market tensions. Intramarginal interventions have been recognized as a useful tool and access to the very-short-term credit facilities for financing such interventions has been eased. The period of credit was lengthened by one month, but the principle remains that international reserves cannot be borrowed for lengthy periods; they must be reconstituted through the generation of a reversal of capital flows which in turn requires early action to establish relative interest rates that can create a sufficient incentive for reflows. The tensions in the EMS after the stock market crash and the resumption of dollar depreciation in early November 1987 provide a good illustration of what can be achieved by determined coordinated action on both interventions and interest rates. Heavy initial interventions in support of the French franc were checked by higher French and lower German money market rates, and the subsequent reflows of capital into France enabled the credits to be repaid within the time frame foreseen in the Nyborg Agreements. This was a successful contrast to the public disagreements and mutual attributions of blame observable in some earlier periods of tension in the EMS, notably in December 1986 and early January 1987 when the absence of a coordinated response forced a realignment which did not in retrospect appear warranted.

Both in terms of general macroeconomic performance and the capacity to manage realignments and the short-term monetary adjustment and financing measures required to underpin a fixed-but-adjustable exchange-rate system in which realignments become gradually smaller and/or more infrequent, the EMS has proved capable of reforming itself without major institutional change. Some will argue that the system could be left to develop further in its informal, *ad hoc* approach to monetary coordination. That would be an overly optimistic assumption in view of the internal and external challenges facing the EMS participants over the next few years.

The internal challenge is that the degree of both real and financial integration aimed for in the EC by 1992 goes well beyond the present framework within which the EMS is functioning. The core of the Internal Market programme is to improve allocation and efficiency and ultimately to make it possible for producers of goods and services to quote uniform prices – net of 'local' taxes – for their products throughout the EC, giving consumers the benefits of more competition and transparency in prices. That aim of real integration is hardly compatible with occasional and cumulatively significant realignments between Europe's monies.

The degree of financial integration, including the removal of remaining controls on short-term capital flows and liberalization of financial services, which is also part of the Internal Market programme also poses a major challenge. Financial flows become potentially much larger, also relative to liberal financing arrangements in the EMS, increasing the risk that the defence of central rates will become more difficult and more quickly abandoned in crises. Only a truly joint monetary policy would provide a robust defence at a time of advanced real and financial integration such as that envisaged for the early 1990s. This is true even if global currency relationships become more stable and the external imbalance of the United States is gradually reduced without further large depreciation of the dollar. The EMS countries – and the EC member states that have not yet joined the system – have a strong incentive to reflect carefully on how they could organize the joint exercise of monetary authority and not to delay such reflections until an advanced degree of political unification has been achieved.

How could the participants move towards a firmer institutional structure that would retain the positive features of the present EMS while making it more robust to the challenges of real and financial integration? There is only limited inspiration to find in earlier blueprints. The Werner Report of 1970 which outlined progress by stages towards Economic and Monetary Union by 1980 comes the closest, but it was not specific on the institutional issues. Nor were the elements of the final stage which corresponds most closely to today's realities fully analyzed. The second stage of the EMS, proposed in 1978 after a two-year introductory phase, focussed excessively on external financing and the pooling of international reserves in a European Monetary Fund and was relatively silent on the internal managerial role of the EMF. The so-called parallel-currency approach which has gained favour in recent years as the private ECU was given an unexpected degree of acceptance in financial markets is a useful complement to other efforts towards monetary unification, but it raises a number of unresolved issues, notably relating to the definition of the unit itself as an average of the component currencies. In the light of the macroeconomic achievements and the close working relationship that has developed among the EMS central banks, it seems more appropriate to focus on the strengthening of these elements and to reflect on how monetary policy could be designed and implemented in a truly joint fashion.

1   Functions and structure of a European Central Banking System

It is easier to outline the main features of an ultimate stage of European monetary integration than to describe the transition towards it. In such a stage national currencies may continue to dominate in use for most purposes within their respective national territories, but their supply would be tightly linked to the supply of a European money, as was largely the case for countries under the gold standard or for a territory with a Currency Board in the Commonwealth. With fixed exchange rate and full convertibility national currencies would essentially be different names for the same monetary unit. The European money would gradually dominate as a contracting unit in intra-European trade and in financial markets. Obviously such a stage would be inconceivable without a European central banking system responsible for the issue of the common money and the regulation of its value through either a quantity rule governing its supply or as a conversion rule into a well-defined asset (or bundle of assets/commodities).

Most observers do not find the design of this ultimate stage relevant to the current debate. They argue that a genuinely common monetary policy, implemented – though possibly with many decentralized features – by a European central bank would imply a jump in both monetary and political cooperation which can not be envisaged as a realistic option within the time span of a few years or even a decade. While this assessment is no doubt correct if one thinks in terms of irrevocably fixed exchange rates and a fully operational European central bank, the implication that one can defer consideration on the basic principles by which a European money should ultimately be supplied and of the institutional framework within which Europe could develop and safeguard an advanced stage of monetary integration seems unwarranted. It is my contention that a restatement of the final objectives of monetary integration and of the relationship of a European central banking system to the political authorities is of relevance in deciding the next steps to be taken in developing the EMS further.

For the process of integration to be attractive also to the most stability-oriented EMS participants the ultimate stage would have to offer not only a common currency and the phasing-out of nominal exchange rate changes, but also a solid prospect of a continuation of the high degree of medium-term price stability which these participants have approached from the mid-1980s. The jointly intended future should, in this respect, not look inferior to what has already been largely achieved. An orientation towards medium-term price stability, explicitly underlined as an objective, needs to be restated to preserve the credibility, achieved implicitly and gradually in the present EMS, of the effort to develop a European currency of high monetary quality, i.e. of predictable and stable purchasing power. Such an affirmation, preferably with reference to the stabilization of a European-based index of traded-goods prices, would clarify the present debate in the EC, in which a quest for more symmetry in the EMS raises a concern that what is sought is some average performance of the present national currencies rather than a monetary standard with more permanent and objective qualities of its own. There is a limit to what can be achieved through monetary policy; the more the emphasis is put on more conjunctural tasks, in frustration over the inability of other policy instruments to achieve a combination of price stability and more rapid growth of output, the greater the risk that European monetary integration will not provide a stable currency. Symmetry is a desirable objective of integration in the sense that monetary policy decisions should ultimately become truly collective. But these decisions will have to be guided by some agreed framework for the discretionary authority to be exercised by a European central banking system.

This point is linked to the second major feature of the ultimate stage which merits early attention. The achievement of an advanced stage of monetary integration prior to political unification – and, in particular, before joint authority over an important part of budgetary powers has been established – would be an experience almost without historical precedent. In national states the formation of a central bank has followed, rather than led, political unification. There are some good reasons for thinking that the usual order could be reversed in the European case: close integration of goods and financial markets, common degrees of sensitivity to shocks from third countries and the visible narrowing of residual divergences in economic performance. All provide arguments for the joint exercise of monetary responsibilities at an earlier date than can be envisaged for budgetary policies. But the reversal of the usual order would require careful specification of the interaction of a European central banking institution with the political authorities at the national and European levels.

Usually this subject is raised by those who insist that an eventual European central bank must be given a degree of autonomy in its policy implementation at least comparable to the position of those national central banks which have the highest degree of autonomy within their national policy-making; the status of the Bundesbank is often referred to. This may miss the point. Inevitably a European central bank would, in the early part of its existence, have a higher degree of autonomy than existing national central banks which in practice are in continuous consultation with their respective governments. There will be no close analogy to this almost symbiotic relationship at the European level prior to political unification and possibly well after that. The challenge is to find, within the firm mandate to the European central banking system to aim for medium-term price stability, an institutional framework which combines auton-omy in policy implementation with political accountability for the central bank.

Inspiration for finding a proper balance between these potentially conflicting considerations is at hand in the structure of the central banks of the United States and the Federal Republic of Germany. In these large Federal countries legislation and habits have had to find a balance of centralization of decision-making with regional participation therein, delegation of operational tasks and political accountability with dialogue.

In the European context one might envisage similarly a definition of the relative competences of a Board (Direktorium), nominated by the Euro-pean Council (or the Council of Ministers) with relatively long terms of office, and a Policy Committee (Bundesbankrat) in which national central bank governors participate in formulating the guidelines for short-term operations in the exchange markets vis-à-vis third currencies and in the financial markets in which the European currency is used. There is no obvious need to build up from the start an institutional capacity at the Board itself to carry out open market operations or foreign exchange interventions; they could, for an initial period, be delegated to national central banks according to the guidelines of the Policy Committee. As in the case in the Federal Reserve System with respect to the execution of foreign exchange interventions and open market operations through the New York Fed, effective delegation of the main operational tasks would imply that the Bundesbank as the institution in the major financial centre within the EMS would have the main executive role at least with respect to the exchange markets.

As regards political accountability the Board could be required to report to the Council of Ministers at regular intervals on the implementation of past policies and the formulation of objectives for the coming period. Such a procedure would be similar to the reports of the Chairman of the Federal Reserve Board to the competent Committees in the US Congress. It might also be envisaged that, in analogy with procedures in Germany, that the President of the Council of Ministers be given the right to attend meetings of the Policy Committee of the bank without a right to vote and that, conversely, the Chairman of the Board be invited to attend meetings in the Council of Ministers where monetary issues figure on the agenda. The Council would have no power to issue directives to the new institution – a possibility in some national systems and in the case of the embryonic European Monetary Cooperation Fund; but the other suggested features could suffice to bring the leading bodies of the new institution into a position where they have to explain their policies so as to gain understanding for them without subjecting them to direct political interference. The continued presence of governors of national central banks in an important policy-making role, though hardly with a majority in the Policy Committee as is the case with the Bundesbankrat in Germany, would also assure that the new institution remained familiar with national views and experience. In short, there are several possible options for giving a content to the autonomy of a European central banking system which do not make it remote from and unresponsive to national and Community policies in the non-monetary area.

Careful attention to these two central features of a European central banking system: its medium-term mandate for stability, and the way in which its leading bodies would be composed and would interact with the political authorities, would greatly clarify the shorter-run steps that lead towards such a system. But it does not answer the question of *when* it becomes desirable to build the structure for the ultimate stage. It is obvious that a European institution has a role when a European currency plays a central role as a common monetary base for the issue of money in Europe, and financial markets in the new unit have developed within Europe as well as internationally. But in the transitional stage in which exchange rates can still change among the participating currencies, could one not leave to the central banks which have been able to develop constructive coordination within the present EMS to get on with this task without early institutional changes? Two arguments can be advanced that this would not be adequate.

One is that institutional changes in the monetary area require, following the adoption of the Single Act by the European Council in 1985, a laborious procedure of national parliamentary ratification. This is natural in view of the importance of such changes, but it implies that proposed changes have to be well ahead of immediate problems, allowing the central banks to develop cooperative habits and operational modifications to evolve within them. This provides an argument for making early changes that are sufficiently farsighted to accommodate, say, a decade of evolutionary cooperation. The basic idea would be to provide a framework only gradually to be filled by the new institution.

The second argument why one can not rely solely on the capacity of the present EMS to cope with the challenges of the next few years lies in the need to reach jointly some monetary decisions which are presently taken at the national level. This applies, in particular, to the *adjustment of relative short-term interest rates*, the central decision in the management of the EMS. As argued above, the German and French authorities did succeed in November 1987 in coordinating their actions on interest rates. But such constructive bilateral or multilateral agreement may be difficult in future similar situations, where a repeat of the mutual political recrimination between Ministers of Finance seen in the exchange-market crisis of December 1986–January 1987 seems more likely. By indicating that the Committee of Central Bank Governors would in the future be expected to exercise authority over short-term interest rate differentials inside the EMS, governments would step back from the limelight of involving themselves directly in short-term management, though they would continue to monitor these developments closely in a joint fashion through their participation in the EC Monetary Committee alongside the central banks.

A second area within which one could envisage more authority to be vested in the Governors' Committee during the transitional stage is that of the *residual small realignments* of currencies. For some years yet such realignments will have to be regarded as necessary, though more and more rarely, to prevent longer-run excessive tensions from building up. A major purpose of having some central banking institutional framework in Europe before a common currency is feasible is to constrain and gradually eliminate realignments. The latter should be sufficiently small to preserve continuity of market exchange rates before and after realignments; this has been an important feature in the containment of speculative pressures in the recent EMS period. By making it clear that major changes in central rates are no longer required within the EMS and by leaving the authority to make the residual smaller ones to the central bankers as part of their task of monetary management, along with changes in interest rate differentials, governments would be giving a clear signal as to the intended tightening of the EMS in the transitional phase.

It should be made clear that such an idea has already been discussed on occasions over the past two years and that the President of the Bundesbank has recently reiterated it (Press conference following the meeting of the Bundesbankrat on May 4, 1988). The difficulty that many other central banks have with it, is that they are not presently the main actors in the discretionary adjustments of exchange rates, however small. This point illustrates that further European monetary integration implies not only some centralization of decision-making at the European level, but also some delegation within most countries participating in the EMS, as in the prospective member countries, to the national central bank of more operational autonomy in a broad sense.

A third task for the Governors' Committee would be to continue to monitor the development of the private ECU-market and discuss further steps that could be taken to encourage it. The ECU itself plays no central role in the strategy here outlined, however, for two main reasons: (1) the ECU is constrained in its evolution towards becoming a parallel currency because, as argued above, it is an average of presently ten, from 1989 probably twelve, currencies some of which are not yet committed to exchange-rate stabilization. As such it can hardly be expected to make major headway in the countries of the stronger EMS-currencies. This is borne out by the experience with the private ECU in Germany since its use was liberalized. (2) Growth in the use of the private ECU and some of the more obvious steps that could be taken to encourage it, notably a linkage of the official and private circuits, are not obviously necessary conditions for arriving at an advanced state of monetary integration. In the coming years the main official efforts should be directed at making the EMS currencies closer substitutes for one another and to make most of them of the same high monetary quality as the most stable national currencies. If that process meets with success, the ECU should develop strongly as a parallel currency. If it does not succeed, efforts to encourage the present basket ECU might not be productive.

There are accordingly some natural tasks for central bank cooperation in the next few years, once the basic ultimate aims of European monetary integration and its institutional framework have been clarified. Progress in these tasks may pave the way for exchange-rate fixity among a substantial group of EC-countries by 1992–93, a natural target data for implementing the more institutional phase to accompany the realization of the Internal Market. One may see the interest expressed over recent months by several European governments in renewed initiatives in the EMS and frequent references to the ultimate objective of a common European currency and a central bank to manage it as an indication that there is no inherent contradiction between pragmatism and a long-term, more visionary approach.

These are in my view the reasons why there may be now sufficient momentum to study how the central banks and the governments in the EC could move towards monetary unification by defining the tasks of a European central banking system. Despite the launching at the Hanover Summit of a committee, presided over by the President of the EC Commission, to study how Economic and Monetary Union could be achieved, there is a danger that the central bankers who dominate the membership of that committee will adopt the attitude that monetary coordination is already sufficiently advanced to warrant no further initiatives, and that, if such initiatives are to be taken, a list of demands on fiscal coordination will first have to be met which is both unnecessarily far-reaching and likely to scare governments, conscious of their need to preserve some visible sovereignty in this area, away from considering institutional steps in the monetary area. There will also be the argument that until all 12 member states are ready to subject themselves to an essentially unified monetary policy, no steps in this direction should be taken. However, the EC has a well-established procedure for dealing with such divergences in initial conditions, most recently applied to the liberalization of capital movements, viz. transitory provisions with a fixed timetable. The design of the EC's future monetary organization will anyway have to be left flexible in order to accommodate new members who seem likely to join over the next decade. It would be a mistake to wait until all present members are fully ready to take further step among those who have already in the present EMS progressed so far.

NOTES

1 'The further development of monetary cooperation in Europe', March 15th, 1988.
2 These comments draw on research done at CEPS and surveyed in Daniel Gros and Niels Thygesen, 'The EMS: Achievements, Current Issues and Directions for the Future'. *CEPS Papers* No. 35, Brussels, March 1988. An earlier version of part of the argument appeared in an article by the author in *EBA Newsletter*, ECU Banking Association.

Index